VIEWPOINTS

*Readings Worth Thinking
and Writing About*

INSTRUCTOR'S EDITION

iewpoints

Readings Worth Thinking and Writing About

Second Edition

W. ROYCE ADAMS
*Santa Barbara City College
Emeritus*

D. C. Heath and Company
Lexington, Massachusetts   Toronto

Address editorial correspondence to:

D. C. Heath and Company
125 Spring Street
Lexington, MA 02173

Cover Design: Dustin Graphics.
Cover Photograph: "Hubble Light—York, Maine," Photo Researchers/
Patrick Grace.

Illustration Credits

p. 4 The American Library Association; p. 138 (top) Stock, Boston/Jerry
Berndt, (bottom) Woodfin Camp & Associates/Jean-Claude Delmas; p. 182
(top) Stock, Boston/Frederick D. Bodin, (bottom) Brown Brothers; p. 230
(top) Stock, Boston/Lionel Delevingne, (bottom) Impact Visuals/Allan Clear;
p. 270 (top) The Image Works/Harriet Gans, (bottom) The Image Works/
Carrie Boretz; p. 310 (top) Stock, Boston/Peter Southwick, (bottom) Stock,
Boston/Virginia Blaisdell; p. 354 Impact Visuals/Rick Reinhard; p. 396 Impact Visuals/Hazel Hankin.

International Standard Book Number: 0–669–27368–6 (Instructor's
Edition)
0–669–27366–X (Student Edition)

Library of Congress Catalog Number: 92–70685

10 9 8 7 6 5 4 3 2 1

Acknowledgments

Molefi Kete Asante. "Putting Africa at the Center" from *Newsweek*, September 23, 1991, p. 46. Reprinted by permission of the author.

Yeghia Aslanian. "A Story of Conflicts" from *Hudson River Edition*, December 1987.

Russell Baker. "School vs. Education," by Russell Baker, the *New York Times*, September 9, 1975. Copyright © 1975 by the New York Times Company. Reprinted by permission.

Dave Barry. "TV or Not TV" from *Dave Barry's Greatest Hits* by Dave Barry. Copyright © 1988 by Dave Barry. Reprinted by permission of Crown Publishers, Inc.

Max Boot. "The Vast Emptiness..." from the *Los Angeles Times*, June 16, 1991. Reprinted with the permission of the author, a graduate student in the Yale University History Department.

Barbara Brandt. "Less is More: A Call for Shorter Work Hours," as appeared in *Utne Reader*, July/August 1991, pp. 81–84.

Forrest Carter. "The Way" from *The Education of Little Tree*, University of New Mexico Press, 1976.

Jeff Cohen. "Bohemian Grove: Off-Limits to News Coverage" from the *Los Angeles Times*, November 26, 1991, B7; original title "The Dilemma of Corporate Media Bosses". Reprinted by permission of the author.

Cara Egan. "The Seven Dwarfs and I" from *Newsweek* (My Turn), September 9, 1991, pp. 8–9.

Barbara Ehrenreich. "Teach Diversity with a Smile" from *Time*, April 8, 1991, p. 84. Copyright 1991 The Time Inc. Magazine Company. Reprinted by permission.

Duane Elgin. "TV + Telephone = Electronic Democracy" from *Utne Reader*, July/August 1991, pp. 70–71. Reprinted by permission of the author.

Nancy Friday. "Mother Love" by Nancy Friday from *My Mother/My Self*. Copyright 1977 by Nancy Friday. Reprinted by permission of International Creative Management, Inc.

Henry Louis Gates, Jr. "Beware the New Pharaohs" originally appeared in *Newsweek*, September 23, 1991, p. 47. Reprinted by permission of Brandt & Brandt Literary Agents, Inc. Copyright © 1991, by Henry Louis Gates, Jr.

Nathan Glazer. "In Defense of Multiculturalism" from *The New Republic*,

September 2, 1991. Reprinted by permission of *The New Republic* © 1991 The New Republic, Inc.

Rick Greenberg. "Escaping the Daily Grind for Life as a House Father" by Rick Greenberg, a Washington, D.C. based writer. Reprinted by permission.

Pete Hamill. "The Wet Drug" as found in *San Jose Mercury News*, March 24, 1983. Copyright © 1983 Pete Hamill. Used with permission of the author.

Langston Hughes. "Salvation" from *The Big Sea* by Langston Hughes. Copyright 1940 by Langston Hughes. Renewed copyright © 1968 by Arna Bontemps and George Houston Bass. Reprinted by permission of Hill and Wang, a division of Farrar, Straus & Giroux, Inc.

Jon D. Hull. "Slow Descent into Hell" from *Time*, February 2, 1987. Copyright 1987 The Time Inc. Magazine Company. Reprinted by permission.

Rachel L. Jones. "What's Wrong with Black English?" by Rachel L. Jones from *Newsweek*, December 27, 1982 from "My Turn" column. Reprinted by permission of the author, a reporter for the *St. Petersburg Times*.

Suzanne Britt Jordan. "Fun. Oh, Boy. Fun. You Could Die From It," by Suzanne Britt Jordan, the *New York Times*, December 23, 1979. Copyright © 1979 by the New York Times Company. Reprinted by permission.

K. Connie Kang, "A Battle of Cultures" from *Asian Week*, May 25, 1990, p. 1.

Sam Keen. "The Importance of Family" (editor's title) from *Fire in the Belly* by Sam Keen. Copyright © 1991 by Sam Keen. Used by permission of Bantam Books, a division of Bantam Doubleday Dell Publishing Group, Inc.

Correta Scott King. "The Death Penalty is a Step Back" by Coretta Scott King. Reprinted by permission of Joan Daves. Copyright © 1981 Cleveland Publishing Company and Coretta Scott King.

Edward I. Koch. "Death and Justice" from *The New Republic*, April 15, 1985. Reprinted by permission of *The New Republic* © 1985 The New Republic, Inc.

Hans Koning. "Don't Celebrate 1492 . . ." from the *New York Times*, August 14, 1990. Copyright © 1990 by the New York Times Company. Reprinted by permission.

Ann Landers. "Dear Ann" and reply by "Gary, Ind." which appeared in the *Los Angeles Times*. Reprinted by permission of Ann Landers and Los Angeles Times Syndicate.

John Leland. "Do You Still Want Your MTV?" from *Newsweek*, August 25, 1991, p. 53.

Tatiana Litvin. "Can Magic Breach the Wall of Denial?" from the *Los Angeles Times*, November 17, 1991, M3. Reprinted by permission of the author.

Terry McMillan. "African-American Literature: Much to be Proud Of" (Editor's title) taken from Introduction to *Breaking Ice*, Editor Preface by John Edgar Wideman. Copyright © 1990 by Terry McMillan, preface, copyright © 1990 by John Edgar Wideman. Used by permission of Penguin, a division of Penguin Books USA Inc.

Nickie McWhirter. "What You Do Is What You Are" from the *San Jose Mercury News*, March 8, 1982.

H. Bruce Miller. "Severing the Human Connection" by H. Bruce Miller from the *San Jose Mercury News*, August 4, 1981. Reprinted with permission from the *San Jose Mercury News*.

Barbara Mujica. "Bilingualism's Goal," by Barbara Mujica, from the *New York Times*, February 26, 1984. Copyright © 1984 by the New York Times Company. Reprinted by permission.

Kathleen Neville. "A Primary Lesson in Sexual Harassment" from *Corporate Attractions*, Acropolis Books, 1990, pp. 159–165. Reprinted by permission of Kathleen Neville.

Steven O'Brien. "One Son, Three Fathers," by Steven O'Brien from the *New York Times*, December 28, 1986. Copyright © 1986 by the New York Times Company. Reprinted by permission.

George Orwell. "A Hanging" from *Shooting an Elephant and Other Essays* by George Orwell, copyright 1950 by Sonia Brownell Orwell and renewed 1978 by Sonia Pitt-Rivers. Reprinted by permission of Harcourt Brace Jovanovich, Inc.

Jeanne Park. "Eggs, Twinkies and Ethnic Stereotypes" from the *New York Times*, April 20, 1990. Copyright © 1990 by the New York Times Company. Reprinted by permission.

Rosa Parks. "A Long Way to Go" by Rosa Parks from the *Los Angeles Times*, June 29, 1986. Reprinted by permission of the author.

Neal R. Peirce. "Murder on the Dial" from the *Los Angeles Times*, April 23, 1989, View 5.

Letty Cottin Pogrebin. "Superstitious Minds" by Letty Cottin Pogrebin from *Ms.* magazine, February 1988. Reprinted by permission of the author, © 1988 by Letty Cottin Pogrebin.

Terry Pristin. "Did the Media Buy a Military Spin on the Gulf War?" from *Los Angeles Times*, April 6, 1991. Copyright, 1991, Los Angeles Times. Reprinted by permission.

Anna Quindlen, "Death Penalty's False Promise," originally titled "Life in the 30's—Death Penalty's False Promise: An Eye for an Eye," from the *New York Times*, September 17, 1986. Copyright © 1986 by the New York Times Company. Reprinted by permission.

Caryl Rivers. "The Issue Isn't Sex, It's Violence" by Caryl Rivers from the *Boston Globe*. Reprinted by permission of the author.

Albert Robbins. "Settling in the Cities" by Albert Robbins from *Coming to America. Immigrants From Northern Europe* Copyright © 1981 by Visual Education Corporation. Reprinted by permission of Visual Education Corporation.

Richard Rodriguez. "America Discovers AIDS." Reprinted by permission of George Borchardt, Inc. for the author. Copyright © 1991 by Richard Rodriguez. First appeared in the *Los Angeles Times*.

Richard Rodriguez. From *Hunger of Memory* by Richard Rodriguez. Copyright © 1981 by Richard Rodriguez. Reprinted by permission of David R. Godine, Publisher.

Roger Rosenblatt. "Sexual Bigotry," from *Life Magazine*, December 1991, p. 33. Copyright © 1991 The Time Inc. Magazine Company. Reprinted with permission.

Mike Royko. "Death to Killers" by Mike Royko from *Chicago Sun Times*. Reprinted by permission of Sterling Lord Literistic, Inc. Copyright © by Mike Royko.

Vincent R. Ruggiero. "Debating Moral Questions" from *The Art of Thinking* by Vincent R. Ruggiero. Copyright © 1984 by Harper & Row Publishers, Inc. Reprinted by permission of HarperCollins Publishers.

Arthur Schlesinger, Jr. "The Cult of Ethnicity, Good and Bad," from *Time*, July 8, 1991, p. 21. Copyright 1991 The Time Inc. Magazine Company. Reprinted by permission.

Jean Shepherd. From *In God We Trust, All Others Pay Cash* by Jean Shepherd. Copyright © 1966 by Jean Shepard. Used by permission of Doubleday, a division of Bantam Doubleday Dell Publishing Group, Inc.

Mary Sherry. "In Praise of the F Word," from *Newsweek*, May 6, 1991.

Debra Sikes and Barbara Murray. "The Practicality of the Liberal Arts Major" by Debra Sikes and Barbara Murray. Reprinted by permission: *Innovation Abstracts* Vol IX, No. 8; Austin, Texas: The University of Texas and the National Institute for Staff and Organizational Development (NISOD).

Bonnie Smith-Yackel. "My Mother Never Worked" by Bonnie Smith-Yackel from *Women: A Journal of Liberation*, 1975.

Kirby W. Stanat. "How to Take a Job Interview" by Kirby W. Stanat from *Job Hunting Secrets and Tactics*, Raintree Publishers.

Brent Staples. "Night Walker" by Brent Staples from *Los Angeles Times Magazine*, December 7, 1986. Reprinted by permission of Brent Staples, Assistant Metropolitan Editor of the *New York Times*.

Roger von Oech. Reprinted by permission of Warner Books/New York from *A Whack on the Side of the Head*. Copyright © 1983 by Roger von Oech.

Sharon Whitley. "Students' Love Affair with Anne Frank" by Sharon Whitley from the *Los Angeles Times*, December 1, 1985. Reprinted by permission of the author.

David Whitman. "Trouble for America's 'Model' Minority." Copyright 1987, *U.S. News and World Report*. Reprinted from issue of February 23, 1987.

Jane Whitney. "Pre-Wedding Syndrome" from the *New York Times*, June 3, 1990 "Hers" section. Copyright © 1990 by the New York Times Company. Reprinted by permission.

Liu Zongren. "After Two Years in the Melting Pot" from *Two Years in the Melting Pot* by Liu Zongren, 1988. Reprinted by permission of China Books & Periodicals.

To The Instructor

The second edition of *Viewpoints: Readings Worth Thinking and Writing About*, like the first, offers two parts. Part I, **Viewpoints on Reading and Writing Essays,** provides students with an overview of the skills necessary for good reading and writing. In Unit 1, students learn about the basic essay structure, its thesis, and various rhetorical arrangements of support. To aid reading comprehension, it emphasizes the advantages of keeping a reading journal and shows how to separate main ideas from supporting details, how to distinguish fact from opinion, and how to draw inferences. Suggestions for marking and summarizing texts are also provided.

Unit 2 covers three basic stages of writing essays: prewriting, drafting, and revising. However, while students become familiar with these stages, this unit reminds them that writing is not a linear procedure, but a recursive one, with all three stages recurring throughout the writing process. How to make a writing assignment one's own, how to find and develop a working thesis, how to arrange supporting evidence, and how to revise and edit are graphically demonstrated through models and illustrations. To strengthen the ties between reading and writing skills, the writing section also draws heavily upon the reading information and rhetorical paragraph patterns presented in Unit 1.

In both units of Part I, reinforcement activities periodically help students interact with the text. After every major concept, students complete a short writing exercise in the form of a journal entry or a homework assignment—whichever you prefer.

Part II, **Readings Worth Thinking and Writing About,** contains eight thematically organized reading units offering a collection of viewpoints on such topics as learning, human behavior, cultural heritage, social concerns, family relationships, work, the media, and two controversial issues: capital punishment and multicultural education. Thirty-two of the sixty-four essays are new to this edition; many deal with multicultural issues or perspectives. I have deliberately chosen diverse viewpoints to provoke student thinking on the issues involved. While many of the essays use the rhetorical forms that many instructors want students to write, the book places greater emphasis on exposing students to viewpoints worth thinking and writing about.

Each thematic unit begins with some prefatory comments and an image that students should read and view in class before you assign readings in that unit. Two or three questions to engage the reader's thoughts on the subject of the essay precede each reading selection. The vocabulary list of words and their definitions can be used any way you see fit. Four sets of questions follow each reading selection: **Understanding the Content, Looking at Structure and Style, Evaluating the Author's Viewpoints,** and **Pursuing Possible Essay Topics.** The questions and suggestions in these four categories require students to draw upon what they learned from Part I. Each unit ends with a student essay written in response to an assignment to write on some aspect of that particular unit's theme. In some cases, I have used early drafts of student essays to illustrate both a writing problem and the correct revision approach needed.

While I have tried to select relatively short readings at a level appropriate for developmental students, I have also included some essays that will be more difficult to read. I believe that if we are to help students grow beyond the developmental stage, we must provide them with both readings and assignments that will challenge them to rise above their present level. One goal of this text, therefore, is to show students how to approach what seems to be difficult reading, rather than avoiding it. As do the reading selections, the questions and suggestions for essays reflect a wide range of ease and difficulty in order to provide for and to challenge the diversity usually found in developmental writing classes. My many years of experience as both a reading and a composition teacher have taught me that developmental students, if taught well, can respond positively to the challenge of material often considered "too difficult."

The **Instructor's Guide** offers suggestions for using the essays. It calls your attention to readings that work well together in pairs. My commentaries on each of the units and individual reading selections may help you decide which ones to assign during the course and in which order.

The Appendix in this edition has been trimmed to allow for more reading selections and now contains Appendix A, Essay Format and Proofreading Guide, and Appendix B, Quoting and Documenting Sources.

I extend my appreciation to those who provided suggestions for this book: Christopher Baker, Lamar University; Domenick Caruso, Kingsborough Community College; Kitty Dean Chen, Nassau Community College; Robert Cosgrove, Saddleback College; Joyce Crawford, Miami-Dade Community College; Ian Cruikshank, St. Louis Community College—Florissant Valley; Kathryn Fitzgerald, University of Utah; Barbara Gold, Westchester Community College; Eric P. Hibbison, J. Sargent Reynolds Community College; William T. Hope, Jefferson Technical College; Myra J. Linden, Joliet Junior College; Susan McKee, California State University—Sacramento; Donna Mealey, Louisiana State University; and Robert E. Yarber, San Diego Mesa College.

Finally, I wish to thank our copyeditor Kathryn Daniel, and the staff at D. C. Heath: editors Paul Smith, Linda Bieze, and most especially Jennifer Raymond, who expertly brought this edition to completion under some trying conditions.

W. Royce Adams

Contents

PART II
READINGS WORTH THINKING AND WRITING ABOUT

Rhetorical Table of Contents

Since few, if any, essays serve as models for one particular rhetorical mode, reading selections containing paragraph examples of several modes appear under more than one category.

Analysis

Illustration and Example

Cause and Effect

Argumentation

VIEWPOINTS

Readings Worth Thinking and Writing About

INSTRUCTOR'S EDITION

PART I

VIEWPOINTS ON READING AND WRITING ESSAYS

Viewpoints on Reading Essays

Take Time To Read... Together

"Reading is to the mind what exercise is to the body."
Joseph Addison

*R*ESEARCH has shown that unless we keep notes and regularly review what we learn we will forget within two weeks over 80 percent of what we thought we knew. That's a big waste, considering the time, energy, and money put into learning. Keeping some type of reading journal for this class is a good way to make certain that you don't lose what you have learned or forget the questions that come up when you are studying. To help you get into the "journal habit," you will be asked periodically to stop reading in this book and to make various types of journal entries.

Keeping a Reading Journal

Buy an 8½″ × 11″ spiral notebook to be used only for this class, as a companion to this textbook. Your journal will be used for three basic functions: (1) **keeping notes** of the key points made in Part I; (2) recording any **reactions, reflections, or questions** you may have regarding what you read; (3) and writing **summaries** of the essays you read in Part II. You will be shown how to write summaries later in this unit. Of course, anything else you want to keep in your journal, such as vocabulary words you want to learn or ideas for possible essays, is up to you. Keeping a journal for this class is not "busy work." It's a vital part of your learning process, and you'll find that you get much more from this class by journaling than you might think.

Reading Essays

If you look at the table of contents in this book, you will see that the reading selections in Part II are grouped into thematic units, such as learning, human behavior, cultural heritage, family, and so on. Each unit contains several readings expressing various viewpoints on that theme. The readings will provide you with at least four uses: (1) information on a theme, (2) ideas for possible essays of your own, (3) examples of ways to write essays, and (4) practice in developing your reading versatility.

In some units, particularly Unit 10, you will find that the authors' viewpoints frequently disagree. Some essays are longer than others; some better written than others; some more interesting to you than others. You will also discover as you read that there are many different styles of writing. But despite these differences, all essays share three particular features: a thesis, support for that thesis, and a logical arrangement of that support. This section shows you what to look for when you read essays; how to look more closely at the methods writers use to express their opinions, feelings, and experiences; and more detailed information on keeping a reading journal.

The Structure of an Essay

Not all essays are structured the same way. Some essays use what might be called the traditional form: the point the author wants to make appears in the first paragraph (the beginning), several paragraphs are used to develop or support that point (the middle), and the last paragraph draws a conclusion or summarizes the support used to make the point (the end). That is basically the form most instructors use to teach beginning writers the essay structure.

In reality, essays don't always follow that form. Creativity enters the writing process! Some writers may choose to withhold their main idea until the last paragraph, building up to the point they want to make. Some essays may begin with an anecdote or a story that consumes several paragraphs before the point is made. In some cases, the point is never stated directly in words, but instead is implied through what the writer says. As a reader, you will see the variety of forms used when you read the essays in Part II. As a beginning writer, you may be asked to work on developing essays by the more traditional approach until you are able to break away from the mold.

Regardless of its form or style, an essay contains the three basic ingredients mentioned earlier: a thesis, either stated or implied; sufficient support of that thesis; and a logic behind the arrangement of that support. As a good reader, you need to identify these ingredients and understand how they function as a whole, no matter what the structure of the essay.

Thesis

Every good essay has a **thesis,** which is the main idea or point an author wants to make about his or her topic. The **topic** of an essay is a broad or general subject, such as teenage drinking. A thesis, on the other hand, is the point the author wants to make about the subject of teenage drinking. A thesis might be "Teenagers should be allowed to drink when they reach age 19" or "Teenagers should not be allowed to drink." In other words, a thesis is what the author thinks or feels about the subject of the essay. It's the purpose for writing, the main point around which everything else is written. If you fail to recognize an author's thesis, you may miss the whole point of the essay.

To help clarify the difference between a topic and a thesis, look at the examples below. Notice that topics are broad, general categories, whereas thesis statements are more specific.

Topics	*Possible thesis statements*
Little League sports	Little League sports can be harmful to a child's sense of sportsmanship.
	The best years of my life were spent playing Little League baseball.
	The Little League soccer coach has a varied background in professional sports.
word processing	All college freshmen should be required to take a word processing course.
	Word processing may be helpful to some but not to me.
	Before buying a word processing program, consider the functions needed, the cost, and the manufacturer's support.
nuclear disarmament	It is too late to worry about nuclear disarmament.
	Everyone should be required to read Jonathan Schell's book on nuclear disarmament, *The Fate of the Earth.*
	Nuclear disarmament would open us up to World War III.

Notice that in each case the thesis statement is a viewpoint about the subject or topic. The thesis deals with a narrower view of the broader subject and makes the author's position clear. You may not agree with the viewpoint, but if the essay is well written, it will support the author's opinion in an effort to convince the reader. A key element in reading, then, is to make certain you understand an author's thesis or viewpoint on the subject of the essay.

Below are some thesis statements. Separate the topic from the writer's viewpoint. In the space provided, write two phrases, one explaining the topic and another explaining the point being made about the topic.

1. A college education may be important, but its value is overemphasized by many employers.

2. We humans have many strange and contradictory behaviors.

3. Our society seems afraid or ashamed of growing old and places too much emphasis on youth.

4. Most of the visuals shown on MTV distract from the music.

Compare the content of your phrases with the following chart:

Topic	Viewpoint expressed
1. college education	value overemphasized by employers
2. human behavior	strange and contradictory
3. aging, growing old	ashamed/afraid of aging, too much value placed on youth
4. MTV	visuals distract from music

Thesis statements are usually clearly stated within the essay; often you can find a sentence or two that directly states the author's views. Other times there is no one sentence you can point to that states the thesis, but the author's viewpoint becomes clear once you have read the supporting evidence. In those cases, it's necessary to form the author's thesis in your own words.

 Writing Exercise

In your reading journal or on a separate sheet, write today's date and the page numbers you just read. In a paragraph, explain the difference between an essay thesis and a topic. Provide two examples of each.

Supporting Evidence

Once a writer has his or her thesis in mind, the next step is to provide **supporting evidence.** If a thesis is controversial, such as whether Little League sports are harmful in some way, then the writer must provide evidence that will at least cause someone who disagrees to look at Little League sports from a new angle. As a reader, you need to look for the reasons given to support the thesis. You may still disagree with the author when you have finished reading, but you will understand why the author feels as he or she does.

Of course, you have to be careful that your own feelings on the subject don't cause you to reject or accept the author's viewpoints without thinking carefully about the evidence presented. Say you coach a Little League team. Because of your own involvement, you immediately resent or reject the thesis that Little League is harmful. Your own bias or prejudice (feelings that keep you from seeing another view) could cause you to miss some valid points that you had never considered before, points that might make you a better coach. It's important to keep an open mind as you read supporting evidence.

In essays, support is given in the form of paragraphs. A paragraph is in some ways similar to a mini-essay. Just as every essay has an implied or stated thesis, a well-written paragraph has an implied or stated **topic sentence.** A topic sentence states the key point or idea of the paragraph. The rest of the sentences support it, just as paragraphs support a thesis.

Good writers use a variety of paragraph types to support their thesis statements. These types are sometimes called **rhetorical modes** or **patterns.** Because humans think in certain basic ways, we can sometimes communicate better with one another if we use these thinking patterns in our writing. Eight common patterns are presented here.

Description is a common writing pattern. This method is used when authors want to reach one or all of our five senses: sight, sound, smell, touch, and taste. See if you can visualize what's being described in this paragraph:

> Whack! A police baton slaps his legs and a voice booms, "Get the hell up, you're outta here. Right now!" Another police officer whacks his nightstick against a metal grating as the twelve men sprawled along the tunnel crawl to their feet. Red pulls himself up and walks slowly up the stairs to the street, never looking back.
>
> Jon D. Hull, "Slow Descent into Hell"

Even though there is no stated topic sentence in the paragraph, it is not difficult for us to understand the point the author wants to make about Red's situation. The author forces us to *hear* the whacks of the police nightstick, to *hear* the roughness and lack of concern in the voice yelling at the twelve men, to *see* Red and the men "crawl to their feet." Their slow movement up the stairs with no comment to the police implies that this event and this treatment are nothing new to Red and the others. The author makes us *feel* what it's like to be one of the homeless. No topic sentence could say what the description itself reveals. The author relies on our reactions to his description to imply (suggest or hint at) his message.

Another paragraph pattern frequently used by writers is **narration.** A paragraph using narration moves from one occurrence to another, generally in chronological order. Narration is often used when authors want to tell a story or relate an anecdote about something that has happened in their lives. Here is an example:

> I was saved from sin when I was going on thirteen. But not really saved. It happened like this. There was a big revival

at my Auntie Reed's church. Every night for weeks there had been much preaching, singing, praying, and shouting, and some very hardened sinners had been brought to Christ, and the membership of the church had grown by leaps and bounds. Then just before the revival ended, they held a special meeting for children, "to bring the young lambs to the fold." ... That night I was escorted to the front row and placed on the mourners' bench with all the other young sinners ....

Langston Hughes, "Salvation"

Here the author uses first-person narration, which means that he tells us his story from his own point of view. He takes us back to his thirteenth year and then proceeds to narrate for us the story of how he was saved, "but not really." As readers we can expect the rest of the story to be told in a chronological fashion, moving from one incident to the next. We might say that the topic sentence is the first one, but to be more accurate the main idea of the paragraph is a combination of the first three sentences.

Still another paragraph pattern is **analysis.** An author may wish to take a subject and examine its parts. For instance, a writer could analyze a poem by looking at the way it is structured, examining the number of lines and stanzas, identifying the rhyme scheme, or weighing the reasons behind the use of certain words. Another author may wish to show how a rotary engine works, which would be called a **process analysis,** a step-by-step explanation of the way the engine works. A paragraph based on an analysis pattern reads like this:

Let us move in for a closer look at how the campus recruiter operates. Let's say you have a 10 o'clock appointment with the recruiter from the XYZ Corporation. The recruiter gets rid of the candidate in front of you at about 5 minutes to 10, jots down a few notes about what he is going to do with him or her, then picks up your résumé or data sheet (which you have submitted in advance).... Although the recruiter is still in the interview room and you are still in the lobby, your interview is under way. You're on. The recruiter will look over your sheet pretty carefully before he goes out to call you. He develops a mental picture of you.

Kirby W. Stanat, "How to Take a Job Interview"

The topic sentence in this paragraph is the first one and the subject is how a job interview works. The paragraph begins analyzing or examining the process. As a reader, we can expect each of the following paragraphs in the essay to continue explaining each part of the job interview process.

Another rhetorical method is the use of **illustration and example.** You probably use this method when you talk. If you are explaining something to someone who doesn't quite understand, you might say, "For instance, . . ." and then proceed to give an example or two to clarify what you mean. The same technique is used in writing. Here is a paragraph that uses the illustration and example pattern:

> Dr. Wayne Dyer, in his book *Your Erroneous Zones,* claims that we have grown up in a culture which has taught us that we are not responsible for our feelings even though the truth is that we always were. He claims we have learned a "host of sayings" to defend ourselves against the fact that we control our feelings. For example, here are some of the utterances that we use over and over to take the blame off ourselves and place it on others:
> "You hurt my feelings."
> "You make me feel bad."
> "I can't help the way I feel."
> "He makes me sick."
> "You're embarrassing me."
> "You made me look foolish."
> Dyer feels that each of these sayings has a built in message that we are not responsible for how we feel, when in fact we are in charge of how we feel.

As is often the case, the topic sentence for the paragraph is the first one. Notice that the main point is to summarize for us what Dr. Wayne Dyer says in his book *Your Erroneous Zones* about growing up in our culture to think that we are not responsible for our feelings. As a reader, it's important to distinguish between what an author is saying and what someone being written about is saying. The author of the paragraph selects examples of sayings Dyer believes we use so frequently that we begin to believe others are responsible for how we feel when, according to Dyer, we are actually in charge. The examples are used to support Dyer's views. These are not the views of the paragraph writer. In fact, we don't know what the author thinks about Dyer's views.

Notice that the **transitional phrase** "for example" alerts us to what is coming. Transitional expressions such as *for instance, also, likewise, in addition, furthermore,* and *more than that* alert us that more examples of the same idea are about to be presented. Words such as *but, however, although,* and *rather* should make us aware that a point is about to be modified or contrasted. When we read *conse-*

quently, so, therefore, in conclusion, thus, or *as a result,* we know that we are about to get a summary or the conclusion of a point. An author's use of transitional words is of great help when we read. Remember to use them in your own writing.

Before learning about any more paragraph patterns, read the paragraphs below. Underline the topic sentence of each, and then in the spaces provided write the paragraph pattern being used and its purpose. Some paragraphs may use more than one pattern.

1.   I looked around the room, and my heart sank. Cobwebs dangled from the ceiling; the once whitewashed walls were yellow with age and streaked with dust. The single naked bulb was coated with grime and extremely dim. Patches of the cement floor were black with dampness. A strong musty smell pervaded the air. I hastened to open the only small window with its rust-pitted iron bars. When I succeeded in pulling the knob and the window swung open, flakes of peeling paint as well as a shower of dust fell to the floor. The only furniture in the room was three narrow beds of rough wooden planks, one against the wall, the other two stacked one on top of the other. A cement toilet was built into one corner.

Nien Cheng, *Life and Death in Shanghai*

pattern used: _____

purpose: _____

2.   Americans, unlike people almost everywhere else in the world, tend to define and judge everybody in terms of the work they do, especially work performed for pay. Charlie is a doctor; Sam is a carpenter; Mary Ellen is a copywriter at a small ad agency....

Nickie McWhirter, "What You Do Is What You Are"

pattern used: _____

purpose: _____

3.   It was at Stanford, one day near the end of my senior year, that a friend told me about a summer construction job he knew was available. I was quickly alert. Desire uncoiled within me. My friend said that he knew I had been looking

for summer employment. He knew I needed some money. Almost apologetically he explained: It was something I probably wouldn't be interested in, but a friend of his, a contractor, needed someone for the summer to do menial jobs. There would be lots of shoveling and raking and sweeping. Nothing too hard. But nothing more interesting either. Still, the pay would be good. Did I want it? . . . I did. Yes, I said, surprised to hear myself say it.

Richard Rodriguez, "Workers"

pattern used: _____

purpose: _____

4.   Grasp the cone with the right hand firmly but gently between the thumb and at least one but not more than three fingers, two-thirds of the way up the cone. Then dart swiftly away to an open area, away from the jostling crowd at the stand. Now take up the classic ice-cream-cone-eating stance: feet from one to two feet apart, body bent forward from the waist at a twenty-five-degree angle, right elbow well up, right forearm horizontal, at a level with your collarbone and about twelve inches from it. But don't start eating yet! Check first to see what emergency repairs may be necessary. Sometimes a sugar cone will be so crushed or broken or cracked that all one can do is gulp at the thing like a savage, getting what he can of it and letting the rest drop to the ground, and then evacuating the area of catastrophe as quickly as possible. . . .

L. Rust Hills, "How to Eat an Ice Cream Cone"

pattern used: _____

purpose: _____

The first paragraph primarily uses description, but it is told through first-person narration. The topic sentence is the first one, with the rest of the paragraph describing why her heart sank. The purpose of the paragraph is to describe the room. Paragraph 2 uses examples to support the topic sentence, which is the first one. The purpose is to show that Americans judge people by the work they do. The third paragraph uses first-person narration with the purpose of telling about a summer job the author accepted. It is difficult to point to any clearly stated topic sentence, but if there is one, it's the first one. The last paragraph uses analysis. Its purpose is to show us the step-by-step process of eating an ice cream cone. Description is also used to help explain the process. There is no stated topic sentence. Make certain you understand these patterns before going on.

✏️ Writing Exercise

In your reading journal or on a separate sheet, write today's date and the page numbers you just read. Define "topic sentence." Then differentiate the four rhetorical modes or patterns you just read about and explain why understanding them can help you read or write better.

Another paragraph pattern often used by writers is **definition.** This pattern is used to clarify words and terms by providing more explanation than a dictionary, or to explain the writer's interpretation of something.

> First, let us get this [American] dream business—and business it now seems to be—straight. The word *dream* is not a synonym for *reality* or *promise*. It is closer to *hope* or *possibility* or even *vision*. The original American dream had only a little to do with material possessions and a lot to do with choices, beginnings and opportunity....
>
> Betty Anne Younglove, "The American Dream"

Here the author is defining the term *American dream* as she sees it. By comparing and contrasting, she defines what it is and is not, implying that there is a new, incorrect definition that has more to do with materialism than its true original meaning.

You will also frequently see a pattern that **divides and classifies** a subject under discussion. Classification is used to divide a subject into groups or parts on the basis of similarities. In the following paragraph, notice how the author divides and classifies "baby boomers," a term applied to people born between 1946 and 1964.

> Understandably, the younger half of the baby boom is much more concerned with finances. Since 1967, UCLA has asked incoming students why they want to go to college; among the choices provided are "to become well off finan-

cially," or "to gain a meaningful life philosophy." In 1967, as the oldest boomers were entering college, nearly 85 percent said they were going to school for philosophical reasons, and less than half went to school to get rich. By 1985, as the youngest boomers were entering school, three-fourths said, "give me the money." Only 44 percent said they wanted a meaningful life philosophy.

Jay Olgilvy, et al., "What's a Baby Boomer?"

The topic sentence, the first one, states that the younger half of the baby boom generation is more concerned with finances. The rest of the paragraph divides the baby boom generation into older and younger groups. It then classifies the younger half as more interested in finances and the older half as more interested in a life philosophy. Support is provided through the UCLA questionnaire.

Comparing and contrasting items is another paragraph pattern that appears frequently in writing. An author uses this pattern to show similarities (comparison) and differences (contrast) in the subjects under discussion. For instance:

Bees get together and build hives, termites build mounds, beavers build dams, and spiders spin webs, but what other animal can change stone and glass into poetry? Other animals can alter their environment at the margins, but only we can set goals for ourselves and then pursue them. . . .

Phil Donahue, "Beauty and the Beast"

Here a comparison and contrast, mostly contrast, is made between what animals and humans can do. Notice the use of the word *but* to show contrast. Key transitional words often used to show comparisons are *similarly, likewise, compared with, both/and,* and *in the same way.* The words *although, however, but, on the other hand, instead of, different from,* and *as opposed to* are used to indicate contrast.

The last pattern we will discuss is **cause and effect.** A cause-effect paragraph explains why something happens or happened. Some key words that serve as clues in such paragraphs are *because of this, for this reason, as a result,* or *resulting in.* Sometimes the effects are presented first and the cause of the effects last; other times it is the other way around.

See if you can distinguish between the cause and the effect in the following paragraph:

Television commercials brought a lot of fun and fun-loving folks into the picture. Everything that people in those commercials did looked like fun: taking Polaroid snapshots, swilling beer, buying insurance, mopping the floor, bowling, taking aspirin. We all wished, I'm sure, that we could have half as much fun as those rough-and-ready guys around the locker room, flicking each other with towels and pouring champagne. The more commercials people watched, the more they wondered when the fun would start in their own lives.

Suzanne Britt, "Fun. Oh, Boy. Fun.
You Could Die from It."

The cause here is watching fun-loving folks in television commercials. The effect is that they made everything look like fun, causing still another effect: people wondered when they would begin having fun.

To make certain you can recognize the writing patterns you just learned about, read the paragraphs below. Underline the topic sentence of each, and then in the spaces provided write the paragraph pattern being used and its purpose. Some paragraphs may use more than one pattern.

1. If you're within a few miles of a nuclear detonation, you'll be incinerated on the spot! And if you survive the blast, what does the future promise? The silent but deadly radiation, either directly or from fallout, in a dose of 400 rems could kill you within two weeks. Your hair would fall out, your skin would be covered with large ulcers, you would vomit and experience diarrhea and you would die from infection or massive bleeding as your white blood cells and platelets stopped working.

Ken Keyes, Jr., *The Hundredth Monkey*

pattern used: _____

purpose: _____

2. An inference is a statement *about* the known made on the basis of what *is* known. In other words, an inference is an educated guess. If a woman smiles when a man tells her she is attractive, he can infer she is pleased. If she frowns and slaps him, he can guess she is not pleased. His inferences are

based on what is known: people generally smile when they are pleased and frown when displeased. However, to know for certain why she slapped him, we would have to ask her.

pattern used: _____

purpose: _____

3.   What do L.A. [Los Angeles] women want? According to the poll, their top two goals in life are having a happy marriage, named by 37%, and helping others, 21%. Those are followed by career and a desire to be creative. Power and fame rank low on the list, with 1% each. But among women who've never been married, career takes top priority, followed by marriage and helping others. Four percent chose fame. A happy marriage appears to be the most popular goal in the Valley and Southeast areas, where it was chosen by 46% of the women—about double the number on the Westside.

Cathleen Decker, "The L.A. Woman"

pattern used: _____

purpose: _____

4.   Every paragraph you write should include one sentence that's supported by everything else in that paragraph. That is the topic sentence. It can be the first sentence, the last sentence, the sixth sentence, or even a sentence that exists only in your mind. When testing your article for topic sentences, you should be able to look at each paragraph and say what the topic sentence is. Having said it, look at all the other sentences in the paragraph and test them to make sure they support it.

Gary Provost, "The 8 Essentials of Nonfiction that Sells"

pattern used: _____

purpose: _____

5.   A trend that began about 10 years ago in Lincoln Heights seems to have hit a critical point now. It's similar to the ethnic

tug-of-war of yesteryear, but different colors, different words are involved. Today Chinese and Vietnamese are displacing the Latinos who, by choice or circumstance, had Lincoln Heights virtually to themselves for two solid generations.... The bank where I opened my first meager savings account in the late 1950s has changed hands. It's now the East-West Federal Bank, an Asian-owned enterprise. The public library on Workman Street, where I checked out *Charlotte's Web* with my first library card, abounds with signs of the new times: It's called "La Biblioteca del Pueblo Heights," and on the door there's a notice that the building is closed because of the Oct. 1 earthquake; it's written in Chinese.

Luis Torres, "Los Chinos Discover El Barrio"

pattern used: _____

purpose: _____

Compare your responses to the paragraphs with these:

1. The topic sentence is the third one. The basic pattern is cause and effect, with description of the effects of the blast provided. The cause is the nuclear bomb and the effect is death. The purpose is to show that you will die from radiation even if the initial blast doesn't kill you.

2. The first sentence is the topic sentence. The pattern is definition, with the example of the man and woman used to clarify the definition. The purpose is to define *inference*.

3. There really isn't a topic sentence. The implied topic sentence is an answer to the question that begins the paragraph, such as "Here is the result of the polls showing what L.A. women want." To show us what they want, the author uses the classification "L.A. women" and divides or groups them according to poll percentages. She further groups the women by areas: the Valley, the Southeast, and the Westside. The purpose is to reveal what L.A. women want, according to the polls.

4. The first sentence is the topic sentence. The author uses both definition and process analysis. He defines what a topic sentence is and its position in the paragraph. Then he shows how to test for an implied or directly stated topic sentence in each paragraph. The purpose is to stress the importance of the topic sentence in writing.

5. The topic sentence is the third one. The rest of the sentences contrast the differences in Lincoln Heights from the time he lived

there to now. Examples such as the library and the bank are used to show the contrast. The purpose is to show that what was once a Latino neighborhood is now being shared by Asians.

Make certain you understand what a topic sentence is and that you can recognize all eight paragraph patterns before reading on.

✍️ Writing Exercise

In your reading journal or on a separate sheet, write today's date and the page numbers you just read. Define the four rhetorical modes or patterns you just read about, and explain why understanding them can help you read or write better.

Order of Support

The third ingredient of a well-structured essay, in addition to thesis and supporting evidence, is the **order or arrangement of the thesis and its supporting evidence.** A good writer will arrange the supporting points for the thesis in a logical, progressive order. What we see when we read an essay is the final product. What we *don't* see are the many different writing drafts the writer went through before deciding which supporting point should go where or which paragraph pattern of development worked best. As a writer, you will need to go through the same process of writing several drafts before deciding which one works best for your audience.

It would be convenient if all essays followed the same writing pattern, but it would also be boring. Part of the pleasure of reading is to experience the various ways writers work with words and ideas. Still, many essays do follow the traditional form, shown in the diagram below. Keep in mind, however, that longer essays may take two or three paragraphs rather than one to introduce their topic and thesis. Most of your student essay writing assignments will probably be short enough to allow you to follow this model.

Introductory Paragraph
- attempts to draw the reader's interest.
- usually states or hints at the subject.
- sometimes states or hints at the thesis.

Paragraph 2

- usually builds on or continues what was said in the introductory paragraph.
- sometimes contains the thesis if it's not in the introductory paragraph.
- uses varying methods of development depending on what point is being made.

Paragraph 3

- is connected to paragraph 2 by a transition.
- provides more support of the thesis.
- uses varying methods of development depending on what works best to clarify supporting point.

Paragraph 4 (plus more paragraphs if needed)

- starts with a transition from paragraph 3 to 4.
- provides more support of thesis.
- uses varying methods of development depending on what best clarifies the point.

Concluding Paragraph

- summarizes points made or draws a conclusion based on the points provided.
- leaves the reader thinking about or reacting to the thesis.

The diagram above represents the basic structure of an essay. Longer essays will, of course, contain more paragraphs. Sometimes an author writes two or three paragraphs of introduction. There may be a dozen supporting paragraphs, and the conclusion may well take more than one paragraph. Sometimes an author's thesis may not be clear until the last paragraph. The typical essay form, however, is much the way it is outlined above, and the diagram probably represents the way your instructor wants you to construct essays in this course.

Before Going On

You have learned that three basic ingredients make up a good essay: a thesis, sufficient support of the thesis, and a logical order or arrangement of the supporting material. Good reading comprehension depends upon being able to identify an author's thesis based on the support that is provided. You have also learned eight different paragraph patterns or rhetorical modes that writers use to express their views: description, narration, analysis, illustration and example, definition, classification and division, comparison and contrast, and cause-effect relationships. Topic sentences are supported through the use of these patterns. In addition, you have learned the basic structure most essays follow to support the thesis. Applying this knowledge can enhance both your reading and writing skills.

 Writing Exercise

In your journal or on a separate sheet of paper, write a one-paragraph summary of the three basic elements that constitute a well-structured essay. Make certain your paragraph has a topic sentence to support. Your instructor may want to see it.

Understanding the Content

Let's look now at the skills you need to better understand what you read. To get the most from your reading, you need to be able to separate main ideas from supporting details, to distinguish fact from opinion and bias, and to draw inferences from implied statements. As you read, all of these skills work together, but for clarification purposes we'll look at each skill separately.

Separating Main Ideas from Supporting Details

The main idea in an essay is the thesis, which we've already discussed on pages 7–9. As you've seen, each paragraph in an essay supports that main idea. You've also learned that each paragraph is, in a way, a mini-essay. Paragraphs, too, have a main idea, expressed through the topic sentence and supported by the rest of the sentences.

Read the following paragraph and underline what you think is the main idea. Determine what paragraph pattern is used.

There are almost as many definitions of meditation as there are people meditating. It has been described as a fourth state of consciousness (neither waking, sleeping, nor dreaming); as a way to recharge one's inner batteries; as a state of passive awareness, of "no mind." Some teachers regard meditation as the complement to prayer: "Prayer is when you talk to God; meditation is when you listen to God." Some say meditation teaches the conscious mind to be still.

Diana Robinson,
"Recharging Yourself Through Meditation"

The point of the paragraph is to show that there are many definitions of meditation. Each of the supporting sentences provides an example of a different definition of meditation to show just how varied they are. An outline of the paragraph might look like this:

Main idea: "There are as many definitions of meditation as there are people meditating."

Support: one definition: fourth state of consciousness (neither waking, sleeping, nor dreaming)

Support: second definition: recharging one's batteries

Support: third definition: state of passive awareness, no mind

Support: fourth definition: complement to prayer

Support: fifth definition: teaches mind to be still

What we see are five different definitions that support the statement made in the first sentence. The first sentence, then, is the topic sentence.

Looking for the main idea in the first sentence of a paragraph is a good place to begin, but as you've already seen, it doesn't always appear there. Read and then underline the main idea in the following paragraph:

In one year, about $3.5 billion is spent for television commercial time. Where does all this money come from, and where does it go? Suppose Ford Motor Company buys $1 million worth of air time from NBC to introduce its new models in the fall. First it hires an advertising agency to actually produce the commercials. Of the $1 million, 15% goes to the agency for its services, and 85% goes to the network. The network in turn uses some of its 85% to pay program costs and some to pay local stations who broadcast the shows on which Ford commercials are carried. This latter payment usually equals about one-third of the local station's base rate (the amount a station would receive for commercial time bought by a local advertiser).

In the above paragraph, the first sentence does *not* state the main idea. Most of the paragraph provides an example of what would happen to one million dollars spent by the Ford Motor Company on television advertising. The example is used to provide a breakdown of where the money spent on television advertising comes from and where it goes, providing an answer to the question in the second sentence of the paragraph: "Where does all this money [$3.5 billion spent on TV advertising] come from, and where does it go?" In a way, then, the main idea is really a combination of the first two sentences of the paragraph. An outline of the paragraph might look something like this:

Main idea: Here's an example of where the $3.5 billion a year spent on advertising comes from and where it goes.

Support: If Ford Motor Company spent $1 million on TV ads:
1. 15% would go to an advertising agency
2. 85% would go to the network, which would pay
   a. program costs
   b. local stations that broadcast the shows on which ads appear (about one-third of the local station's base advertising rate)

In this paragraph, then, there is no one topic sentence expressing the main idea, but by combining the first two sentences, we can form a topic sentence of our own.

Here is another paragraph. Underline what you think is the main idea.

> The Upjohn Company is studying anti-cholesterol therapy that would actually reverse some coronary artery injury. They are also doing some exciting research in combating hypertension. In addition, they are working on important advances against deadly heart arrhythmias, or irregular heartbeat rhythms, plus a new way to zero in on blood clots with fewer side effects. These are just a few of the research projects against heart disease that Upjohn is working on.

The main idea in the paragraph appears in the last sentence. It sums up the purpose of each of the other sentences—to provide examples of the research projects Upjohn is working on in the area of heart disease. An outline of the paragraph might look like this:

Main idea: Here are a few examples of Upjohn's research projects against heart disease.

Support: anti-cholesterol therapy to reverse coronary artery injury

Support: ways to combat hypertension

Support: advances against heartbeat irregularities (arrhythmias)

Support: ways to treat blood clots with fewer side effects

Thus, we see that it doesn't matter where a topic sentence is placed; first, last, or somewhere in between, it will always contain the main idea of the paragraph.

When you have difficulty separating main ideas from the details of a paragraph, you may need to stop and outline the passage that is giving you trouble. Remember that reading entails a combination of skills, only one of which is separating main ideas from supporting details. But identifying the main idea, whether in a paragraph or an essay, is crucial to good comprehension.

Separating Fact from Opinion

Once you have identified the main ideas from supporting details, you need to separate facts from opinions. A **fact** is usually defined as something that can be proven. We accept something as a fact only when many different people come to the same conclusion after years of observation, research, and experimentation. Evidence that supports a fact is generally arrived at objectively. An **opinion**, on the other hand, is a belief, feeling, or judgment made about something or someone that a person may hold as fact but cannot prove. Evidence that supports an opinion is usually subjective. *Beautiful/ugly, wonderful/terrible, nice/disgusting, greatest/worst* are examples of subjective words writers often use to express their views. When you see them, you're reading opinions, even if you agree with the author.

But separating facts from opinions is not always easy. One reason is that facts change. At one time in history, it was a "fact" that the earth was flat (members of the Flat Earth Society still believe it); it was a "fact" that the sun revolved around the earth; it was a "fact" that the atom couldn't be split; it was a "fact" that no one would ever walk on the moon. Today, enough evidence has been gathered to prove that these and many other "facts" are wrong. Who knows what "facts" of today may be laughed at by future generations?

Another reason that separating fact from opinion is difficult is that opinion statements can be made to sound factual. We might read in one anthropology book that the first inhabitants of North America arrived "around 25,000 years ago." Another book might say North America was first inhabited "over 35,000 years ago." Which is the correct figure? Since no one who lived back then kept records, and since anthropologists disagree on the exact date the first native Americans came, we have to be careful that we don't accept such information as actual fact. We could take the trouble to read several anthropology journals and textbooks in order to get an overview of what various anthropologists believe, but until there is more factual evidence, we can't accept either date as fact. In the future, there may be enough evidence gathered to prove a particular date.

Another reason for the difficulty in separating fact from opinion is our personal bias or prejudice. Frequently, we allow our feelings and beliefs to interfere with our acceptance of facts. Certain ideas and thoughts are instilled in us as we grow up. Family, friends, and people we admire all influence our thinking. Sometimes we unknowingly accept someone's opinion as fact simply because of our faith in that person.

Let's look now at some statements of fact and opinion. In the following paragraph, underline any verifiable facts (those statements that can be supported with objective evidence).

> In the U.S., 1 in 6 couples has difficulty conceiving or bearing a child. About 27 percent of women between ages 15 and 44 can't have children because of physical problems. The sperm count of U.S. males has fallen more than 30 percent in 50 years. Some 25 percent of men are considered functionally sterile. Experts suspect that environmental pollution is a cause.
>
> Stanley N. Wellborn, "Birth"

In this case the entire paragraph should have been underlined. You may have hesitated marking the last sentence as fact. But the sentence doesn't say that environmental pollution *is* a cause; it merely says that experts suspect it is, and it can be verified that experts do suspect it is a cause. All of the paragraph can be accepted as factual. The author of the paragraph does not offer his opinion; he merely presents objective, statistical data.

Read the following paragraph and underline any statements in it that seem to be factual or that could be verified as fact:

> It's hard to believe, but in the ninth decade of the 20th Century, *The Catcher in the Rye*, *Of Mice and Men*, *Huckleberry Finn*, and *The Diary of Anne Frank*, among other books, are still the objects of censorship in the nation's public schools. And the incidence of book bannings is going up, according to a report by People for the American Way, the liberal watchdog group. In the last year, the study found, there were efforts to ban books in schools in 46 of the 50 states, including California. Many of them succeeded.
>
> Editorial, *Los Angeles Times*

The opening four words, "It's hard to believe," constitute a statement of opinion, but the majority of the paragraph can be verified as fact. We could do research on censorship to see if the books mentioned are "still objects of censorship in the nation's public schools." We could read the study mentioned by People for the American Way to see if the numbers quoted are correct. We can investigate the group that did the study to see if they are reliable. If we disagree with the statement because we don't want to believe it, that's because of personal bias; basically, there's no reason we shouldn't accept the statement as verifiable.

Now read this paragraph and underline any statements that appear to be facts:

> The purpose of education is to teach students to think, not to instill dogma or to train them to respond in predictable ways. Far from being banned, controversial material should be welcomed in schools. Students should be taught the critical ability to evaluate different ideas and to come to their own conclusions. It is a disservice to them and to society to restrict instructional material to a single viewpoint.
>
> Editorial, *Los Angeles Times*

If you underlined anything in the above paragraph, you didn't underline any facts. Regardless of how true or false you think the ideas in the paragraph are, they are all opinions. On a personal level, we may agree with the statements made, but that doesn't make them facts. Not everyone agrees with the purpose of education as stated above; many people do not want controversial materials presented to their children. In fact, some parents select certain schools for their children *because* only one viewpoint is taught.

Here's one more statement on censorship. Again, read it and underline any statements that seem to be factual.

> Everyone older than 50 grew up in a time when Hollywood films were strictly censored by the industry itself to exclude explicit sexual scenes, gruesome violence, and vulgar language. The Supreme Court in the 1950s struck down movie censorship. It extended to film makers the First Amendment protection traditionally enjoyed by newspapers and book publishers. The court also redefined the anti-pornography and anti-obscenity statutes into meaninglessness.
>
> Those decisions were praised as liberal advances, but their consequences were unforeseen and disastrous. . . . Unless they

are reversed, the coarsening and corrupting of the nation's youth will continue.

William Shannon, "Shield Our Youth with Censorship"

A mixture of fact and opinion appears here. At one time, the film industry *did* censor itself; in the 1950s the Supreme Court *did* rule against movie censorship by expanding the interpretation of the First Amendment; some people *did* praise this as a liberal advance. This can all be verified. The last sentence, however, is opinion. There is no verifiable proof that the lack of censorship in the movies is the cause for the "coarsening and corrupting of the nation's youth," nor is there verifiable proof that unless the decisions the author cites are reversed, the corruption of youth will continue. He uses facts to make his opinions appear true.

As a careful reader, you will want to use the essays in Part II as a means of practicing the separation of facts from opinions.

Drawing Inferences

Another reading skill essential to effective reading is **drawing inferences.** Sometimes writers don't state directly what they mean; they imply or suggest their meaning. When that happens, we have to draw inferences from what they do say.

Drawing an inference is sometimes called "making an educated guess." Based on what an author tells us, we can often guess what other thoughts, feelings, and ideas the author may have that are not stated directly. For instance, what are some things you can tell about the writer of the following paragraph that are not directly stated?

> In 1987, we commemorated the 100th anniversary of Sherlock Holmes's "birth." The great sleuth made his first appearance in 1887, and right from the start was so popular that when his creator killed him off after twenty-four adventures, followers eventually forced Conan Doyle to bring him back to life. Even today, the intrepid duo of Holmes and his stalwart companion Dr. Watson continue to delight each new generation of readers.

The author doesn't say it straight out, but we can infer from what is said that the writer is very knowledgeable about the Sherlock Holmes stories because of the facts that are presented. We also suspect that the author has probably read most or all of the stories and likes them very much; notice the use of such phrases as "great sleuth," "intrepid duo," and "continues to delight." Finally, based on the vocabulary and structural organization used, we can infer that the writer is fairly literate. These inferences help us get a sense of the person writing, a sense that goes beyond what is actually written. We may not always be right, but the more we practice, the more our inferences will be good educated guesses.

Read the following paragraph and see what inferences you can draw about the author. In the space that follows, write what you infer.

> We say that it is our right to control our bodies, and this is true. But there is a distinction that needs to be made, and that distinction is this: Preventing a pregnancy is controlling a body—controlling your body. But preventing the continuance of a human life that is not your own is murder. If you attempt to control the body of another in that fashion, you become as a slave master was—controlling the lives and bodies of his slave, chopping off their feet when they ran away, or murdering them if it pleased him.
>
> Ken Lonnquist, "Ghosts"

You probably can infer that the author of the paragraph is against abortion. While he agrees with pro-abortionists that we have a right to control our bodies, he draws the line after conception. We can infer, then, that he defines human life as beginning at the moment sperm and egg fuse. We can also infer he is opposed to slavery. We might even suspect that his use of the unpleasant image of slave masters cutting off the feet of runaways in connection with abortion is done deliberately to win readers to his way of thinking. If we are pro-abortionists, we might still disagree with him, but we will better understand the reasons for his views.

Now let's put together all of this section on understanding content. Read the next paragraph, underline what you think is the main idea, and see what you can infer about the author:

> Controversy—the heart of politics—has gotten a bad name in the textbook business, and publishers have advised their writers to avoid it. This fear of controversy is distorting our children's education, leaving us with biology texts that neglect evolution history and texts that omit the important influence of religion. Similarly, in civics and government texts, it is treatment of such volatile events as the Vietnam war, the Watergate scandal, the civil rights movement, and the school prayer debate that is "dulled down" to the point of tedium, or minimized to the point of evasion.
>
> Arthur J. Kropp, "Let's Put an End
> to Mediocre Textbooks"

If you underlined the first sentence as the main idea, you are partly right. But there are parts of the second sentence that also apply. One paragraph method used here is cause-effect: the cause, the fear of publishers to deal with controversial issues in textbooks; the effect, a distortion of children's education. Although the author mentions that publishers have advised their writers to avoid certain issues in textbooks, the paragraph does not support that point. The support statements that are provided are instead examples of issues that are either left out or watered down in textbooks, which the author believes then distort children's education. Thus, the paragraph uses a combination of cause-effect and illustration-example. Here is a possible outline of the paragraph:

Main idea: Fear among publishers to deal with controversial issues has resulted in a distortion of children's education. (cause-effect)

Support: biology texts that neglect evolution history

Support: omission of the important influence of religion

Support: civics and government texts that "dull down" or minimize
a. Vietnam war
b. Watergate scandal
c. civil rights movement
d. school prayer debate

Though he does not directly state it, we can infer that the author is against censorship and that he believes children should be exposed to controversy. We can infer that he does not want everything in textbooks to be watered down to show only the "smooth" side of life. We can also infer that the author believes publishers are responsible for producing books that do not challenge students. This, we might guess, is from the fear that controversial subjects in textbooks might offend some people who would then put pressure on the schools not to buy those books.

As written, most of what is stated is opinion. To prove or disprove what he says and implies, we would need to examine textbooks in many of the areas he mentions, or do further research on the subject of textbook censorship.

Use the following passage to practice all of the reading skills you have learned.

> Adaptability and lifelong learning are now the corner-stones of success. What direction does a person take to prepare for a lifetime of change? The one degree which provides training which never becomes obsolete is the liberal arts degree; it teaches you how to think. It also teaches you how to read, write and speak intelligently, get along with others, and conceptualize problems. For the first time in several decades, the liberal arts degree is coming to the forefront of the employment field.
>
> Growing ranks of corporate executives are lamenting that college students are specializing too much and too early. What corporate America really needs, according to chief executive officers of major corporations, is students soundly grounded in the liberal arts—English, especially—who then can pick up more specific business or technical skills on the job. Few students, however, seem to be listening to this message. Today's best selling courses offer evidence that students want to take the courses that provide direct job related skills rather than the most basic survival skills in the workplace: communication and thinking skills. They want courses they can parlay into jobs—and high-paying ones at that....
>
> Debra Sikes and Barbara Murray, "The Practicality
> of the Liberal Arts Major"

✍️ Writing Exercise

In your journal, answer the following questions about the two paragraphs you just read. You may look back if you need to do so.

1. What writing pattern is used in the first paragraph?
2. In your own words, write a one-sentence statement of the main idea of the first paragraph.

3. List the support provided for the main idea of the first paragraph.
4. In your own words, write a topic sentence for the second paragraph.
5. What inference can you draw regarding the authors' attitude toward a liberal arts degree?
6. Is the passage mostly fact or opinion? Explain.
7. What does the passage imply about most of today's college students?

Wording will be different, of course, but compare your answers with these:

1. Examples of the benefits of a liberal arts education make up the bulk of the paragraph; thus the illustration and example pattern is used.

2. A combination of the first three sentences is needed to cover the major point of the paragraph, so the main idea is, "The one degree that provides adaptability and lifelong learning skills is the liberal arts degree."

3. The liberal arts degree (1) teaches you how to (a) think, (b) read, write, and speak intelligently, (c) get along with others, and (d) conceptualize problems; and (2) it is coming to the forefront of the employment field.

4. The basic idea is, "Corporate executives feel that college students are coming into business too specialized, but students don't seem to be listening."

5. The authors seem in favor of the degree.

6. The passage is mostly opinion. (However, you should be aware that the passage is taken from an article that is based on the findings of research conducted with corporate executives.)

7. The last two sentences imply that most of today's college students are more interested in obtaining job skills that they think will land them high-paying jobs. They are more interested in making money than preparing for lifelong change and adaptability.

Make your goal the ability to read well enough to answer correctly these types of questions when you read. Part II will provide ample practice.

Before Going On

You have learned that reading critically requires the ability to distinguish main ideas from supporting details, to separate fact from opinion, and to draw inferences from authors' direct statements.

✍️ Writing Exercise

In your journal or on a separate sheet of paper, write a one-paragraph statement explaining what major field of study you have selected, why you selected it, and what you hope to learn. If you have not yet selected a major, write a paragraph that discusses areas of study you are considering and why. Make certain that you have a clearly stated topic sentence and adequate support. Your instructor may want to see this exercise.

Marking as You Read

To improve your comprehension and concentration, read the essays in Part II with a pen or pencil in hand, making notations in the margins. Marking as you read slows you down; it helps you to get engaged with the author, to catch your thoughts and put them in writing before you forget them. How you mark or take notes as you read is up to you, but you might want to consider doing all or some of the following:

1. Underline only major points or statements. Don't underline almost everything as some students do. Force yourself to read so carefully that you are sure that a statement or phrase is important before you mark it. Identifying the paragraph method used may help you see the difference between main ideas and supporting points.

2. Use numbers in the margins when a series of points is listed or discussed. This, too, will help you distinguish the main ideas from supporting points.

3. Think about and react to what you are reading. In the margins, write your reactions, such as "Good point!" or "Never thought of that" or "Where's the proof?" if you don't believe a statement.

4. If there's not much room in the margins, create your own kind of shorthand: Use an exclamation mark [!] when a statement surprises you, a question mark [?] when you don't understand a

point, or abbreviations, such as "ex" for example or "prf" for proof—anything that will remind you of your reaction.

5. Write a one-paragraph summary of the reading selection. If you can't, then you may need to read it again.

These are just suggestions. You or your instructor may have other methods for marking. Feel free to mark your books in any way that will help your reading concentration. Whatever the method, the reasons for marking are to gain control of concentration and to develop close, analytical reading.

Try to cultivate an interest in the assigned readings. If you don't know anything about the subject of a reading selection, keep asking questions as you read, such as: "What does the author mean by this statement?" and "How do I know if this is true?" and "What's the point of this comment?" Asking questions about what you are reading will keep you involved. Don't try to read for too long a period of time. And don't try to read assignments when you are tired; you won't concentrate very well. Good reading requires a fresh mind.

Here's a reading selection typical of the kind in Part II of this book. Read it through once. Then read it again, marking it up as suggested above or using your own marking techniques.

The Wet Drug

PETE HAMILL

1   Among the worst bores in the Western world are religious converts and reformed drunks. I have never been knocked off a horse on the way to Damascus, but I did give up drinking more than a dozen years ago. This didn't make me feel morally superior to anyone. If asked, I would talk about going dry but, from the first, I was determined to preach no sermons and stand in judgment of no human being who took pleasure in the sauce.

2   But I must confess that lately my feelings have begun to change. Drinking and drunks now fill me with loathing. Increasingly, I see close friends—human beings of intelligence, wit and style—reduced to slobbering fools by liquor. I've seen other friends ruin their marriages, brutalize their children, destroy their careers. I've also reached the age when I've had to help bury a few people who allowed booze to take them into eternity.

3   In the past few weeks, two ghastly episodes have underlined for

me the horror that goes with alcohol. In New Bedford, Mass., a 21-year-old woman was beaten and repeatedly raped by a gang of drunks in a bar called Big Dan's. There were at least 15 onlookers to her violation; they did nothing to prevent it. All of them were drunk or drinking.

4 In New York, four teen-age boys were killed when a car driven by a fifth kid smashed into a concrete wall at 90 mph. They were all under the legal drinking age of 19; nevertheless, they had managed to spend a long night drinking in a public bar, and got drunk enough to die. When it was over, and they had pried the human pieces out of the torn rubber and steel, the driver was charged with four counts of manslaughter. His worst punishment may be that he lived.

5 These are not isolated cases. This year more than 25,000 Americans will die in auto accidents caused by alcohol. And the roads are not the only site of the horror. Studies indicate that alcohol is a factor in 86 percent of our homicides, 83 percent of our fatal fires, 72 percent of robberies, 52 percent of wife-beatings, 38 percent of cases of child abuse. We can never be certain how many on-the-job accidents are caused by drinking, how many drownings, how many suicides.

6 All of this is bizarre. We live in a culture that certifies alcohol as an acceptable drug and places marijuana smokers or coke dealers in jail. Presidents and statesmen toast each other with the wet drug. It's advertised on radio and TV. Popular music is full of references to it. But when the mellow moments, the elegant evenings are over, there are our kids, smashing themselves into eternity with the same drug.

7 I'm not suggesting here any bluenose return to Prohibition. But I wish we would begin to make it more and more clear that drinking to drunkenness is one of the more disgusting occupations of human beings.

8 For every beer commercial showing all those he-men getting ready to drink, we should show footage of destroyed teenagers, their bodies broken and bleeding, beer cans filling what's left of the back seat. For every high fashion couple toasting each other with wine, show men and women puking on their shoes, falling over tables, sliding away into violence.

9 If cigarette advertising could be banned from TV, so should commercials for the drug called alcohol. Cigarette smokers, after all, usually kill only themselves with their habit. Drunks get behind the wheels of their cars and kill strangers.

10 At night now, driving along any American road, you come across these vomiting slaughterers, slowly weaving from lane to lane, or racing in confused fury to the grave at 90 mph. They don't know the

rest of us exist and, what's more, they don't care. They are criminal narcissists, careening around until they kill others and themselves.

11   We Americans should begin immediately to remind ourselves that when we drink we are entering the company of killers and fools.

Here again is the essay you just read. Compare your markings with those below. Your markings will be different, but compare what you underlined as main ideas and what you marked as supporting points with those marked in the model. They should be similar.

The Wet Drug   *what's a wet drug?*

PETE HAMILL

Among the worst bores in the Western world are religious converts and reformed drunks. <u>I have never been knocked off</u> *ask instructor what this means*

? <u>a horse on the way to Damascus,</u> but I did give up drinking more than a dozen years ago. This didn't make me feel morally superior to anyone. If asked, I would talk about going dry but, from the first, I was determined to preach no sermons and *changed his mind. Why?* stand in judgment of no human being who took pleasure in the <u>sauce.</u> *Booze? Ah, the wet drug!*

transition (But) I must confess that lately my feelings have begun to change. <u>Drinking and drunks</u> now <u>fill me with loathing.</u> Increasingly, I see close friends—human beings of intelligence, wit and style—reduced to slobbering fools by liquor. I've seen other friends <u>ruin their marriages,</u> <u>brutalize their children,</u> <u>destroy their careers.</u> I've also reached the age when I've had to help <u>bury a few people</u> who allowed booze to take them into eternity.

1. foolish acting
2. ruined marriages
3. child beating
4. ruined careers
5. death

In the past few weeks, <u>two ghastly episodes</u> have underlined for me the horror that goes with alcohol. In New Bedford, Mass., a 21-year-old woman was beaten and repeatedly raped by a gang of drunks in a bar called Big Dan's. There were at least 15 onlookers to her violation; they did nothing to prevent it. <u>All</u> of them were <u>drunk</u> or <u>drinking.</u>

example of drunks in bar — beating/raping woman

In New York, <u>four teen-age boys</u> were <u>killed</u> when a car driven by a fifth kid smashed into a concrete wall at 90 mph. They were all under the legal drinking age of 19; nevertheless, they had managed to spend a long night drinking in a public bar, and got drunk enough to die. When it was over, and they had <u>pried the human pieces</u> out of the <u>torn rubber and steel,</u> the driver was charged with four counts of manslaughter. His worst punishment may be that he lived.

example of teenage death 4 teenage drunk from driving

Yuk! (descriptive)

These are not isolated cases. This year more than 25,000 Americans will die in auto accidents caused by alcohol. And the roads are not the only site of the horror. Studies indicate that alcohol is a factor in 86 percent of our homicides, 83 percent of our fatal fires, 72 percent of robberies, 52 percent of wife-beatings, 38 percent of cases of child abuse. We can never be certain how many on-the-job accidents are caused by drinking, how many drownings, how many suicides.

[margin: statistics on damage from drinking problems 1. auto accidents 2. homicides 3. fires 4. robberies 5. wife beating 6. child abuse]

All of this is bizarre. We live in a culture that certifies alcohol as an acceptable drug and places marijuana smokers or coke dealers in jail. Presidents and statesmen toast each other with the wet drug. It's advertised on radio and TV. Popular music is full of references to it. (But) when the mellow moments, the elegant evenings are over, there are our kids, smashing themselves into eternity with the same drug.

[margin: good point → if alcohol is so damaging why legal?]
[margin: examples of acceptability contrasted with problem]

I'm not suggesting here any bluenose return to Prohibition. (But) I wish we would begin to make it more and more clear that drinking to drunkenness is one of the more disgusting occupations of human beings.

For every beer commercial showing all those he-men getting ready to drink, we should show footage of destroyed teenagers, their bodies broken and bleeding, beer cans filling what's left of the back seat. For every high fashion couple toasting each other with wine, show men and women puking on their shoes, falling over tables, sliding away into violence.

[margin: compare contrast / strong images]
[margin: wants to counter all "acceptable" drinking images with un madd, negativa, "realistic" ones]

If cigarette advertising could be banned from TV, so should commercials for the drug called alcohol. Cigarette smokers, after all, usually kill only themselves with their habit. Drunks get behind the wheels of their cars and kill strangers.

[margin: wants to ban alcohol ads]

At night now, driving along any American road, you come across these vomiting slaughterers, slowly weaving from lane to lane, or racing in confused fury to the grave at 90 mph. They don't know the rest of us exist and, what's more, they don't care. They are criminal (narcissists) careening around until they kill others and themselves.

[margin: strong image]
[margin: ?]

We Americans should begin immediately to remind ourselves that when we drink we are entering the company of killers and fools.

[margin: forceful ending! sounds fed up.]

- ask teacher about "... way to Damascus" in first ¶
- look up narcissist
- strong argument -- uses personal appeal, emotional appeal, facts & figures
- guess booze is a wet drug - never thought about it before

If you aren't used to this type of reading, it may take one or two practices before you feel confident about what you are doing. But it's a practice worth your time.

Writing Summaries

Another habit worth developing is to write a one-paragraph summary in your journal of each essay you are assigned to read. Doing so requires that you put to use all the reading skills discussed earlier. To write an accurate summary, you need to recognize the main idea of the essay (the thesis), identify its supporting points, separate fact from opinion, and draw inferences. You then use this information to write an objective summary, including only what the author says, not your opinions. When you write a summary in your journal, follow these steps:

1. Think about what you want to say first. Try writing down the author's thesis in your own words and then listing the supporting points. Use this as an outline for your summary.

2. Don't write too much, about 200 words or less. One paragraph is usually enough, although there may be times when two paragraphs are needed. The idea of a summary is to present only the main idea and supporting points.

3. Be objective; that is, don't give your own opinions or value judgments.

4. In your first sentence, provide the author's name, the title of the work, and an indication of what the essay is about. Once you have stated the author's name, you don't need to repeat it in your summary.

5. Use your own words, except for phrases you feel are important to include for clarity of a point. These phrases should have quotation marks around them.

6. Avoid using phrases such as "the author believes" or "another interesting point is." Just state what the author says.

✍️ Writing Exercise

As practice, write a one-paragraph summary in your journal of the essay you just read, Pete Hamill's "The Wet Drug." You will probably want to look over your markings or reread the essay before you begin.

Naturally, your wording will be different, but see if your summary contains the same basic points as this one:

> Excessive drinking is disgusting and harmful, says Pete Hamill in his essay, "The Wet Drug." Although he had vowed not to moralize or pass judgment on those who still drank after he quit, Hamill has changed his mind after witnessing the harm he has seen from the "drinking to drunkenness" of friends and others. As support, Hamill provides examples of what excessive drinking has done to some of his friends, such as acting foolish, ruined marriages and careers, child beating, and even death. He then cites two recent news accounts of harm from excessive drinking, one regarding a woman who was beaten and raped by a gang in a bar, another of four teens killed in an auto accident. Finally, the author presents some national statistics on the effects drinking has on auto accidents, homicides, fatal fires, wife-beatings, child abuse, and on-the-job accidents. Because we live in a society that "certifies alcohol as an acceptable drug," we should counter all acceptable images of drinking with more realistic images of the results of drunkenness. Commercials for alcohol, like those for cigarettes, should be banned from TV.

Notice that the summary's first sentence includes the author, title, and thesis of the essay. It includes the evidence Hamill uses to support his thesis: examples of the effects drinking has had on Hamill's friends, recent "horror stories" in the news of crime and violence related to drinking, and statistics on the harm caused by drinking. The summary concludes with Hamill's suggestion for countering the "acceptable" media images of drinking with more realistic ones.

The summary is objective; the only opinions used are those of Hamill, the author of the essay. Notice, too, that when the summary uses words from the essay, those words are identified with quotation marks.

You can write a good summary only when you truly understand what you have read. Writing good summaries in your journal ensures that you have read carefully. In addition, the summaries serve as good resources if you ever need to go back to review what you've read.

Writing Reflections

Writing your reflections on what you read is another useful type of journal entry to consider. Writing summaries requires objectivity;

but you also need also to capture on paper your subjective reactions, ideas, and questions that arise from the reading selections assigned. Here is where you write whatever you want. There's no right or wrong remark. You might, for instance, disagree with Pete Hamill's thesis that commercials for alcoholic beverages should be banned. Write it down in this section of your journal before you forget your reaction. Or, maybe you agree with Hamill because his essay reminds you of someone who was harmed physically or mentally because of drinking problems. Maybe the essay causes you to wonder why "the wet drug" is legal when other drugs, such as marijuana, are not. Write it down. You might be able to use your entry as the basis for an essay of your own. Write down any reactions you have or ideas that the essay causes you to think about—even those that don't directly relate to the essay. The point is not to lose any good ideas while they are on your mind.

Reflection entries are also a good place to write down some examples of the way writers work. For instance, maybe you were impressed with Hamill's use of language; write down passages that struck you, such as: "I've had to help bury a few people who allowed booze to take them to eternity," "...these vomiting slaughterers, slowly weaving from lane to lane," or "...when we drink we are entering the company of killers and fools." On the other hand, if you think these statements are too dramatic, write them down as examples of overdramatic writing. Such entries help you pay more attention to a writer's style and use of language. In turn, you will be more conscious of your own word choices when you write.

This is also a good place for questions you might want to pursue later or ask your instructor. Some of the questions might come from your marking as you read; others might come after you have finished reading. As you were reading the first paragraph in "The Wet Drug," you might have marked as a question, "What does 'knocked off a horse, on the way to Damascus' refer to?" Maybe you don't understand what Hamill means in paragraph 7 when he uses the phrase "bluenose." Write down, "What is a 'bluenose'?" Perhaps you've heard much about Prohibition but don't really know what it was or when it occurred. Write it down. Some of your questions can be answered by asking your instructor; others can be answered by using a dictionary or doing a little research in the library.

It's important to capture our thoughts, ideas, and questions in writing while we are thinking about them. If we don't, chances are we'll forget them when we get involved in another assignment. Making reflective journal entries of this type right after reading prevents the loss of our thoughts and questions.

Collecting Words to Learn

It is a good idea to set aside a section in your journal where you keep a list of the words you know you should learn. The only way you're going to enlarge your vocabulary is to take the time to expand it. You need a strong vocabulary not only to handle sophisticated reading, but also to express yourself in your own writing.

How you can best develop your vocabulary is something only you know, but just collecting a list of words is not going to help you learn them. You need to do something with the list.

As you know, words often have more than one meaning; their definitions depend on their contextual usage; that is, how they are used in a given sentence. So don't merely accumulate unknown words from the reading selections. Write down the entire sentence or at least the phrase in which the word appears. That way, when you look up the word in a dictionary, you can pick from among the various meanings the definition that fits. Once you have looked up the word to learn, write a sentence of your own using it in the proper context. Show your sentences to your instructor to make certain you are using the words correctly. Then use as many as possible in your own writing until they become as familiar as the words you already use. Yes, this takes time, but how else are you going to develop your vocabulary?

Before Going On

In order to understand better what you read, and remember it longer, be an active reader by carrying on a dialogue with the author. Make brief notations and marks in your books as you read. In addition, keep a reading journal where you can write objective summaries of the readings. Also use the journal as a place to record your reactions, ideas, and questions prompted by the reading selections. Finally, in order to enlarge your vocabulary, keep a list of new words from the readings and learn as many as you can.

✒️ Writing Exercise

In your reading journal or on a separate sheet, write today's date and the page numbers you just read. Summarize the important points in Unit I. Use your previous journal entries as a guide.

Viewpoints on
Writing Essays

Calvin and Hobbes

by Bill Watterson

"Writing is manual labor of the mind:
a job, like laying pipe."

John Gregory Dunne

*I*N THE previous unit "Viewpoints on Reading Essays," you looked at some methods and qualities of a good essay reader. Now you'll learn what it takes to be a good essay writer. What you learned about an essay's thesis, supporting paragraphs, and organization will be useful in writing essays. In fact, much of that information will sound familiar. The difference is that you will now look at the essay from a writer's point of view rather than a reader's. As a reader, you see only the final efforts of a writer; in this section, you'll see each of the various writing stages that lead to the finished product.

Three basic writing steps are presented here: how to get started, how to get your ideas in writing, and how to rewrite or polish what you write. But good writing is seldom a quick one-two-three process. It involves starting and stopping, eagerly writing away and angrily throwing away, moving along and stalling, feeling pleased and feeling frustrated, thinking you're finished and then realizing you need to start again. Sometimes a writing assignment may seem to come effortlessly; more often you will have to work very hard at it.

Writers go about writing in various ways. Hundreds of books exist on how to write, each one offering "the right way." But regardless of their differences, most of them cover at least three basic stages of writing: methods for getting started, methods for writing a first draft, and methods for revising and editing. These three stages in the writing process will be presented in that order in this section, but the order in which you follow them may vary with each essay you write. Once you increase your knowledge of what goes into writing an essay, you may modify the stages to suit yourself.

This basic three-step approach should make writing easier for you. It will give you a sense of direction and an understanding of what is expected of you as a writer. Let's look at each of these steps more closely.

Getting Started: Finding a Working Thesis (Stage 1)

As you learned in the section on reading, essays are structured around a thesis, the main idea an author wants to develop. The thesis is what the author wants to say about the topic or subject of the essay. Sometimes an instructor gives you a topic for an essay. In that case, you have to decide what you want to say about it and what thesis will guide what you want to say. Sometimes you are left on your own and must come up with both an essay topic and a thesis.

Once you've been given a writing assignment, make the topic interesting for yourself. Finding a slant that interests you will make it easier to write about the subject assigned. Also, unless the assignment requires research, think about the assignment in terms of what you already know. Depending upon the topic, that's not always easy, but here are some methods for selecting and making a topic your own.

Using Your Reading Journal

Your reading journal is one of the best places to start searching for a topic and thesis. If your instructor asks you to write an essay dealing with the general topic of an assigned reading selection, you may have already written down some reactions, ideas, or questions that you can use as a starting point. So look over your journal entries. Also, look over any textbook markings you made when you read the assignment. Just by keeping in mind that you have to write on something from that particular reading selection, you might see other essay possibilities in your markings that didn't occur to you before. By using your reflections on what you read, you will have not only a possible topic and working thesis, but also an essay that is based on your feelings and opinions.

Let's say you are assigned to read Pete Hamill's "The Wet Drug" from Unit 1. The writing assignment is to agree or disagree with the author's opinion that advertisements for alcoholic beverages should be banned from television. In this case, both your topic and thesis have been given to you. By checking your journal entry for the essay, you discover you wrote down your reaction, a notation that you agree (or disagree) with the author. You might begin by writing down a working thesis: "I agree (or disagree) with Pete Hamill in his essay

'The Wet Drug' when he says advertisements for alcoholic beverages should be banned from television." Then look again at each of Hamill's supporting points and show why you agree or disagree with his points. Such an approach at least gets you started. You may even change your mind once you begin. That's why the term *working thesis* is used at this stage. It's quite normal to discover you want to go in a different direction after writing several hundred words. Just accept that forced flexibility as part of the writing process.

At other times you may be assigned a broader topic that you must write about. Let's say that an instructor wants you to write a 500-word essay on some aspect of television commercials. A review of your journal entry on Hamill's essay shows you wrote some questions: "Where did Hamill get his statistics?" "Doesn't Hamill know that hard liquor ads are already banned on TV?" "How much of an effect do beer and wine ads on TV have on teens? adults?" "Why should such ads be banned from TV but allowed in magazines?" Looking for answers to your own questions is also a good place to find a topic and a thesis. You can see how important thoughtful journal entries can be to stimulate your own writing.

Brainstorming

When the topic is too broad for a short essay, you have to narrow it down. How do you whittle down a topic to something you can handle if you can't even think of something to write about? **Brainstorm.** There are at least two ways to brainstorm for ideas: one way is to create a list of your ideas, and another is to cluster them. Let's look at **creating a list** first.

You've probably participated in brainstorming sessions at one time or another. If so, you know it is important to follow the rules. Done correctly, brainstorming can be used to help you select a topic. For instance, if the general writing assignment is to write about television commercials, then take a sheet of paper and start writing down whatever ideas about the topic pop into your head. The trick here is not to be critical as you jot down your thoughts; just put your ideas on paper even if you don't like them at the time. It's important not to interrupt the flow of thoughts by stopping to ask yourself if what you've written is a good idea or not; you can decide that later. Just let your brain "storm." Once you have exhausted all your thoughts about the topic, then look at your list and see which ones are useful.

Sometimes it's helpful (and fun) to work with other classmates as a team. Getting together with two or three others to brainstorm brings out ideas for the assigned topic that you might not have thought about on your own.

Here's an example of a brainstorming list a student wrote on television commercials:

TV Commercials

pretty stupid
miller Lite bar scenes
lots of automobile ads
seem louder than program
   being watched
repetitive, get boring
some seem sexy
have you driven a Ford
   lately?
hate the interruptions
What does an ad cost?
Doublemint gum twins
Some are funny (Isuzu)
truck splashing through
   rivers, up hills

are they necessary?
music used is hot
   sometimes
one after the other
Obnoxious but memorable
attractiveness of some
   makes you want to
   buy
causes dissatisfaction
   with what you don't
   have
Saturday morning kids'
   ads

As you can see, some of these entries provide a sense of direction for an essay on television commercials. Some are slogans and scenes from TV commercials that she remembers. Others are her opinions about commercials. A closer look at the list may reveal that some items are dated or unusable. It doesn't matter. Making the list prompted her to think about the assigned subject.

It may be that once you decide upon a topic, such as Saturday morning kids' ads, you may need to do more brainstorming. Another brainstorming session dealing with the chosen topic should provide more specific ideas on it. If few ideas come, it may be that you shouldn't use that topic. Making a brainstorming list is useful because it helps prevent writer's block and gets ideas flowing. Discovering and narrowing down a possible topic through brainstorming saves you from false starts.

Try a little brainstorming. In the following space, brainstorm for three minutes on the topic "sports." Remember to write down everything that comes to your mind, even if it doesn't seem related. Don't be critical of any ideas; just list as many as you can in the time your instructor allows.

SPORTS

Now look over your brainstorming list. Sports is obviously a broad subject, too broad to write about in an essay. Circle any items on your list that could serve as a narrower topic for an essay dealing with some aspect of sports. For instance, you might have listed the name of your favorite athlete, or the disappointing basketball game you attended last night, or a memorable moment in a game you might have played in high school, or your favorite sport.

Once you have decided on a narrower topic in your brainstorming list, place a checkmark beside any other items that might help support your topic. If you can't find many, brainstorm again on the new topic you've chosen. Gradually, you will begin to narrow a topic down to a size you can handle with ideas for supporting points.

In the space below, list two topics from your final brainstorming session that you might use for an essay topic and create a working thesis statement for each.

topic: _____

working thesis statement: _____

topic: _____

working thesis statement: _____

Another brainstorming method is called **clustering.** In her book *Writing the Natural Way*, Gabriel Rico claims that we have two minds, our "Design mind" and our "Sign mind." Most of us have learned to write through our Sign mind, the part of the brain that deals with rules and logic. Our Sign mind criticizes, censors, and corrects errors. Because most of our training in writing deals with the Sign mind, our Design mind—the creative, less critical side of our brain—doesn't get developed much. This often leaves our creative side blocked and unused. A good piece of writing requires that both minds work together. Using an analogy with music, Rico says our Sign mind "attends to the notes," whereas our Design mind "attends to the melodies."

Clustering is a way to tap into the Design mind, the part of the brain that doesn't care about rules. It helps bring out our more creative side. A type of brainstorming, clustering brings to the surface our hidden thoughts. Rather than merely making a list of ideas, clustering creates a design, a pattern of thought.

Here's how clustering works. Write down a word or phrase in the center of a page (the **nucleus thought),** and then allow your mind to flow out from the center, like ripples created by a stone thrown into water. Rapidly write down and circle whatever comes to mind, connecting each new word or phrase with a line to the previous circle. When a new thought occurs, begin a new "ripple," or branch.

An example of clustering on the topic "TV commercials" appears on the facing page. Notice that there are five branches stemming from the nucleus thought: "dumb," "costly," "emotional appeal," "harmful," and "none?" Each one of these leads the writer closer to a workable subject. If one of these branches seems interesting enough to write about, that branch can become the nucleus for a new clustering to gain more specific details. A few minutes of clustering on an assigned topic frequently provides a sense of direction that is truly your own. Chances are your essay will be different from the norm because clustering has brought forth ideas in your mind that your usual approach to writing would not have touched.

Give clustering a try. In your journal or on a separate sheet of paper, use the clustering technique for three minutes on the topic "social problems." Write the nucleus thought "social problems" in the middle of the page and circle it. Then begin branching and clustering your ideas on the subject.

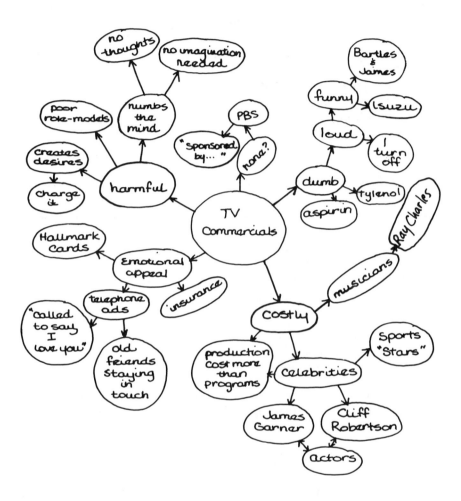

Look over your clustering. Pick two of the branches from the cluster that could serve as a narrower essay topic than "social problems." For instance, you might have a cluster branch on AIDS education, rising unemployment, inner-city gangs, racial bigotry, or police brutality. Make certain your branch contains some support for that issue. If not, you may need to take one of your branches and do some more clustering on that branch.

In the spaces below, write in two possible topics from your clustering that you could use for an essay and create a working thesis statement for each.

topic: _____

working thesis statement: _____

_____

topic: _____

working thesis statement: _____

_____

✍️ *Writing Exercise*

In your journal or on a separate sheet, write a summary of what you just read about brainstorming and its usefulness in finding a usable topic for an essay.

Freewriting

In his book *Writing with Power,* Peter Elbow recommends freewriting as still another way to focus on a writing topic or to break writer's

KUDZU by Doug Marlette, by permission of Doug Marlette and Creators Syndicate.

block. Elbow claims that practicing freewriting for ten minutes a day increases writing skills within a few weeks. Freewriting isn't polished writing, but it helps open you up to the thinking-writing process without the worrying about mechanical errors that often blocks thinking. As Elbow states in his book, what's important about freewriting is not the end product, but the process.

To freewrite, simply start writing words on a page and see what comes out. There are only two rules: don't stop to think about what you are saying, and don't stop to worry about errors in writing. Just try to write down as fast as you can exactly what's going through your mind. If you can't think of anything, write, "I can't think of anything." Repeat the phrase until you do think of something. It won't take long. You'll be surprised to see how many useful ideas for topics often emerge as you read what you've freewritten.

Here's an example of freewriting done by a student who was asked to freewrite about television commercials for a few minutes. The errors aren't important here; the ideas are.

Freewrite about TV commercials, huh? O.K. I'll give it a try but I don't know what to say, what am I suppose to say about TV commercials, anything I guess. But I don't watch much television and I hate commercials. maybe I could write about how much I hate commercials. I always watch them because I'm to lazy to get up and turn them off or down wish we had a gizmo— what its called— remote box or something that you just press a button and the sound goes off or you could change the channel. Channel 10 is that public station, they don't have any commercials but I don't like much of what I see on it always animals or nature or lots of talking. I did see a TV commercial I liked the one with the guy who lies about the car, don't remember the name of the car, but its kind a funny. Could I write about that ad? probably not, but maybe I need to watch some TV commercials and really look at them.

Notice that the student didn't stop to fix spelling or grammatical mistakes made during the freewriting. What matters in freewriting is *what* is being said. If you look carefully at the sample, you'll notice that after a bit of spinning around and going nowhere, some ideas started to come out: the advantage of owning a remote control device, the kind of programming on stations that don't air commercials, writing about funny ads, and the need to watch some television commercials closely before trying to write. Even the last idea provides a sense of direction for the writing assignment. At least four ideas for possible essays surfaced from just a few minutes of freewriting.

A ten-minute freewriting session is also useful for reasons other than finding a topic. A freewriting session before you begin to write an essay can get you warmed up to writing. It can discipline you to write when you don't feel like it. It helps you get words on paper without worrying about the writing process itself. And it helps bring out ideas and thoughts buried in your subconscious.

Some students like to freewrite for a few minutes in their journals after completing a reading assignment. It helps them capture ideas, experiences, feelings, and reactions prompted by the reading assignment and exercises. You might want to make this a part of your assignments, too.

Freewriting is an especially good technique to use if you work with a word processor. You can turn off the monitor light, and since you won't see anything on the screen, you can concern yourself only with writing your thoughts. When finished, turn up the monitor light and read what you have written. Chances are that you will find a topic you can handle.

Use a page in your journal to see how freewriting works. Write for just five minutes on the topic "family." Remember, keep writing the whole time. Don't stop to think about what you are saying; just write whatever comes to your mind, even if it's not about family. Don't worry about mistakes in spelling or grammar. Come back here when you have finished.

Now look over your freewriting. In your journal, write down all possible essay topics that you see in it. Then pick two possible topics you could use for an essay and write a working thesis statement for each.

topic: _____

working thesis statement: _____

_____

topic: _____

working thesis statement: _____

_____

Before Going On

You now know some approaches for finding an essay topic on your own. One way is to look over your journal entries for possible topics. Another is to brainstorm for topics, either by making a list or by clustering. Still another is to freewrite. If you experience difficulty selecting a topic for an essay, try one or all of these approaches. Feel free to modify them to fit your style of thinking and writing.

Writing Exercise

In your journal or on a separate sheet of paper, write a paragraph that explains and describes one of the four methods for finding an essay topic: using journal entries, listing, clustering, or freewriting. In a second paragraph, tell which one you prefer, and why. Your instructor may want you to turn this exercise in.

Getting It on Paper: Supporting Your Thesis (Stage 2)

Refining Your Thesis

Sometimes it's possible to sit down and write an essay from beginning to end. But more often than not, you'll find yourself surrounded by crumpled sheets of paper containing false starts, because you tried to write before you and your thesis were ready.

Here's a more practical and productive way to get your ideas on paper. Let's say that after clustering for ideas on the broad topic of television commercials, you narrow your subject to harmful television commercials. That branch of your cluster contains three reasons you think they are harmful: "create desires," "poor role models," and "numbs the mind." You realize now that when you wrote "numbs the mind" you were really thinking about television in general, not just commercials. So that leaves only two points.

Now you are wondering exactly what you meant about "role models" and decide it's not something you could easily write about.

That leaves only one point: "creates desires." You consider forgetting the whole idea, but you scribble down a possible working thesis: "Television advertisements create desires for things we don't need and often can't pay for." That, you think, is something you can write about because you have experienced those desires.

Had you gone ahead and started writing a draft on the three items of the cluster "leg," you would have eventually realized you couldn't do it, but not before you wasted a lot of time, effort, and paper. In most cases, it pays to think before you write.

Even now, with a working thesis, you still aren't ready to write a first draft. To defend your thesis as stated, you'd have to show that TV ads create a desire for things we don't need and sometimes can't pay for. Do all television ads do this? No, so you change your thesis: "*Some* television advertisements create desires for things we don't need and often can't pay for." Now, which ones do that? You remember a television advertisement you saw for the Mazda pickup truck. The ad made the truck look so good that you went out and bought one, even though there was nothing wrong with your old car, and even though you really couldn't afford it. In fact, you had to get your parents to cosign the loan. Further, you bought new speakers for the truck's stereo, which you didn't need either.

As you think about your working thesis, it dawns on you: you use a toothpaste and after-shave lotion because you've been influenced by commercials on television! You never used after-shave lotion until that ad appeared. Even last night, you called in to order a collection of 1950s rock-and-roll music advertised on television. Suddenly your thesis really applies to *you!* You don't actually know about everyone else, so you change your working thesis again: "Some television advertisements create desires *in me* for things I don't really need and often can't pay for." But the thesis sounds awkward, so you refine it: "Sometimes I am influenced by television advertisements and buy things I don't need and often can't afford." Now you can see why the term *working thesis* is used at this stage of essay writing.

In the process of developing a thesis, the ideas used to form it often become part of the support.

> **Working thesis:** Sometimes I am influenced by television advertisements and buy things I don't need and often can't afford.
> **Support:** the Mazda truck I bought
> **Support:** the toothpaste I use
> **Support:** the after-shave lotion I started using
> **Support:** the rock-and-roll records I ordered

Rather than writing a draft at this point, it would be better to brainstorm a bit more. What other ads have given you the "wants"? You soon come up with these:

Support: subscription to *TIME* magazine (a free watch came with it)

Support: subscription to *Sports Illustrated* (a free videotape came with it)

Support: new speakers for the truck

Support: Reebok tennis shoes

Support: a survival knife I didn't need

By now, you are embarrassed by the growing list; that's enough support to prove your point.

Before going on, make certain you understand what is meant by a working thesis and support. Some of the statements below are working thesis statements; others are not. Circle the number of any thesis statements and then explain in the space provided what the topic is and what support would be needed.

1. First impressions of people can be misleading.

2. Smaller colleges are better than large universities.

3. The value of pets

4. Participating in college athletics builds character.

5. The problems of today's students

6. Making mistakes has an educational value.

Compare your answers with these. Item 1 could be used as a working thesis. The essay topic is first impressions of people. The key word requiring support is "misleading." Examples are needed to support how first impressions can be misleading. Item 2 is also a possible working thesis. The topic is smaller colleges and support must be given to show why they are better. Item 3 should not have been circled. The value of pets is a topic, but there is no statement about the value of pets. Item 4 is usable. The subject is participation in college athletics; the support required is evidence that it builds character. Item 5 is only a topic, not a thesis statement. What about the problems of today's student? Are there any? If so, what? Item 6 should have been circled. The subject or topic is making mistakes; the support must reveal its educational value.

Grouping Your Ideas

Even after deciding on a working thesis, you're not quite ready to begin your first draft. You can't simply go down the list of supporting ideas and write a sentence about each one, and connect the sentences into an "essay." You need to organize the list in some way. So you group the items this way:

Group 1	Group 2	Group 3	Group 4
truck	toothpaste	*TIME* subscription	records
truck's stereo speakers	after-shave tennis shoes	*Sports Illustrated* subscription	knife

Group 1 deals with the truck; Group 2, personal items; Group 3, magazine subscriptions; and Group 4, miscellaneous items.

Outlining Your Support

Using the reasoning behind your grouping, you must now write down an **informal outline** to follow when you begin your first draft.

> **Thesis:** Sometimes I am influenced by television advertisements and buy things I don't need and often can't afford.
> **Major support:** unnecessary truck purchase
>   —didn't need it; old car OK
>   —parents had to cosign
>   —didn't need new speakers either
> **Major support:** unnecessary personal items
>   —changed toothpaste
>   —started using after-shave
>   —bought Reebok tennis shoes; already had new Pumas

Major support: unnecessary magazine subscriptions
–subscribed to *TIME* for the watch; already have one
–subscribed to *Sports Illustrated* for the free videotape of sports events
Major support: unnecessary miscellaneous purchases
–rock-and-roll records, could have borrowed them from friends and made tapes
–survival knife, for what?

This informal outline provides a structure for getting your ideas on paper. Following it ensures organized support of the thesis.

There may be times when an instructor requires you to attach a more **formal outline** to your essay. In that case, you should submit something along these lines:

Main idea: Sometimes I am influenced by television advertisements and buy things I don't need and often can't afford.

  I. Unnecessary truck purchase
    A. didn't need it; old car fine
    B. couldn't afford it
      1. parents had to cosign
      2. stuck with payments
    C. spent even more on unnecessary new speakers

  II. Unnecessary changes in personal items
    A. switched brand of toothpaste
    B. started using after-shave lotion
    C. bought Reebok tennis shoes because of ad

  III. Unnecessary magazine subscriptions
    A. subscribed to *TIME* for the free watch
    B. subscribed to *Sports Illustrated* for the free videotape

  IV. Unnecessary miscellaneous purchases
    A. rock-and-roll records
    B. survival knife

Regardless of what form an outline takes, it is, like a thesis, usually a working outline. Once you start writing, new ideas may surface and you may add, delete, or change what you have on your outline. Until the final essay draft, nothing written should be considered permanent.

For practice, pick one of the topics you got from brainstorming or clustering on pages 49–50 and 52. In the space provided, write a working thesis and list your support. If you don't have at least eight supporting points, do more brainstorming or clustering.

topic: _____

working thesis: _____

support: _____

support: _____

support: _____

support: _____

support: _____

support: _____

support: _____

support: _____

In your journal group your support into some type of organizational pattern you could follow to write your first draft.

Nutshell Statements

You could begin writing your first draft at this point, but first you might want to write a nutshell statement. A nutshell statement is a one-paragraph statement of the **purpose** of your essay, the **support** you will use, and the **audience** for whom you are writing. A nutshell statement for an essay based on the outline on page 59 might read:

> The purpose of my essay is to show how I am influenced by television commercials to buy things I don't need and often can't pay for. As support, I will reveal some of the items I have purchased recently because of ads I have seen, such as my new truck, personal items, magazine subscriptions, and other miscellaneous things. My intended audience will be other buyers like myself, who have yet to realize the power television ads have on us.

Notice that the statement of purpose contains the thesis. The statement regarding support summarizes the major groups or categories of evidence to be discussed. The statement about audience provides a picture of the real or imaginary people interested in the subject or those you want to make more aware of your subject.

Your audience is an important factor whenever you write. A quick note regarding your whereabouts using sentence fragments and no punctuation may be acceptable to your roommate, but certainly inappropriate for your boss. When planning an essay, then, it is necessary that you give thought to its purpose and audience. Suppose, for instance, your audience is not other buyers like yourself, but parents of young children. Your revised nutshell statement might read like this:

> The purpose of my essay is to show the negative influence of television commercials aimed at young children. As support, I will describe some of the advertisements that appear on children's early morning and Saturday programming that brainwash children and turn them into would-be consumers. My intended audience will be parents who allow their children to watch television unsupervised.

Notice the changes that need to be made as a result of your new audience. Now the thesis goes beyond the personal influence of television advertising to its influence on younger children. A different set of advertisements will be necessary for support of the thesis. Since the intended audience is now parents, even the language of the essay will need to be more formal and, given your purpose, more convincing.

Here is still another nutshell statement dealing with television commercials:

> The purpose of my essay is to write an argument in rebuttal to an article that appeared in the *Boston Globe*'s editorial pages today that claims that television commercials do not influence us. As support, I will use my own experiences, as well as factual information taken from my library research. My intended audience is the author of the article with whom I disagree and other *Globe* newspaper readers.

In this case, the final piece will be an argumentative essay that explains what the article in the *Globe* says and then provides proof that those comments about television commercials are wrong. Since the audience interested in the topic will be a fairly literate group of newspaper readers, the language selected must be appropriate, the arguments persuasive, and the other author shown to be wrong.

Even though your ultimate "audience" is your instructor who will read and grade your essay, you should write for an audience that either is interested in your thesis or needs to be made aware. Thinking about audience before you write can help you determine the type of vocabulary to use, what arguments to present, and what to assume your audience may know about the subject. For instance, if your intended audience is fifth-grade students, you will have to write at a level they can understand. The words you use, your sentence structure, and the content will have to be geared to that group. On the other hand, if you are writing to convince anti-abortionists to change their minds, you will need to understand their reasoning and provide counterarguments. You will have to imagine what they might say in reaction to what you say. You will have to decide what approach will get them to even listen to your views. Should you use sarcasm? sympathy? medical terms?

A nutshell statement requires that you have your purpose, support, and audience in mind before you begin writing. If you can complete a nutshell statement, then you are ready to begin your first draft.

In your journal or in the space provided, write a one-paragraph nutshell statement for an essay based on the outline you completed on pages 59–60.

Once you have your thesis, support, and audience in mind, you're ready to start your first draft.

Patterning Your Paragraphs: The Beginning

As readers we only see the finished product of a writer, not all the changes that went into creating it. What finally appears as a beginning or introductory paragraph may actually be the last paragraph an author writes. In other words, it is not infrequent that the opening paragraph you write in a first draft is *not* the opening paragraph in the final draft. In fact, that first paragraph may not even be used in the final draft, or it could be changed so much it no longer resembles what you started with. By the time revisions are made and the support has been established, your old introductory paragraph may be obsolete.

Most of us, however, begin writing our first drafts with what we think will be our introduction. It helps us formulate and state our thesis. Such a paragraph might help *us* get started, but it may not get our readers interested in what we have to say. What, then, are some effective ways to begin an essay?

Here are some suggestions that may work for you, depending on your essay audience and purpose. Many of the essays in this book use these methods. Check out the essays mentioned to see each strategy at work.

1. Get right to the point, stating your thesis and your general reasons for feeling or believing as you do. One drawback to this approach is that unless your thesis is stated in such a way that your audience will be interested in reading on, it could be a boring opening. Examine Albert Robbins's essay "Settling in the Cities," Letty Cottin Pogrebin's "Superstitious Minds," and Vincent Ryan Ruggiero's "Debating Moral Questions" to see how they use this direct technique.

2. Use a quotation that relates to your thesis, one by someone respected by most everyone, one that supports your point of view, or one that you disagree with and want to disprove in your essay. Rachel L. Jones does this in "What's Wrong with Black English."

3. Tell a brief anecdote or story that relates in some way to or introduces the point of your thesis. For examples, look at the introductory paragraphs used in Roger von Oech's "To Err Is Wrong," Langston Hughes's "Salvation, and Brent Staples's "Night Walker."

4. Use one or more questions that cause the reader to think about your topic, questions that you intend to answer in the body of your essay. Jeanne Park's opening paragraph in "Eggs, Twinkies and Ethnic Stereotypes" is a question. Sikes and Murray use questions in their first two opening paragraphs in "The Practi-

cality of the Liberal Arts Major." See also Liu Zongren's opening paragraph in "After Two Years in the Melting Pot."

5. Provide some startling statistics or information that will get your readers' attention and that will appeal to their good sense. Notice how this is done in Sharon Whitley's "Students' Love Affair with Anne Frank" and Mary Sherry's "In Praise of the F Word."

6. Describe a scene that gets attention and pulls your reader into the subject. Jon D. Hull does this very well in "Slow Descent into Hell" as does H. Bruce Miller in "Severing the Human Connection."

7. Be creative and use a combination of the above.

The introductory paragraph is an important one. Make certain that whatever method you use, your opening draws your reader's interest, fits into the point of your essay, and gets the reader involved in your subject.

Patterning Your Paragraphs: The Middle

As a means for better reading comprehension, Unit 1 presented some paragraph methods that writers use. Now let's look at those same paragraph patterns from the writer's angle.

Recall that the **topic sentence** in a paragraph serves the same function as the thesis statement in an essay. Just as what you say in your essay depends on the point of your thesis, what you say and how you say it depend on the topic sentence of your paragraph. Here are some possible topic sentences for paragraphs. Notice that the way they are written pretty much determines the paragraph pattern:

Topic sentence	*Best pattern*
The Mazda truck commercial was very appealing.	**description** Descriptive details should be provided to create an image in the reader's mind of the commercial's appeal.
Yesterday, I went from one truck dealership to the next looking for the best deal.	**narration** A narrative would take the reader from one dealership experience to the next relating what happened at each.

I now recognize three reasons why I buy many things I don't really need.	**analysis** Each of the three reasons for the buying problem needs to be examined.
I recently bought several things I don't need.	**illustration-example** Evidence needs to be provided to illustrate the unnecessary items purchased. Examples of the things not needed or a narrative about the buying of unnecessary items is required.
Pat's mother says he is the perfect example of an impulsive buyer.	**definition** The term *impulsive buyer* needs to be defined so readers understand what Pat is an example of.
The commercial showed the four basic types of auto stereo speakers.	**division-classification** The topic sentence divides the speakers into four basic types, each of which needs to be named and discussed.
The Mazda truck commercial appealed to Jim more than the one for Chevrolets.	**comparison-contrast** While some description of the two truck ads may be needed, the topic sentence calls for a comparison of the two ads to show why Jim prefers one over the other.
Because the Mazda commercial was so well done, I bought one of their trucks.	**cause-effect** The cause here is the ad, and the effect is the purchase; description of the well-done ad may be needed to help explain the cause.

It is important to see here that the way you state a topic sentence requires that you structure your paragraph with a pattern that supports it. Of course, all the examples above are "working" topic sentences. After you have developed your support, you may need to change the wording of the topic sentence to fit what you wrote. You may decide that the topic sentence is best placed at the end of the paragraph or in the middle, or that it should be implied rather than stated. Remember, revision is not limited to any one particular stage.

It occurs at all points during the writing process. But if writing does not come easily for you, try writing a topic sentence that you can use as the first sentence in the paragraph and work from there.

Here are some topic sentences taken from the reading selections in this book. In the space provided, write a one-sentence statement that tells what pattern or method should be used to develop the paragraph and why.

1. "Compared to the animals around us, there's no doubt we are a remarkable phenomenon."

2. "I will never forget that Sunday as long as I live."

3. "Behind a Dumpster sits a man who calls himself Red enjoying the last drops of a bottle of wine called Wild Irish Rose."

4. "There are four reasons for practicing freewriting."

5. "After the dishes have soaked in water hot enough to deform small plastic implements, I begin my attack."

6. "We humans live with contradictions in our behavior."

7. "Irony is not easy to explain."

8. "Television journalism has recently stimulated political conservatism."

Compare your statements with these. Wording may be different, but the explanations should contain the same ideas.

1. The **comparison-contrast** method will show why humans are a phenomenon compared with other animals.
2. **A narration** will tell us about that unforgettable Sunday.
3. The topic sentence introduces us to Red and calls for more **description** of him.
4. **Division-classification** is required to show each of the four reasons for practicing freewriting.
5. The "attack" on the dishes is a process calling for a **step-by-step analysis.**
6. **Examples and illustrations** of contradictory behavior are needed for support.
7. An extended **definition** of irony should show why it isn't easy to define.
8. If television journalism has stimulated political conservatism, some proof or support of this **cause-effect** relationship is required.

If you had trouble with these, you may want to review the section on paragraph patterns in Unit 1.

Patterning Your Paragraphs: The End

As with essay introductions, there is no one way to conclude an essay. Many students tend to repeat almost verbatim in their closing paragraph what they said in their opening one. However, the concluding paragraph of an essay should not simply duplicate what has already been written. Instead, you will usually want to do one of these three things in your last paragraph, depending on what your thesis is:

1. Summarize the major points of the essay. This can be tricky. Try to summarize by using different wording to restate the points you've made in a fresh but familiar way. Don't use this method in a short essay with only three or four supporting paragraphs. This approach works best when you have written a longer piece with many points. Your summary will help your reader pull them all together.

2. Draw a conclusion based on the information you have presented. This method works best when you have been arguing for a particular viewpoint and have presented evidence that needs to be highlighted in order to draw a conclusion for the reader. Usually, you begin your paragraph with words such as, "Thus, we can see from these facts that . . . ," or "For these reasons we must conclude that . . . ," and then you state your conclusion. [Note: Don't confuse the word "conclusion" meaning "the end," with "drawing a conclusion," or making a judgment based on information provided.]

3. Emphasize the need for change or more attention on the subject. Make a pitch for what needs to be done, based on the information you have presented in your essay. Call upon your readers to think more, care more, or act more on the subject of your essay now that you have successfully made your case.

Many of the paragraph patterns already discussed can be used effectively in concluding paragraphs.

✍️ Writing Exercise

In your journal or on another sheet, summarize the information on writing beginning, middle, and ending paragraphs. Make certain you understand pages 63–68 before going on.

First Draft

Let's say that you decide to follow the formal outline on page 59 about the effect of television commercials. The first draft might look something like this:

First Draft

1   I have a tendency to buy things I see on television commercials even though I don't need them and often can't pay for them. The other night I was putting myself to sleep by watching a late movie on TV when an ad with a fast-talking announcer began describing a new collection of rock-and-roll records. You've probably seen the kind I mean. You get to hear little pieces of music with famous singers singing one or two lines then they cut to the next song. Anyway, I like all of the songs they played, and when the announcers said, "Call this 800 number now and get these fabulous songs not sold in any record store," I called and ordered the record set. This is not unusual behavior for me.

2   I bought my Mazda truck because of a TV commercial. It seemed like every time I watched TV I'd see the same ad for the truck. It showed the truck going through mud, climbing hills, and carrying heavy loads. Then it showed a guy and his girlfriend all dressed up pulling up in front of some fancy restaurant in the truck all shined up. The girl was something else and every time the ad came on I caught myself looking at her and not the truck. Anyway, the next thing I knew I had talked my folks into cosigning the loan for me even though they tried to talk me out of it. Banks don't loan money to college students to buy trucks. There wasn't anything wrong with my old car. But I came up with this crazy idea I could get some parttime

work hauling or something to help make the payments. I think that's what convinced them to help out. Anyway, now I can't afford to take a girl out because I'm too busy with classes, homework, and an evening job I have to keep to make my truck payments.

3   I also have two magazine subscriptions that I don't even have time to read. When TIME showed an ad on TV for a good deal on a subscription, plus a free watch, I called their toll-free number. Then Sports Illustrated ran an ad for their magazine offering a free videocassette of famous sports plays if you subscribed to them. Of course, I called their toll-free number. Now unread magazines are stacking up around my room. Not only that, they sent me a Beta videocassette and we've got VHS.

4   I realize now that I have even been persuaded by TV ads to buy items I never used before. My family has always used Crest. After seeing all those ads for Closeup and having kissable breath, I got my mom to buy some for me. I even use an after-shave lotion now because of ads. I use to do like my dad and just put on a little of mom's skin cream after I shaved. And even though I didn't need them, I bought a new pair of Reebok tennis shoes because a TV commercial for a local shoe store had them on sale.

5   Last night there was a commercial on TV for a good deal on a neat looking survival knife. It looked like something the commandos use. It had a big blade, a compass in the handle, with a fish hook and line, matches and the sheath had a little pocket with a sharpening stone in it. Naturally, I ordered one.

6   When my mom heard about this she called me an "impulsive complusive buyer." When I asked her what she meant, she

just yelled look it up. After looking it up, I realize she's right. I need to belong to a "buyers anonymous" group or something.

Even though the outline wasn't followed exactly, it served to get the ideas into a rough draft in essay form. Of course, this is just the first draft. There's more to be done.

This is a good place to make another pitch for word processing. If you don't know how already, you should learn to write on a word processor. Making changes, doing revisions, and producing neat essays is so much easier once you learn word processing. A recent study done by a professional organization of English teachers revealed that students who submitted typed papers usually got a letter grade higher than those who submitted handwritten papers. But more importantly, word processing enables you to make changes without having to retype your entire essay. It's something to think about.

Whatever you use for your first drafts—pencil, pen, typewriter, or word processor—don't worry about mistakes in punctuation, word choice, spelling, and the like. At this point, you just want to get your essay ideas into words on paper. If you stop to make too many corrections as you write, you may lose your train of thought. Worry about the nitty-gritty later. On the other hand, if there's an error you can quickly change, go ahead and do it, but never at the expense of thoughtful content.

Before Going On

Remember that a working thesis statement is open to changes based on your supporting ideas. Before writing a first draft, make certain you have sufficient support to develop your thesis. Once you are satisfied you do, organize or outline the support as a writing guide. Writing a nutshell statement before you begin your draft helps you focus on your thesis, support, and audience. As you write your draft, be aware that all paragraphs should have an implied or directly stated topic sentence. The wording of your topic sentence can often provide a clue as to the best paragraph pattern to use. However, don't let concern over paragraph patterns or mechanical errors get in the way of getting your ideas on paper. Changes and corrections can be made during the revision and editing process.

✍️ Writing Exercise

Look again at the draft of the student essay on television commercials. Apply the information on reading essays from Unit 1. Mark and take notes as you read. Then, in your journal or on a separate sheet of paper, write what you would tell the student about the essay, offering your suggestions for improvement and indicating errors that should be changed. Your instructor may want to see your paper.

Getting It Right: Revising and Editing (Stage 3)

It can't be said too often that good writing frequently requires many rewrites. Don't be impatient. Revision is necessary, expected, and part of the writing process. A final draft may look nothing like the first one. There's much to do before turning in your masterpiece.

Revising

Here's a checklist to guide revision of your first draft:

1. *Have you made your point?*
   Make sure your thesis is clear. Stated or implied, your purpose should be clear to the reader. Have someone read your draft; if he or she doesn't understand the point you're trying to make, rewrite until it becomes clear. It's even possible that you will need to change your entire thesis once a first draft is completed.

2. *Does your support move smoothly from one point to the next?*
   Rearrange what you have written so that the ideas flow easily from one to the next. You may need to "cut and paste," or move a sentence or paragraph from one place to another. Use scissors and literally cut up your draft, moving parts around where you want them. (Here again, word processing helps. With a word processor you can easily move whole paragraphs without having to cut or retype.) To move smoothly and logically from one point to the next, use transitional words and phrases such as these:

however	thus	in addition
although	on the other hand	first
therefore	in conclusion	next
furthermore	in other words	finally
moreover	for instance	as a result
consequently	for example	also

3. *Have you developed each paragraph fully?*

   Look closely at the topic sentence of each paragraph. Do you provide enough support to fully develop the topic sentence? You may need to add more information or to take out information that does not relate to the topic sentence. You may need to rewrite your topic sentence to fit the content of the paragraph.

4. *Will your essay interest your audience?*

   Try to make your essay interesting for your audience. Your opening paragraph should grab the readers' attention and make them want to read on. Try to get a picture in your mind of your audience and talk to them in writing. Sometimes the opening paragraph doesn't take shape until several drafts are completed.

5. *Is the tone of your essay consistent?*

   Use the same **tone of voice** throughout your essay. For instance, the tone of the student's rough draft on television commercials is personable and friendly. Using contractions (such as **don't** instead of **do not**) is acceptable in informal writing. The essay is not written for the audience of a scholarly or professional journal. If it were, it would need more formal language, less personal narrative, and a thesis that dealt more broadly with television commercials and cited sources other than personal experience.

6. *Have you said everything you want and need to say and nothing else?*

   Make certain you have said everything necessary to support your thesis. On the other hand, you may need to cut out passages that aren't relevant or that repeat what you've already said.

Let's apply the above checklist to the rough draft on television commercials. Here's what it might look like:

I have a tendency to buy things I see on television commercials even though I don't need them and often can't pay for them. *[move to the end]*

The other night I was putting myself to sleep by watching a late movie on ~~TV~~ *television* when ~~an ad~~ *a commercial* with a fast-talking announcer began describing a new collection of rock-and-roll records. You've probably seen the kind I mean. ~~You get to hear~~ *They play* little ~~pieces~~ *snippets* of ~~music with~~ *of a song you recognize* famous singers singing one or two lines, then they cut to the next song. ~~Anyway,~~ I like all of the songs they played, ~~and~~ *so* when the

announcers said, "Call this 800 number now and ~~get these~~ *order this* fabulous ~~songs~~ *record set* not sold in any ~~record~~ store," I ~~called and ordered the~~ *did.*
start new ¶ ~~record set.~~ This is not unusual behavior for me. *For instance,*

I bought my Mazda truck because of a TV commercial. It
seemed like every time I watched TV I'd see the same ad for the
truck. It showed the truck *at work during the day* going through mud, climbing hills, and
carrying heavy loads. Then it showed *the truck at night cleaned and polished,* ~~a guy and his girlfriend all~~
~~dressed up~~ pulling up in front of ~~some fancy~~ *a plush* restaurant. ~~in the~~ *As the driver got*
out, a smiling doorman helped the woman out. Both of them looked elegant, but she
~~truck all shined up. The girl was something else and~~ every time *really got to me.*
the ad came on I caught myself looking at her and not the truck.
I realize now it wasn't the truck I wanted.
¶ Anyway, the next thing I knew I had talked my folks into cosign-
ing ~~the~~ *a* loan for ~~me even though~~ *a new truck since* ~~they tried to talk me out of it~~ *since*
Banks don't loan money to college students to buy trucks. There
wasn't anything wrong with my old car. But I came up with this
crazy idea I could get some parttime work hauling or ~~something~~ *delivering*
to help make the payments. I think that's what convinced them to
help out. ~~Anyway,~~ now *I wish I hadn't been so convincing.* I can't afford to take a girl out because I'm
too busy with classes, homework, and an evening job I have to
keep to make my truck payments.
Thanks to TV commercials,
I also have two magazine subscriptions that I don't even have
time to read. When ~~TIME showed an ad on TV~~ *I saw a commercial* for a ~~good deal~~ *reduced price* on a
subscription *for TIME* plus a free watch, I called their toll-free number. The
Sports Illustrated ~~ran an ad for their magazine offering~~ *offered a low-priced subscription and* a free
videocassette of famous sports plays if you subscribed to them. Of
course, I called their toll-free number. Now unread magazines are
stacking up around my room. Not only that, they sent me a Beta
videocassette and we've got VHS.

I realize now that I have even been persuaded by TV ads to
buy items I never used before. My family has always used Crest.
After seeing all those ads for Closeup and ~~having~~ *the need for* kissable breath,

I got my mom to buy some for me. I even ~~use~~ began using an after-shave lotion now because of ~~ads.~~ the influence of commercials, I use to do like my dad and just put on a little of mom's skin cream after I shaved. And even though I didn't need them, I bought a new pair of Reebok tennis shoes because a TV commercial for a local shoe store had them on sale.

Last night there was a commercial on TV for a good deal on an interesting ~~neat~~ looking survival knife, similar to the ones ~~It looked like something~~ the commandos use. It has a big blade, a compass in the handle, with a fish hook and line, matches and the sheath had a little pocket with a sharpening stone in it. Naturally, I ordered one. *end here*

When my mom heard about this she called me an "impulsive complusive buyer." When I asked her what she meant, she just *move up* yelled look it up. After looking it up, I realize she's right. I need to belong to a "buyers anonymous" group or something.

Look more closely at some of the changes being considered for the next draft. Sentences are to be moved or removed. Wording has been changed, in some cases to keep from repeating words, in others to be more descriptive or clear. New paragraphs have been started in different places, and the last paragraph has been moved. While none of the support has changed, more attention has been paid to the flow of support with smoother transitions from one idea to the next. Attention to such details is the basis for the second draft. And even after that draft is completed, it may be necessary to write still another.

After applying the revision checklist to several different drafts, you might have a paper resembling this one:

About to doze off while watching an old movie on television the other night, a commercial caught my eye. The sound came up as a fast-talking announcer began describing a new collection of rock-and-roll records. You've probably seen the kind I mean. They play little snippets of singers singing one or two seconds of a song that made them famous, cutting quickly from one to the next. I like all the tunes they played, so when the announcer urged, "Call this toll-free number now ... operators are standing by ... order this fabulous set of records not available in any store," I did.

This, I'm sorry to say, is not unusual behavior for me. For instance, when I saw a television commercial offering a free digital watch along with a reduced price on a subscription to TIME, I called their toll-free number. Then Sports Illustrated offered a low price subscription along with a free videocassette of some famous sports plays. Of course, I had to call their toll-free number too. Now I have unread magazines stacking up around my room. Not only that, the videocassette they set me is for a Beta machine, we've got VHS.

TV commercials have influenced me so much that I even use personal items I have never used before, my family has used Crest toothpaste ever since I can remember. But after all those ads for Close-up (I think its the kissable breath idea) I had my mom buy some just for me. And, like my dad, I used to just apply a little of moms skin cream on my face after I shaved. But now, thanks to the influence of television commercials, I have tried several beands of after-shave lotion.

The biggest purchase I ever made because of a TV commercial is my truck. It seemed like every time I watched TV I'd see the same ad for Mazda pickup trucks. It showed the truck at work during the day going through mud, climbing hills, and carrying heavy loads. Then it showed the truck at night, cleaned and polished, pulling up in front of a plush restaurant. As the driver got out, a doorman helped his date step out. Both of them looked elegant. But it was the woman that got me. Every time the commercial comes on, I caught myself looking at her, not the truck. Anyway, the next thing I knew I had talked my folks into cosign-

ing a loan for a new truck, since banks don't loan money to unemployed college students to buy new trucks. They tried to talk
me out of it because there wasn't anything wrong with my old
one. But you know how it is when you really want something. I
rationalized that I could get part-time work hauling or delivering
to help make payments. I think that's what convinced my mom
and dad to help out.

Now I wish I hadn't been so convincing. I can't afford to go
out on a date because I'm too busy with classes, homework, and
an evening job. If I don't make my truck payments, my parents
said they would sell my truck. They don't want to be stuck with
the payments. I can't blame them.

Recently a local shoe store announced on television that Reebok tennis shoes were on sale. The next day, I bought a pair, even
though I had just bought a pair of Pumas a week before. When my
mom heard, she called me an "impulsive compulsive buyer". When
I asked her what she meant, she yelled, "Look it up!" and mumbled something about my need to join a "buyers anonymous"
group or quit watching so much TV.

She's right I have a tendency to buy things I see on television
even though I don't need them or can't really afford them. Even
last night, there was a commercial for a survival knife similar to
the type commandos use. The knife has a big blade, a hollow handle with a fish hook, some line, a few matches, a compass that
screws on top of the knife handle, and the sheath has a little
pocket on the side with a sharpening stone, I just couldn't resist
calling there toll-free number.

This draft still retains the same thesis and support, but it is structured differently. The position of the thesis has been moved from the
opening paragraph to the end. The first draft opened with the thesis

statement and then provided examples of "impulsive compulsive" buying. This draft opens with a narrative anecdote that reflects the subject and thesis of the essay, rather than directly stating it. The narrative now builds on one purchase after the other and ends with the thesis statement. This seems to work better because the thesis itself doesn't deal with any resolution of the problem, only an awareness of the influence of television commercials on the author.

Other changes in the position of the supporting materials have been made. The largest purchase, the truck, has been moved toward the end of the essay, with smaller purchases leading up to it. The placement of the Reebok purchase after the truck purchase works well because it reflects the mother's exasperation with her son's buying habits. It also serves as a transition to the last paragraph, which now contains the thesis and an acknowledgement that the author's mother is right: another needless purchase, the survival knife, is made. The essay ends with a touch of humor, yet leaves the reader with a feeling of pity for the author.

While the student essay is not perfect, it is an honest essay based on experience and it fits the assignment given: to write an essay on some aspect of television. Had the assignment been more specific, such as one requiring research on the effects of television advertising, then this first-person essay would not do.

As improved as this draft is over the first, there is still more to do before the student can turn it in. The essay needs editing.

Editing

Once you are satisfied that your essay's organizational structure and thesis are clear and fully developed, you need to edit your essay for errors in punctuation and mechanics. Of course, as you do this you may also see other problems or errors that need revision. Revision is a continual process, even though you may be focusing on making specific corrections.

Here is a list of questions to ask yourself when you edit your latest draft:

1. *Have you given yourself some time off between drafts?*
   Put your essay aside for at least a couple of hours before editing. In fact, it's a good idea to do this between each draft. You need to get away from what you've written so you can come back to it with "fresh eyes."

2. *Have you read each sentence aloud to hear how it sounds?*
   Begin editing by reading aloud the *last* sentence of your essay. Once you're satisfied it is the best you can do, read aloud the

next-to-last sentence and evaluate it the same way. Gradually work your way to the beginning of the essay sentence by sentence. It sounds odd, but doing so forces you to look at each sentence out of context, as a separate piece of writing. Listen to the way the sentence sounds. If it is difficult to read or sounds awkward, rewrite it. Make certain each sentence is complete, not a fragment, a piece of a sentence.

3. *Have you used proper punctuation?*
   Don't form a comma splice by putting a comma [,] between two sentences. If you aren't sure where a comma belongs, it's probably best to leave it out. Place periods [.] at the ends of sentences, not at the end of phrases or introductory clauses. Use apostrophes ['] to show possession (Tom's house, the grandparents' house). Watch for *you're* (you are) as opposed to *your* (belonging to), and *it's* (it is) as opposed to *its* (belonging to it).

4. *Do your verbs agree with their subjects?*
   Watch for sentences that contain singular subjects and plural verbs. For instance, in the following sentence the subject is singular, but a plural verb is used:
   > A set of books are missing.
   Because *set* is the subject, not *books*, the verb *is* should be used. Look also for sentences that contain plural subjects but singular verbs, such as:
   > Boxes of computer software was everywhere.
   The sentence should use the verb *were* to agree with the subject *boxes*. Such mistakes are easy to make.

5. *Are your pronoun references correct?*
   Look at each pronoun (his, her, their, its, etc.) and make sure it agrees with what it refers to. For instance, it's incorrect to write:
   > Everyone in the group must buy their own lunch.
   Since *everyone* is singular, the plural pronoun *their* can't be used. It should read:
   > Everyone in the group must buy his or her own lunch.
   [Note: Avoid sexist usage. Don't use *his* when the reference being made is to a group containing both men and women.] Don't confuse *there* (not here), *they're* (they are), and *their* (belonging to them).

6. *Have you repeated the same word too often?*
   If you don't own a thesaurus, a dictionary of synonyms (words that mean the same thing), you should buy one. Several are published in paperback editions. A good thesaurus will not only define words for you, but will also provide synonyms and antonyms (words that are opposite in meaning). When you notice that you are repeating a word, look it up and use a synonym.

7. *Do you have a title that reflects your thesis?*
A title, like a thesis, should not be too general. It should reflect the purpose and the content of your paper. A title should also fit the tone of your essay. If your essay is serious in tone, it's probably best to have a title that is direct; if your essay is light or humorous, try a catchy title.

For practice in editing, apply the steps of the preceding editing checklist to the last draft of the student essay on pages 75–77. Change any errors you find and give the essay an appropriate title.

✍️ Writing Exercise

In your journal or on a separate sheet of paper, write a one-paragraph summary of the editing checklist. Make certain you have a topic sentence that allows you to discuss all the steps. Your instructor may want to see your summary.

Here is what the next draft of the essay might look like after editing and minor revisions. Compare your markings with those below.

Trouble with Toll-Free Numbers

About to doze off while watching an old movie on television the other night, a commercial caught my eye. The sound came up as a fast-talking announcer began describing a new collection of rock-and-roll records. You've probably seen the kind I mean. They play little snippets of singers singing one or two seconds of a song that made them famous, cutting quickly from one to the next. I like all the tunes they played, so when the announcer urged, "Call this toll-free number now ... operators are standing by ... order this fabulous set of records not available in any store," I did.

This, I'm sorry to say, is not unusual behavior for me.

For instance, when I saw a television commercial offering a free digital watch along with a reduced price on a subscription to TIME, I called their toll-free number. Then Sports Illustrated offered a low-price subscription along with a free videocassette of some famous sports plays. Of course, I had to call their toll-free number too. Now I have unread magazines stacking up around my room. Not only that, the videocassette they sent me is for a Beta machine; we've got VHS.

[margin: underline magazine titles]
[margin: comma splice, replace comma with semicolon.]

TV commercials have influenced me so much that I even use personal items I have never used before; my family has used Crest toothpaste ever since I can remember. But after all those ads for Close-up (I think it's the kissable breath idea), I had my mom buy some just for me. And, like my dad, I used to just apply a little of mom's skin cream on my face after I shaved. But now, thanks to the influence of television commercials, I have tried several brands of after-shave lotion.

[margin: comma splice. Replace comma with period. Cap M.]
[margin: comma after intro phrase]
[margin: possessive]

The biggest purchase I ever made because of a TV commercial is my truck. It seemed ~~like~~ *that* every time I watched TV I'd see the same ad for Mazda pickup trucks. It showed the truck at work during the day going through mud, climbing hills, and carrying heavy loads. Then it showed the truck at night, cleaned and polished, pulling up in front of a plush-*looking* restaurant. As the driver got out, a doorman helped ~~his date step out~~ *his date was helped by a doorman*. Both of them looked elegant. But it was the woman ~~that~~ *who* got me. Every time the commercial ~~comes~~ *came* on, I caught myself looking at her, not the truck. Anyway, the next thing I knew I had talked my ~~folks~~ *parents* into cosigning a loan for a new truck, since banks

[margin: use who to refer to people]
[margin: past tense]

don't loan money to unemployed college students to buy new trucks. They tried to talk me out of it, because there wasn't anything wrong with my old one. But you know how it is when you really want something. I rationalized that I could get part-time work hauling or delivering to help make payments. I think that's what convinced my mom and dad to help out.

Now I wish I hadn't been so convincing. I can't afford to go out on a date because I'm too busy with classes, homework, and an evening job. If I don't make my truck payments, my parents said they would sell my truck. They don't want to be stuck with the payments. I can't blame them.

Recently a local shoe store announced on television that Reebok tennis shoes were on sale. The next day I *necessary?* bought ~~a pair~~ them, even though I had just bought a pair of *pair used twice* Pumas a week before. When my mom heard, she called me an "impulsive compulsive buyer." When I asked her what *end punctuation, goes inside quotation marks.* she meant, she yelled, "Look it up!" and mumbled something about my need to join a "buyers anonymous" group or quit watching so much TV.

She's right, I have a tendency to buy things I see on *run on needs period.* television even though I don't need them or can't really afford them. Even last night, there was a commercial for a survival knife similar to the type commandos use. The knife has a big blade, a hollow handle with a fish hook, some line, a few matches, a compass that screws on top of the knife handle, and the sheath has a little pocket on the side with a sharpening stone, I just couldn't resist calling *their* ~~there~~ toll-free number. *wrong word*

At this point you are ready to type up the final draft to submit to your instructor.

Proofreading

Once you write, type, or print out your final draft, you should proofread your paper for typing and spelling mistakes. It's possible that even then you might notice changes that have to be made. Remember that revising and editing, even though presented here as Stage 3, can happen at any stage of the writing process.

If the final copy of your essay has many mistakes, you may need to recopy or retype it. However, if it has only a few minor errors, use the proofreading guide in the Appendix to make your corrections. Your final copy might be marked like this after proofreading:

Trouble with Toll-Free Numbers

The other night I was about to doze off while watching an old movie on television when the sounds of a commercial caught my attention. A fast-talking announcer began describing a new collection of rock-and-roll records. You've probably seen the kind I mean. They play little snippets of singers singing one or two seconds of a song that made them famous, cutting quickly from one to the next. I like all the tunes they played, so when the announcer urged, "Call this toll-free number now ... operators are standing by ... order this fabulous set of records not available in any store," I did.

This, I'm sorry to say, is not unusual behavior for me. For instance, when I saw a television commercial offering a free digital watch along with a reduced price on a subscription to TIME, I called their toll-free number. Then Sports Illustrated offered a low-priced subscription along with a free videocassette of famous sports plays. Of course, I had to call their toll-free number, too. Now I have stacks of unread magazines around my room. Not only that, the cassette they sent me is for Beta; we have VHS.

TV commercials have influenced me so much that I even use personal items I never used before. My family has brushed with Crest toothpaste ever since I can remember. But after all those ads for Close-up (I think it's the kissable breath idea), I had mom buy some just for me. And, like my dad, I used to just apply a little of mom's skin cream on my face after I shaved. But now, thanks to the influence of television commercials, I have tried several bands of after-shave lotion.

The biggest purchase I ever made because of a TV commercial was my truck. Almost every time I watched TV, I'd see the same ad for Mazda pickup trucks. It showed the truck at work during the day going through mud, climbing hils, and carrying heavy loads. Then it showed the truck at night, cleaned and polished. Neon signs reflected off the truck as it pulled in front of a plush-looking restaurant. As the driver, now dressed in his finest, got out, a doorman helped ~~his~~ the driver's elegant-looking date step from the truck. But it was the woman who got me. Every time the commercial came on, I caught myself looking at her, not the truck.

Anyway, the next thing I knew I had talked my parents into cosigning a loan for a new truck, since banks don't loan money to unemployed college students to buy new trucks. They tried to discourage me because there wasn't anything wrong with my old one. But you know how it is when you think you really want something. I rationalized that I could get part-time work hauling or delivering to help make payments. I think that's what convinced my mom and dad to help out.

Now I wish I hadn't been so convincing. I can't afford to go out on a date because of my truck payments. After attending classes, doing my homework, and working an evening job, I'm too tired to do anything but watch TV. If I don't make my Mazda payments, my parents said they ~~would~~ ^{will} sell my truck. They don't want to be stuck with the payments. I can't blame them.

But my buying hasn't stopped there. Recently a local shoe store announced on television that Reebok tennis shoes were on sale. The next day, I bought them, even though I had just bought a pair of Pumas a week before. When my mom heard, she called me an "impulsive compulsive buyer." When I asked her what she meant, she yelled, "Look it up" and mumbled something about my need to join a "buyers anonymous" group or quit watching so much TV.

She's right; I have a tendency to buy things I see on television even though I don't need them or can't really afford them. Even last night, there was a commercial for a survival knife similar to the type commandos use. It has a big blade, a hollow handle with a fish hook, some line, a few matches, a compass that screws on top of the handle, and the sheath has a little pocket on the side with a sharpening stone. When their toll-free number was announced, I just couldn't resist calling.

Using the proper proofreading marks relieves you of retyping or recopying your entire essay. One of the reasons for double spacing each page is to leave room to make corrections neatly. Of course, if there are so many corrections that the paper is too messy to read, you will have to redo it.

To practice your proof-marking skill, use these standard proofreading symbols to correct the paragraph below the list.

to remove a letter	rea**l**lly
to insert a word or letter	lib**r**ary
to insert punctuation	professor**'**s book
to insert space	the model**#**essay
to reverse letters	rev**er**se
to change a word	a little ~~larger~~ ^{smaller}
to close up space	re⌒verse

Lets say you are assigned to do research on what critics have said abuot John Updikes novel <u>The Witches of Eastwick</u>. In such a case secondary sources will be called for in your pa per. If, on the other hand the assignment calls for your own analysis of the novel, you will neeed to stick to the primary source, the novel Reading secondarysources on the novel, however, may provide you with ideas arguments that could be useful in supporting your own analysis of the book.

Compare your markings with the following to see how well you did.

Lets say you are assigned to do research on what critics have said about John Updikes novel <u>The Witches of Eastwick</u>. In such a case, secondary sources will be called for in your paper. If, on the other hand, the assignment calls for your own analysis of the novel, you will need to stick to the primary source, the novel. Reading secondary sources on the novel, however, may provide you with ideas *and* arguments that could be useful in supporting your own analysis of the book.

Before submitting an essay that has this many corrections in one paragraph, you should retype it. The corrections get in the way of the content.

Your instructor may require that you follow a particular format regarding size of margins, position of name, title, and page numbers, and so on. If not, you will find information on form and style beginning on page 461.

Before Going On

Remember that revising and editing are necessary and vital to good writing. Use the revision stage to make certain your essay makes its point, that the point is supported adequately, that each paragraph is developed fully, that your tone is consistent, and that you have done your best to make the essay interesting to your audience. When editing, look at each sentence separately. Make certain each sentence is complete and that it sounds correct. Check for correct punctuation, subject-verb agreement, pronoun agreement, and overuse of certain words. Consult the Appendix for the proper essay format and proof-reading guide.

✍ *Writing Exercise*

In your journal or on a separate sheet of paper, write three paragraphs summarizing the major points of each of the three stages of writing presented in this section. Make certain each paragraph has a topic sentence and that each paragraph is developed fully. Apply the three writing stages to this writing exercise. Your instructor may want you to turn in this exercise.

Brief Version of the Revision Checklist on Pages 72–73

When you revise the various drafts of an essay, ask yourself the following:

_____ 1. Have you made your point? Is your thesis clear?

_____ 2. Does your support move smoothly from one point to the next? Is your support logically arranged? Do you use transitional words and phrases to aid the reader?

_____ 3. Have you fully developed each paragraph? Does each paragraph have a topic sentence? Have you added or cut information if necessary?

_____ 4. Will your essay interest your audience? Does your opening paragraph grab the reader's attention?

_____ 5. Is the tone of your essay consistent? Do you use the same tone throughout? Is the language appropriate for your audience?

_____ 6. Have you said everything you need to say? Is your thesis fully developed? Does everything relate to the thesis?

Brief Version of the Editing Checklist on Pages 78–80

When you edit the various drafts of an essay, ask yourself the following:

_____ 1. Have you given yourself some time off between drafts? Have you put your essay aside for at least two hours?

_____ 2. Have you read each sentence aloud to hear how it sounds? Did you read each sentence from last to first?

_____ 3. Have you used proper punctuation?

_____ 4. Do your subjects and verbs agree in tense and number?

_____ 5. Are your pronoun usages correct?

_____ 6. Have you avoided repeating the same word too often?

_____ 7. Do you have a title that reflects your thesis or subject?

PART II

READINGS WORTH THINKING AND WRITING ABOUT

Viewpoints on Learning

DOONESBURY

G. B. TRUDEAU

"*Most teachers would agree that
the primary goal of education
is to teach students
how to learn on their own.*"
Kenneth Graham and H. Alan Robinson

IMAGINE what your life would be like if you woke up one morning and everything you had ever learned was gone from your head. You wouldn't be able to get out of bed, dress yourself, feed yourself, or find the bathroom, much less know how to use it. You wouldn't be able to talk, read, or write. You wouldn't know what a television was, how to drive a car, or how to use a telephone. In other words, you'd be helpless.

We all know that learning is important. But what exactly is it? A dictionary might tell you that learning is acquiring knowledge through experience or study (sounds all right); a teacher might tell you that it's memorizing what you need to know for a test (we could argue that one); your boss might tell you that it's mastery of the task you're hired to do (OK, if the pay's good); a psychology book might tell you that learning is a relatively permanent change in behavior due to past experience (that one could use some examples); your parents may tell you that learning is achieved by a "Do as I say, not as I do" approach (no comment).

Obviously, learning takes place in many ways and forms. Hardly a day goes by that we don't learn something, either directly or indirectly. For instance, from television you will "learn" that minorities are generally criminals, victims, service workers, or students (come on, now!) and you might "learn" from a friend that smoking is "cool" (but what about the surgeon general?). The tendency, however, is to link learning with school. Then, of course, we can think about the definition of school. Is is a building labeled elementary, junior, or senior high school? Is it the ivy-walled institution called college or university? Is it the warehouse converted into an adult education center? Is it Sunday school, the synagogue, or church? Is it the media—from television to the *National Enquirer?* Is it the city streets? Some type of schooling certainly occurs in all these places.

This unit does not provide any definitive answers to what learning and schooling are. Instead, reading selections with various viewpoints on learning are offered. As you practice your reading skills, let your reactions to the ideas and the exercises provide some ideas for essays of your own.

📖 Preparing to Read

Take a minute or two to look over the following reading selection. Note the title and author, read the opening paragraph, and check the length. Make certain you have the time now to read it carefully and to do the exercises that follow it. Then, in the spaces provided, answer the following questions.

1. With what experience in the life of the author will this selection deal?

_____

2. What will the tone of the selection be (funny, sad, serious, etc.)? Why do

   you think so? _____

_____

Vocabulary

Good comprehension of what you are about to read depends upon your understanding of the words below. The number following each word refers to the paragraph where it is used.

revival (1) a meeting for the purposes of reawakening religious faith

fold (1) a fenced enclosure for sheep; here, a group gathered as if enclosed for safety.

dire (3) dreadful, warning of disaster

work-gnarled (4) misshapen and swollen from work

rounder (6) a dishonest person

deacons (6,11) assistants to a minister

knickerbockered (11) wearing loose pants gathered just below the knees

ecstatic (14) very enthusiastic

Now read the essay.

Salvation

LANGSTON HUGHES

1   I was saved from sin when I was going on thirteen. But not really saved. It happened like this. There was a big revival at my Auntie Reed's church. Every night for weeks there had been much preaching, singing, praying, and shouting, and some very hardened sinners had been brought to Christ, and the membership of the church had grown by leaps and bounds. Then just before the revival ended, they held a special meeting for children, "to bring the young lambs to the fold." My aunt spoke of it for days ahead. That night I was escorted to the front row and placed on the mourners' bench with all the other young sinners, who had not yet been brought to Jesus.

2   My aunt told me that when you were saved you saw a light, and something happened to you inside! And Jesus came into your life! And God was with you from then on! She said you could see and hear and feel Jesus in your soul. I believed her. I had heard a great many old people say the same thing and it seemed to me they ought to know. So I sat there calmly in the hot, crowded church, waiting for Jesus to come to me.

3   The preacher preached a wonderful rhythmical sermon, all moans and shouts and lonely cries and dire pictures of hell, and then he sang a song about the ninety and nine safe and in the fold, but one little lamb was left out in the cold. Then he said: "Won't you come? Won't you come to Jesus? Young lambs, won't you come?" And he held out his arms to all of us young sinners there on the mourners' bench. And the little girls cried. And some of them jumped up and went to Jesus right away. But most of us just sat there.

4   A great many old people came and knelt around us and prayed, old women with jet-black faces and braided hair, old men with work-gnarled hands. And the church sang a song about the lower lights are burning, some poor sinners to be saved. And the whole building rocked with prayer and song.

5   Still I kept waiting to *see* Jesus.

6   Finally all the young people had gone to the altar and were saved, but one boy and me. He was a rounder's son named Westley. Westley and I were surrounded by sisters and deacons praying. It was very hot in the church, and getting late now. Finally Westley said to me in a whisper: "God damn! I'm tired o' sitting here. Let's get up and be saved." So he got up and was saved.

7   Then I was left all alone on the mourners' bench. My aunt came and knelt at my knees and cried, while prayers and songs swirled all around me in the little church. The whole congregation prayed for

me alone, in a mighty wail of moans and voices. And I kept waiting serenely for Jesus, waiting, waiting—but he didn't come. I wanted to see him, but nothing happened to me. Nothing! I wanted something to happen to me, but nothing happened.

8   I heard the songs and the minister saying: "Why don't you come? My dear child, why don't you come to Jesus? Jesus is waiting for you. He wants you. Why don't you come? Sister Reed, what is this child's name?"

9   "Langston," my aunt sobbed.

10   "Langston, why don't you come? Why don't you come and be saved? Oh, Lamb of God! Why don't you come?"

11   Now it was really getting late. I began to be ashamed of myself, holding everything up so long. I began to wonder what God thought about Westley, who certainly hadn't seen Jesus either, but who was now sitting proudly on the platform, swinging his knickerbockered legs and grinning down at me, surrounded by deacons and old women on their knees praying. God had not struck Westley dead for taking his name in vain or for lying in the temple. So I decided that maybe to save further trouble, I'd better lie, too, and say that Jesus had come, and get up and be saved.

12   So I got up.

13   Suddenly the whole room broke into a sea of shouting, as they saw me rise. Waves of rejoicing swept the place. Women leaped in the air. My aunt threw her arms around me. The minister took me by the hand and led me to the platform.

14   When things quieted down, in a hushed silence, punctuated by a few ecstatic "Amens," all the new young lambs were blessed in the name of God. Then joyous singing filled the room.

15   That night for the last time in my life but one—for I was a big boy twelve years old—I cried. I cried, in bed alone, and couldn't stop. I buried my head under the quilts, but my aunt heard me. She woke up and told my uncle I was crying because the Holy Ghost had come into my life, and because I had seen Jesus. But I was really crying because I couldn't bear to tell her that I had lied, that I had deceived everybody in the church, and I hadn't seen Jesus, and that now I didn't believe there was a Jesus any more, since he didn't come to help me.

You may want to write a summary in your journal of the reading selection as described on page 38 before answering the following questions.

Understanding the Content

Feel free to reread all or parts of the selection to answer the following questions.

1. For what reason was Langston Hughes at the revival?

2. Why didn't Hughes go to the altar with the rest of the children to be saved?

3. Why did Westley finally go down to the altar? What effect did this have on Hughes?

4. What kind of pressure was put on Hughes to be saved? By whom?

5. Why did Hughes cry that night? What had he learned?

6. What is the thesis? Is it implied or stated?

Looking at Structure and Style

1. Why are the first three sentences of the essay important? What information is provided that is necessary to understanding what happens?

2. How important is the information in paragraph 2? How does it prepare us as readers for the last paragraph?

3. Paragraphs 3 and 4 are basically descriptive. To what senses does the description appeal? How do these passages serve to explain the emotional pressure put on the children to be saved?

4. Paragraphs 8–10 use dialogue. Why did Hughes include direct quotations? How effective are they in helping us feel the pressure being put on the author?

5. How important to the story is paragraph 11? For what purpose is Westley described?

6. What is the effect of having paragraphs 5 and 12 consist of just one sentence?

7. Hughes is writing as an adult about his experience as a twelve-year-old. How does he manage to develop a tone and an attitude that fits the experience?

8. In the last paragraph, do we hear the adult or the twelve-year-old talking?

Evaluating the Author's Viewpoints

1. How do you think Hughes's adult attitude toward revivals differs from when he was "going on thirteen"?

2. Hughes didn't believe he could tell his Auntie Reed the truth about why he was crying. Do you think he was right? Explain.

3. Compare the young Hughes's literal definition of "seeing Jesus" with that of his adult aunt's. In your view, is he making fun of himself, of adults, of both, of neither? Explain.

4. Explain what attitudes are revealed in the following excerpts from the essay:

    a. "I believed her. I had heard a great many old people say the same thing and it seemed to me they ought to know." (2)

    b. "The preacher preached a wonderful rhythmical sermon, all moans and shouts and lonely cries and dire pictures of hell ..." (3)

    c. "Suddenly the whole room broke into a sea of shouting, as they saw me rise. Waves of rejoicing swept the place." (13)

    d. "That night for the last time in my life but one—for I was a big boy twelve years old—I cried." (15)

Pursuing Possible Essay Topics

1. Write an essay about an experience you had that caused you to become hurt or disillusioned. What did you learn from the experience that changed you?

2. Describe a time in your life when you could not tell your parents how you really felt because you didn't think they would understand. Were you right?

3. Write a new ending for the essay that allows Hughes to say what you think he wants to say to his Auntie Reed.

4. Write a narrative essay that recalls a time when you went along with the crowd and did not follow your true convictions. What did you learn from the experience?

5. Discuss whether or not disillusionment is a necessary part of learning about life.

6. If you don't like these, find a topic of your own on some aspect of learning.

Preparing to Read

Take a minute or two to look over the following reading selection. Note the title and author, read the opening paragraph, and check the length. Make certain you have the time now to read it carefully and to do the exercises that follow it. Then, in the spaces provided, answer the following questions.

1. What do you think the title means? _____

    _____

2. Do you think the author believes in book censorship, especially censorship

of *The Diary of Anne Frank?* Explain. _____

_____

3. With which of the books mentioned in the opening paragraph are you

   familiar? _____

_____

Vocabulary

Good comprehension of what you are about to read depends upon your understanding of the words below. The number following each word refers to the paragraph where it is used.

deprived (2) underprivileged, needy

migrant (2) moving about, not permanently settled

offhand (2) not well thought out, on the spur of the moment

plight (7) difficult situation or condition

optimistic (7) having a bright outlook, positive

cropping up (8) appearing unexpectedly

empathy (11) sympathy, understanding

multitude (12) great number (of individuals)

tyranny (12) dictatorship, a government where the power rests in one individual

Now read the essay.

Students' Love Affair with Anne Frank

SHARON WHITLEY

1   There it was, among books listed as "objectionable, filthy, dirty and inappropriate" by several groups: *The Diary of Anne Frank.* I couldn't believe it. The list of books facing censorship in some public schools (which included *The Catcher in the Rye* by J. D. Salinger, *Of Mice and Men* by John Steinbeck, Mark Twain's *Huckleberry Finn,* and William Shakespeare's *Romeo and Juliet*) was recently published in a New York Times News Service article. According to the article,

the groups objecting to use of these books in schools include Phyllis Schlafly's Eagle Forum, Jerry Falwell's Moral Majority, the national Pro-Family Forum, and a few with "other political perspectives."

2   All I could think of was the fifth-grade class I taught 10 years ago in the dusty, hot, socially and economically deprived desert town of Coachella, Calif. The 36 Latino children in my class, mostly from migrant farming families, were a handful. Eleven couldn't speak English, and I was a young and inexperienced teacher. I'll never forget that scorching September day when my charges trooped noisily into the classroom after lunch. I made an offhand remark that they could never keep as quiet as Anne Frank had for more than two years.

3   "Anne Frank? Who's that? Does she go here?"

4   As they settled down into the after-lunch routine and placed their hands, grimy from play, on the desks, I told them the story of Anne Frank: how she hid with her family from Hitler's Nazis, how she was persecuted because she was Jewish (none of my Mexican-heritage Roman Catholic students had ever heard of a Jew), how Anne wrote a diary, and about her death in the Bergen-Belsen concentration camp.

5   I had just returned from a summer vacation in Europe, and the highlight for me was seeing the small rooms in the Amsterdam factory where Anne and her family had hidden. I described them to the children: the yellowed wallpaper, the tiny kitchen sink, the photos of movie stars and Queen Elizabeth and Princess Margaret as children; the pencil markings on the doorway where Anne's mother measured the growth of Anne and her sister, Margot; the attic where Peter, Anne's first love, stayed; the bookcase that hid the stairs leading up to the secret hide-out. I told them about the guest register at the Anne Frank Museum next door where visitors from all over the world had written their feelings and thoughts, and that when it was my turn I picked up the pen but was too overwhelmed to put any words down.

After-Lunch Ritual

6   The children were wide-eyed and quiet as I told them the tale of Anne. But that was not enough: "Read the diary to us!" they excitedly demanded.

7   So that became our ritual every day after lunch for the next several weeks. With heads on their desks, the only sound in the class was the whir of the fan on the hot September afternoons and my reading from the yellowed, torn copy I had owned since sixth grade. Stopping only now and then to clarify some of Anne's sophisticated vocabulary, I was prodded on by the children who wanted to hear more and more. The diary opened up a whole new world for these

children in the Coachella Valley. They understood prejudice. Now they knew there were many different kinds. They identified with Anne and her plight. They grew to love her as she described her pre-war birthday parties, receiving her first diary, her friends, falling in love, and her still optimistic view of the world: "In spite of everything, I still believe that people are really good at heart."

8   As I continued reading the diary every afternoon, I soon noticed more of the diaries cropping up in class. One by one, the children had bought their own copies of the book—even Spanish versions— and were quietly following along with me, or looking intently at the sad-eyed picture of Anne on the cover. When we completed reading the diary, they wanted more. "Please help us write a play about Anne that we can put on!" they begged.

9   So for the next month, in a flurry of excitement over the class project, we spent several hours after school, rehearsing our condensed version of *The Diary of Anne Frank*. (The Broadway version in 1955 was awarded the Pulitzer Prize, the New York Drama Critics Circle Award and the Antoinette Perry Award.) The night we performed our amateur version in the school auditorium, 100 members of the community turned out to see it.

10   Several years later, when I had moved to San Diego to teach high school special education, one of my former Coachella fifth-graders— then in high school—called excitedly to tell me that *The Diary of Anne Frank* was on television that night. I was thrilled that she had remembered our special class project from years before.

11   To this day, *The Diary of Anne Frank* continues to be an important teaching tool in my classes. It is the ultimate in lesson plans—teaching listening skills, silent and oral reading, vocabulary, history, religion and customs, race relations, thoughts for the future, boy-girl relationships, empathy for others, comparison of our experiences with Anne's and the experiences of others, drama and role play, and understanding ourselves, our friends, and parents.

Tribute from Kennedy

12   As John F. Kennedy wrote Sept. 15, 1961: "Of the multitude who throughout history have spoken for human dignity in times of great suffering and loss, no voice is more compelling than that of Anne Frank. . . . Her words, written as they were in the face of a monstrous tyranny, have significant meaning today as millions who read them live in the shadow of fear of another such tyranny. . . . It is indeed a gift for all mankind to receive from a child growing into womanhood the greatest truth of all—that as man rises from the brute, the kind and hopeful and the gentle are the true makers of history."

13   And Eleanor Roosevelt had commented, "This is one of the wisest

and most moving commentaries on war and its impact on human beings that I have ever read."

14   As Anne wrote, "I can feel the sufferings of millions and yet, if I look up into the heavens, I think that it will all come right, that this cruelty too will end, and that peace and tranquility will return again" (July 15, 1944).

15   More than 10 million copies of *The Diary of Anne Frank* have been printed in 38 different languages in 48 countries. We *must* keep Anne in the classroom.

Understanding the Content

Feel free to reread all or parts of the selection to answer the following questions.

1. Who was Anne Frank? What do you learn about her life?

2. What groups object to the use of *The Diary of Anne Frank* in the classroom? To what other books do they object?

3. How did Whitley get her students interested in *The Diary of Anne Frank?* Describe her students at the time.

4. Why does Whitley believe that *The Diary of Anne Frank* is an important teaching tool, "the ultimate in lesson plans"?

5. What is Whitley's thesis?

Looking at Structure and Style

1. How is the opening paragraph used to introduce the subject of the essay? How is the author's attitude toward her subject revealed?

2. Paragraph 2 serves as a "flashback" to Whitley's past. How is this done?

3. Whitley carefully describes her students in paragraphs 2, 4, and 7. Is it important to her discussion of Anne Frank? Why? What inferences might we draw from her description of her students?

4. In paragraph 9, Whitley mentions the prizes the Broadway version of *The Diary of Anne Frank* won. What function does her remark serve? Why does she put this information in parentheses?

5. What function do paragraphs 12–13 serve? Are these important to the author's viewpoint? In what way?

6. How does Whitley's concluding paragraph bring us back to her opening remarks?

7. To whom is Whitley writing? Explain.

Evaluating the Author's Viewpoints

1. Whitley is shocked to see *The Diary of Anne Frank* listed by some groups as an "objectionable, filthy, dirty and inappropriate" book. Does she convince you it is not? Explain.

2. Look at paragraph 11. Do you feel that all of the lessons listed should be taught and discussed in the classroom? Explain. What items on Whitley's list might some persons or groups not want discussed or taught in class? Would you agree with them? Why?

3. In paragraph 12, John F. Kennedy is quoted as saying of Anne Frank, "It is indeed a gift for all mankind to receive from a child growing into womanhood the greatest truth of all—that as man rises from the brute, the kind and hopeful and the gentle are the true makers of history." Explain what he means. Do you agree? Why?

4. Respond to the quote from Anne Frank's diary in paragraph 4. Do you hold such an optimistic view of life? Explain.

Pursuing Possible Essay Topics

1. Write an essay about a book or play you have read that had a profound effect on your life. Why is it memorable? What did you learn? What emotions were aroused? Why would you recommend it be taught to others?

2. Some parents think that schools should teach only what are often called "the basic skills"—reading, writing, math. Agree or disagree with such a viewpoint.

3. Pretend that some parents in Whitley's classroom are demanding that she stop using *The Diary of Anne Frank* in her classes. Choose a side and write a defense of your argument.

4. Find a copy of *The Diary of Anne Frank* or one of the other books listed in Whitley's opening paragraph as "objectionable" and read it. Argue for or against its being taught in schools.

5. What is the role of public education today? What skills should public schools emphasize? Should such subjects as sex education, race relations, facing moral dilemmas, marriage and the family, and driver's education be required? Are we asking too much of our schools and teachers?

6. Brainstorm or freewrite on one or more of the following:

   a. reading to learn   d. loving to learn
   b. book censorship   e. the real basic skills
   c. keeping a diary   f. stimulating teaching

7. Forget these and find your own topic on some aspect of learning.

Preparing to Read

Take a minute or two to look over the following reading selection. Note the title and author, read the opening paragraph, and check the length. Make certain you have the time now to read it carefully and to do the exercises that follow it. Then, in the spaces provided, answer the following questions.

1. What does the title mean to you? _____

_____

2. What do you think this selection will have to say about making mistakes?

_____

_____

3. How do you feel about making mistakes? _____

_____

_____

Vocabulary

Good comprehension of what you are about to read depends upon your understanding of the words below. The number following each word refers to the paragraph where it is used.

plateau (1) an elevated, stable state

cultivates (3) fosters, nurtures

embedded (3) planted, fixed firmly

incentive (3) drive, desire, motivation (in this case, the grading system)

penalizes (4) subjects to penalty, places a disadvantage on

garners (4) acquires, gains

stigma (4) mark of shame or disgrace

adherence (8) desire to stick with or cling to

germinal phase (8) beginning or earliest stage

erroneous (9,10) mistaken, based on error

exemplifies (10) serves as an example

phenomenon (10) a perceivable occurrence or fact

combust (11) burn

analogous (11) alike in certain ways

Brittany (16) an area on the northern coast of France across the English Channel from England

precedence (18) awareness of prior existence, priority

innovators (18) creators or introducers of something new

diverging (24) branching out, departing from the norm

deleterious (25) damaging, harmful

amoeba (25) shapeless, microscopic, one-celled organism

atrophy (26) waste away

Now read the essay.

To Err Is Wrong

ROGER VON OECH

Hits and Misses

1   In the summer of 1979, Boston Red Sox first baseman Carl Yastrzemski became the fifteenth player in baseball history to reach the three thousand hit plateau. This event drew a lot of media attention, and for about a week prior to the attainment of this goal, hundreds of reporters covered Yaz's every move. Finally, one reporter asked, "Hey Yaz, aren't you afraid all of this attention will go to your head?" Yastrzemski replied, "I look at it this way: in my career I've been up to bat over ten thousand times. That means I've been unsuccessful at the plate over seven thousand times. That fact alone keeps me from getting a swollen head."

2   Most people consider success and failure as opposites, but they are actually both products of the same process. As Yaz suggests, an activity which produces a hit may also produce a miss. It is the same with creative thinking; the same energy which generates good creative ideas also produces errors.

3   Many people, however, are not comfortable with errors. Our educational system, based on "the right answer" belief, cultivates our thinking in another, more conservative way. From an early age, we are taught that right answers are good and incorrect answers are bad. This value is deeply embedded in the incentive system used in most schools:

Right over 90% of the time = "A"
Right over 80% of the time = "B"

Right over 70% of the time = "C"
Right over 60% of the time = "D"
Less than 60% correct, you fail.

From this we learn to be right as often as possible and to keep our mistakes to a minimum. We learn, in other words, that "to err is wrong."

Playing It Safe

4   With this kind of attitude, you aren't going to be taking too many chances. If you learn that failing even a little penalizes you (e.g., being wrong only 15% of the time garners you only a "B" performance), you learn not to make mistakes. And more important, you learn not to put yourself in situations where you might fail. This leads to conservative thought patterns designed to avoid the stigma our society puts on "failure."

5   I have a friend who recently graduated from college with a Master's degree in Journalism. For the last six months, she has been trying to find a job, but to no avail. I talked with her about her situation, and realized that her problem is that she doesn't know how to fail. She went through eighteen years of schooling without ever failing an examination, a paper, a midterm, a pop-quiz, or a final. Now, she is reluctant to try any approaches where she might fail. She has been conditioned to believe that failure is bad in and of itself, rather than a potential stepping stone to new ideas.

6   Look around. How many middle managers, housewives, administrators, teachers, and other people do you see who are afraid to try anything new because of this fear of failure? Most of us have learned not to make mistakes in public. As a result, we remove ourselves from many learning experiences except for those occurring in the most private of circumstances.

A Different Logic

7   From a practical point of view, "to err is wrong" makes sense. Our survival in the everyday world requires us to perform thousands of small tasks without failure. Think about it: you wouldn't last very long if you were to step out in front of traffic or stick your hand into a pot of boiling water. In addition, engineers whose bridges collapse, stock brokers who lose money for their clients, and copywriters whose ad campaigns decrease sales won't keep their jobs very long.

8   Nevertheless, too great an adherence to the belief "to err is wrong" can greatly undermine your attempts to generate new ideas. If you're more concerned with producing right answers than generating orig-

inal ideas, you'll probably make uncritical use of the rules, formulae, and procedures used to obtain these right answers. By doing this, you'll by-pass the germinal phase of the creative process, and thus spend little time testing assumptions, challenging the rules, asking what-if questions, or just playing around with the problem. All of these techniques will produce some incorrect answers, but in the germinal phase errors are viewed as a necessary by-product of creative thinking. As Yaz would put it, "If you want the hits, be prepared for the misses." That's the way the game of life goes.

Errors As Stepping Stones

9   Whenever an error pops up, the usual response is "Jeez, another screwup, what went wrong this time?" The creative thinker, on the other hand, will realize the potential value of errors, and perhaps say something like, "Would you look at that! Where can it lead our thinking?" And then he or she will go on to use the error as a stepping stone to a new idea. As a matter of fact, the whole history of discovery is filled with people who used erroneous assumptions and failed ideas as stepping stones to new ideas. Columbus thought he was finding a shorter route to India. Johannes Kepler stumbled on to the idea of interplanetary gravity because of assumptions which were right for the wrong reasons. And, Thomas Edison knew 1800 ways *not* to build a light bulb.

10   The following story about the automotive genius Charles Kettering exemplifies the spirit of working through erroneous assumptions to good ideas. In 1912, when the automobile industry was just beginning to grow, Kettering was interested in improving gasoline-engine efficiency. The problem he faced was "knock," the phenomenon in which gasoline takes too long to burn in the cylinder—thereby reducing efficiency.

11   Kettering began searching for ways to eliminate the "knock." He thought to himself, "How can I get the gasoline to combust in the cylinder at an earlier time?" The key concept here is "early." Searching for analogous situations, he looked around for models of "things that happen early." He thought of historical models, physical models, and biological models. Finally, he remembered a particular plant, the trailing arbutus, which "happens early," i.e., it blooms in the snow ("earlier" than other plants). One of this plant's chief characteristics is its red leaves, which help the plant retain light at certain wavelengths. Kettering figured that it must be the red color which made the trailing arbutus bloom earlier.

12   Now came the critical step in Kettering's chain of thought. He asked himself, "How can I make the gasoline red? Perhaps I'll put

red dye in the gasoline—maybe that'll make it combust earlier." He looked around his workshop, and found that he didn't have any red dye. But he did happen to have some iodine—perhaps that would do. He added the iodine to the gasoline and, lo and behold, the engine didn't "knock."

13   Several days later, Kettering wanted to make sure that it was the redness of the iodine which had in fact solved his problem. He got some red dye and added it to the gasoline. Nothing happened! Kettering then realized that it wasn't the "redness" which had solved the "knock" problem, but certain other properties of iodine. In this case, an error had proven to be a stepping stone to a better idea. Had he known that "redness" alone was not the solution, he may not have found his way to the additives in iodine.

Negative Feedback

14   Errors serve another useful purpose: they tell us when to change direction. When things are going smoothly, we generally don't think about them. To a great extent, this is because we function according to the principle of negative feedback. Often it is only when things or people fail to do their job that they get our attention. For example, you are probably not thinking about your kneecaps right now; that's because everything is fine with them. The same goes for your elbows: they are also performing their function—no problem at all. But if you were to break a leg, you would immediately notice all of the things you could no longer do, but which you used to take for granted.

15   Negative feedback means that the current approach is not working, and it is up to you to figure out a new one. We learn by trial and error, not by trial and rightness. If we did things correctly every time, we would never have to change direction—we'd just continue the current course and end up with more of the same.

16   For example, after the supertanker *Amoco Cadiz* broke up off the coast of Brittany in the spring of 1978, thereby polluting the coast with hundreds of thousands of tons of oil, the oil industry rethought many of its safety standards regarding petroleum transport. The same thing happened after the accident at the Three Mile Island nuclear reactor in 1979—many procedures and safety standards were changed.

17   Neil Goldschmidt, former Secretary of Transportation, had this to say about the Bay Area Rapid Transit (BART):

It's gotten too fashionable around the country to beat up on BART and not give credit to the vision that put this system in place. We have learned from BART around the country.

The lessons were put to use in Washington, in Atlanta, in Buffalo, and other cities where we are building mass transit systems. One of the lessons is not to build a system like BART.

We learn by our failures. A person's errors are the whacks that lead him to think something different.

Trying New Things

18 Your error rate in any activity is a function of your familiarity with that activity. If you are doing things that are routine and have a high likelihood of correctness, then you will probably make very few errors. But if you are doing things that have no precedence in your experience or are trying different approaches, then you will be making your share of mistakes. Innovators may not bat a thousand—far from it—but they do get new ideas.

19 The creative director of an advertising agency told me that he isn't happy unless he is failing at least half of the time. As he puts it, "If you are going to be original, you are going to be wrong a lot."

20 One of my clients, the president of a fast-growing computer company, tells his people: "We're innovators. We're doing things nobody has ever done before. Therefore, we are going to be making mistakes. My advice to you: make your mistakes, but make them in a hurry."

21 Another client, a division manager of a high-technology company, asked his vice president of engineering what percentage of their new products should be successful in the marketplace. The answer he received was "about 50%." The division manager replied, "That's too high. 30% is a better target; otherwise we'll be too conservative in our planning."

22 Along similar lines, in the banking industry, it is said that if the credit manager never has to default on any of his loans, it's a sure sign he's not being aggressive enough in the marketplace.

23 Thomas J. Watson, the founder of IBM, has similar words: "The way to succeed is to double your failure rate."

24 Thus, errors, at the very least, are a sign that we are diverging from the main road and trying different approaches.

Nature's Errors

25 Nature serves as a good example of how trial and error can be used to make changes. Every now and then genetic mutations occur—errors in gene reproduction. Most of the time, these mutations have a deleterious effect on the species, and they drop out of the gene pool. But occasionally, a mutation provides the species with something beneficial, and that change will be passed on to future generations.

The rich variety of all species is due to this trial and error process. If there had never been any mutations from the first amoeba, where would we be now?

Summary

26   There are places where errors are inappropriate, but the germinal phase of the creative process isn't one of them. Errors are a sign that you are diverging from the well-traveled path. If you're not failing every now and then, it's a sign you're not being very innovative.

Tip #1:
If you make an error, use it as a stepping stone to a new idea you might not have otherwise discovered.

Tip #2:
Differentiate between errors of "commission" and those of "omission." The latter can be more costly than the former. If you're not making many errors, you might ask yourself, "How many opportunities am I missing by not being more aggressive?"

Tip #3:
Strengthen your "risk muscle." Everyone has one, but you have to exercise it or else it will atrophy. Make it a point to take at least one risk every twenty-four hours.

Tip #4:
Remember these two benefits of failure. First, if you do fail, you learn what doesn't work; and second, the failure gives you an opportunity to try a new approach.

Understanding the Content

Feel free to reread all or parts of the selection to answer the following questions.

1. Does von Oech believe "to err is wrong"? Why?

2. How does von Oech feel about the traditional grading system in schools? Why?

3. According to the author, what is wrong with "playing it safe"?

4. What are some of the "useful purposes" of making mistakes?

5. Explain what von Oech means when he says in his conclusion that we should differentiate between errors of "commission" and those of "omission"?

6. What two benefits of failure does the author propose?

7. To what audience do you think the author is writing? Why?

8. Is there an implied or stated thesis? What is it?

Looking at Structure and Style

1. How does von Oech use the first two paragraphs to lead us into his subject and thesis?

2. What is the cause-effect relationship discussed in paragraph 4?

3. What is the function of paragraphs 5 and 6?

4. What is being compared/contrasted in paragraphs 7 and 8?

5. Is this essay mostly formal or informal? Pick out some words or phrases that support your answer.

6. For what purpose does the author use paragraphs 9–13? Are they effective?

7. What writing pattern is used in paragraphs 14, 16, and 17?

8. How would you describe the author's attitude and tone?

Evaluating the Author's Viewpoints

1. Do you agree or disagree with von Oech's comments regarding the traditional educational grading system? Why?

2. In paragraph 6, the author says, "Most of us have learned not to make mistakes in public. As a result, we remove ourselves from many learning experiences except for those occurring in the most private of circumstances." Is this true? Is it true of you?

3. Respond to paragraph 25. What does von Oech mean? Do you agree?

4. Do you agree with von Oech that we should take at least one risk every twenty-four hours? Why? What kind of risks does he have in mind?

5. Where and when are errors inappropriate?

Pursuing Possible Essay Topics

1. Make a list of von Oech's arguments for the positive side of making errors. Write an essay that agrees with his thesis, but provide examples of your own. Or, write an essay that disagrees with him.

2. Write about a time when you learned from an error you made.

3. Discuss your viewpoints on the traditional grading system. What are the pros and cons? How has it affected your learning?

4. Use this statement from the essay as the thesis for your own essay: "Most people consider success and failure as opposites, but they are actually both products of the same process."

5. In his book *Escape from Childhood*, educator John Holt states:

> Young people should have the right to control and direct their own learning, that is, to decide what they want to learn, and when, where, how, how much, how fast, and with what help they want to learn it. To be still more specific, I want them to have the right to decide if, when, how much, and by whom they want to be *taught* and the right to decide whether they want to learn in a school and if so which one and for how much of the time.

Write an essay that supports or refutes Holt's radical statement about learning. How would his ideas work? How would such an approach change the present educational system?

6. Write an essay about your own learning style. How do you learn best? What kind of teaching seems to help you learn best?

7. Freewrite or brainstorm on one or more of the following:
   a. making mistakes   d. nature's errors
   b. famous errors   e. negative feedback
   c. grades   f. trying new things

8. Ignore these and find your own topic on some aspect of learning.

📖 Preparing to Read

Take a minute or two to look over the following reading selection. Note the title and author, read the opening paragraph, and check the length. Make certain you have the time now to read it carefully and to do the exercises that follow it. Then, in the spaces provided, answer the following questions.

1. What do you think the title means? _____

_____

_____

2. What will be the subject of this essay? _____

_____

3. What might you learn from reading it? _____

_____

Vocabulary

Good comprehension of what you are about to read depends upon your understanding of the words below. The number following each word refers to the paragraph where it is used.

semiliterate (1) having only an elementary level of reading and writing ability

impediments (4) obstacles, barriers, hindrances

trump card (4) a card from the suit in a card game that outranks all other suits for the duration of the game

composure (6) self-possession, calmness

chemical dependency (9) addiction to drugs

Now read the essay.

In Praise of the F Word

MARY SHERRY

1   Tens of thousands of 18-year-olds will graduate this year and be handed meaningless diplomas. These diplomas won't look any different from those awarded their luckier classmates. Their validity will be questioned only when their employers discover that these graduates are semiliterate.

2   Eventually a fortunate few will find their way into educational-repair shops—adult-literacy programs, such as the one where I teach basic grammar and writing. There, high-school graduates and high-school dropouts pursuing graduate-equivalency certificates will learn the skills they should have learned in school. They will also discover they have been cheated by our educational system.

3   As I teach, I learn a lot about our schools. Early in each session I ask my students to write about an unpleasant experience they had in school. No writers' block here! "I wish someone would have had made me stop doing drugs and made me study." "I liked to party and no one seemed to care." "I was a good kid and didn't cause any trouble, so they just passed me along even though I didn't read well and couldn't write." And so on.

4   I am your basic do-gooder, and prior to teaching this class I blamed the poor academic skills our kids have today on drugs, divorce and other impediments to concentration necessary for doing well in school. But, as I rediscover each time I walk into the classroom, before a teacher can expect students to concentrate, he has to get their attention, no matter what distractions may be at hand. There are many ways to do this, and they have much to do with teaching style. However, if style alone won't do it, there is another way to show who holds the winning hand in the classroom. That is to reveal the trump card of failure.

5   I will never forget a teacher who played that card to get the attention of one of my children. Our youngest, a world-class charmer, did little to develop his intellectual talents but always got by. Until Mrs. Stifter.

6   Our son was a high-school senior when he had her for English. "He sits in the back of the room talking to his friends," she told me. "Why don't you move him to the front row?" I urged, believing the embarrassment would get him to settle down. Mrs. Stifter looked at me steely-eyed over her glasses. "I don't move seniors," she said. "I flunk them." I was flustered. Our son's academic life flashed before my eyes. No teacher had ever threatened him with that before. I regained my composure and managed to say that I thought she was right. By the time I got home I was feeling pretty good about this. It was a radical approach for these times, but, well, why not? "She's going to flunk you," I told my son. I did not discuss it any further. Suddenly English became a priority in his life. He finished out the semester with an A.

7   I know one example doesn't make a case, but at night I see a parade of students who are angry and resentful for having been passed along until they could no longer even pretend to keep up. Of average intelligence or better, they eventually quit school, concluding they were too dumb to finish. "I should have been held back," is a comment I hear frequently. Even sadder are those students who are high-school graduates who say to me after a few weeks of class, "I don't know how I ever got a high-school diploma."

8   Passing students who have not mastered the work cheats them and the employers who expect graduates to have basic skills. We excuse this dishonest behavior by saying kids can't learn if they come from terrible environments. No one seems to stop to think that—no matter what environments they come from—most kids don't put school first on their list unless they perceive something is at stake. They'd rather be sailing.

9   Many students I see at night could give expert testimony on unemployment, chemical dependency, abusive relationships. In spite of

these difficulties, they have decided to make education a priority. They are motivated by the desire for a better job or the need to hang on to the one they've got. They have a healthy fear of failure.

10   People of all ages can rise above their problems, but they need to have a reason to do so. Young people generally don't have the maturity to value education in the same way my adult students value it. But fear of failure, whether economic or academic, can motivate both.

11   Flunking as a regular policy has just as much merit today as it did two generations ago. We must review the threat of flunking and see it as it really is—a positive teaching tool. It is an expression of confidence by both teachers and parents that the students have the ability to learn the material presented to them. However, making it work again would take a dedicated, caring conspiracy between teachers and parents. It would mean facing the tough reality that passing kids who haven't learned the material—while it might save them grief for the short term—dooms them to long-term illiteracy. It would mean that teachers would have to follow through on their threats, and parents would have to stand behind them, knowing their children's best interests are indeed at stake. This means no more doing Scott's assignments for him because he might fail. No more passing Jodi because she's such a nice kid.

12   This is a policy that worked in the past and can work today. A wise teacher, with the support of his parents, gave our son the opportunity to succeed—or fail. It's time we return this choice to all students.

Understanding the Content

Feel free to reread all or parts of the selection to answer the following questions.

1. What is the "F Word" discussed in the essay?

2. What is Sherry's attitude toward the F word?

3. What reasons does the author give for believing that the threat of flunking students is a positive teaching tool?

4. What choice does the author want to give to students? Why is she particularly interested in the subject?

5. What is the point of this selection? What does it have to do with the subject of learning?

Looking at Structure and Style

1. How does paragraph 2 help to support paragraph 1?

2. What is the point of paragraph 3?

3. How does Sherry use paragraphs 5 and 6 to support her viewpoint?

4. What is the point of paragraphs 9 and 10?

5. What audience do you think the author had in mind when she wrote this essay?

Evaluating the Author's Viewpoints

1. Do you agree with the author that "flunking as a regular policy has just as much merit today as it did two generations ago" (11)? Why?

2. What are some good arguments for *not* flunking students?

3. The author contends that fear of failure can motivate students. Explain why you do or do not agree.

4. Explain why you would or would not like to have Sherry as a teacher.

Pursuing Possible Essay Topics

1. Recall a time when fear of failure motivated you to accomplish something.

2. Summarize the reasons why the author is in praise of the F word.

3. Write an essay that takes the opposite viewpoint regarding the F word.

4. Explore the pros and cons of withholding high school diplomas from students who lack the ability to learn, despite fear of failure.

5. Brainstorm or freewrite on one or more of the following:
   a. fear of failure
   b. flunking
   c. educational priorities
   d. impediments to doing well in school
   e. literacy
   f. the grading system

6. Forget these and find your own topic on some aspect of learning.

📖 Preparing to Read

Take a minute or two to look over the following reading selection. Note the title and author, read the opening paragraph, and check the length. Make certain you have the time to read it carefully and to do the exercises that follow it. Then, in the spaces provided, answer the following questions.

1. What will the essay have to say about school vs. education? _____

   _____

   _____

2. What might you learn from reading this essay? _____

   _____

   _____

3. Do you think this selection will be serious or humorous? _____

Vocabulary

Good comprehension of what you are about to read depends upon your understanding of the words below. The number following each word refers to the paragraph where it is used.

armaments (2) weapons

violate (3) break (a law, for example)

social cohesion (5) group togetherness (here, of parents who share the same concerns)

pigmentation (5) skin coloration (refers here to racial differences)

nightstick (5) a club used by policemen

subduing (5) overpowering, bringing under control

incentive (8) drive, desire, motivation

the bar (13) jargon for the legal profession, law practice

"the race is to the cunning and ... the unprincipled" (13) the "winners" are crafty, shrewd, and without morals (a possible allusion or reference to John Davidson's poem "War Song": "The race is to the swift;/The battle to the strong.")

emerges (14) comes out

melodrama (14) plays or movies that rely heavily on sensational events, sentimentality, or coincidence instead of strong characterization

porcelain (15) a hard, white ceramic

inclination (15) desire

Now read the essay.

School vs. Education

RUSSELL BAKER

1   By the age of six the average child will have completed the basic American education and be ready to enter school. If the child has been attentive in these preschool years, he or she will already have mastered many skills.

2   From television, the child will have learned how to pick a lock, commit a fairly elaborate bank holdup, prevent wetness all day long, get the laundry twice as white, and kill people with a variety of sophisticated armaments.

3   From watching his parents, the child, in many cases, will already know how to smoke, how much soda to mix with whiskey, what kind of language to use when angry, and how to violate the speed laws without being caught.

4   At this point, the child is ready for the second stage of education, which occurs in school. There, a variety of lessons may be learned in the very first days.

5   The teacher may illustrate the economic importance of belonging to a strong union by closing down the school before the child arrives. Fathers and mothers may demonstrate to the child the social cohesion that can be built on shared hatred by demonstrating their dislike for children whose pigmentation displeases them. In the latter event, the child may receive visual instruction in techniques of stoning buses, cracking skulls with a nightstick, and subduing mobs with tear gas. Formal education has begun.

6   During formal education, the child learns that life is for testing. This stage lasts twelve years, a period during which the child learns that success comes from telling testers what they want to hear.

7   Early in this stage, the child learns that he is either dumb or smart. If the teacher puts intelligent demands upon the child, the child learns he is smart. If the teacher expects little of the child, the child learns he is dumb and soon quits bothering to tell the testers what they want to hear.

8   At this point, education becomes more subtle. The child taught by school that he is dumb observes that neither he, she, nor any of the many children who are even dumber, ever fails to be promoted to the next grade. From this, the child learns that while everybody talks a lot about the virtue of being smart, there is very little incentive to stop being dumb.

9   What is the point of school, besides attendance? the child wonders. As the end of the first formal stage of education approaches,

school answers this question. The point is to equip the child to enter college.

10   Children who have been taught they are smart have no difficulty. They have been happily telling testers what they want to hear for twelve years. Being artists at telling testers what they want to hear, they are admitted to college joyously, where they promptly learn that they are the hope of America.

11   Children whose education has been limited to adjusting themselves to their schools' low estimates of them are admitted to less joyous colleges which, in some cases, may teach them to read.

12   At this stage of education, a fresh question arises for everyone. If the point of lower education was to get into college, what is the point of college? The answer is soon learned. The point of college is to prepare the student—no longer a child now—to get into graduate school. In college, the student learns that it is no longer enough simply to tell the testers what they want to hear. Many are tested for graduate school; few are admitted.

13   Those excluded may be denied valuable certificates to prosper in medicine, at the bar, in the corporate boardroom. The student learns that the race is to the cunning and often, alas, to the unprincipled.

14   Thus, the student learns the importance of destroying competitors and emerges richly prepared to play his role in the great simmering melodrama of American life.

15   Afterward, the former student's destiny fulfilled, his life rich with Oriental carpets, rare porcelain, and full bank accounts, he may one day find himself with the leisure and the inclination to open a book with a curious mind, and start to become educated.

Understanding the Content

Feel free to reread all or parts of the selection to answer the following questions.

1. What does Baker see as the difference between school and education?

2. List Baker's "stages of education." What does he say is learned in each stage?

3. What is Baker's thesis? Is it stated or implied?

4. Describe Baker's attitude toward school. What early passages reflect this attitude?

5. Is Baker's tone serious or humorous? How do you know?

6. What can we infer about Baker's attitude toward television? toward parents? toward schools? toward American life?

Looking at Structure and Style

1. Divide Baker's essay into each "stage of education." What transitional techniques does he use to move from one stage to the next? Are they effective?

2. What is the topic sentence of paragraph 5? What paragraph pattern is used?

3. Explain or rewrite in your own words the following passages from the essay:
   a. paragraph 5, second sentence
   b. " ... The child learns that success comes from telling testers what they want to hear." (6)
   c. paragraph 11
   d. paragraph 14

4. Explain Baker's conclusion in paragraph 15. How effective is it?

5. What suggestions for revision, if any, would you offer the author?

Evaluating the Author's Viewpoints

1. How strong is Baker's support for his thesis? Look again at each "stage." Are his viewpoints on television, parents, and school balanced or has he overlooked something?

2. Do you agree that "during formal education, the child learns that life is for testing" (6)? Explain.

3. Do you agree or disagree with paragraph 10? Why?

4. Explain what Baker means in paragraphs 13 and 14. Do you agree with him?

5. Baker's tone is very cynical in this essay. To what degree do you think he means what he says? Explain.

Pursuing Possible Essay Topics

1. Agree or disagree with one of Baker's "stages of education."

2. Summarize Baker's definition of education and defend or argue against his position.

3. Discuss what children learn from watching television. You may want to narrow this down to what they learn from commercials, cartoons, soap operas, crime shows, or whatever. Don't try to cover too much.

4. Discuss what preschool children learn from their parents, directly or indirectly, that schools don't teach. You might want to use yourself as your subject.

5. Baker says that students learn that "destroying competitors" (14) is the way to win. In what ways do schools teach students the importance of and the strategies for winning?

6. Brainstorm or freewrite on one or more of the following:
   a. learning to read   c. learning to lose
   b. learning to win   d. learning prejudice

7. Write a reaction to the following quotation:

   Thank God there are no free schools or printing; ... for learning has brought disobedience and heresy into the world, and printing has divulged them.... God keep us from both.

   Sir William Berkeley
Governor of Virginia, 1677

8. Write about the first educational experience you can remember. What did you learn? Where? Why is it memorable?

9. If you don't like these, try your own topic related to learning.

📖 Preparing to Read

Take a minute or two to look over the following reading selection. Note the title and author, read the opening paragraph, and check the length. Make certain you have the time now to read it carefully and to do the exercises that follow it. Then, in the spaces provided, answer the following questions.

1. How do you define "bilingualism"? _____

   _____

2. What do you think the author will say about bilingual education? ____

   _____

   _____

3. Do you think schools should teach bilingual classes? Why? _____

   _____

   _____

Vocabulary

Good comprehension of what you are about to read depends upon your understanding of the words below. The number following each word refers to the paragraph where it is used.

instilling (1) introducing gradually, teaching bit by bit

inculcate (2) instill, teach

advocate (3) speak in favor of, recommend

alienated (3) excluded

simulated (3) imitated, reproduced

encompasses (6) includes

curricula (6) courses of study offered by schools (plural of **curriculum** [7])

notoriously (8) famously, but unfavorably so

median (8) at the middle, average

menial (9) appropriate to a servant

vulnerable (9) capable of being harmed

exploitation (9) the act of being taken advantage of

Now read the essay.

Bilingualism's Goal

BARBARA MUJICA

1   Mine is a Spanish-speaking household. We use Spanish exclusively. I have made an effort not only to encourage use of the language but also to familiarize my children with Hispanic culture. I use books from Latin America to teach them to read and write, and I try to maintain close contacts with Spanish-speaking relatives. Instilling in my children a sense of family and ethnic identity is my role; it is not the role of the school system.

2   The public schools, supported by public funds, have the responsibility to teach skills needed in public life—among them the use of the English language. They also must inculcate an appreciation of all the cultures that have contributed to this country's complex social weave. To set one ethnic group apart as more worthy of attention than others is unjust, and might breed resentment against that group.

3   I differ with educators who advocate bilingual education programs whose goal is to preserve the Spanish language and culture among children of Hispanic families. These professionals argue that in an English-speaking environment, Spanish-speaking children often

feel alienated and that this causes them to become withdrawn and hostile. To prevent this reaction, they say, the home environment must be simulated at school.

4   Imagine how much more alienated these youngsters will feel, however, if they are kept in special bilingual programs separate from the general student body, semester after semester. How much more uncomfortable they will feel if they are maintained in ghettos in the school. Youngsters feel a need to conform. They imitate each other in dress and in habit. To isolate Spanish-speaking children from their English-speaking peers may prove more psychologically damaging than hurling them into an English-speaking environment with no transition courses at all.

5   The purpose of bilingual education must be to teach English to non-English-speaking youngsters so that they will be able to function in regular classes.

6   The term "bilingual education" encompasses a huge variety of programs ranging from total immersion to special classes for foreigners to curricula that offer courses in mathematics and history in the child's native language. The most effective bilingual education programs have as their goal the gradual incorporation of non-English-speaking students into regular programs in which English is used.

7   Not all children of Spanish-speaking parents need bilingual education. Many Spanish-speaking parents oppose the placement of their children in special programs; the wishes of these parents should be respected. Furthermore, very young children are able to learn a foreign language rapidly; bilingual programs for the nursery, kindergarten and early primary years should be kept to a minimum. Older children who have done part of their schooling in a foreign country often need to be eased into an English-speaking curriculum more gently. For them, it is helpful to offer certain subjects in their native tongues until they have learned English; otherwise, they may feel so lost and frustrated that they will drop out of school. High school dropouts have less chance than others of finding satisfying careers and are more likely to find themselves in trouble and unemployed.

8   Hispanics are now the fastest-growing minority in the United States. According to the Population Reference Bureau, a private organization, Hispanics, counted at 14.6 million in the 1980 census, may well number 47 million by the year 2020. Yet, they are notoriously underrepresented in the arts, sciences, professions and politics. Economically, as a group, they tend to lag behind non-Hispanics. According to March 1983 Federal figures, the median income for Hispanics is $16,227; for non-Hispanics, $23,907. Certainly, part of the remedy is educational programs that give young people the preparation and confidence necessary to pursue satisfying careers.

9   To get better jobs, young people must be fluent in English. Without English, they will be stuck in menial positions. Without English, they will be unable to acquire advanced degrees. Without English, they will be unable to protest to the proper authorities if they are abused. Non-English-speaking individuals are vulnerable to not only economic but also political exploitation. Too often, politicians who speak their language claim unjustly to represent their interests.

10   The primary goal of bilingual education must be mainstreaming of non-English-speaking children through the teaching of English. But while the schools teach my children English, I will continue to teach them Spanish at home, because Spanish is part of their heritage. Ethnic identity, like religion, is a family matter.

Understanding the Content

Feel free to reread all or parts of the selection to answer the following questions.

1. How does Mujica define "bilingual education"?

2. What is her opinion of bilingual education?

3. How does Mujica differentiate the responsibilities of the school and the home in education?

4. What arguments or support does Mujica provide for her position on bilingual education?

5. Mujica refers to a 1980 census that shows Hispanics are the fastest-growing minority in the United States. What conclusion does the author draw from the statistics in paragraph 8?

Looking at Structure and Style

1. What is the function of paragraph 1? Why does Mujica place so much emphasis on her Spanish-speaking household? Does this help her argument? Why?

2. How do paragraphs 1 and 2 function as a unit?

3. How do paragraphs 3 and 4 function as a unit?

4. In paragraphs 5 and 6, Mujica fleshes out her definition of "bilingual education" and its goal. What other educational goal does she think the schools should have? Where does she state it? Is this an appropriate place? Explain.

5. What are Mujica's arguments in paragraphs 8 and 9? What are causes and what are effects?

6. How do Mujica's opening and closing paragraphs make her position clear? Describe her tone and attitude in these paragraphs.

7. To what audience is the author writing? Explain.

8. Is Mujica's essay mostly fact or opinion? Explain.

Evaluating the Author's Viewpoints

1. Mujica makes it clear that she feels that developing a sense of ethnic identity should occur in the home, not in the school. Is her argument convincing? Explain why you do or do not agree with her.

2. One of Mujica's claims is that placing Spanish-speaking children in bilingual classes actually makes them feel as if they are "in ghettos in the school" (4). What does she mean? Is this really a possibility?

3. Reread paragraph 5. Is this a valid definition of "bilingual education"? Should it include more? Explain.

4. Do you agree with Mujica's last sentence? Can ethnic identity and religion be made analogous (treated the same) in this case? Explain.

Pursuing Possible Essay Topics

1. Write a rebuttal to Mujica's viewpoints.

2. Write an essay that reflects the points regarding bilingual education on which you and Mujica might agree/disagree. Use quotations from the essays.

3. Write a description of bilingual education as you think it should be offered in school systems.

4. Write an argument against/for bilingual education.

5. If you have experienced instruction in a bilingual program, write about your views of that program. Was it a profitable experience? Was it taught correctly? Would you support more programs like it?

6. Research the present governmental support for bilingual education. Write your views of the program. In addition to the card catalog and the *Reader's Guide to Periodical Literature,* you might want to use the *Monthly Catalog of United States Government Publications* and *The New York Times Index* for more current sources on bilingual education.

7. What if the Hispanic population got so large that English became a second language in the United States? Write about the possible changes that might take place. How would it affect your life?

8. If you don't like these ideas, write an essay that deals with another aspect of learning.

📖 *Preparing to Read*

Take a minute or two to look over the following reading selection. Note the title and author, read the opening paragraph, and check the length. Make certain you have the time now to read it carefully and to do the exercises that follow it. Then, in the spaces provided, answer the following questions.

1. What do you think the title means? What is a liberal arts major? _____

_____

_____

2. What is the difference between the way our fathers prepared for their careers and the way entering college freshmen will prepare? _____

_____

_____

3. What might you learn about preparing for your own career? _____

_____

Vocabulary

Good comprehension of what you are about to read depends upon your understanding of the words below. The number following each word refers to the paragraph where it is used.

trends (1) movements, tendencies to go in a certain direction

apprenticed (1) placed under a skilled craftsman to learn a trade

obsolete (2) no longer useful

lamenting (3) complaining, regretting, showing sorrow

grounded (3) based

parlay (3) use an asset to its greatest advantage (from gambling lingo)

ivory tower (4) a place or attitude of retreat from the practical world where one is more occupied with intellectual considerations

extolling (4) praising highly

diversity (5,8) variety

validate (5) verify, prove

plethora (5) an excessive amount, more than enough

all encompassing (5) all inclusive, touching all bases

augment (5) supplement, add to

vehicle (7) means

steeped (8) saturated, subjected thoroughly

voluminous (9) of great size

alluded (9) referred

smorgasbord (9) a wide variety

Now read the essay.

The Practicality of the Liberal Arts Major

DEBRA SIKES and BARBARA MURRAY

1   Current trends indicate that by the year 2000 the average person will change careers at least twice during a lifetime. How does the entering college student prepare for career mobility which has never before been necessary? Our fathers decided what they wanted to do in life, which was very often what their fathers had done—went to college or apprenticed themselves, and pursued the same career until retirement. Our mothers assumed one of the nurturing roles in society, if they assumed a role outside of the home at all. Things have certainly changed. No longer is life so simple.

2   Adaptability and lifelong learning are now the cornerstones of success. What direction does a person take to prepare for a lifetime of change? The one degree which provides training which never becomes obsolete is the liberal arts degree; it teaches you how to think. It also teaches you how to read, write and speak intelligently, get along with others, and conceptualize problems. For the first time in several decades, the liberal arts degree is coming to the forefront of the employment field.

3   Growing ranks of corporate executives are lamenting that college students are specializing too much and too early. What corporate America really needs, according to chief executive officers of major corporations, is students soundly grounded in the liberal arts—English, especially—who then can pick up more specific business or technical skills on the job. Few students, however, seem to be listening to this message. Today's best selling courses offer evidence that students want to take courses that provide direct job related skills rather

than the most basic survival skills in the workplace: communication and thinking skills. They want courses they can parlay into jobs—and high paying ones at that. Certainly, we can understand this mentality when we consider trends indicating that this generation will be the first who will not be able to do better economically than their parents. They don't want to leave anything to chance. Historically, the liberal arts degree was good insurance for a poverty level existence. Students are looking to history to provide some answers it simply cannot give. They would do well to examine the present.

4   One of the big problems in the liberal arts community is that we do not market what we have to offer. Students very often fail to see the practicality of studying Shakespeare as preparation for a career in the business community. Perhaps some of us have locked ourselves in the ivory tower a little too long extolling the virtues of a liberal education as preparation for citizenship and life only to the neglect of it as preparation for career or careers. Education for education's sake is noble but impractical to today's college student who is facing a competitive and rapidly changing job market. They want and deserve to know how their courses will help them get a job. We as educators owe them some answers; we must be accountable not only for learning but also for providing information regarding the transferability of classroom skills into the workplace.

5   In an attempt to provide answers, we conducted a research project in the Dallas metroplex last year, assuming the role of the liberal arts graduate seeking employment in the fields of government, banking, business, and industry. Using informational interviewing as our method of job hunting and obtaining data, we conducted twenty-five interviews with a diversity of executive officers, ranging from personnel directors to the chairman of the board of an exclusive department store and the state governor. We wished to validate, through practical and current research, that not only does the liberal arts degree provide the best preparation for a lifetime of change, but it also provides a plethora of employment opportunities. We do not claim our research to be all encompassing, but we do feel its practicality was rewarding. We gathered data as to how the liberal arts major should present himself on paper and in person, where her best chances for employment are, and what he can do to augment the liberal arts degree. We were able to draw several conclusions as to how the liberal arts community could better prepare students for professional mobility.

The Liberal Arts Degree Is Marketable

6   Ninety percent of those interviewed responded they would hire a liberal arts major for an entry level position which could lead to

the executive suite if the position itself were not executive level. The chairman of the board of a major department store in Dallas responded to the question, "For what position would you hire a liberal arts graduate?" with a direct, "Any position in the company." When asked if a buyer wouldn't need to have special skills, he replied, "Taste is acquired or learned, and the liberal arts major could certainly learn this skill on the job." This interview is typical of the responses.

Skills Acquired with a Liberal Arts Background Are Most Desired by Employers

7   We were not at all surprised to learn that the skills cited as the most desirable in an employee are those skills acquired from a liberal arts background. The cited skills are listed below in order of importance.

1. Oral communication
2. Written communication
3. Interpersonal
4. Analytical thinking
5. Critical thinking
6. Leadership

Although these skills are not solely acquired through the mastery of an academic discipline, the discipline serves as a vehicle for developing or refining these skills.

Liberal Arts Majors Can Enhance Their Credentials

8   Adaptability and lifelong learning are the cornerstones of success in today's complex and rapidly changing society. No longer can the person who is steeped in one academic discipline, but knows nothing about anything else, meet today's demands. Based on the data we accumulated, our recommendations for the liberal arts major are the following:

1. A basic knowledge of accounting
2. Computer literacy
3. Second major in a business field
4. Multiple minors
5. Advanced degree in another field

The key here is adaptability and diversity. Contrary to what most people believe, the higher a skill level an individual can claim, the more marketable he is. About those individuals who complain that they are "overeducated" we can only assume that they are marketing themselves on the wrong level. "Overeducation" is a term whose time will not come in the foreseeable future. The problem many individuals will face is a narrowness of education rather than "overeducation."

9   Unlike Aristotle who is believed to have known everything there was to know at the time he lived, it is impossible for us to deal with the voluminous amounts of information which are produced daily. The lifelong learning which we have alluded to will not always be acquired through the traditional sixteen-week college course. We in the community college need to provide a smorgasbord of opportunities for individuals who wish to increase their mobility and options.

10   The time has come to rethink what education really is and how it relates to the functions of society. Perhaps what a liberal education does for an individual, which is more important than anything else, is to prepare him for more learning. The liberal arts background equips one with thinking skills; and those, coupled with the desire to learn, are the best preparation for career and life that any of us can possess.

Understanding the Content

Feel free to reread all or parts of the selection to answer the following questions.

1. By the year 2000 (judging from current trends), how many times will the average person change careers during a lifetime? How does this differ from past generations?

2. The authors claim that lifelong learning and adaptability are now the cornerstones of success. What do they mean? What degree provides training that is never obsolete?

3. According to the authors, what does corporate America want and need from its college graduates?

4. Upon what evidence have the authors based their information? Are their sources reliable? Objective?

5. What skills are cited as the most desirable in an employee?

6. Based on their findings, what recommendations do the authors make for the liberal arts major to consider?

7. Do the authors believe it is possible to be "overeducated"? Explain.

Looking at Structure and Style

1. How do paragraphs 1 and 2 work together to establish the subject and thesis of the essay?

2. What is the basic function of paragraphs 3 and 4? How do they support the essay's thesis?

3. Why are paragraphs 5 and 6 important for thesis support? How strong would the essay be without these two paragraphs?

4. Paragraphs 7 and 8 both use lists. Is this effective? Explain.

5. To what audience do you think the authors direct their essay? How do paragraphs 4, 9, and 10 help reveal audience?

6. How would you describe the essays's tone and attitude toward the subject? What words or phrases reveal tone and attitude?

Evaluating the Authors' Viewpoints

1. Do the authors convince you that a liberal arts education is important to your future career? Explain.

2. In paragraph 2, the authors state that the most basic survival skills in the workplace are communication and thinking skills. Why would these be more important than, say, learning how to program a computer if your goal is to be a computer programmer?

3. Look again at the skills listed in paragraph 7. Do these skills seem important to you? Evaluate your skills in those areas. In which skill do you need the most improvement?

4. Look again at the list in paragraph 8 of the basic knowledge the authors urge for enhancing a liberal arts major. Discuss the importance of each item.

5. The authors conclude by stating that perhaps the best thing a liberal arts education can do is to prepare one for more learning. How does such a statement fit your definition of what you think education is all about?

Pursuing Possible Essay Topics

1. Argue for or against the need for a liberal arts education.

2. Discuss what you think are the most important job skills necessary for the career you have chosen or are thinking of entering. Explain why you think each is important.

3. Define what is meant by a "liberal arts major." You may want to consult your college catalog for information on the course work required or talk with a counselor on campus.

4. Explain your reasons for wanting to attend college.

5. Discuss some aspect of yourself as a student: your study skills, your attitude, your self-image, your best learning style, your needs, your expectations, and so on.

6. Explain what you consider "the best preparation for career and life that any of us can possess."

7. Brainstorm or freewrite on one or more of the following:
   a. college life   d. a good teacher
   b. your favorite class   e. student responsibility
   c. high school vs. college   f. lifelong learning

8. Ignore these and find a topic of your own related to learning.

✍️ Student Essay

The following essay was written by a graduating senior from the University of California, Berkeley, and published in the *Los Angeles Times*. As you read it, look for answers to these questions:

1. Would this essay satisfy a writing assignment on some aspect of learning?

2. Why do you think the author wrote it?

3. Does the writer follow the writing suggestions provided in Unit 2, "Viewpoints on Writing Essays"?

4. What grade would you give this essay?

The Vast Emptiness at the Core of
Today's Liberal Arts Education
Max A. Boot

1   With this year's graduation season drawing to a close, we won't have to listen to many more commencement speakers. Usually, they tell the graduating seniors how lucky they were to spend four years acquiring wisdom. As a graduating senior at UC Berkeley, I have a somewhat different perspective—one that wasn't heard often at this year's commencement ceremonies but that contains a great deal more truth about the state of American higher education today.

2   I have done relatively well academically at Berkeley. Even so, I don't think I've received a true liberal education—at least not in the way that a well-educated man of the 19th Century would have understood it. Back then, a university was sup-

posed to provide nourishment for mind, body and soul. American colleges stopped catering to the latter too long ago, when mandatory attendance in chapel and at physical-education classes was abolished. Now, Berkeley and other leading research universities have even stopped feeding students' minds.

3   What I've missed is an education that integrates philosophy, history, literature and the other humanities into a coherent whole. Part of the fault is my own: I did not seek out some classes that I should have. But a large share of the burden lies with the university, which lacks a core curriculum—for example, "Great Books"—that could provide a general education.

4   Instead, Berkeley, like many other large universities, offers a host of overly specialized courses that seem to have little connection. The history department offers a class on Theodore Roosevelt; English has a course on science fiction; philosophy offers a class on Hegel. That's it. Almost no courses attempt to bridge the gulf between these areas. Those that should—that is, introductory courses aimed at freshmen—only offer the same content as the upper-division courses. They have an added drawback: They are taught by inaccessible professors in giant auditoriums before thousands of bored students.

5   The man responsible for this deplorable state of affairs is Clark Kerr, UC president during the 1960s and one of the most influential figures of post-World War II higher education. Kerr dreamed that the college would become all things to all people—a "multiversity." Instead, it wound up serving almost everybody inadequately.

6   Nobody is sure what the university's mission is anymore: Is it to educate elite students? To create a social melting pot? To conduct graduate-level research? Partisans of all three

viewpoints have waged intermittent battles on the Berkeley campus for decades, leaving all the players profoundly dissatisfied.

7   Undergraduates are therefore denied the opportunity to pursue a comprehensive curriculum. Instead, they are left, like shoppers in a giant supermarket, to wander the aisles, picking products at random, never sure that their selections will add up to a nutritious meal. Laissez faire may work in the economy, but it's no way to run a university.

8   This loss of mission has also allowed a weird collection of nuts and cranks to assume prominent positions at Berkeley, as they have at other leading U.S. colleges. Deconstructionists in the English department teach that words have no intrinsic meaning. Revisionists in the history department teach that the Constitution was the result of a capitalist cabal. Newly minted Ph.D.'s in the ethnic-studies field teach that America has waged genocidal war against its racial minorities for centuries. Instructors in the "Peace and Conflict Studies" department teach strategies for nonviolent protest. A sociology professor instructs students on the "plantation system" in professional sports today.

9   This is education? Thankfully, I've been able to avoid most of these professors with an ax to grind. I have managed to study almost exclusively with professors who believe in old-fashioned academic standards and the importance of Western civilization. But most students don't fare as well. The lucky ones merely miss the chance to be educated. The unlucky ones are indoctrinated by unscrupulous lecturers.

10   It's safe to say, then, that the reality of college education today is a far cry from the dreamy land of learning and higher

thinking described by commencement speakers. Just ask any recent graduate.

Reaction

In the space below or in your writing journal, write your reaction to the student essay. What would you tell this student about his essay?

Commentary

It is fairly obvious that the essay does indeed fit a writing assignment on some aspect of learning. Boot's subject is the lack of integration of the various academic disciplines offered at a university. His thesis is best stated in the last paragraph: "the reality of college education today is a far cry from the dreamy land of learning and higher thinking described by commencement speakers." If we use the checklist on page 87 as a guide, we can see that the author does follow the rules for good essay writing.

The opening paragraph, although not stating the thesis directly, establishes Boot's disagreement with what commencement speakers usually have to say about "how lucky they [students] were to spend four years acquiring wisdom." He states, "I have a somewhat different perspective."

He moves smoothly to his second paragraph, letting us know he has done well academically, but "I don't think I've received a true liberal education—at least not in the way that a well-educated man of the 19th Century would have understood it." He uses the transitional words "back then" to describe what he thinks a university's goals once were and brings us to the present with "Now, Berkeley and other leading universities have even stopped feeding students' minds."

His next paragraph describes what he has missed in his education and smoothly moves into paragraph 4 with the transition "Instead." There Boot lists specific examples of overly specialized and unconnected courses offered by many universities today.

Having presented certain effects, in paragraph 5 Boot reveals what he regards to be the cause of the problem, following up in paragraph 6 with how this has led to decades of confusion as to what the university's mission is. Paragraphs 7 and 8 deal with further effects: the lack of a comprehensive curriculum and the rise of what he calls "a collection of nuts and cranks to assume prominent positions."

Paragraph 9 contrasts his ability to avoid most of the "professors with an axe to grind," with the luck of most students, who "don't fare as well" as he has.

His last paragraph states his thesis quite clearly and ties in nicely with the comments in his opening paragraph.

Not everyone will agree with the author's viewpoints; nevertheless, the essay does make some valid points and does adhere to the checklist.

*V*iewpoints on *Human Behavior*

"What a piece of work is man!"
William Shakespeare

DEAR ANN: For most of the 14 years that my wife and I have been married she has been undressing in the closet. At first it bothered me, but I never said anything because I knew she was shy by nature and I didn't want to upset her. Well, last week she started to sleep in the closet and this is more than I can take.

I don't understand how she can be comfortable in there, but she says it is just fine and that I shouldn't worry about her.

I ought to tell you that we have two beautiful children and a good marriage. We love and respect each other even though our sex life isn't terrific. Her mother told her when she got married that sex was a duty and to lie back and think of England.

I feel guilty in a nice, comfortable bed while my wife is on the floor with a shoe rack and a laundry bag. Please advise.

GARY, IND.

WHAT makes us behave the way we do? Sociologists and psychologists, among others, are still trying to find an answer to this question. Some answers have been found. It's clear that we humans have the ability to reason and make choices. But many aspects of our physical and social environment limit the choices available to us. Still, sociologists claim that given our options and our preferences, we choose to do what we expect will be most rewarding. Whether the rewards are candy, fame, money, a better life in the future, or affection, we act or choose primarily for self-interest.

The idea of self-interest as a motive for human behavior is one that many social scientists use to try to explain our actions. Economists, observing that we seek a variety of goods for ourselves, developed their theories of supply and demand. And the success of advertising certainly depends on the self-interest of the consumer. Psychologists believe that behavior is shaped by reinforcement. That is, we repeat actions or behaviors that produce the results we desire. If our parents praise us for certain actions, we continue to act to please. Our reward is the praise we get from their pleasure. Sociologists believe that we seek what we expect will reward us and avoid what we perceive will cost us. Making our parents angry "costs" us; touching a hot fire "costs" us. If we are "normal," then we learn to behave based on these norms.

According to social scientists, we learn to see ourselves as others see us. In a sense, we look at ourselves from the outside. As infants and young children, we are not able to understand the meaning of the behavior of those around us. As we grow, we learn to know what we are like by seeing ourselves in others. We form an idea of what others want and expect and how they react to us. We settle into a pattern of behavior through interactions with others; we learn the "rules" of behavior for our particular environment. And even though we have choice, our behavior is frequently influenced by what those around us want or expect us to do.

Of course, we don't always follow the norm. Those who regularly don't follow the rules are considered abnormal. Some abnormal behavior is funny, some sad, some self-destructive, some dangerous to others. The essays in this unit deal with a variety of behavior: the good and the bad, the misunderstood, the so-called abnormal, the funny, and the unexplainable. You will recognize some behavioral actions described and wonder at others, but they are all part of the complex creatures called humans. It is hoped that you will both learn from the variety of readings and be stimulated by them to write your viewpoints on the subject.

Oh, in case you're interested, here is Ann Landers's reply to the letter from Gary, Indiana:

> DEAR GARY: I've heard of shy women undressing in the closet, but sleeping there is a new one on me.
>
> Is it possible that you aren't as careful about your personal hygiene as you might be? Do you snore? Are your sexual demands excessive or kinky?

If you can answer no to all of the above I suggest that you sit down with your wife and have a quiet talk. A woman who prefers the closet floor to a bed needs to explain herself.

📖 *Preparing to Read*

Take a minute or two to look over the following reading selection. Note the title and author, read the opening paragraph, and check the length. Make certain you have the time now to read it carefully and to do the exercises that follow it. Then, in the spaces provided, answer the following question.

1. What do you think is meant here by the title "The Seven Dwarfs and I"?

_____

_____

_____

2. What do you think will be the point of this essay? _____

_____

_____

_____

3. What might you learn from reading this selection? _____

_____

_____

_____

Vocabulary

Good comprehension of what you are about to read depends upon your understanding of the words below. The number following each word refers to the paragraph where it appears.

embedded (1) fixed firmly in place

mutation (2) variation, alteration, change

disproportionately (2) in a way that lacks proper balance

surreal (2) dreamlike or unreal in quality

disdainful (4) superior, haughty, insolent

acquiesced (5) yielded, gave in, submitted

diminutive (6) very small

discern (8) understand, recognize, realize

animosity (8) hatred, resentment, hostility

Now read the essay.

The Seven Dwarfs and I

CARA M. EGAN

1   During a recent trip to Walt Disney World, I searched through a gift shop hoping to find a set of Seven Dwarfs dolls I had as a child; I wanted to get the same set for my nephew. This may not sound unusual—the story of Snow White is embedded in most everyone's childhood memories; at Disney World, the adults I saw squirming alongside the children were just as eager as their kids to pose for a snapshot with their favorite dwarf. The ironic part about this episode in the gift shop is that I myself am a dwarf. And I'm nothing like those seven friends of Snow White.

2   "The Wizard of Oz" used to be one of my favorite movies as a child, until I got older and realized that the munchkins were like me. Except they're not. I don't have an accelerated voice; I don't wear funny clothes; I don't have pointed ears or pointed feet. I do have something called achondroplasia, which is a type of dwarfism. Achondroplasia is caused by a spontaneous gene mutation that occurs early in fetal development. The mutated gene has affected my overall bone structure, affecting my height, but also causing my arms and legs to be disproportionately smaller than the rest of my body. This happens to one in 10,000 people all over the world. There is nothing comical or magical about it, or tragic for that matter, but most people have been led to believe there is, due to the lingering surreal images of the Seven Dwarfs and the munchkins.

3   As I have grown older, I've realized that Americans have a distorted idea of what a short-statured person is. Movies like "Snow White and the Seven Dwarfs," "The Wizard of Oz" and the more recent "Willow" contribute to this problem. These entertainments,

with their fanciful, mystical short people, dehumanize the short-statured men and women actors. The films depict dwarfs as dwellers of forests and glens, places where the average-size person is a strange intruder. In reality, dwarfs are often born into average-size families, from average-size parents. We interact socially and professionally with average-size people. Movies and TV prefer not to show this reality. It's rare to see a short-statured person playing any kind of role on TV besides Santa's helper in an electric-razor commercial around Christmastime. TV and movies were not the first to depict us as a weird phenomenon. It started long ago at carnival sideshows when people lined up to see "the shortest man alive"—the "freak"—not quite animal, not quite human.

4   We have not progressed far from the days when the short-statured were held up on display as objects of disdainful laughter. Even now, there are bars that feature "dwarf tossing" as a main attraction. Why is it amusing to toss a human being in the air as far as you can as if he were a Frisbee or a football?

5   I have experienced a similiar insult in my own life. All through school, but especially during college, people had an uncontrollable urge to pick me up. Often people would greet me by saying, "You're so cute!" as if I were a doll they couldn't resist squeezing. Mostly they would want to lift me and spin me around. Sometimes they asked and sometimes they did not. I can't believe it now, but there were times when I acquiesced. I remember once being swept up unexpectedly by some drunken dancer who undoubtedly could not hear my screams or feel my kicks as I tried to free myself. I remember how scared I was at the powerlessness I felt, and after that I never let anyone lift me again.

Sinister and Hurtful

6   People are even more confused about what to call me. The word "midget" is the word used the most, although in my case it is incorrect. A midget is someone exceptionally diminutive in size, with everything—arms, legs, etc.—in proportion. The problem with the word midget can be compared to that of the word "bitch." Both words have justifiable meanings in the proper context, but over time they have acquired associations that are sinister and hurtful. Sometimes I'll be walking down the street and I will hear someone snicker, "Hey, look at that *midget*." When this happens, the word takes on a non-human aspect, as well as connotations of stupidity and unworthiness; as if the deficiency in my height equates with a deficiency in my intelligence or character, or negates my right to walk down the street altogether. When people use the word in this way they are indirectly refusing to recognize me as a human being, and this frightens me.

7   A few years ago I happened to answer the front door when my sister brought her boyfriend to meet me for the first time. I wondered if my sister had told him about me earlier in order to prevent shock or surprise. When I asked her about it later she responded, "Why? I wouldn't go out of my way to tell him the color of your hair or the shade of your eyes." From that moment I've tried to look at my situation that way. I am not a doll or toy, or some alien being. I'm a person who happens to be exceptionally short. That's it.

8   When I got back from Walt Disney World my sister expressed surprise that I had been the one to purchase the dolls for her son. I hadn't really thought about it until she asked, but then I realized it is because I am able to discern the difference between the Seven Dwarfs and me. I have no animosity toward them, but that doesn't make me one of them, either. This realization has probably been the biggest part of my growing up. But it hasn't come easily. I've spent 24 years learning to accept it. Now it's time for the rest of you.

Before answering the following questions, you may want to write a summary in your journal of the reading selection.

Understanding the Content

Feel free to reread all or parts of the selection to answer the following questions.

1. What is the difference between a midget and a dwarf?

2. What is achondroplasia?

3. What is Egan's objection to movies like *Snow White and the Seven Dwarfs* and *The Wizard of Oz*?

4. What is it about the word "midget" that Egan doesn't like?

5. What is the thesis of this selection? Is it implied or stated?

Looking at Structure and Style

1. How does Egan use her trip to Walt Disney World to introduce her subject?

2. What is the function of paragraph 2?

3. Which writing pattern shapes paragraph 3?

4. How do paragraphs 4 and 5 work together? What point do they make?

5. Explain the effectiveness of the last sentence in paragraph 7.

6. In what paragraph is the thesis best stated or implied?

7. What suggestions for improving this essay, if any, would you give the author?

Evaluating the Author's Viewpoints

1. The author states, "As I have grown older, I've realized that Americans have a distorted idea of what a short-statured person is" (3). Explain why you do or don't agree.

2. Do you believe, as the author does, that the movies she mentions contribute to a negative image of short-statured people? Defend your opinion.

3. Egan claims that few movies or television shows depict dwarfs as anything less than a "freak." If so, why do you think this is?

4. If you've ever seen a dwarf, how did you react? Why?

Pursuing Possible Essay Topics

1. Think about a behavior trait you have that you would like to change. Discuss how that trait developed, what effect it has had on you, and how you might change it.

2. Do a little research on achondroplasia and explain it more fully.

3. Write about a time when your feelings were hurt because of a name someone called you.

4. If you had an opportunity to change just one negative trait you find in humans, what would it be? Why would you change it, and into what?

5. Brainstorm or freewrite on one or more of the following:
   a. hurtful words
   b. "dwarf tossing"
   c. beastly behavior
   d. the human animal
   e. giants
   f. reacting to appearance

6. Come up with your own topic that deals with human behavior.

📖 Preparing to Read

Take a minute or two to look over the following reading selection. Note the title and author, read the opening paragraph, and check the length. Make certain you have the time now to read it carefully and to do the exercises that follow it. Then, in the spaces provided, answer the following questions.

1. What do you think is meant here by the title "Sexual Bigotry"?

_____

_____

_____

2. What do you think will be the point of this essay? _____

_____

_____

_____

3. What might you learn from reading this selection? _____

_____

_____

_____

Vocabulary

Good comprehension of what you are about to read depends upon your understanding of the words below. The number following each word refers to the paragraph where it appears.

bigotry (title, 2) intolerance toward others

overbearing (1) bossy, oppressive, dominating

fraught (3) loaded, burdened

derision (6) ridicule, scorn, negativity

Klansman (18) a member of the Ku Klux Klan, an organization that advocates white supremacy

Now read the essay.

Sexual Bigotry

ROGER ROSENBLATT

1   The reason people are having so much trouble identifying sexual harassment these days is that the offense has less to do with sex than gender. Ever since Professor Anita Hill accused Supreme Court nominee Judge Clarence Thomas of lewd and overbearing conduct toward her, the country has been trying to determine the difference between innocent fun and genuine pain.

2   But the pain felt by a woman who suffers indignities from men in a place of work rarely has anything to do with the men's sexual

desires. The pain is experienced because women are made to feel inferior—inferior intellectually, emotionally, professionally—in a situation where they have every right to feel equal. They are not so much sex objects as targets of bigotry.

3   Now, bigotry between sexes, unlike bigotry between races, is fraught with a lot of biological tension that can make it seem something other than it is. And sex often does involve the deliberate exertion of leverage or power.

4   But when some guy calls a female colleague "honey" and does nothing else suggestive, I think it's a stretch to assume that "honey" is a sign of his wanting to roll in the hay. When the word is dropped into, say, a professional disagreement, or a competition of views, however, it has the edge of an attack.

5   "That's all well and good, honey, but if you had as much experience with these things as I . . . ."

6   In that sort of case, which is far more common than a man's making a pass, the term of endearment is actually a term of derision, of purposeful belittling. Not very subtly, the male in the office wants to tell the female: "O.K. You've got a big, responsible job now. But this is still a man's world, *honey*, and I'm going to try and make you feel as uncomfortable in it as I possibly can."

7   The movie *Tootsie* brought out this kind of sexual bigotry as well as anything. Dustin Hoffman, passing as a woman, and playing an actress in a soap opera, chews out "her" director, played by Dabney Coleman (America's favorite male chauvinist pig), when Coleman uses the supposedly affectionate nickname of Tootsie. Coleman isn't interested in squeezing Tootsie's body but in squeezing her mind. He wants to make her feel she does not belong, or that she exists at his sufferance.

8   That, I think, is the real and brutal motive behind most sexual harassment—to keep a woman in her "place" whenever she emerges into a "man's place."

9   These recent years have been kind of hard on the old boys' network. (I know, I'm an old boy myself.) In the 1990s men are finally beginning to realize that the women's movement has moved; it has happened. With the economy requiring two wage earners in a family, and the general enlightenment that follows a right idea, nothing is going to make it *un*-happen.

10   Some men take the news well, some grudgingly, some angrily. Some take it angrily who only appear to take it well.

11   These are the ones you often find leering like Red Riding Hood's wolf over the watercooler or reaching out to make a pinch. They don't want sex, they want dominance. They want to set back the office clock to when those desks and nameplates were all theirs.

12   We have seen this type of bigotry before, of course, but it was in the South before the 1960s, at swimming pools and lunch counters, when American blacks were told they were not Americans.

13   And we saw it at the start of the century, when American Irish, Slavs, Jews, Italians and others were told they were not Americans either: "Irish need not apply." American Hispanics are told the same thing today, as are American Asians and American Indians, and American homosexuals and the American handicapped.

14   With civil rights laws in place, bigots have nowhere to turn except toward lesser forms of tyranny. The matter often lies in intention. Most male bigots intend to bring women down, all right—not in the bed, in the whole society. They hope to injure a woman's self-esteem by bringing her low. It is one sure way such men can think better of themselves.

15   Like conventional bigots, too, they will treat the targets of their bigotry as inferior because of fear. Usually men who behave badly toward women coworkers are afraid of them, afraid that women will show them up as less capable or that the women will band together in a sorority as clannish and exclusionary as men's clubs. You wouldn't want *that.*

16   Many observers feel that the gray area in the harassment issue lies where a woman misinterprets a man's intentions. I think that is so. Many men, myself sorrowfully included, are bumblers when it comes to knowing what's cute and what's rude or worse.

17   But I also think that the misinterpretation of intentions is far more likely when it comes to sexual desires than when it comes to bigotry.

18   No law can prove it, but the heart knows when it is being assaulted as something less, not worthy, not human. The man who does anything—anything at all—to intentionally make a woman feel not human is no different from the coward Klansman hiding his hatred under a sheet. He's not making love, he's making war.

Understanding the Content

Feel free to read all or parts of the essay in order to answer the following questions.

1. What does Rosenblatt mean by "sexual bigotry"? How does it differ from sexual harassment?

2. What does Rosenblatt believe is "the real and brutal motive" (8) behind most sexual harassment? Why does he think this?

3. To what other types of bigotry does the author liken the bigotry of some men toward women?

4. Explain what Rosenblatt means by "the gray area in the harassment issue" (16).

5. What does Rosenblatt feel is at the root of bigotry?

Looking at Structure and Style

1. Is Rosenblatt's thesis stated or implied? If stated, where do you find it?

2. Discuss the author's use of comparison and contrast with uses of the term "honey" in paragraphs 4–6. How do these paragraphs help support his thesis?

3. What is the function of paragraph 7? How does it support Rosenblatt's thesis?

4. Why did the author include the parenthetical comment in paragraph 9?

5. Why is the last word in paragraph 15 italicized? How should the sentence be read?

6. Is the last paragraph effective? Explain.

Evaluating the Author's Viewpoints

1. Rosenblatt says that women who suffer indignities at the work place are not so much sex objects as targets of bigotry. Is he correct? Why?

2. Reread paragraph 8. Do you agree? Why?

3. Do you agree with Rosenblatt's claims in paragraph 14? Why?

4. Fear, contends the author, is a factor in bigotry. Explain what he means. What kind of fear? Do you agree?

5. "Many men, myself sorrowfully included, are bumblers when it comes to knowing what's cute and what's rude or worse," says Rosenblatt (16). Is this an acceptable excuse? Is he using it as one here? Explain.

6. Do you agree or disagree with Rosenblatt's concluding remarks? Why?

Pursuing Possible Essay Topics

1. Agree or disagree with Rosenblatt's thesis in a persuasive essay.

2. Write an essay about another type of bigotry you detest. Define your terms and use examples and illustrations to support your thesis.

3. Write an essay that deals with sexual bigotry toward males.

4. Write a narrative about a time when you were made to feel inferior. What was the motive behind the incident? How did you deal with your feelings?

5. Have you ever made someone feel inferior? Write about it. Why did you do it? What were the results?

6. Brainstorm or freewrite on one or more of the following:
   a. your fears   d. jealousy
   b. sex objects   e. behavior
   c. hatred   f. false intentions

7. Find your own topic on some aspect of human behavior, normal or abnormal.

Preparing to Read

Take a minute or two to look over the following reading selection. Note the title and author, read the opening paragraph, and check the length. Make certain you have the time now to read it carefully and to do the exercises that follow it. Then, in the spaces provided, answer the following questions.

1. What is the author's attitude toward superstitions? _____

   _____

2. How would you define a "superstitious mind"? _____

   _____

3. Are you superstitious? In what way? Why? _____

   _____

Vocabulary

Good comprehension of what you are about to read depends upon your understanding of the words below. The number following each word refers to the paragraph where it appears.

amulets (1) lucky charms

incantations (1) words believed to have magic powers to cast spells

occult (2) supernatural, unearthly, mystical

excising (3) removing, ridding

evasion (4) avoidance

deference (4) honor, respect

shroud (5) a cloth used to wrap a person for burial

pinafore (5) a young girl's dress

melodramatic (6) exaggeratedly emotional

idiom (6) an expression of speech having a meaning different from the literal meaning of the words

prolong (7) extend

ironically (8) oppositely or differently from what is expected

matrilineal heritage (8) those things inherited from the mother's side of the family

askew (9) crooked

Now read the essay.

Superstitious Minds

LETTY COTTIN POGREBIN

1   I am a very rational person. I tend to trust reason more than feeling. But I also happen to be superstitious—in my fashion. Black cats and rabbits' feet hold no power for me. My superstitions are my mother's superstitions, the amulets and incantations she learned from *her* mother and taught me.

2   I don't mean to suggest that I grew up in an occult atmosphere. On the contrary, my mother desperately wanted me to rise above her immigrant ways and become an educated American. She tried to hide her superstitions, but I came to know them all: Slap a girl's cheeks when she first gets her period. Never take a picture of a pregnant woman. Knock wood when speaking about your good fortune. Eat the ends of bread if you want to have a boy. Don't leave a bride alone on her wedding day.

3   When I was growing up, my mother often would tiptoe in after I seemed to be asleep and kiss my forehead three times, making odd noises that sounded like a cross between sucking and spitting. One night I opened my eyes and demanded an explanation. Embarrassed, she told me she was excising the "Evil Eye"—in case I had attracted its attention that day by being especially wonderful. She believed her kisses could suck out any envy or ill will that those less fortunate may have directed at her child.

4   By the time I was in my teens, I was almost on speaking terms with the Evil Eye, a jealous spirit that kept track of those who had "too much" happiness and zapped them with sickness and misery to even the score. To guard against this mischief, my mother practiced

rituals of interference, evasion, deference, and above all, avoidance of situations where the Evil Eye might feel at home.

5   This is why I wasn't allowed to attend funerals. This is also why my mother hated to mend my clothes while I was wearing them. The only garment one should properly get sewn *into* is a shroud. To ensure that the Evil Eye did not confuse my pinafore with a burial outfit, my mother insisted that I chew a thread while she sewed, thus proving myself very much alive. Outwitting the Evil Eye also accounted for her closing the window shades above my bed whenever there was a full moon. The moon should only shine on cemeteries, you see; the living need protection from the spirits.

6   Because we were dealing with a deadly force, I also wasn't supposed to say any words associated with mortality. This was hard for a 12-year-old who punctuated every anecdote with the verb "to die," as in "You'll die when you hear this!" or "If I don't get home by ten, I'm dead." I managed to avoid using such expressions in the presence of my mother until the day my parents brought home a painting I hated and we were arguing about whether it should be displayed on our walls. Unthinking, I pressed my point with a melodramatic idiom: "That picture will hang over my dead body!" Without a word, my mother grabbed a knife and slashed the canvas to shreds.

7   I understand all this now. My mother emigrated in 1907 from a small Hungarian village. The oldest of seven children, she had to go out to work before she finished the eighth grade. Experience taught her that life was unpredictable and often incomprehensible. Just as an athlete keeps wearing the same T-shirt in every game to prolong a winning streak, my mother's superstitions gave her a means of imposing order on a chaotic system. Her desire to control the fates sprung from the same helplessness that makes the San Francisco 49ers' defensive more superstitious than its offensive team. Psychologists speculate this is because the defense has less control; they don't have the ball.

8   Women like my mother never had the ball. She died when I was 15, leaving me with deep regrets for what she might have been—and a growing understanding of who she was. *Superstitious* is one of the things she was. I wish I had a million sharp recollections of her, but when you don't expect someone to die, you don't store up enough memories. Ironically, her mystical practices are among the clearest impressions she left behind. In honor of this matrilineal heritage— and to symbolize my mother's effort to control her life as I in my way try to find order in mine—I knock on wood and I do not let the moon shine on those I love. My children laugh at me, but they understand that these tiny rituals have helped keep my mother alive in my mind.

9   A year ago, I awoke in the night and realized that my son's window blinds had been removed for repair. Smiling at my own compulsion, I got a bed sheet to tack up against the moonlight and I opened his bedroom door. What I saw brought tears to my eyes. There, hopelessly askew, was a blanket my son, then 18, had taped to his window like a curtain.

10   My mother never lived to know David, but he knew she would not want the moon to shine upon him as he slept.

Understanding the Content

Feel free to reread all or parts of the selection to answer the following questions.

1. Pogrebin says that she is a rational person, but superstitious in her own way. In what way is she superstitious?

2. The author mentions several of her mother's superstitions. What were some of them?

3. What was the reason Pogrebin's mother would never mend her clothes while she was wearing them?

4. The term "Evil Eye" is used several times. How would the author's mother have defined the term?

5. Pogrebin says that she now understands her mother's superstitions. How does she explain them?

6. How does Pogrebin explain away her own practice of some of her mother's "tiny rituals" if she is a "rational person"?

Looking at Structure and Style

1. How well does the opening paragraph establish the author's subject and her attitude toward that subject? What do we know after reading it?

2. What writing pattern is used in paragraph 2? Explain it.

3. What writing pattern is used in paragraph 3? Explain it.

4. What is the function of paragraph 7?

5. What is the function of paragraph 9? What inferences can you draw from the episode?

6. Explain or rewrite the following passages from the essay:
   a. "By the time I was in my teens, I was almost on speaking terms with the Evil Eye, a jealous spirit that kept track of those who had 'too much' happiness and zapped them with sickness and misery to even the score." (4)

b. "This was hard for a 12-year-old who punctuated every anecdote with the verb 'to die,' as in 'You'll die when you hear this!' ..." (6)
c. "Experience taught her that life was unpredictable and often incomprehensible." (7)
d. "Women like my mother never had the ball." (8)

7. How would you describe the tone of this essay?

Evaluating the Author's Viewpoints

1. Pogrebin says that her mother's "desire to control the fates sprung from the same helplessness that makes the San Francisco 49ers' defensive more superstitious than its offensive team. Psychologists speculate this is because the defense has less control; they don't have the ball" (7). Explain why this is or isn't a good analogy. Can you think of another?

2. Do you get the feeling that the author is as superstitious as her mother was? Explain.

3. For what reason do you think Pogrebin chose to write about her mother's superstitions? Is she embarrassed or ashamed of them? What is her point?

Pursuing Possible Essay Topics

1. Write about a superstition of your own or a family member's. How strong is it? Where does it come from?

2. Talk to someone from another country about superstitions. Are their superstitions similar to those you know?

3. Look up "superstitions" in your library card catalog, and look through one or two references that seem interesting. You may get some ideas for an essay.

4. Brainstorm or freewrite on one or more of the following:
   a. black magic
   b. voodoo
   c. the occult
   d. silly superstitions
   e. ESP
   f. astrological forecasts

5. Attempt to explain why many people like to view movies that frighten them.

6. Ignore these and write on some aspect of strange human behavior.

Preparing to Read

Take a minute or two to look over the following reading selection. Note the title and author, read the opening paragraph, and check the length. Make certain you have the time now to read it carefully and to do the exercises that follow it. Then, in the spaces provided, answer the following questions.

1. What is suggested by the title? _____

_____

2. What do you think the essay will be about? _____

_____

3. Does the opening paragraph make you want to read on? Why? _____

_____

_____

Vocabulary

Good comprehension of what you are about to read depends upon your understanding of the words below. The number following each word refers to the paragraph where it appears.

affluent (1) wealthy, well-to-do

impoverished (1) drained of wealth, poor

discreet (1) cautious, careful

uninflammatory (1) not arousing anger or emotion

unwieldy (2) difficult to handle

quarry (2) a hunted animal, prey

dismayed (2) unnerved, rattled, taken aback

accomplice (2) one who aids a criminal

tyranny (2) absolute power, usually unjust and cruel; here, the power muggers have to terrorize women

elicit (3) bring out or cause

avid (4) enthusiastic, eager

taut (4) strained, tense

warrenlike (5) describing a *warren*, a place where small animals live, but also referring to places overcrowded with people

bandolier-style (5) like a soldier's bullet belt

perpetrators (5) those who commit crimes

solace (5) comfort

in retrospect (6) looking back on the past

bravado (6) false bravery

perilous (7) dangerous

ad hoc posse (7) a group formed for a special purpose (in this case, to chase him); *ad hoc* is Latin for "for this"

skittish (9) nervous

congenial (9) friendly, cooperative

constitutionals (10) healthy walks

Now read the essay.

Night Walker

BRENT STAPLES

1   My first victim was a woman—white, well dressed, probably in her early 20s. I came upon her late one evening on a deserted street in Hyde Park, a relatively affluent neighborhood in an otherwise mean, impoverished section of Chicago. As I swung onto the avenue behind her, there seemed to be a discreet, uninflammatory distance between us. Not so. She cast back a worried glance. To her, the youngish black man—a broad six feet two inches with a beard and billowing hair, both hands shoved into the pockets of a bulky military jacket— seemed menacingly close. She picked up her pace and was soon running in earnest. Within seconds she disappeared into a cross street.

2   That was more than a decade ago. I was 22 years old, a graduate student newly arrived at the University of Chicago. It was in the echo of that terrified woman's footfalls that I first began to know the unwieldy inheritance I'd come into—the ability to alter public space in ugly ways. It was clear that she thought herself the quarry of a mugger, a rapist, or worse. Suffering a bout of insomnia, however, I was stalking sleep, not defenseless wayfarers. As a softy who is scarcely able to take a knife to a raw chicken—let alone hold one to a person's throat—I was surprised, embarrassed, and dismayed all at once. Her flight made me feel like an accomplice in tyranny. It also made it clear that I was indistinguishable from the muggers who occasionally seeped into the area from the surrounding ghetto. I soon gathered that being perceived as dangerous is a hazard in itself: Where fear and weapons meet—and they often do in urban America—there is always the possibility of death.

3   In that first year, my first away from my hometown, I was to

become thoroughly familiar with the language of fear. At dark, shadowy intersections, I could cross in front of a car stopped at a traffic light and elicit the *thunk, thunk, thunk, thunk* of the driver—black, white, male, female—hammering down the door locks. On less traveled streets after dark, I grew accustomed to but never comfortable with people crossing to the other side of the street rather than pass me. Then there were the standard unpleasantries with policemen, doormen, bouncers, cabdrivers, and others whose business it is to screen out troublesome individuals *before* there is any nastiness.

4   I moved to New York nearly two years ago and I have remained an avid night walker. In central Manhattan, the near-constant crowd covers the tense one-on-one street encounters. Elsewhere, things can get very taut indeed.

5   After dark, on the warrenlike streets of Brooklyn where I live, I often see women who fear the worst from me. They seem to have set their faces on neutral, and with their purse straps strung across their chests bandolier-style, they forge ahead as though bracing themselves against being tackled. I understand, of course, that the danger they perceive is not a hallucination. Women are particularly vulnerable to street violence, and young black males are drastically overrepresented among the perpetrators of that violence. Yet these truths are no solace against the alienation that comes of being ever the suspect, an entity with whom pedestrians avoid making eye contact.

6   It is not altogether clear to me how I reached the ripe old age of 22 without being conscious of the lethality nighttime pedestrians attributed to me. Perhaps it was because in Chester, Pa., the small, angry industrial town where I came of age in the 1960s, I was scarcely noticeable against a backdrop of gang warfare, street knifings, and murders. I grew up one of the good boys, had perhaps a half-dozen fistfights. In retrospect, my shyness of combat has clear sources. As a boy, I saw countless tough guys locked away; I have since buried several, too. They were babies, really—a teen-age cousin, a brother of 22, a childhood friend in his mid-20s—all gone down in episodes of bravado played out in the streets. I chose, perhaps unconsciously, to remain a shadow—timid, but a survivor.

7   The fearsomeness mistakenly attributed to me in public places often has a perilous flavor. The most frightening of these confusions occurred in the late 1970s and early 1980s, when I worked as a journalist in Chicago. One day, rushing into the office of a magazine I was writing for with a deadline story in hand, I was mistaken for a burglar. The office manager called security and, with an ad hoc posse, pursued me through the labyrinthine halls, nearly to my editor's door. I had no way of proving who I was. I could only move briskly toward the company of someone who knew me.

8   Relatively speaking, however, I never fared as badly as another black male journalist. He went to nearby Waukegan, Ill., a couple of summers ago to work on a story about a murderer who was born there. Mistaking the reporter for the killer, police officers hauled him from his car at gunpoint and but for his press credentials would probably have tried to book him. Such episodes are not uncommon. Black men trade tales like this all the time.

9   Over the years, I learned to smother the rage I felt at so often being mistaken for a criminal. Not to do so would surely have led to madness. I now take precautions to make myself less threatening. I move about with care, particularly late in the evening. I give a wide berth to nervous people on subway platforms during the wee hours. If I happen to be entering a building behind some people who appear skittish, I may walk by, letting them clear the lobby before I return, so as not to seem to be following them. I have been calm and extremely congenial on those rare occasions when I've been pulled over by the police.

10   And on late-evening constitutionals I employ what has proved to be an excellent tension-reducing measure: I whistle melodies from Beethoven and Vivaldi and the more popular classical composers. Even steely New Yorkers hunching toward nighttime destinations seem to relax, and occasionally they even join in the tune. Virtually everybody seems to sense that a mugger wouldn't be warbling bright, sunny selections from Vivaldi's "Four Seasons." It is my equivalent of the cowbell that hikers wear when they are in bear country.

Understanding the Content

Feel free to reread all or parts of the selection to answer the following questions.

1. What point is Staples making in his essay? Is his thesis implied or stated?

2. What happened that caused Staples to learn that "being perceived as dangerous is a hazard in itself" (2)? What does he mean?

3. How old was the author at the time? What was his reaction?

4. What other events have made him "thoroughly familiar with the language of fear" (3)?

5. Why does Staples feel that he is "often being mistaken for a criminal" (9)?

6. What tactics or precautions does he take to avoid being mistaken for a potential criminal?

Looking at Structure and Style

1. How effective is the author's first paragraph? Does it create an interest in the essay? Why?

2. Why does Staples wait until the middle of paragraph 2 to explain what was actually happening, that he was merely taking a walk?

3. What is the function of paragraph 3? What paragraph pattern is used there?

4. What attitude do you think is expressed in paragraph 9? What inferences can you draw from the author's statements?

5. Rewrite or explain the following passages from the essay:

    a. "It was in the echo of that terrified woman's footfalls that I first began to know the unwieldy inheritance I'd come into...." (2)

    b. "Where fear and weapons meet—and they often do in urban America—there is always the possibility of death." (2)

    c. "...I could cross in front of a car stopped at a traffic light and elicit the *thunk, thunk, thunk, thunk* of the driver—black, white, male, female—hammering down the door locks." (3)

    d. "They seem to have set their faces on neutral, and with their purse straps strung across their chests bandolier-style, they forge ahead as though bracing themselves against being tackled." (5)

    e. "It is my equivalent of the cowbell that hikers wear when they are in bear country." (10)

6. How effective is the title? Explain.

7. What suggestions for revision, if any, would you offer the author?

Evaluating the Author's Viewpoints

1. In paragraph 2, Staples says that he learned at twenty-two that he had "the ability to alter public space in ugly ways." Explain what he means. Might the woman he describes in the opening paragraph be just as afraid of a white man in the same situation?

2. Reread the last sentence in paragraph 3. What attitude does the author reflect when he alludes to "standard unpleasantries" with people in authority? Is he exaggerating?

3. In paragraph 5, Staples says that "young black males are drastically overrepresented among the perpetrators of...violence." Where do you think he believes this overrepresentation takes place? Do you agree?

4. Staples reveals to his audience negative attitudes toward black males that he has experienced firsthand and does not deserve. What is your reaction to the way he has responded?

Pursuing Possible Essay Topics

1. Write about a time when your identity was questioned or you were mistakenly accused of something. How were you made to feel? How did you react?

2. Write about a time when you were frightened or felt threatened by someone. Was the fear or threat real or imagined? What led up to the situation or incident? How was it resolved?

3. Brainstorm or freewrite on one or more of the following:
   a. fear   d. gangs
   b. anger   e. danger
   c. prejudice   f. tension

4. Skim through a newspaper for two or three days to see how many episodes of street violence are reported. What effect do these reports have on people's fears? Is street violence exaggerated?

5. Staples is a victim of stereotyping. Write an essay about the way you may knowingly or unknowingly stereotype a certain ethnic group. Examine the cause or basis for your doing so.

6. Examine a characteristic of yourself or someone you know that you don't like. How did the trait or attitude develop? What harm has it caused? What can you do about it?

7. Ignore these and come up with your own topic on some aspect of human behavior.

Preparing to Read

Take a minute or two to look over the following reading selection. Note the title and author, read the opening paragraph, and check the length. Make certain you have the time now to read it carefully and to do the exercises that follow it. Then, in the spaces provided, answer the following questions.

1. Explain your reaction to the title. _____

   _____

   _____

2. What do you think will be the point of the essay? _____

   _____

   _____

3. What is your reaction to the opening paragraph? _____

_____

Vocabulary

Good comprehension of what you are about to read depends upon your understanding of the words below. The number following each word refers to the paragraph where it appears.

Dumpster (1) a huge trash container

gaunt (2) thin and bony

incisor (2) the sharp, pointed tooth used for cutting and tearing

maze (3) a confusing series of pathways

canine unit (4) a patrol group using dogs

recesses (4) alcoves

baton (5) a club or nightstick

acrid (6) bitter, harsh

Now read the essay.

Slow Descent into Hell

JON D. HULL

1   Behind a Dumpster sits a man who calls himself Red enjoying the last drops of a bottle of wine called Wild Irish Rose. It's 1 a.m., and the thermometer hovers around 20°, with a biting wind. His nickname comes from a golden retriever his family once had back in Memphis, and a sparkle comes to his eyes as he recalls examples of the dog's loyalty. One day he plans to get another dog, and says, "I'm getting to the point where I can't talk to people. They're always telling me to do something or get out of their way. But a dog is different."

2   At 35, he looks 50, and his gaunt face carries discolored scars from the falls and fights of three years on the streets. An upper incisor is missing, and his lower teeth jut outward against his lower lip, giving the impression that he can't close his mouth. His baggy pants are about five inches too long and when he walks, their frayed ends drag on the ground. "You know something?" he asks, holding up the bottle. "I wasn't stuck to this stuff until the cold got to me. Now I'll freeze without it. I could go to Florida or someplace, but I know this town and I know who the creeps are. Besides, it's not too bad in the summer."

3   Finishing the bottle, and not yet drunk enough to sleep out in the cold, he gathers his blanket around his neck and heads for the subways beneath city hall, where hundreds of the homeless seek warmth. Once inside, the game of cat-and-mouse begins with the police, who patrol the maze of tunnels and stairways and insist that everybody remain off the floor and keep moving. Sitting can be an invitation to trouble, and the choice between sleep and warmth becomes agonizing as the night wears on.

4   For the first hour, Red shuffles through the tunnels, stopping occasionally to urinate against the graffiti-covered walls. Then he picks a spot and stands for half an hour, peering out from the large hood of his coat. In the distance, the barking of German shepherds echoes through the tunnels as a canine unit patrols the darker recesses of the underground. Nearby, a young man in a ragged trench coat stands against the wall, slapping his palms against his sides and muttering, "I've got to get some paperwork done. I've just got to get some paperwork done!" Red shakes his head. "Home sweet home," he says. Finally exhausted, he curls up on the littered floor, lying on his side with his hands in his pockets and his hood pulled all the way over his face to keep the rats away. He is asleep instantly.

5   Whack! A police baton slaps his legs and a voice booms, "Get the hell up, you're outta here. Right now!" Another police officer whacks his nightstick against a metal grating as the twelve men sprawled along the tunnel crawl to their feet. Red pulls himself up and walks slowly up the stairs to the street, never looking back.

6   Pausing at every pay phone to check the coin-return slots, he makes his way to a long steam grate whose warm hiss bears the acrid smell of a dry cleaner's shop. He searches for newspaper and cardboard to block the moisture but retain the heat. With his makeshift bed made, he curls up again, but the rest is short-lived. "This s.o.b. used to give off more heat," he says, staring with disgust at the grate. He gathers the newspapers and moves down the block, all the while muttering about the differences among grates. "Some are good, some are bad. I remember I was getting a beautiful sleep on this one baby and then all this honking starts. I was laying right in a damn driveway and nearly got run over by a garbage truck."

7   Stopping at a small circular vent shooting jets of steam, Red shakes his head and curses: "This one is too wet, and it'll go off sometimes, leaving you to freeze." Shaking now with the cold, he walks four more blocks and finds another grate, where he curls up and fishes a half-spent cigarette from his pocket. The grate is warm, but soon the moisture from the steam has soaked his newspapers and begins to gather on his clothes. Too tired to find another grate, he sets down more newspapers, throws his blanket over his head and sprawls across the grate. By morning he is soaked.

Understanding the Content

Feel free to reread all or parts of the selection to answer the following questions.

1. What is the subject of the essay?
2. What is the thesis or point of the essay? Is it stated or implied?
3. Can you infer where the incident takes place? How?
4. What is the "the game of cat-and-mouse" people like Red play?
5. For how long has Red been living as he does?
6. Why does Red stay when he could "go to Florida or someplace" (2)?
7. Describe Red.

Looking at Structure and Style

1. What is the author's attitude toward Red?
2. Is the essay told mostly subjectively or objectively? Explain. Is this an effective approach in this case? Why?
3. On occasion, the author lets Red speak for himself. How does hearing Red's own words help us get a better picture of him in paragraph 1? paragraph 2? paragraph 4? paragraph 6?
4. Describe the transition used between paragraphs 4 and 5.
5. Pick out some passages from the essay that you think are particularly well written. What makes them noteworthy?
6. What is the basic writing mode used in this essay? How else might the author have chosen to write about Red? Would that style have the same effect?
7. Explain the significance of the title.
8. What suggestions for revision, if any, would you offer the author?

Evaluating the Author's Viewpoints

1. Hull does not directly state his viewpoints, but a look at his title implies a point of view toward Red's existence. What is it? Do you agree?
2. What seems to be Red's attitude toward his own lifestyle?
3. How does Hull portray the police? What do they think of Red?
4. What do you think are Hull's feelings toward Red and others like him? Sympathy? Disgust? Concern? Interest? Explain.

Pursuing Possible Essay Topics

1. Pretend you are Red. Write a narrative that explains why you are living where you are and as you are. Be as descriptive as you can.

2. Investigate your city's laws and its attitude toward the homeless. Go to the city hall or ask your librarian for information. Write an analysis of your findings.

3. Do some library research on the homeless. Look in the latest issues of the *Reader's Guide to Periodical Literature* under the heading "homeless." It will direct you to current magazine articles or essays. Do some reading and then react to what you read in an essay of your own.

4. Explain what you would do about the homeless situation if you had the power.

5. Visit an organization such as the Salvation Army that attempts to help the homeless. Interview someone who works for the organization and report their viewpoints on homeless people's behavior. How do they see the situation?

6. Brainstorm or freewrite on one or more of the following:

   a. runaways   d. shelters
   b. drunks   e. the human bond
   c. street people f. destitution

7. Ignore these and find your own topic on some aspect of human behavior.

📖 Preparing to Read

Take a minute or two to look over the following reading selection. Note the title and author, read the first *three* paragraphs, and check the length. Make certain you have the time now to read it carefully and to do the exercises that follow it. Then, in the spaces provided, answer the following questions.

1. What seems to be the author's attitude toward fun? _____

   _____

2. Do you think the essay is serious or humorous? Why? _____

   _____

3. Guess the thesis of the essay. _____

   _____

Vocabulary

Good comprehension of what you are about to read depends upon your understanding of the words below. The number following each word refers to the paragraph where it appears.

Puritans (3) those who practice strict moral rules and regard luxury and fun as sinful

fetish (5) an object to which one is overattached or obsessed

traipsing (8) walking about idly

licentiousness (9) immorality, lustfulness

epitome (11) perfect example

blaspheme (13) speak irreverently of

Now read the essay.

Fun. Oh, Boy. Fun. You Could Die from It.

SUZANNE BRITT

1 Fun is hard to have.

2 Fun is a rare jewel.

3 Somewhere along the line people got the modern idea that fun was there for the asking, that people deserved fun, that if we didn't have a little fun every day we would turn into (sakes alive!) Puritans.

4 "Was it fun?" became the question that overshadowed all other questions: good questions like: Was it moral? Was it kind? Was it honest? Was it beneficial? Was it generous? Was it necessary? And (my favorite) was it selfless?

5 When pleasure got to be the main thing, the fun fetish was sure to follow. Everything was supposed to be fun. If it wasn't fun, then by Jove, we were going to make it fun, or else.

6 Think of all the things that got the reputation of being fun. Family outings were supposed to be fun. Sex was supposed to be fun. Education was supposed to be fun. Work was supposed to be fun. Walt Disney was supposed to be fun. Church was supposed to be fun. Staying fit was supposed to be fun.

7 Just to make sure that everybody knew how much fun we were having, we put happy faces on flunking test papers, dirty bumpers, sticky refrigerator doors, bathroom mirrors.

8 If a kid, looking at his very happy parents traipsing through that very happy Disney World, said, "This ain't no fun, ma," his ma's

heart sank. She wondered where she had gone wrong. Everybody told her what fun family outings to Disney World would be. Golly gee, what was the matter?

9   Fun got to be such a big thing that everybody started to look for more and more thrilling ways to supply it. One way was to step up the level of danger or licentiousness or alcohol or drug consumption so that you could be sure that, no matter what, you would manage to have a little fun.

10   Television commercials brought a lot of fun and fun-loving folks into the picture. Everything that people in those commercials did looked like fun: taking Polaroid snapshots, swilling beer, buying insurance, mopping the floor, bowling, taking aspirin. We all wished, I'm sure, that we could have half as much fun as those rough-and-ready guys around the locker room, flicking each other with towels and pouring champagne. The more commercials people watched, the more they wondered when the fun would start in their own lives. It was pretty depressing.

11   Big occasions were supposed to be fun. Christmas, Thanksgiving and Easter were obviously supposed to be fun. Your wedding day was supposed to be fun. Your wedding night was supposed to be a whole lot of fun. Your honeymoon was supposed to be the epitome of fundom. And so we ended up going through every Big Event we ever celebrated, waiting for the fun to start.

12   It occurred to me, while I was sitting around waiting for the fun to start, that not much is, and that I should tell you just in case you're worried about your fun capacity.

13   I don't mean to put a damper on things. I just mean we ought to treat fun reverently. It is a mystery. It cannot be caught like a virus. It cannot be trapped like an animal. The god of mirth is paying us back for all those years of thinking fun was everywhere by refusing to come to our party. I don't want to blaspheme fun anymore. When fun comes in on little dancing feet, you probably won't be expecting it. In fact, I bet it comes when you're doing your duty, your job, or your work. It may even come on a Tuesday.

14   I remember one day, long ago, on which I had an especially good time. Pam Davis and I walked to the College Village drug store one Saturday morning to buy some candy. We were about 12 years old (fun ages). She got her Bit-O-Honey. I got my malted milk balls, chocolate stars, Chunkys, and a small bag of M&M's. We started back to her house. I was going to spend the night. We had the whole day to look forward to. We had plenty of candy. It was a long way to Pam's house but every time we got weary Pam would put her hand over her eyes, scan the horizon like a sailor and say, "Oughta reach

home by nightfall," at which point the two of us would laugh until we thought we couldn't stand it another minute. Then after we got calm, she'd say it again. You should have been there. It was the kind of day and friendship and occasion that made me deeply regret that I had to grow up.

15 It was fun.

Understanding the Content

Feel free to reread all or parts of the selection to answer the following questions.

1. Britt's essay subject is *fun*. What is her thesis?

2. What are some examples Britt provides to support her thesis?

3. What are some of her objections to the idea of fun?

4. What is Britt's definition of "fun"?

Looking at Structure and Style

1. Britt opens and closes with very short, one-sentence paragraphs. How effective is this technique? Explain.

2. How does the use of "(sakes alive!)" in paragraph 3 help create the author's tone? What are some other examples of her use of certain words or phrases to create tone?

3. What is the function of paragraphs 4–11?

4. What is the function of paragraphs 12 and 13?

5. How does Britt use paragraph 14 to define fun? Is her definition effective? Explain.

6. How appropriate is her title?

7. Explain or rewrite the following passages from the selection:
   a. "Just to make sure that everybody knew how much fun we were having, we put happy faces on flunking test papers, dirty bumpers, sticky refrigerator doors, bathroom mirrors." (7)
   b. "The more commercials people watched, the more they wondered when the fun would start in their own lives. It was pretty depressing." (10)
   c. "I don't mean to put a damper on things." (13)
   d. "The god of mirth is paying us back for all those years of thinking fun was everywhere by refusing to come to our party." (13)
   e. "It [fun] may even come on a Tuesday." (13)

Evaluating the Author's Viewpoints

1. Does Britt convince you that her views on fun are correct? Explain.

2. In paragraph 4, Britt supplies some questions she feels we should ask in place of "Was it fun?" Do you agree with her? Why?

3. Look through paragraphs 6–11 at the many examples of what the author says we have come to expect to be "fun." With how many of these items do you agree? Why?

4. Do you agree with Britt's definition of fun? Explain. How has she changed your view of fun?

Pursuing Possible Essay Topics

1. Write your own essay on the meaning of "fun." Avoid dictionary definitions and try to use examples to illustrate your definition.

2. Look closely at some television commercials. Is Britt right? Do advertisers attempt to make everything look like fun? Analyze the fun behavior portrayed in a particular commercial.

3. Write about a time when you expected to have fun and were disappointed. What did you learn?

4. What was the most fun you have ever had? Why was it fun? What does it say about you and your values?

5. "Are we having fun yet?" (commonly seen bumper sticker)

6. Brainstorm or freewrite on one or more of the following:

   a. the pursuit of happiness   d. jokes
   b. Is everybody happy?   e. pleasure vs. fun
   c. the funniest person alive   f. funny behavior

7. If these aren't fun enough, come up with your own topic on some aspect of human behavior.

Preparing to Read

Take a minute or so to look over the following reading selection. Note the title and author, read the first *two* paragraphs, and check the length. Make certain you have the time now to read it carefully and to do the exercises that follow it. Then, in the spaces provided, answer the following questions.

1. What is your reaction to the title of the reading selection?

_____

_____

2. With what subject do you think the reading selection will deal?

_____

_____

Vocabulary

Good comprehension of what you are about to read depends upon your understanding of the words below. The number following each word refers to the paragraph where it appears.

torrent (1) a turbulent, overwhelming flow

Castoria (1) a laxative

ciphers (1) those without influence or value; literally, "zeroes"

purported (2) professed, rumored, alleged, supposed

sidled (2) moved along sideways

ribald (6) vulgar, indecent

feckless (6) ineffective, careless

sartorial (8) having to do with clothing

eaves (8) the parts of the roof that hang over the edge of the building

voluminously (8) with great fullness and size

bilge-green (21) the color of the water that collects in the bottom of a boat (not a pretty color!)

bluchers (23) high laced shoes or half-boots

nonchalantly (29) casually, in a carefree way

car cards (30) advertisments on cardboard posters in streetcars

thorax (32) chest

crescendo (40) a gradual increase in sound

Now read the essay.

The Endless Streetcar Ride into the Night, and the Tinfoil Noose

JEAN SHEPHERD

1   When I was fourteen, Life was flowing through me in a deep, rich torrent of Castoria. How did I know that the first rocks were just ahead, and I was about to have my keel ripped out on the reef?

Sometimes you feel as though you are alone in a rented rowboat, bailing like mad in the darkness with a leaky bailing can. It is important to know that there are at least two billion other ciphers in the same boat, bailing with the same leaky can. They all think they are alone and are crossed with an evil star. They are right.

2 I'm fourteen years old, in my sophomore year at high school. One day Schwartz, my purported best friend, sidled up to me edgily outside of school while we were waiting on the steps to come in after lunch. He proceeded to outline his plan:

3 "Helen's old man won't let me take her out on a date on Saturday night unless I get a date for her girlfriend. A double date. The old coot figures, I guess, that if there are four of us there won't be no monkey business. Well, how about it? Do you want to go on a blind date with this chick? I never seen her."

4 Well. For years I had this principle—absolutely *no* blind dates. I was a man of perception and taste, and life was short. But there is a time in your life when you have to stop taking and begin to give just a little. For the first time the warmth of sweet Human Charity brought the roses to my cheeks. After all, Schwartz was my friend. It was little enough to do, have a blind date with some no doubt skinny, pimply girl for your best friend. I would do it for Schwartz. He would do as much for me.

5 "Okay. Okay, Schwartz."

6 Then followed the usual ribald remarks, feckless boasting, and dirty jokes about dates in general and girls in particular. It was decided that next Saturday we would go all the way. I had a morning paper route at the time, and my life savings stood at about $1.80. I was all set to blow it on one big night.

7 I will never forget that particular Saturday as long as I live. The air was as soft as the finest of spun silk. The scent of lilacs hung heavy. The catalpa trees rustled in the early evening breeze from off the Lake. The inner Me itched in the nameless way, that indescribable way that only the fourteen-year-old Male fully knows.

8 All that afternoon I had carefully gone over my wardrobe to select the proper symphony of sartorial brilliance. That night I set out wearing my magnificent electric blue sport coat, whose shoulders were so wide that they hung out over my frame like vast, drooping eaves, so wide I had difficulty going through an ordinary door head-on. The electric blue sport coat that draped voluminously almost to my knees, its wide lapels flapping soundlessly in the slightest breeze. My pleated gray flannel slacks began just below my breastbone and indeed chafed my armpits. High-belted, cascading down finally to grasp my ankles in a vise-like grip. My tie, indeed one of my most prized possessions, had been a gift from my Aunt Glenn upon the state occasion of grad-

uation from eighth grade. It was of a beautiful silky fabric, silvery pearly colored, four inches wide at the fulcrum, and of such a length to endanger occasionally my zipper in moments of haste. Handpainted upon it was a magnificent blood-red snail.

9   I had spent fully two hours carefully arranging and rearranging my great mop of wavy hair, into which I had rubbed fully a pound and a half of Greasy Kid Stuff.

10   Helen and Schwartz waited on the corner under the streetlight at the streetcar stop near Junie Jo's home. Her name was Junie Jo Prewitt. I won't forget it quickly, although she has, no doubt, forgotten mine. I walked down the dark street alone, past houses set back off the street, through the darkness, past privet hedges, under elm trees, through air rich and ripe with promise. Her house stood back from the street even farther than the others. It sort of crouched in the darkness, looking out at me, kneeling. Pregnant with Girldom. A real Girlfriend house.

11   The first faint touch of nervousness filtered through the marrow of my skullbone as I knocked on the door of the screen-enclosed porch. No answer. I knocked again, louder. Through the murky screens I could see faint lights in the house itself. Still no answer. Then I found a small doorbell button buried in the sash. I pressed. From far off in the bowels of the house I heard two chimes "Bong" politely. It sure didn't sound like our doorbell. We had a real ripper that went off like a broken buzz saw, more of a BRRRAAAAKKK than a muffled Bong. This was a rich people's doorbell.

12   The door opened and there stood a real, genuine, goldplated Father: potbelly, underwear shirt, suspenders, and all.

13   "Well?" he asked.

14   For one blinding moment of embarrassment I couldn't remember her name. After all, she was a blind date. I couldn't just say:

15   "I'm here to pick up some girl."

16   He turned back into the house and hollered:

17   "JUNIE JO! SOME KID'S HERE!"

18   "Heh, heh...." I countered.

19   He led me into the living room. It was an itchy house, sticky stucco walls of a dull orange color, and all over the floor this Oriental rug with the design crawling around, making loops and sworls. I sat on an overstuffed chair covered in stiff green mohair that scratched even through my slacks. Little twisty bridge lamps stood everywhere. I instantly began to sweat down the back of my clean white shirt. Like I said, it was a very itchy house. It had little lamps sticking out of the walls that looked like phony candles, with phony glass orange flames. The rug started moaning to itself.

20   I sat on the edge of the chair and tried to talk to this Father. He

was a Cub fan. We struggled under water for what seemed like an hour and a half, when suddenly I heard someone coming down the stairs. First the feet; then those legs, and there she was. She was magnificent! The greatest-looking girl I ever saw in my life! I have hit the double jackpot! And on a blind date! Great Scot!

21   My senses actually reeled as I clutched the arm of that bilge-green chair for support. Junie Jo Prewitt made Cleopatra look like a Girl Scout!

22   Five minutes later we are sitting in the streetcar, heading toward the bowling alley. I am sitting next to the most fantastic creation in the Feminine department known to Western man. There are the four of us in that long, yellow-lit streetcar. No one else was aboard; just us four. I, naturally, being a trained gentleman, sat on the aisle to protect her from candy wrappers and cigar butts and such. Directly ahead of me, also on the aisle, sat Schwartz, his arm already flung affectionately in a death grip around Helen's neck as we boomed and rattled through the night.

23   I casually flung my right foot up onto my left knee so that she could see my crepe-soled, perforated, wing-toed, Scotch bluchers with the two-toned laces. I started to work my famous charm on her. Casually, with my practiced offhand, cynical, cutting, sardonic humor I told her about how my Old Man had cracked the block in the Oldsmobile, how the White Sox were going to have a good year this year, how my kid brother wet his pants when he saw a snake, how I figured it was going to rain, what a great guy Schwartz was, what a good second baseman I was, how I figured I might go out for football. On and on I rolled, like Old Man River, pausing significantly for her to pick up the conversation. Nothing.

24   Ahead of us Schwartz and Helen were almost indistinguishable one from the other. They giggled, bit each other's ears, whispered, clasped hands, and in general made me itch even more.

25   From time to time Junie Jo would bend forward stiffly from the waist and say something I could never quite catch into Helen's right ear.

26   I told her my great story of the time that Uncle Carl lost his false teeth down the airshaft. Still nothing. Out of the corner of my eye I could see that she had her coat collar turned up, hiding most of her face as she sat silently, looking forward past Helen Weathers into nothingness.

27   I told her about this old lady on my paper route who chews tobacco, and roller skates in the backyard every morning. I still couldn't get through to her. Casually I inched my right arm up over the back of the seat behind her shoulders. The acid test. She learned forward, avoiding my arm, and stayed that way.

28   "Heh, heh, heh...."

29   As nonchalantly as I could, I retrieved it, battling a giant cramp in my right shoulder blade. I sat in silence for a few seconds, sweating heavily as ahead Schwartz and Helen are going at it hot and heavy.

30   It was then that I became aware of someone saying something to me. It was an empty car. There was no one else but us. I glanced around, and there it was. Above us a line of car cards looked down on the empty streetcar. One was speaking directly to me, to me alone.
                                    DO YOU OFFEND?

31   Do I *offend?!*

32   With no warning, from up near the front of the car where the motorman is steering I see this thing coming down the aisle directly toward *me.* It's coming closer and closer. I can't escape it. It's this blinding, fantastic, brilliant, screaming blue light. I am spread-eagled in it. There's a pin sticking through my thorax. I see it all now.

33   *I* AM THE BLIND DATE!

34   *ME!!*

35   *I'M* the one they're being nice to!

36   I'm suddenly getting fatter, more itchy. My new shoes are like bowling balls with laces; thick, rubber-crepe bowling balls. My great tie that Aunt Glenn gave me is two feet wide, hanging down to the floor like some crinkly tinfoil noose. My beautiful hand-painted snail is seven feet high, sitting up on my shoulder, burping. Great Scot! It is all clear to me in the searing white light of Truth—My friend Schwartz, I can see him saying to Junie Jo:

37   "I got this crummy fat friend who never has a date. Let's give him a break and. . . ."

38   *I* AM THE BLIND DATE!

39   They are being nice to *me!* She is the one who is out on a Blind Date. A Blind Date that didn't make it.

40   In the seat ahead, the merriment rose to a crescendo. Helen tittered; Schwartz cackled. The marble statue next to me stared gloomily out into the darkness as our streetcar rattled on. The ride went on and on.

41   *I AM THE BLIND DATE!*

42   I didn't say much the rest of the night. There wasn't much to be said.

Understanding the Content

Feel free to reread all or parts of the selection to answer the following questions.

   1. How old was the author, Shepherd, when the events of the narrative took place? Why is his age important?

   2. What was Shepherd's reaction when Schwartz asked him to go on a blind date?

3. Describe the way Shepherd dressed for the date.

4. What was his reaction upon seeing his blind date, Junie Jo? Why? What was Junie Jo's reaction to Shepherd? Why?

5. Shepherd was struck with a sudden revelation or awareness on the streetcar ride. What was it and how did it occur?

6. What is the implied thesis?

Looking at Structure and Style

1. Except for the first paragraph, the reading selection is a first-person narrative. What is the purpose of the first paragraph? How does it help set the tone of the essay?

2. How do paragraphs 8 and 9 help us to understand some of Junie Jo's reaction to Shepherd?

3. What function do paragraphs 23, 26, 27, and 28 serve?

4. Why does Shepherd make paragraphs 31, 33, 34, and 35 so short?

5. What is the effect of capitalizing and repeating "*I* AM THE BLIND DATE!" three times, in paragraphs 33, 38, and 41?

6. Explain the effectiveness of the following descriptive passages from the selection:

   a. "Sometimes you feel as though you are alone in a rented rowboat, bailing like mad in the darkness with a leaky bailing can." (1)
   b. "The inner Me itched in that nameless way, that indescribable way that only the fourteen-year-old Male fully knows." (7)
   c. "The door opened and there stood a real, genuine, gold-plated Father: potbelly, underwear shirt, suspenders, and all." (12)
   d. "On and on I rolled, like Old Man River, pausing significantly for her to pick up the conversation. Nothing." (23)

7. Pick out some descriptive phrases or passages that you think are particularly effective. What makes them so?

8. How well does the title fit? Why?

Evaluating the Author's Viewpoints

1. How does Shepherd view being fourteen years old? Do you agree with him?

2. At the end of paragraph 1, Shepherd says, "It is important to know that there are at least two billion other ciphers in the same boat, bailing with the same leaky can. They all think they are alone and are crossed with an evil star. They are right." What does he mean? Do you agree?

3. How different would this selection be if it were told from the viewpoint of Schwartz? Junie Jo?

Pursuing Possible Essay Topics

1. Brainstorm or freewrite on one or more of the following:
   a. blind dates   d. teenage friendship
   b. Do you offend?   e. first date
   c. fourteen-year-olds f. my usual topics of conversation

2. Pretend you are Junie Jo. Write your version of the "endless streetcar ride."

3. Write an essay about a time when you had a sudden discovery about yourself, something that startled you or made you more aware of yourself.

4. If you have ever had a blind date, write about how you got into it, what it was like, how it turned out, and so on.

5. Write an essay about the difficulties of being an early teenager. What changes occur both physically and mentally? What does life seem to be all about at that age? Do typical behavior patterns characterize that age?

6. Write an essay that prepares parents for dealing with their child's fourteen-year-old behavior.

7. These don't do it for you? Then try your own ideas.

Student Essay

The following student essay was written in response to an assignment to write on some aspect of human behavior. As you read it, look for answers to these questions:

1. Does the essay satisfy the assignment?

2. How well does the author know her subject?

3. Does the author provide good support and transitions?

Man and Woman: A Soap Opera with Real Soap

Cindy Evans

1   Anyone who doesn't believe in aggressiveness in the gentle sex and gentleness in the aggressive sex has never watched the two sexes do housework.

2   Take washing dishes at my house, for example. No gladiator ever entered the arena with more grim determination than I have before I plunge into the dinner dishes. First, with firm

jaw and a steely-eyed glint, I don my pink rubber gloves. Not the cheap kind you see your fingernails through. Oh, no. Nothing but heavy-duty, industrial-strength, cotton-lined Playtex gloves can protect these hands from the counterful of foes mustered before them. From my arsenal under the sink, I draw at least three weapons of germ destruction: the grease-cutting dishwashing detergent, a sponge with two textures, and the ubiquitous nylon net ball, that kitchen staple so often praised by Heloise in her household hints column.

3   After the dishes have soaked in water hot enough to deform small plastic implements, my attack begins. Wielding the scratchy side of my sponge, I aim first at my opponents' weakest link—the glasses. I dig at the rim for lipmarks, scrape the insides for milk rings, and feverishly rub the outside for fingerprints. Weakened, they are then subjected to a severe rinsing. For silverware, the strategy is to divide and conquer. Each individual piece gets scraped, soaked, scratched, and scrubbed until no germ would dream of polluting that shiny metal surface. Then the plates are treated like an automatic sander gone mad. By the time I get to the pans, the sink is a rolling cauldron of flying suds and steaming metal. My hair snakes around my face and the swoosh of steel wool against metal underscores the fanatical gleam in my eyes as the pot-rubbing reaches a frenzied crescendo. In the end, the dripping survivors of the massacre are left hanging in the drying rack, glistening and quivering in the dark.

4   Compare this domestic Dante's Inferno to an Easter sunrise service and you get some idea of how my husband approaches this selfsame task of doing the dinner dishes. The acts of the Pope blessing the crowd, Mother Teresa tending the

sick, and Buddha contemplating his navel pale in comparison to the tender rites my beloved performs over our dirty dishes. It is truly a transcendent experience to even watch him approach the sink, as he moves reverently toward the unwashed masses awaiting him on the counter. First, as though divinely inspired, he slowly turns on the tap, adjusting the temperature equal to that of, say, day-old communion wine. Then with a beneficent wave of his hand, he casts drops of detergent onto the tepid waters. Gazing with kind eyes, he begins the ritual by gently blessing our encrusted crockery with the soft side of the sponge.

5   With a trembling hand, he brings up a palmful of silverware, being careful not to separate them during washing and rinsing, lest they get lonely for their metallic mates before they reach their resting place.

6   No mother bathing a newborn was ever more tender with her baby than my husband is when washing our pots. Mind you, this is the same bearded brute who smashed innocent fuzzy tennis balls so hard his racket strings broke. And this is the same man of iron who rode 60 miles uphill on a bicycle and called it "fun." My hairy leviathan, who thought nothing of repeatedly carrying his own weight in boxes on his bride's moving day, turns into a moon-struck mystic over a sinkful of dirty dishes, gazing at them lovingly, caressing them gently and making sure the rinse water is neither too hot nor too cold for the delicate Corningware. In another generation, he would have found a devout following among my grandmother's fine bone China.

7   So, under the care of St. Michael of the Dishes, our plates end up resting contentedly on the drying rack with their little

souls cleansed—but not much else. Whoever says men can't be gentle and women aggressive should buy a ringside ticket to our sink. Group discounts available.

Reaction

In the space below or in your writing journal, write your reaction to the student essay. What would you tell this student about her essay?

Commentary

Evans's essay is a good example of making a topic your own. Assigned to write an essay on some aspect of human behavior, she uses something she knows well. By comparing the way she washes dishes with the way her husband does, Evans uses as the basis for her essay something most readers can relate to. She puts a twist on the human behavior aspect by describing herself instead of "the man of the house" as the more aggressive sex—at least when it comes to doing dishes.

Some students try to write about things they have not experienced or don't really know enough about. The results are usually flat, uninteresting, forced pieces of writing churned out in time for an assignment deadline. Evans takes a very simple task, doing dishes, and by contrasting the way two different people approach the task, makes a statement about human behavior. She shows that you can write interesting, readable essays by writing about what you know.

In her comparison of the dishwashing approaches, Cindy also uses description well. Notice in paragraph 2 how she equates herself with a gladiator with "grim determination . . . firm jaw . . . and a steely-eyed glint." Her "pink rubber gloves" are "nothing but heavy-duty, industrial-strength." The dishes are her "foes." From her "arsenal under the sink," she chooses "three weapons of germ destruction." In paragraph 3, her "attack begins," as she "digs . . . scrapes . . . and feverishly rubs" the dishes clean "until no germ would dream of polluting" her kitchenware. She's "an automatic sander gone mad." The overwhelming visual image is of a warrior in battle.

In paragraph 4, she begins the comparison of her approach, which she calls a "domestic Dante's Inferno" (a reference to a classical work by Alighieri Dante in which he depicts various levels of punishment suffered by people damned to Hell) to her husband's methods, which are more like the "Pope blessing the crowd, . . . Mother Teresa, . . . or Buddha. . . ." Against her rough methods, he "slowly turns on the tap," adjusting the temperature "equal to that of . . . day-old communion wine." Unlike her, he is "beneficent," has "kind eyes" and makes the whole process more like a gentle blessing than a gladiator fight. Yet, in paragraph 6 she provides ample evidence of her "bearded brute's" ability to smash "innocent fuzzy tennis balls," ride a bike 60 miles, and lift heavy weights. She lets us know he's no wimp, despite his gentle approach to the dishes.

Because the subject matter (washing dishes) is familiar to her, Evans says she had more time to devote to her use of language, rather than needing to investigate or learn more about a new subject. Her attention to word choice helps make this an amusing look at a very basic level of human behavior.

V iewpoints on
Cultural Heritage

"Give me your tired, your poor
Your huddled masses yearning to breathe free,
The wretched refuse of your teeming shore.
Send these, the homeless, tempest-tost to me,
I lift my lamp beside the golden door!"
Emma Lazarus

THE HISTORY of the United States is filled with accounts of people who came from all over the world to settle here. Many came willingly to find a better life, some were forced to come as slaves or to be used as cheap labor, some were driven from their homelands for political reasons, some fled from war, and still others came hoping to get rich quickly and then go back home. Immigration, especially of people from western and southern Europe, was high between 1870–1920. Between the years 1880–1900 alone, a half million people came to this country *each year*. During the next fourteen years, over a million people immigrated to America *each year*. Whether born here or an immigrant, everyone living in America felt widespread cultural and institutional changes. The rise of an urban-industrial way of life that attracted thousands of people to cities, the growing interest in scientific knowledge and research, and the variety of new cultures that the immigrants brought with them all had an effect on education, science, fashion, food, music, art, literature, publishing, and politics. People referred to America as "a melting pot," a place where people of all types could blend together.

Immigration was somewhat restricted during the 1940s and 1950s, but another surge in immigration occurred in the 1970s, although not always through normal channels. According to Charles M. Dollar's *America: Changing Times*, estimates of illegal aliens arriving during this ten-year period matched the number of legal aliens, four million.

Most of the "new" immigration of the seventies came from the Western hemisphere and Asian nations. Statistics showed Mexico to be the leading source, with over 550,000 legal entrants from 1970–1978; the Philippines and Korea each accounted for about 300,000 in the same period, and Cuba, over 250,000. Other sources of more than 100,000 immigrants (1970–1978) included China (Taiwan), India, the Dominican Republic, Jamaica, and Vietnam. These immigrants, as well as hundreds of thousands of illegal newcomers every year . . . put great strains on the ability of the American Government to cope with such numbers. . . .

Because it is difficult to determine the number of illegal entries to the United States, these figures are probably low.

What will be the make-up of America's population by the year 2000? By the mid-1980s, it was estimated that there were between twelve and fifteen million people of Spanish origin here. The United States is now the fifth largest Spanish-speaking country in the world, following Mexico, Spain, Argentina, and Colombia. Hispanics, three out of every five from Mexico, are the second largest and fastest growing minority group in this country. In addition, Asian immigration is also on the rise. By the year 2000, it is estimated that as many as twelve million Asians will have immigrated here.

Some sociologists are concerned that America is no longer "a melting pot," but "a salad bowl." Unlike most earlier immigrants who were willing to learn English and wanted to "melt" into American life, many of today's immigrants don't see the need to assimilate, or blend in. How will all this affect America's future?

The reading selections in this unit reflect various viewpoints on this country's rich cultural heritage. Broad in scope and attitude, they will provide you with information on this country's cultural heritage and encourage you to think about your own.

Preparing to Read

Take a minute or two to look over the following reading selection. Notice the title and author, read the opening paragraph, and check the length. Make certain you have the time now to read it carefully and to do the exercises that follow it. Then, in the spaces provided, answer the following questions.

1. What will this reading selection cover? _____

2. What might you learn from reading this selection? _____

_____

_____

3. What do you already know about the topic? _____

_____

Vocabulary

Good comprehension of what you are about to read depends upon your understanding of the words below. The number following each word refers to the paragraph where it is used.

bustling urban centers (1) fast-growing, busy cities

the Old World (2) European countries, as contrasted with the New World, America

appalled (2) shocked, dismayed, horrified

prodigal (2) recklessly extravagant

ironically (3) oppositely or differently from what is expected

densely (3) thickly

prostrate (3) physically helpless

congregate (5) come together

fostered (7) helped cause to happen or occur

assimilation (7) a mixing or bringing together into one

Now read the essay.

Settling in the Cities

ALBERT ROBBINS

1   While most of the northern European immigrants who came to America prior to the Civil War were farmers, many city dwellers came to the new land as well. These newcomers were attracted to the bustling urban centers of the New World, and as a result, American cities expanded enormously. New York, for example, which had a population of only sixty thousand in 1800, grew to a city of more than one million people by 1860. As urban settlers moved west, they helped to change cities like St. Louis, Chicago, and Cincinnati from minor frontier outposts to major metropolitan centers. For a time St. Louis doubled its population every nine years; Cincinnati every seven years.

2   As with immigrants who came to America to farm, urban immigrants were drawn to the rapidly growing cities by the promise of economic improvement. The Old World looked on the New as a land of abundance, a magical place where "the streets were paved with gold." And to many northern European newcomers, America indeed lived up to that promise. Some, however, were appalled by what they saw as American wastefulness. Edward Bok, a Dutch immigrant who came to the United States as a boy of six and went on to become famous as the editor of the *Ladies' Home Journal*, described in his memoirs how different life in the New World was from life in his native Holland:

> I had been taught in my home across the sea that thrift was one of the fundamentals in a successful life. My family had come from a land (the Netherlands) noted for its thrift; but we had been in the United States only a few days before the realization came home strongly to my father and mother that they had brought their children to a land of waste.
>
> Where the Dutchman saved, the American wasted. There was waste, and the most prodigal waste, on every hand. In every street-car and on every ferry-boat the floors and seats were littered with newspapers that had been read and thrown away or left behind. If I went to a grocery store to buy a peck of potatoes, and a potato rolled off the heaping measure, the grocery-man, instead of picking it up, kicked it into the gutter for the wheels of his wagon to run over. The butcher's waste filled my mother's soul with dismay. If I bought a scuttle of coal at the corner grocery, the coal that missed the scuttle [a bucket], instead of being shovelled up and put back into the bin, was swept into the street. My young eyes quickly saw this; in the evening I gathered up the coal thus swept away, and during the course of a week, I collected a scuttleful....[1]

3   Bok's account, based on recollections of his boyhood in the 1870s, ignores another consequence of mass immigration to the cities—the growth of the urban slum, beginning in the 1840s. Municipal services we take for granted—a safe water supply, police and fire protection, public transportation, and garbage collection—either were not provided or were primitive. With the extra demands made by expanding populations, these services often broke down. Housing was in short supply, and overcrowding was common—especially in poor immi-

[1]*The Americanization of Edward Bok: The Autobiography of a Dutch Boy Fifty Years After* (New York: Charles Scribner's Sons, 1922), 434–435.

grant neighborhoods. Ironically, the growth of the slums was viewed as a sign of material progress in the young industrial age because the increased population provided much of the labor for industry. The immigrants in the poor neighborhoods, however, often paid a high price:

> The ... Ward was densely crowded with working classes ... [and] showed a high rate of sickness and mortality, owing to the overcrowded and ill-ventilated dwellings....
>
> The tenants are all Germans.... They are exceedingly filthy in person and their bedclothes are as dirty as the floors they walk on. Their food is of the poorest quality, and their feet and hands, doubtless their whole bodies are suffering from what they call rheumatism, but which in reality is a prostrate nervous system, the result of foul air and inadequate supply of nutritious food.... Not one decent sleeping apartment can be found on the entire premises and not one stove properly arranged.... The rooms are 6 by 10 feet. The inhabitants lead a miserable existence, and their children wilt and die in their infancy.[2]

4   Harsh as life could be in the cities, the immigrant's attitude toward the new country was generally not one of despair, but of accomplishment. The immigrants had made a hard and dangerous voyage to America. If poverty welcomed them on their arrival, at least it was no worse than the poverty they had left behind in Germany, Holland, or Scandinavia. And in America, unlike Europe, an immigrant could quickly improve his economic condition through hard work and diligence....

5   To become in the majority, immigrants tended to congregate in neighborhoods where people from the Old World could create a little of what they had left behind. Their neighbors spoke their language, the stores sold the kind of goods they were used to, and traditional holidays could be observed with the same spirit and gusto. In Cincinnati in the nineteenth century, for example, almost fifty thousand Germans lived in a section of the city called "Over the Rhine." The same pattern was repeated in St. Louis, Milwaukee, almost everywhere immigrants tended to settle. One visitor to New York City in the 1860s described its German section, then called *Kleindeutschland*, or Little Germany:

---

[2]Quoted in Isaac A. Hourwitch, *Immigration and Labor: The Economic Aspects of European Immigration to the U.S.* (New York: G. P. Putnam's Sons, 1912), 232–233.

New York has about 120,000 German-born inhabitants. Two-thirds of these live in Kleindeutschland. They come from every part of Germany.... Naturally the Germans were not forced by the authorities, or by law, to settle in this specific area. It just happened.... The Germans like to live together; this permits them to speak their own language and live according to their own customs.

Life in Kleindeutschland is almost the same as in the Old Country. Bakers, butchers, druggists—all are Germans. There is not a single business which is not run by Germans. Not only the shoe-makers, tailors, barbers, physicians, grocers, and innkeepers are German, but the pastors and priests as well. There is even a German lending library where one can get all kinds of German books. The residents of Kleindeutschland need not even know English in order to make a living.... [3]

6   Immigrants tended to feel comfortable in neighborhoods like these. Their children, however, often felt different. They found themselves torn between two worlds—an America that demanded conformity to get ahead and the desires of their immigrant parents to pass on their European heritage. The result was often confusion and shame, as one college-educated daughter of a German immigrant expressed:

My father made me learn German and always was wanting me to read it. I hated to have anything to do with it. It seemed to me something inferior. People in the West call a thing "Dutch" as a term of scorn. It was not till I was in college that I realized what German literature and philosophy have meant to the world, and that to be a German is not a thing to be ashamed of.[4]

7   Tensions like these, between generations, fostered the process of assimilation through which the children of immigrants could more easily enter the American mainstream. Old habits die hard, however, and the immigrant neighborhoods, sitting like ever-shrinking ethnic islands in an American sea, survived to give comfort and shelter to new arrivals.

---

[3]Quoted in Howard B. Furer, ed., *The Germans in America, 1607–1970: A Chronology and Fact Book* (Dobbs Ferry, NY: Oceana Publications, 1973), 117–118.
[4]Quoted in Emily Balch, *Our Slavic Fellow Citizens* (New York: Arno Press and the *New York Times*, 1969), 414.

Understanding the Content

Feel free to reread all or parts of the selection to answer the following questions.

1. Why did European immigrants settle mostly in the cities rather than on farms during the 1800s?

2. What was city life like for most nineteenth-century immigrants? Does it differ much from city life today?

3. Edward Bok, who was to become an editor for the *Ladies' Home Journal*, describes some differences he found between life in his native Holland and in "the New World." What differences surprised him?

4. Why did many immigrants tend to create neighborhoods of their own when they arrived in the cities? What were the primary advantages and disadvantages of this trend?

5. What unique problems existed for children of the first-generation immigrants?

6. What is Robbins's thesis? Is it stated or implied?

7. What can we infer about the author's attitude toward the immigrants of the 1800s?

8. Circle the letters of the statements from the essay that are factual or can be verified as fact:
   a. "New York, for example, which had a population of only sixty thousand in 1800, grew to a city of more than one million people by 1860." (1)
   b. "The Old World looked on the New as a land of abundance, a magical place where 'the streets were paved with gold.'" (2)
   c. "The immigrants had made a hard and dangerous voyage to America." (4)

Looking at Structure and Style

1. What is the topic sentence of the first paragraph? How is it supported?

2. Paragraph 2 uses a long quotation. (Notice how it is indented and clearly set off from the rest of the paragraph.) What is the purpose of the quotation? Why does it belong where it is?

3. How does the first sentence of paragraph 3 make a transition from the quotation in the previous paragraph? What becomes the point of the third paragraph?

4. Paragraph 3 includes another long quotation from another source. How does the excerpt help Robbins develop his topic sentence?

5. How effective are the quotations used in paragraphs 5 and 6?

6. Explain or rewrite the following passages from the reading selection:

   a. "Ironically, the growth of the slums was viewed as a sign of material progress in the young industrial age because the increased population provided much of the labor for industry." (3)

   b. "They found themselves torn between two worlds—an America that demanded conformity to get ahead and the desires of their immigrant parents to pass on their European heritage." (6)

   c. " ...The immigrant neighborhoods, sitting like ever-shrinking ethnic islands in an American sea, survived to give comfort and shelter to new arrivals." (7)

7. Why does Robbins provide the sources of the quotations he uses in his essay?

Evaluating the Author's Viewpoints

1. Robbins states in his last paragraph that the tensions created between first- and second-generation immigrants "fostered the process of assimilation through which the children of immigrants could more easily enter the American mainstream." What does he mean? How would such tension help?

2. After discussing the life in *Kleindeutschland* or Little Germany, Robbins says immigrants tended to feel comfortable in neighborhoods like these. What evidence does he have for this viewpoint?

3. The European immigrants of the mid-1800s experienced many hardships, but according to Robbins, their attitude was not one of despair. To what does he attribute their optimism and success?

Pursuing Possible Essay Topics

1. In paragraph 2, Edward Bok compares the thrift in his native homeland with the waste in America he observed in the 1870s. Write an essay on waste in America today.

2. Look in the library for one of the works mentioned in the essay or read selections from Albert Robbins's book *Coming to America: Immigrants from Northern Europe* (one in a series of six books). Then write an essay on some aspect of the European immigrants' life: the emotional impact of leaving their homeland, the hard voyage, the shock of discovering America did not have "streets paved with gold," the difficulties with language, getting through customs, or whatever strikes you as you read from one of the sources.

3. Interview someone who may be a recent immigrant to America. Ask that person to compare his or her experiences with those Robbins discusses.

4. Interview older members of your family who may have come or may have known others from the Old World. Write an essay that uses quotations from their stories and experiences.

5. Think of a country that you have always wanted to visit or live in for a while. Pretend you are willing to leave your home and family and emigrate to that country to start a new life. What hardships would you have to undergo? How would it feel to leave your roots?

6. By consulting family members or using the library, research your own heritage. How far back can you trace your roots? What blood lines have you inherited?

7. Discuss the differences and/or similarities between immigrants coming to America today and those who came in the 1800s. From what countries are most of today's immigrants?

8. Pretend you are an immigrant coming to America. Describe in an essay how you might feel as your ship sails into New York Harbor past the Statue of Liberty or under the Golden Gate Bridge in San Francisco.

9. Brainstorm or freewrite on one or more of the following:

   a. the Statue of Liberty
   b. the border patrol
   c. immigration hardships

   d. two different neighborhoods
   e. city culture
   f. starting a new life

10. If you don't like these, find your own topic on some aspect of cultural heritage.

Preparing to Read

Take a minute or two to look over the following reading selection. Notice the title and author, read the opening paragraph, and check the length. Make certain you have the time now to read it carefully and to do the exercises that follow it. Then, in the spaces provided, answer the following questions.

1. What do you think the essay will say about celebrating Columbus Day?

   _____

2. What do you think the author means by the title? _____

   _____

   _____

3. What might you learn from reading this essay? _____

   _____

_____

_____

Vocabulary

Good comprehension of what you are about to read depends upon your understanding of the words below. The number following each word refers to the paragraph where it is used.

counter (1) contrary, opposing

quincentennial (1) five-hundred-year anniversary

tentatively (1) for the time being, temporarily

genocide (6) the systematic killing of a cultural or racial group

substantiated (7) proven, confirmed

lore (8) legend, stories, tales

Now read the essay.

Don't Celebrate 1492— Mourn It

HANS KONING

1   Throughout the country, groups are organizing counter-celebrations of the quincentennial of the year 1492. They are preparing to counteract the official celebrations of the 500th anniversary of Columbus's landing in the Americas. A New York group, tentatively called Columbus In Context, had its first meeting last month. This is our opening statement:

2   We are not spoilsports. We are not out to spoil innocent fun, happy parading, dressing up in old costumes and selling Santa Maria souvenirs.

3   However, the fun is not innocent. "You are spoiling the pleasure of our children," a woman said to an American Indian who was demonstrating outside a 1992 exhibition already circulating in the Southeast. That exhibition is called "First Encounters."

4   The miserable truth is that those first encounters on the Indian side quickly led to last encounters. The Indians of the Caribbean were

destroyed within two generations by the Spanish discoverers. Not one of them was converted to the Catholic faith, which was supposedly a prime motive of those voyages. They died when they were hanged, in rows of 13, "in honor of the Redeemer and His twelve Apostles," according to the original Spanish documents.

5   They had their hands cut off when they did not bring in their quarterly quota of gold dust. Their chiefs were roasted on fires of green wood. When their cries kept the Spaniards awake, they were silenced with wooden slats put over their tongues. Ten years after the first landing, the miserable native survivors started killing themselves by eating poisoned roots.

6   Yes, Christopher Columbus was the first European to sail to America in recorded history. But Columbus set into motion a sequence of greed, cruelty, slavery and genocide that, even in the bloody history of mankind, has few parallels. He organized an extermination of native Americans. He was also as mean, cruel and greedy in small matters as he was in vast ones.

7   I am not giving any radical opinions here. These aren't new facts. You can find them substantiated in the logs of Columbus's son, in the writing of Bartolomé de las Casas, a Spanish bishop and historian of the time, and in plenty of other period documents.

8   It may seem a pity to let go of dear national lore. But we can no longer in good faith celebrate this man and this occasion. We must look at our own past with open eyes.

9   We must end the phony baloney about the white man bringing Christianity, and about Columbus the noble son of the humble weaver. Our false heroes and a false sense of the meaning of courage and manliness have too long burdened our national spirit.

10   We must set out for a new harmony of races, for an atonement of past crimes. In that way, we have a truly New World to discover.

Understanding the Content

Feel free to reread all or parts of the selection to answer the following questions.

1. What is the function of the group called "Columbus in Context"? What is its exhibition "First Encounters" about?

2. Why do some people resent the group's intentions?

3. For what reasons do many Indians and others oppose celebrating the 500th anniversary of Columbus's sailing to America?

4. What sources does Koning cite to support his views of Columbus?

5. What does Koning call "phony baloney"? Why does he feel this way?

6. Explain what Koning means when he says, "Our false heroes and a false sense of the meaning of courage and manliness have too long burdened our national spirit" (9).

Looking at Structure and Style

1. What are some of the words Koning uses to help develop a negative tone toward Columbus and his contemporaries?

2. How does Koning's last sentence in paragraph 3 help make his point in paragraph 4?

3. What is the function of paragraphs 4 and 5? Are they effective?

4. What is the function of paragraph 7 in connection with paragraph 6?

5. In paragraphs 8, 9, and 10, the author uses the phrase "We must..." three times. What is the effect of the repetition?

6. Is the thesis stated or implied? If it is stated, where does it appear?

7. How effective is the title? Does it fit the thesis?

Evaluating the Author's Viewpoints

1. In his title, Koning tells us we should mourn 1492, not celebrate it. Explain why you do or do not agree.

2. What does Koning mean by the statement in paragraph 8, "We must look at our own past with open eyes"? Do you agree? How can we do this?

3. Koning calls Columbus a "false hero"? Is he, do you think?

4. What might you read to learn more about Columbus, from other viewpoints, so that you can form your own opinions?

5. Explain whether or not most people would agree with Koning. Do you think Columbus Day should continue to be celebrated?

Pursuing Possible Essay Topics

1. Research the library for material about Columbus and/or early Spanish colonization. Compare what you find with what Koning claims.

2. Take the opposite view of Columbus's discovery and write an essay that states why we should *not* mourn, but continue to celebrate, 1492.

3. Write an essay arguing against the celebration of some other holiday, giving reasons for discontinuing it. Be serious or be sarcastic.

4. Brainstorm or freewrite on one or more of the following for ideas:

   a. your heritage   d. cultural heroes
   b. childhood heros   e. explorers
   c. religious differences   f. holidays

5. Go to the library and find one of the following titles. Read all or parts of one and then write an essay on some aspect of native Americans you never knew about before. Use Robbins's "Settling in the Cities" as a model.

   a. Dee Brown, *Bury My Heart at Wounded Knee*
   b. Vine Deloria, Jr., *Custer Died for Your Sins*
   c. Alvin M. Josephy, Jr., *The Indian Heritage of America*
   d. John G. Neihardt, *Black Elk Speaks*
   e. Dale Van Every, *Disinherited*

6. Ignore these ideas and come up with your own topic on some aspect of cultural differences.

Preparing to Read

Take a minute or two to look over the following reading selection. Note the title and author, read the opening paragraph, and check the length. Make certain you have the time now to read it carefully and to do the exercises that follow it. Then, in the spaces provided, answer the following questions.

1. What will this essay be about? _____

   _____

2. What does the title mean? _____

   _____

3. What might you learn from reading this selection? _____

   _____

Vocabulary

Good comprehension of what you are about to read depends upon your understanding of the words below. The number following each word refers to the paragraph where it is used.

eccentric (1) strange, peculiar, bizarre

horde (2) great number, multitude

Malcolm X (4) black civil rights leader assassinated in the 1960s who taught himself how to read while serving a prison sentence

counterparts (5) equals, equivalent to

provocative (5) intriguing, stimulating, interesting

flamboyant (6) showy, ornate

vignettes (11) short literary pieces

bohemians (12) those with artistic or literary interests who disregard conventional standards of behavior

inherent (12) natural, inborn

philanthropy (12) an action designed to promote human welfare

inconsequential (12) meaningless, trivial

Now read the essay

African-American Literature: Much to Be Proud Of*

TERRY MCMILLAN

1   As a child, I didn't know that African-American people wrote books. I grew up in a small town in northern Michigan, where the only books I came across were the Bible and required reading for school. I did not read for pleasure, and it wasn't until I was sixteen when I got a job shelving books at the public library that I got lost in a book. It was a biography of Louisa May Alcott. I was excited because I had not really read about poor white folks before; her father was so eccentric and idealistic that at the time I just thought he was crazy. I related to Louisa because she had to help support her family at a young age, which was what I was doing at the library.

2   Then one day I went to put a book away, and saw James Baldwin's face staring up at me. "Who in the world is this?" I wondered. I remember feeling embarrassed and did not read his book because I was too afraid. I couldn't imagine that he'd have anything better or different to say than Thomas Mann, Henry Thoreau, Ralph Waldo Emerson, Nathaniel Hawthorne, Ernest Hemingway, William Faulkner, etc., and a horde of other mostly white male writers that I'd been introduced to in Literature 101 in high school. I mean, not only had there not been any African-American authors included in any of those textbooks, but I'd never been given a clue that if we did have anything

---

*Editor's title

important to say that somebody would actually publish it. Needless to say, I was not just naïve, but had not yet acquired an ounce of black pride. I never once questioned why there were no representative works by us in any of those textbooks. After all, I had never heard of any African-American writers, and no one I knew hardly read *any* books.

3   And then things changed.

4   It wasn't until after Malcolm X had been assassinated that I found out who he was. I know I should be embarrassed about this, but I'm not. I read Alex Haley's biography of him and it literally changed my life. First and foremost, I realized that there was no reason to be ashamed of being black, that it was ridiculous. That we had a history, and much to be proud of. I began to notice how we had actually been treated as less than human; began to see our strength as a people whereas I'd only been made aware of our inferiorities. I started thinking about my role in the world and not just on my street. I started *thinking*. Thinking about things I'd never thought about before, and the thinking turned into questions. But I had more questions than answers.

5   So I went to college. When I looked through the catalog and saw a class called Afro-American Literature, I signed up and couldn't wait for the first day of class. Did *we* really have enough writers to warrant an entire class? I remember the textbook was called *Dark Symphony: Negro Literature in America* because I still have it. I couldn't believe the rush I felt over and over once I discovered Countee Cullen, Langston Hughes, Ann Petry, Zora Neale Hurston, Ralph Ellison, Jean Toomer, Richard Wright, and rediscovered and read James Baldwin, to name just a few. I'm surprised I didn't need glasses by the end of the semester. My world opened up. I accumulated and gained a totally new insight about, and perception of, our lives as "black" people, as if I had been an outsider and was finally let in. To discover that our lives held as much significance and importance as our white counterparts was more than gratifying, it was exhilarating. Not only had we lived diverse, interesting, provocative, and relentless lives, but during, through, and as a result of all these painful experiences, some folks had taken the time to write it down.

6   Not once, throughout my entire four years as an undergraduate, did it occur to me that I might one day *be* a writer. I mean, these folks had genuine knowledge and insight. They also had a fascination with the truth. They had something to write about. Their work was bold, not flamboyant. They learned how to exploit the language so that readers would be affected by what they said and how they said it. And they had talent.

7   I never considered myself to be in possession of much of the above,

and yet when I was twenty years old, the first man I fell in love with broke my heart. I was so devastated and felt so helpless that my reaction manifested itself in a poem. I did not sit down and say, "I'm going to write a poem about this." It was more like magic. I didn't even know I was writing a poem until I had written it. Afterward, I felt lighter, as if something had happened to lessen the pain. And when I read this "thing" I was shocked because I didn't know where the words came from. I was scared, to say the least, about what I had just experienced, because I didn't understand what had happened.

8   For the next few days, I read that poem over and over in disbelief because *I* had written it. One day, a colleague saw it lying on the kitchen table and read it. I was embarrassed and shocked when he said he liked it, then went on to tell me that he had just started a black literary magazine at the college and he wanted to publish it. Publish it? He was serious and it found its way onto a typeset page.

9   Seeing my name in print excited me. And from that point on, if a leaf moved on a tree, I wrote a poem about it. If a crack in the sidewalk glistened, surely there was a poem in that. Some of these verbose things actually got published in various campus newspapers that were obviously desperate to fill up space. I did not call myself a poet; I told people I wrote poems.

10   Years passed.

11   Those poems started turning into sentences and I started getting nervous. What the hell did I think I was doing? Writing these little go-nowhere vignettes. All these beginnings. And who did I think I was, trying to tell a story? And who cared? Even though I had no idea what I was doing, all I knew was that I was beginning to realize that a lot of things mattered to me, things disturbed me, things that I couldn't change. Writing became an outlet for my dissatisfactions, distaste, and my way of trying to make sense of what I saw happening around me. It was my way of trying to fix what I thought was broken. It later became the only way to explore personally what I didn't understand. The problem, however, was that I was writing more about ideas than people. Everything was so "large," and eventually I had to find a common denominator. I ended up asking myself what I really cared about: it was people, and particularly African-American people.

12   The whole idea of taking myself seriously as a writer was terrifying. I didn't know any writers. Didn't know how you knew if you "had" it or not. Didn't know if I was or would ever be good enough. I didn't know how you went about the business of writing, and be-

sides, I sincerely wanted to make a decent living. (I had read the horror stories of how so few writers were able to live off of their writing alone, many having lived like bohemians.) At first, I thought being a social worker was the right thing to do, since I was bent on saving the world (I was an idealistic twenty-two years old), but when I found out I couldn't do it that way, I had to figure out another way to make an impact on folks. A positive impact. I ended up majoring in journalism because writing was "easy" for me, but it didn't take long for me to learn that I did not like answering the "who, what, when, where, and why" of anything. I then—upon the urging of my mother and friends who had graduated and gotten "normal" jobs—decided to try something that would still allow me to "express myself" but was relatively safer, though still risky: I went to film school. Of course what was inherent in my quest to find my "spot" in the world was this whole notion of affecting people on some grand scale. Malcolm and Martin caused me to think like this. Writing for me, as it's turned out, is philanthropy. It didn't take years for me to realize the impact that other writers' work had had on me, and if I was going to write, I did not want to write inconsequential, mediocre stories that didn't conjure up or arouse much in a reader. So I had to start by exciting myself and paying special attention to what I cared about, what mattered to me.

13   Film school didn't work out. Besides, I never could stop writing, which ultimately forced me to stop fighting it. It took even longer to realize that writing was not something you aspired to, it was something you did because you had to.

Understanding the Content

1. Why had McMillan never read any African-American literature in high school?

2. What book does McMillan say changed her life? Why did it?

3. Who are some of the authors McMillan was introduced to in her college literature course?

4. What happened that turned McMillan into a writer?

5. McMillan says, "I did not call myself a poet; I told people I wrote poems" (9). What does she mean?

6. How did McMillan use writing for her personal growth?

7. Why did McMillan give up journalism as a career?

8. What is the thesis of this selection?

Looking at Structure and Style

1. What is the main function of paragraphs 1 and 2?

2. Why is paragraph 3 only one sentence? Is it effective?

3. What is the function of paragraph 4?

4. Paragraph 6 serves as a transitional point in the reading selection. What shift in focus occurs at this point?

5. Examine the use of punctuation marks in paragraph 12 (quotation marks, parentheses, dashes) and explain why they are used as they are.

6. Is the thesis stated or implied? Explain.

Evaluating the Author's Viewpoints

1. In paragraph 2, McMillan says she did not read James Baldwin's book when she first saw it in the library because "I was too afraid." What does she mean? What did she fear?

2. In paragraph 7, McMillan says writing her first poem was "more like magic" than intentional. What does she mean? Do you understand her reaction? Why?

3. In paragraph 9, the author tells us that some of her writings were published in various campus newspapers "that were obviously desperate to fill up space." What do you infer from that statement?

4. McMillan concludes with this realization: "that writing was not something you aspired to, it was something you did because you had to" (13). Explain what you think she means.

Pursuing Possible Essay Topics

1. Write an essay about something you've read that has had a great impact on or has changed your life.

2. Write an essay about an author or authors who have a similar cultural background to yours. Do they give you pride in your cultural heritage? Do you learn anything about yourself from reading them?

3. Write an essay called "Much to Be Proud Of" in which you discuss your pride in your cultural background.

4. Read a piece by an author mentioned in the selection and write what you learned from your reading. You might begin by looking for a copy of the textbook McMillan mentions, *Dark Symphony: Negro Literature in America*.

5. Brainstorm on one or more of the following:
   a. language and culture   c. cultural diversity
   b. cultural pride   d. racial prejudice

6. If these lack appeal, find your own topic on some aspect of cultural differences.

Preparing to Read

Take a minute or two to look over the following reading selection. Note the title and author, read the opening paragraph, and check the length. Make certain you have the time now to read it carefully and to do the exercises that follow it. Then, in the spaces provided, answer the following questions.

1. What will this essay be about? _____

   _____

2. What does the title mean? _____

   _____

3. What might you learn from reading this selection? _____

   _____

Vocabulary

Good comprehension of what you are about to read depends upon your understanding of the words below. The number following each word refers to the paragraph where it is used.

Mao jacket (2) a Chinese-style coat designed and worn by virtually everyone during the reign of Mao Zedong in the People's Republic of China

conspicuous (2) obvious, unmistakably apparent

pigment (6) coloring

Taiwan (8) an island off the southeast coast of mainland China where many Nationalist Chinese fled after the revolution led by Mao Zedong

Now read the essay.

After Two Years in the Melting Pot

LIU ZONGREN

1   There were many American customs which puzzled me. I was very impatient with table formality. Why do people have to remember to change plates, forks, knives, and spoons so many times in one meal? I was especially bothered by that piece of cloth called a napkin. English gentlemen tuck a white napkin under their chins during a meal and Americans put one on their laps. I had trouble remembering to do this even a year and a half after I had arrived and had been to a number of fancy restaurants. Even if I did place it on my lap, it always slipped onto the floor. I often remembered to use my napkin only when I saw someone wipe his mouth with one; I then hastily picked mine up and spread it across my lap, stealing a look to see if others had noticed my lack of etiquette.

2   The concept of [the Mao] jacket conforms with the Chinese teaching of modesty, taught very early to children. They are told not to differ from others in appearance, not to be conspicuous, or they will provoke gossip. "She is frivolous," people might say if a woman did her hair in a fancy way; or, if she wore western clothing, they might comment, "Her blouse is too open at the neck!"

3   Of course, this is not the way Americans judge each other. Everyone tries to be different—and sometimes this goes to an extreme. One morning I glanced out of a classroom window to see a bright-colored figure walking across the lawn in front of University Hall. The sun glistened on her scarlet dress and bright red boots; her huge gold earrings sparkled, yet the part that caught the sunshine most was her hair. It was dyed half-red and half-yellow. In China, even a crazy woman would not dare walk out in the open looking like that.

4   In America, the overriding need to be recognized as an individual is so often expressed in the way one dresses. The exceptions are the teenagers who choose to dress alike and happily submit to the styles dictated by their peers. Parents and schools may not approve of certain fads in clothing yet they find it virtually impossible to control the dress codes. Other than the teenagers, I discovered no restrictions on how people should dress. I never saw two persons dressed identically, except by choice; the businessmen and bank workers on LaSalle Street dressed in three-piece suits and ties, all wearing their wing-tipped shoes. Still, they had enough variety in their outfits to appear different from one another. A young professor at Circle wore a different tie and shirt every day, even if he wore the same suit. With

all the clothing changes they made every day, there was little chance that two professors would show up looking alike....

5   I bought few clothes in the United States, not wanting to spend two hundred dollars for a suit I would never wear back in China. Most of my western Chicago clothes would go into a storage trunk, as my father's had—mere reminders of his ten-year period of service abroad. I wore the same jacket and two pairs of pants all through the seasons, just as I had in Beijing. I thought little of this until two Chinese colleagues from Illinois State University told me they felt embarrassed when they wore the same clothes two days in a row. "Everyone in America changes every day," they said. "We don't have many clothes but we don't want to look shabby. We learned a trick— don't laugh at us. We take off the clothes we wear today and hang them in the closet. Tomorrow we put on another set. The day after tomorrow, we will wear the first set again; then next day, we mix the two sets up and we thus have a new set of clothes."

6   I laughed, not at my two colleagues, but at people who spend time worrying about what clothes they should wear. It is a waste of time for people to fuss over clothes, and it is also a waste for Chinese to try to find ways to restrict others' manner of dress. I hope that Chinese society will become more open, as America is, about the matter of clothing. A few western suits and blue jeans can hardly change centuries of Chinese teaching—history has already proved that. A billion people are like an immense ocean which can easily accommodate a few drops of foreign pigment without changing color. Western life is very appealing to many young Chinese today, who think that a better life can be achieved by adopting western life-styles. Let them try—they will soon learn.

7   Home now meant much more than just my wife and our son. It also meant the life I was born into, the surroundings and environment that looked Chinese, the people with whom I shared a culture, and the job at my office which I had, in the past, sometimes resented. I longed for them all. As one Chinese saying goes, all water returns to the sea; all leaves go back to their roots. My roots were in China, in Beijing, in my family. It was time I went home....

8   I reflected on the fact that most of the successful Chinese I had met in Chicago—doctors and professors—never thought of themselves as Americans. "China is my country. Someday I will go back," one professor told me. These Chinese have a deeper sense of homeland than members of other ethnic groups I met in the United States. They have preserved more ancient Chinese customs and traditions than have the Chinese on either the mainland or Taiwan. It appears easier for a European immigrant to adjust to American society; a Chinese always thinks of his homeland. It is not merely a difference of skin

color; it is cultural. I was glad to have become more aware of the importance of upholding my cultural values....

9   After twenty months of observing American life, I had become more satisfied with the idea of my simple life in China, and I hoped that our country would never be one in which money is of first importance. I would never in my lifetime have the many possessions my middle-class American friends have. Yet, it seemed to me as if they were really only living the same cycle of life that I do in China, except on a higher economic rung of the ladder. We shared the same fundamental needs: family, friends, a familiar culture.

Understanding the Content

Feel free to reread all parts of the reading selection to answer the following questions.

1. From what country is the author? How long and where did he live in America? Why?

2. What problems did he have with our table etiquette?

3. Explain how the Mao jacket conforms to the teaching of modesty in China.

4. According to Zongren, what is the major difference between the way adults and teenagers dress in the United States?

5. What is the difference between Chinese and American attitudes toward clothes? What is Zongren's attitude toward Western wear?

6. What difference does Zongren find between Chinese and European immigrants to the United States?

7. What is the thesis of this selection?

Looking at Structure and Style

1. Is the thesis stated or implied? If stated, where?

2. How does paragraph 3 support paragraph 2?

3. What is the function of paragraph 6? What inferences can we draw from that paragraph?

4. What comparisons are made in paragraphs 8 and 9?

Evaluating the Author's Viewpoints

1. What are some of the American customs Zongren rejects?

2. Reread paragraph 4. Explain why you agree or disagree with him.

3. Zongren says in paragraph 6, "Western life is very appealing to many young Chinese today, who think that a better life can be achieved by adopting western life-styles. Let them try—they will soon learn." What does he think they will learn?

4. Do you agree with Zongren that it is a waste of time to fuss over clothes? Explain.

5. What is the author's opinion regarding what Americans hold most important? (9) Is he correct?

Pursuing Possible Essay Topics

1. Argue for conformity in dress. How would society benefit if everyone wore the same type of clothes?

2. Write an essay that describes how your neighborhood has changed since you were ten years old.

3. Write a comparison/contrast essay that shows cultural differences you noticed when you traveled to a foreign country.

4. Explain in an essay what country you would like to visit and why.

5. Research Chinese customs that you find interesting or unusual.

6. What effect would it have on the world if the Chinese people, the largest population in the world, became "Americanized" (drove cars, built freeways, became consumer oriented, and so on)?

7. Read Liu Zongren's book, *Two Years in the Melting Pot*, and report on other American customs he found strange.

8. Freewrite or brainstorm on one or more of the following:
   a. old vs. new generations
   b. what is culture?
   c. ethnic differences in food
   d. the melting pot vs. salad bowl
   e. universal, fundamental needs
   f. family habits

9. You don't like these? Come up with your own topic on cultural differences.

Preparing to Read

Take a minute or two to look over the following reading selection. Note the title and author, read the opening paragraph, and check the length. Make certain you have the time now to read it carefully and to do the exercises that follow it. Then, in the spaces provided, answer the following questions.

1. What do you think the author means by "black English"? _____

_____

2. Do you think the essay will deal with what is "wrong" with black English? Explain. _____

_____

3. What do you think the essay has to do with cultural heritage, the subject

of this unit? _____

_____

Vocabulary

Good comprehension of what you are about to read depends upon your understanding of the words below. The number following each word refers to the paragraph where it appears.

linguist (1) a specialist in the study of the nature and structure of human speech

patois (1) regional dialect, substandard speech

peers (2) equals

L. Frank Baum (3) author of *The Wizard of Oz*

Ray Bradbury (3) author of numerous science fiction stories and novels, among them *Fahrenheit 451* and *The Martian Chronicles*

doggedly (4) stubbornly, relentlessly

Valley Girl jargon (5) slang and speech pattern attributed to teenage girls living in the San Fernando Valley

articulate (6) clear and expressive in speech

staples (6) major parts

academic abstractions (6) intellectual, theoretical discussions

Malcolm X, Martin Luther King, Jr. (7) black civil-rights leaders, both victims of assassination

Toni Morrison, Alice Walker, James Baldwin (7) famous contemporary black authors (Morrison, *Beloved*; Walker, *The Color Purple*; Baldwin, *Go Tell It on the Mountain*)

ethnic dialects (8) speech patterns of a particular cultural group

Now read the essay.

What's Wrong with Black English

RACHEL L. JONES

1   William Labov, a noted linguist, once said about the use of black English, "It is the goal of most black Americans to acquire full control of the standard language without giving up their own culture." He also suggested that there are certain advantages to having two ways to express one's feelings. I wonder if the good doctor might also consider the goals of those black Americans who have full control of standard English but who are every now and then troubled by that colorful, grammar-to-the-winds patois that is black English. Case in point—me.

2   I'm a 21-year-old black born to a family that would probably be considered lower-middle class—which in my mind is a polite way of describing a condition only slightly better than poverty. Let's just say we rarely if ever did the winter-vacation thing in the Caribbean. I've often had to defend my humble beginnings to a most unlikely group of people for an even less likely reason. Because of the way I talk, some of my black peers, look at me sideways and ask, "Why do you talk like you're white?"

3   The first time it happened to me I was nine years old. Cornered in the school bathroom by the class bully and her sidekick, I was offered the opportunity to swallow a few of my teeth unless I satisfactorily explained why I always got good grades, why I talked "proper" or "white." I had no ready answer for her, save the fact that my mother had from the time I was old enough to talk stressed the importance of reading and learning, or that L. Frank Baum and Ray Bradbury were my closest companions. I read all my older brothers' and sisters' literature textbooks more faithfully than they did, and even lightweights like the Bobbsey Twins and Trixie Belden were allowed into my bookish inner circle. I don't remember exactly what I told those girls, but I somehow talked my way out of a beating.

4   I was reminded once again of my "white pipes" problem while apartment hunting in Evanston, Illinois, last winter. I doggedly made out lists of available places and called all around. I would immediately be invited over—and immediately turned down. The thinly concealed looks of shock when the front door opened clued me in, along with the flustered instances of "just getting off the phone with the girl who was ahead of you and she wants the rooms." When I finally found a place to live, my roommate stirred up old memories when

she remarked a few months later, "You know, I was surprised when I first saw you. You sounded white over the phone." Tell me another one, sister.

5   I should've asked her a question I've wanted an answer to for years: how does one "talk white"? The silly side of me pictures a rabid white foam spewing forth when I speak. I don't use Valley Girl jargon, so that's not what's meant in my case. Actually, I've pretty much deduced what people mean when they say that to me, and the implications are really frightening.

6   It means that I'm articulate and well-versed. It means that I can talk as freely about John Steinbeck as I can about Rick James. It means that "ain't" and "he be" are not staples of my vocabulary and are only used around family and friends. (It is almost Jekyll and Hyde-ish the way I can slip out of academic abstractions into a long, lean, double-negative–filled dialogue, but I've come to terms with that aspect of my personality.) As a child, I found it hard to believe that's what people meant by "talking proper"; that would've meant that good grades and standard English were equated with white skin, and that went against everything I'd ever been taught. Running into the same type of mentality as an adult has confirmed the depressing reality that for many blacks, standard English is not only unfamiliar, it is socially unacceptable.

7   James Baldwin once defended black English by saying it had added "vitality to the language," and even went so far as to label it a language in its own right, saying, "Language [i.e., black English] is a political instrument" and a "vivid and crucial key to identity." But did Malcolm X urge blacks to take power in this country "any way y'all can"? Did Martin Luther King, Jr. say to blacks, "I has been to the mountaintop, and I done seed the Promised Land"? Toni Morrison, Alice Walker and James Baldwin did not achieve their eloquence, grace and stature by using only black English in their writing. Andrew Young, Tom Bradley and Barbara Jordan did not acquire political power by saying, "Y'all crazy if you ain't gon vote for me." They all have full command of standard English, and I don't think that knowledge takes away from their blackness or commitment to black people.

8   I know from experience that it's important for black people, stripped of culture and heritage, to have something they can point to and say, "This is ours, *we* can comprehend it, *we* alone can speak it with a soulful flourish," I'd be lying if I said that the rhythms of my people caught up in "some serious rap" don't sound natural and right to me sometimes. But how heartwarming is it for those same brothers when they hit the pavement searching for employment? Studies have proven that the use of ethnic dialects decreases power

in the marketplace. "I be" is acceptable on the corner, but not with the boss.

9   Am I letting capitalistic, European-oriented thinking fog the issue? Am I selling out blacks to an ideal of assimilating, being as much like whites as possible? I have not formed a personal political ideology, but I do know this: it hurts me to hear black children use black English, knowing that they will be at yet another disadvantage in an educational system already full of stumbling blocks. It hurts me to sit in lecture halls and hear fellow black students complain that the professor "be tripping dem out using big words dey can't understand." And what hurts most is to be stripped of my own blackness simply because I know my way around the English language.

10   I would have to disagree with Labov in one respect. My goal is not so much to acquire full control of both standard and black English, but to one day see more black people less dependent on a dialect that excludes them from full participation in the world we live in. I don't think I talk white, I think I talk right.

Understanding the Content

Feel free to reread all or parts of the selection to answer the following questions.

1. What is Jones's position toward "black English"?

2. What reasons or support does Jones give for her argument? Are they valid reasons?

3. What do people mean when they accuse Jones of "talking white"?

4. What is Jones's rebuttal to James Baldwin's defense of black English as being a "political instrument" and a "crucial key to identity" (7)?

5. Does Jones have anything positive to say about black English?

6. Does Jones agree or disagree with the linguist Labov?

Looking at Structure and Style

1. Is the thesis stated or implied? If stated, where?

2. For what reasons does Jones begin and end her essay with a quote from and reference to William Labov, "a noted linguist"? Is this an effective writing method? Explain.

3. What is the importance of paragraph 2 to Jones's argument? Is it important that she provides this information? Why?

4. What is the function of paragraphs 3 and 4?

5. In paragraph 9, Jones asks two rhetorical questions. How well does she answer them?

6. For what reason does Jones begin paragraph 9 with questions? To what audience is she directing the questions?

7. Even if you were not familiar with Andrew Young, Tom Bradley, or Barbara Jordan, mentioned in paragraph 7, what can you infer about them from the context?

8. Describe Jones's tone.

Evaluating the Author's Viewpoints

1. Jones says, "Studies have proven that the use of ethnic dialects decreases power in the marketplace" (8). Do you agree? Should Jones have provided the names of the studies to verify her statement?

2. James Baldwin disagrees with Jones regarding black English. Whose argument is more convincing to you? Explain.

3. Jones asks in paragraph 9, "Am I letting capitalistic, European-oriented thinking fog the issue?" What does she mean? How do you answer her question?

4. Jones says her goal is "to one day see more black people less dependent on a dialect that excludes them from full participation in the world we live in" (10). Do you think that not speaking standard English excludes people from full participation in the world we live in? Does this apply only to blacks? Explain your views.

Pursuing Possible Essay Topics

1. Support or refute Jones's position.

2. Discuss the need for everyone in this country to know standard English, regardless of their cultural heritage. If you disagree, take the opposite viewpoint.

3. React to the idea that knowing one's ethnic language is a "vivid and crucial key to identity."

4. Because of the large Hispanic and Asian population now in the United States, many states provide voter information, driver's license applications, and public transportation information in other languages. Argue for or against this practice. What effect will expanding or abolishing it have on our culture?

5. Should people who come to the United States seeking citizenship be required to learn English? Write an essay supporting your position.

6. It is predicted that large cities, such as Miami, New York, and Los Angeles,

will soon have more Spanish speakers than English speakers. Write an essay on what effects this will have or already is having in such areas.

7. Brainstorm or freewrite on one or more of the following:

   a. your cultural heritage   d. language and culture
   b. ethnic dialects   e. what your speech says about you
   c. rapping   f. bilingualism

8. You may want to read one or more of the works written by the black authors mentioned in Jones's essay and write an evaluation of what you read. Here are some other suggested sources your school library may have:

   a. James A. Emanuel and Theodore L. Gross, *Dark Symphony: Negro Literature in America*
   b. Charles L. James, ed., *From the Roots: Short Stories by Black Americans*
   c. Terry McMillan, *Breaking Ice: An Anthology of Contemporary African Black Fiction*

9. If these lack appeal, find your own topic on some aspect of cultural heritage.

Preparing to Read

Take a minute or two to look over the following reading selection. Note the title and author, read the opening paragraph, and check the length. Make certain you have the time now to read it carefully and to do the exercises that follow it. Then, in the spaces provided, answer the following questions.

1. What kinds of conflicts do you think the essay will discuss? _____

   _____

   _____

2. What nationality is the author? _____

   _____

3. What do you think you will learn from reading this essay? _____

   _____

   _____

Vocabulary

Good comprehension of what you are about to read depends upon your understanding of the words below. The number following each word refers to the paragraph where it appears.

Armenia (1) once an Asian kingdom, now a region in present-day northeast Turkey, southeast European Russia, and sections of Iranian Azerbaijan

predominantly (1) mostly, primarily

stigma (1) shame, marked with disgrace

grapple (1) struggle

subjugated (3) overpowered, subdued, lessened

milieu (3) environment, surroundings

pondering (5) thinking about, meditating on

excruciating (6) unbearable, intense

subsiding (7) decreasing, lessening

ESL (7) English as a Second Language

Now read the essay

A Story of Conflicts

YEGHIA ASLANIAN

1   Mine is a story of conflicts. I was born into an Armenian (consequently Christian) family in Isfahan, Iran, a town with a predominantly Islamic culture. I had to cope with the stigma of being a "bad" Armenian or a "dirty" Armenian (depending on who was doing the cursing). Although by the 1960s and '70s you could see Armenians in socially prominent positions, when I was a child we were often looked upon as an alien ethnic group who were not supposed to mingle with Muslims. There was a separate Armenian section of Isfahan, but because the language of instruction at elementary school was Persian (or Farsi), I had two languages and two cultures to grapple with. Having to struggle to catch up with classmates whose mother tongue was Persian, I felt Armenian to be a hindrance to my social progress and social image. As soon as I'd open my mouth to say something, they'd know I was not one of them, so the conversation would end right there and then.

2   Childhood humiliation can make or break a person; it made me. When I realized that my social image was at stake, at school or in the street, I plotted against myself. I began to devote myself to Per-

sian—reading, copying and memorizing long stretches of Persian texts. I studied my school subjects day in and day out and managed in this way to get a head start over my classmates, rehashing what I had learned for those of them not in the mood to apply themselves. Little by little, I gained acceptance at school—at the expense of my Armenian.

3   During my first six years of school, I had lessons in Armenian only a few hours a week. In high school the situation was worse, for it was a government school and I was taught no Armenian at all. My Armenian identity was increasingly subjugated. The only place I had a slight possibility of using Armenian was at home—if there was anything parents and children could talk about in a cultural milieu in which children were supposed to be seen and not heard.

4   My parents were functionally illiterate in Persian, and so if I read a doctor's prescription (which was always in Persian) for them, they considered me worthy of all the money they'd spent on me and all the troubles they'd endured for me. I always suspect that my desire for learning was a response to my parents' being illiterate. That I graduated from school with honors heightened their confidence in me, and it also made it clear to me that I could maintain my self-esteem in my little world without Armenian. And yet, because I had not achieved the proficiency in my parents' language that other Armenian students normally acquired by high school, if I ran into a friend who "knew" Armenian, I'd feel inferior to him. The two languages and the two cultures were tearing me apart.

5   When it was time to go to the university, I stayed awake many a night pondering my future. What to do? Wishing to preserve both my self and my image, I could not choose between my two equally powerful cultural heritages, in both of which I thought I had somehow failed. An answer presented itself in English, which I had studied as a foreign language in high school, with enough success so that from the very beginning I thought, or at least my teachers thought, that I had a special ability for languages. In fact, the pull of English had been so irresistible that I enrolled in a night school to study it further. Now, thinking it would resolve my dilemma, I made English language and literature my undergraduate major. I devoted myself completely to this third route, shutting off the other two, except for the occasional required course in Persian and answering some friends' letters in Armenian. I felt great relief and was finally at peace with myself. Or was I?

6   I received a BA in English language and literature from Tehran University, an MA in Teaching English as a Second Language from the American University in Beirut, and a doctorate from Columbia's Teachers College in Teaching English to Speakers of Other Languages.

But when I finished this last degree, I realized that I wasn't at peace with my English identity either, that abandoning the two worlds that had formed me had cost [caused] me excruciating pain, and that to be truly happy with myself I had to recapture the Armenian and Persian languages. I made up my mind to regain my origins. I began to read, write, and translate from English to Persian and vice versa. I opened my long-forgotten Armenian books—I have very few of them!—reading them very slowly. And as I've grown a bit more comfortable, I've started reading Armenian classic and modern literature. I feel I'm coming alive again.

7   If all goes well, my daughter will have to learn four languages: English, Armenian, Italian (my wife is Italian), and Persian. I think the idea of using only English in this country ignores the cultural wealth and linguistic variety that immigrants have always brought with them. A society like this one should be able to tolerate differences and make the best of them. I'm aware of how our ESL students are enriched by their struggle to learn a new language and adapt to a new culture at the same time they work to preserve their own heritage. I myself rarely miss the two weekly one-hour radio programs in Armenian and Persian on WEVD, "the station that speaks your language." And as I try hard to grow in my three languages and cultures, I find my inner conflicts gradually subsiding. Or at least I think so, and thinking is a reality.

Understanding the Content

Feel free to reread all or parts of the selection to answer the following questions.

1. What is Aslanian's cultural background?

2. What is Farsi?

3. Why did Aslanian decide to study English?

4. Why does Aslanian call his essay "a story of conflicts"? What are the conflicts?

5. How does Aslanian feel about people learning and using only English in the United States?

6. What is Aslanian doing that makes him say, "I feel I'm coming alive again" (6)?

Looking at Structure and Style

1. How well does the opening paragraph establish Aslanian's conflict? Why?

2. What is the topic sentence of paragraph 2? Is it well supported?

3. What is the point of paragraph 3? How does it help explain or support the thesis?

4. What is the main point being made in paragraph 4?

5. How effective is the last sentence in paragraph 5? How well does it serve as a transitional device?

6. Why does the author mention his degrees in paragraph 6? How does that information affect your judgment of him and his opinions?

7. Based on his thesis, how effective is the concluding paragraph?

Evaluating the Author's Viewpoints

1. Aslanian says that childhood humiliation can make or break a person. Explore what he means and explain why you agree or disagree with him.

2. How much of the author's conflicts are based on his concern about his social image? Is his concern understandable? Why?

3. What can you infer from the author's statement, "The only place I had a slight possibility of using Armenian was at home—if there was anything parents and children could talk about in a cultural milieu in which children were supposed to be seen and not heard" (3)?

4. The writer contends that "the idea of using only English in this country [U.S.] ignores the cultural wealth and linguistic variety that immigrants have always brought with them" (7). Explain why you agree or disagree with him.

Pursuing Possible Essay Topics

1. Write about a time in your childhood when "childhood humiliation" made or broke you.

2. Discuss in an essay a time when you were concerned about your social image and what effects that anxiety had on you.

3. Argue for or against English being the only language people living in America should speak.

4. Explain in an essay why you want to learn a particular language.

5. Write a personal account of a cultural conflict you have faced, or a time when you had difficulty making a choice about something.

6. Research more information on one of the following and write about it:

   a. Armenia   f. Hindu
   b. Farsi   g. Zen
   c. Persia   h. Beirut
   d. Muslim   i. ESL
   e. Christian

7. Brainstorm or freewrite on one or more of the following:

    a. humiliation   d. peer pressure

    b. cultural clashes   e. childhood conflicts

    c. languages   f. social image

8. Come up with a topic of your own if these suggestions seem foreign to you.

📖 *Preparing to Read*

Take a minute or two to look over the following reading selection. Note the title and author, read the opening paragraph, and check the length. Make certain you have the time now to read it carefully and to do the exercises that follow it. Then, in the spaces provided, answer the following questions.

1. What do you think is the point of this reading selection? _____

_____

_____

2. What do you already know about the topic? _____

_____

3. What might you learn from reading this? _____

_____

_____

Vocabulary

Good comprehension of what you are about to read depends upon your understanding of the words below. The number following each word refers to the paragraph where it is used.

    centennial (1) marking a 100-year anniversary

    Indochinese boat person (1) a refugee who fled by boat from the area of Southeast Asia that includes Vietnam, Cambodia, Thailand, Laos, Burma, and the Malay Peninsula

    sham (2) something phony or fake

    deposed (3) removed from office or power

    upper-echelon (3) high-ranking

flourishing entrepreneurs (3) successful business people

precarious (4) dangerously unstable

bolster (4) support

traumas (4,11) severe shocks to the mind or body

Pol Pot's Cambodia (4) a 1970s period of ruthless government rule in Cambodia

"...play well in Peoria" (5) satisfy the expectations of conservative, white, middle-class Americans

the dole (6) welfare, public assistance

shamans (8) priests, medicine men

sieges (10) prolonged periods

genocide (10) planned, systematic killing of a group or race

harrowing (11) extremely distressing, agonizing

atypical (11) unusual

exemplary (12) commendable, worthy of imitation

Now read the essay.

Trouble for America's "Model" Minority

DAVID WHITMAN

1   When 12-year-old Hue Cao shyly read her prize-winning essay at last year's nationally televised Statue of Liberty centennial celebration, she seemed the very model of a thriving Indochinese boat person. Only six years before, Hue, her mother, four brothers and two sisters fled Vietnam in a fishing boat, and now she was the center of national attention, having bested 2,000 other children in a highly competitive essay contest. "This nation has given my family a brand-new life," Hue recited proudly as tens of millions of equally proud Americans looked on.

2   Unfortunately, however, what they saw on their TV screens was something of a sham. Far from flourishing in the U.S., the Cao family turned out to be on welfare, unable even to accept the contest prize— a new automobile—because it would have meant surrendering their public-assistance benefits. "The girl's mother was in tears," recalls Reg Schwenke of the Aloha Liberty Foundation, sponsor of the essay contest. "She was both anxious and ashamed."

3   The problems of Hue Cao and her family illustrate a major but long-hidden difference in social backgrounds between the two groups

that make up the more than 800,000 Indochinese who sought refuge in the U.S. in the past 11 years. The first wave of 130,000 refugees— those who arrived in the immediate aftermath of the fall of Saigon in 1975—was largely an elite group. They were officials of the deposed South Vietnamese government, employees of the American military, dependents of U.S. servicemen and upper-echelon staffers of multinational corporations. Given their experience and contacts, these refugees made a relatively easy transition to life in the U.S. and created a near mythic image of the Indochinese as brilliant students, flourishing entrepreneurs and altogether successful symbols of the American dream. After only four years in the U.S., the first wave of Indochinese refugees earned 18 percent more than the average American.

Behind the Myth

4   The story, however, is far different for the second wave, the 640,000 who arrived in the U.S. following Vietnam's invasion of Cambodia in 1978. For many of them, life in America has been far less satisfying and considerably more precarious. In contrast to those who preceded them, the second wave of refugees had little education and few skills to bolster them in their new homes. Instead of sophisticated city dwellers, they were mostly rural people—farmers, fishers, small merchants and mountain tribespeople—many unable to speak English and illiterate in their own language. Half came from Laos and Cambodia, nations considerably poorer and socially less developed than Vietnam. And unlike the earlier refugees, those in the second wave often suffered brutal physical and psychological traumas before arriving in the United States. Many had been imprisoned in Vietnamese re-education camps, nearly starved and tortured in Pol Pot's Cambodia, or raped, beaten and robbed by the Thai pirates who preyed on the boat people in the Gulf of Thailand.

5   "This was the the largest nonwhite, non-Western, non–English-speaking group of people ever to enter the country at one time," says Peter Rose, a Smith College professor who has written widely on the refugees. "The public assumed they succeeded just because the first wave did." Adds Ruben Rumbaut, director of the Indochinese Health and Adaptation Research Project at San Diego State University: "The Southeast Asian success stories play well in Peoria. Those of the losers don't."

6   Even when compared with depressed minorities in the U.S., "second wave" Indochinese fare poorly. A staggering 64 percent of the Indochinese households headed by refugees who arrived after 1980 are on public assistance—three times the rate of American blacks and four times that of Hispanics. And among refugee groups as a

whole, the newly arrived Indochinese are by far the most dependent upon the dole.

7   *"In our old country, whatever we had was made or brought in by our hands," says Chong Sao Yang, 62, a former farmer and soldier who moved to San Diego from Laos. Yang and three family members have been on welfare for seven years. "We are not born on earth to have somebody give us food. Here, I'm sure we're going to starve, because since our arrival there is no penny I can get that is money I earn from work. I've been trying very hard to learn English, and at the same time look for a job. But no matter what kind of job—even a job to clean people's toilets—still people don't trust you or offer you such work. I'm not even worth as much as a dog's stool. Talking about this, I want to die right here so I won't see my future."*

8   Many in the newer wave of refugees grew up in Laos and Cambodia without electricity, running water, clocks or stoves—much less banks, savings accounts and credit cards. And Hmong tribesmen like Yang from the highlands of Laos feel even more isolated because of their illiteracy and traditional beliefs in witchcraft and shamans. "What we have here are 16th-century people suddenly thrust into 20th-century life," says Ernest Velasquez of the welfare department in Fresno, Calif., home for an estimated 18,000 Hmong....

9   *Nao Chai Her was the respected head of a Hmong village of more than 500 people in Laos. Here, he is on welfare and shares a cramped three-bedroom apartment with 20 relatives. "We are just like the baby birds," says Nao, 61, "who stay in the nest opening their mouths, waiting only for the mother bird to bring the worms. When the government doesn't send the cash on time, we even fear we'll starve. I used to be a real man like any other man, but not any longer. The work I used to do, I can't do here. I feel like a thing which drops in the fire but won't burn and drops in the river but won't flow."*

10   Many Indochinese experience similar sieges of depression but manage to carefully disguise the condition behind a mask of hard work and traditional courtesy. In one standardized psychological test given in San Diego, 45 percent of the adult refugees showed distress symptoms serious enough to require clinical treatment, four times the proportion among the population at large. Cambodian women, many left husbandless by Pol Pot's genocide, are especially troubled. Lay Plok, 34, of Arlington, Va., lost her husband in 1977 when they fled the famine in Cambodia. "I'm down," she says quietly, "and yet I don't know what would make life feel better."

11   Like U.S. veterans with painful memories of Vietnam, some Indochinese refugees suffer repeated nightmares and evidence a variety of stress-related disorders. Indeed, emotional trauma among the new arrivals is so extensive and little understood that Dr. Richard Mollica and social worker James Lavelle of St. Elizabeth's Hospital set up

the Indochinese Psychiatry Clinic in 1981 in Boston just to assist refugees. One woman treated at the clinic wandered from city to city in the U.S., fearful that her Communist jailers were out to recapture her. She told clinic doctors a harrowing but not atypical story of having been repeatedly raped, tortured and given mind-altering drugs while imprisoned.

12   For all their problems, however, the newer refugees don't fully fit the underclass stereotype. Most cherish hard work and stress the value of family and education. Divorce and out-of-wedlock pregnancy are still taboo. Drug and alcohol abuse is minimal. Studies of the refugee children, including those with illiterate Hmong parents, indicate they do quite well in school. And even where most of the family gets public-assistance payments, at least one member has a paying job, sometimes off the books. "The refugees make exemplary use of the welfare system," argues Nathan Caplan of the University of Michigan, an expert on the second wave of refugees. "They tend to have large families, so they pool resources to finance education and training. And they rely on welfare less as time goes by."

13   In the end, however, whatever their cultural liabilities, the refugees' greatest asset may be simply that they are survivors. Puthnear Mom, 22, also of Arlington, lost her husband while crossing the Cambodian border to Thailand. She can't read or write, and has been unemployed for two years. "I'm unhappy to receive welfare," she says through a translator, "but life is better now than in Cambodia or the refugee camp. I can learn anything here I want. Freedom does matter."

Understanding the Content

Feel free to reread all or parts of the selection to answer the following questions.

1. Distinguish between the first and second "wave" of Indochinese immigrants.

2. What were some of the hardships Indochinese immigrants suffered in their homelands?

3. Why are many of the "second wave" Indochinese in worse shape than most other minorities on public assistance?

4. What does Ernest Velasquez of the welfare department in Fresno, California, mean when he says that many of the 18,000 Hmongs living there are "16th-century people suddenly thrust into 20th-century life"(8)?

5. What percentage of adult refugees tested in San Diego showed distress symptoms serious enough to require clinical treatment? Why does being on welfare contribute to this depression for some Hmongs?

6. In what way do many of the "second wave" refugees make "exemplary use of the welfare system"(12)?

7. How well does the title reflect the point of the reading selection?

Looking at Structure and Style

1. How do paragraphs 1 and 2 work together? What is their function in relation to the main point of the reading selection?

2. How does the first sentence of the third paragraph work as a transition from paragraphs 1 and 2?

3. Is the essay mostly fact or opinion? What paragraphs can be verified as factual?

4. How do the quotations that comprise paragraphs 7 and 9 support the main point of the essay?

5. List the "troubles" for Indochinese mentioned in the essay. Are they presented in any particular order?

6. From paragraphs 12 and 13, list the positive attributes that characterize "the newer refugees." Why do you think Whitman waits until the end of the essay to mention these points?

Evaluating the Author's Viewpoints

1. In paragraphs 3 and 4, Whitman contrasts the first and second waves of Indochinese refugees, offering reasons for the second group's lack of success. Do these reasons make sense?

2. Look over the reading selection carefully for Whitman's sources. What are they? Are they reliable?

3. In paragraph 9, Nao Chai Her is quoted as saying, "I feel like a thing which drops in the fire but won't burn and drops in the river but won't flow." Explain what he means.

4. In paragraph 12, Whitman says, "For all their problems, however, the newer refugees don't fully fit the underclass stereotype." Based on his examples, what does he think the underclass stereotype is?

5. Whitman calls the refugees "survivors." Based on what you have read and know, do you agree with him? Define "survivors."

Pursuing Possible Essay Topics

1. Compare/contrast the experiences of refugees coming from Europe in the 1800s (see Robbins's "Settling in the Cities") with those of Indochinese refugees in the 1980s.

2. Do some research on Indochinese immigrants, first or second wave, and

write an essay on any differences between the two groups that strike you as interesting or important for native-born Americans to know. Refer to the library's card catalog as well as the *Reader's Guide to Periodical Literature*, 1970s editions to the present.

3. Research Pol Pot's Cambodian regime to see what occurred that would cause so many refugees to flee to America. A good source is *Haing Ngor: A Cambodian Odyssey* by Haing Ngor, a Cambodian refugee. Your library's card catalog will list other books and sources under "Cambodia" and "Pol Pot."

4. Interview an Indochinese refugee on your campus. Compare some aspect of that person's culture with your own, such as homelife, education, religion, marriage customs, holidays, and the like.

5. Research one of the Indochinese countries. Find an intriguing aspect of that culture to describe.

6. Pretend you are one of the "16th-century people suddenly thrust into 20th-century life" (8). What are some of the strange lifestyles to which you would have to become accustomed?

7. Discuss whether or not Indochinese refugees should be allowed to collect welfare, or discuss your feelings about the welfare system in general.

8. Ignore these ideas and come up with your own topic on the subject of cultural heritage.

Student Essay

Read the following narrative essay, written by a student who is in the process of learning English as a second language. As you read, look for answers to these questions:

1. Does the essay's subject fit the assignment to write about some aspect of cultural heritage?

2. How well does the narrative hold your interest?

3. Is the thesis clear and supported well?

Coming to America

Hieu Huynh

1   My coming to America in 1979 was not very pleasant. When I was twelve, my parents had to leave my homeland, Vietnam. We lived near My Tho all my years and I did not want to leave, but they said we must. My two sisters were younger, four and seven,

and they did not know what it meant to leave. My mother said that we must not tell any of our friends, that our going was a secret. It was hard for me to think I would never see my home or some of my family again. Some of my story I tell here I remember well, but some is not clear and is from stories my family tells.

2   I was very sad the day we left my house. We could not take many things with us because we did not want the authorities to know we were trying to leave Vietnam. So we pretended that we were visiting my mother's sister and husband who lived in a fishing village in the Mekong Delta. Many times we were stopped by soldiers and officials who wanted to know where we were going. My sisters and I were afraid often. Finally, we reached their village.

3   We stayed there for several days. Our four cousins played with us and we did not really know what the family was planning. But after a few days, we were awakened one night and told to be quiet. My family, along with my uncle and aunt and cousins, all boarded a smelly fishing boat. The children were all told to go inside and sleep. There were already other people I did not know on the boat, but I found room for my sisters and they were tired and went to sleep. I couldn't because of all the hushed talking and I sensed fear.

4   Soon the boat started moving. It was still night and I wondered how anyone could see where the boat was going. Everyone was very quiet. I remember feeling sick from the smell of the boat and the smell of fear. When light broke, I felt the boat stop and many loud voices up above. Soon, my mother and two other women came down in the boat and went through our things, taking out gold and silver pieces. They whispered to be still and

went back up. Soon we were moving again. I learned later that my parents had to pay much gold and silver to the harbor authorities in order to let us continue.

5   I forget how many days we tossed about on the ocean. Almost everyone got sick. There was not much water so we had to drink sparingly. The boat leaked because it was old and the water was sometimes very rough. We could not always cook food. Sometimes we only ate uncooked rice. The younger children cried a lot. I wanted to but did not. My parents said I must be brave for my sisters.

6   The next part of the story I do not like to tell. A large boat with Thai men who had guns and knives stopped us and made us all go on their ship. They were very mean to everybody. They ripped at our clothes thinking that we might be hiding money and jewelry, which we were. When they found some gold in one woman's blouse, they made all of us take off our clothes. When my father and other men tried to stop them, they shot a man I didn't know. They hit my father with a gun and made us all get on our knees. The evil men were shouting and my sisters were screaming and crying for my mother, but she told us to do as the men say. I could not believe all this was happening. It was so terrible it did not seem real. But it was.

7   After they ripped up our clothes and took our valuables, they told all the men and children to go back to our boat. They threw the man they shot into the water and we never saw him again. They kept my mother and two other women on their boat. We could hear them weeping and we called to her, afraid we would never see her again. My father made all the children go down into the boat. He put his arms around us and he cried silently. Later, the women were put back on our boat and we were happy

to see her alive. But she was never the same after that happened.

8   One or two days later one of the women died and it was decided to throw the body overboard. Her children cried and wanted to be thrown overboard too, but their father held them tight.

9   We all thought we would die soon on the ocean. But a Malaysian police boat found us. They were not nice, but they didn't harm us. Of course we had nothing left to be taken, and I think my mother no longer cared what happened. But they took us to Bidong Island where thousands of other refugees like us had already been taken.

10   We spent many months there. It was not easy and food was scarce. There was not much water to go around. People were sick and dying. I got sick myself and often did not know what was happening.

11   Finally, our family was interviewed by authorities. Fortunately, my father's older brother was already in the United States. Somehow things worked out, and our family finally arrived in America. But getting here was not easy. We are all some happier, but there is a part of our lives we would like to never remember again.

Reaction

In the space below and on the following page, write your reaction to the student essay. What would you tell this student about his essay?

Commentary

Hieu's essay stands as a good example of a first-person narrative. Originally, he was not certain he wanted to write about this experience, but he says he is now glad he did. This is his fourth draft and it could still use some more revision. However, because of the painful subject matter, Hieu was not required to do so at this point.

Hieu had spoken and written English only since his arrival in the United States eight years earlier, and so was provided tutorial help with some of his wording. Other than that, though, the essay is his own work. Writing in English is not easy for him, but he wants to put this draft away for a while and perhaps come back later to rewrite some of the sentences when he feels he has developed a more sophisticated vocabulary. Not happy with his opening, he wants to write in such a way that the reader "sees and feels" the difficulties his family underwent rather than his "just telling" us.

What holds the audience's attention is both the subject matter and the simple, straightforward way it is presented. It is written in a chronological fashion and his paragraphs move easily from one episode to the next. It was no doubt difficult for him to retell this part of his "coming to America" (his title), but he wrote about something he knew. As mentioned before, students too often attempt to write about something they really have not felt, experienced, or learned anything about. The results are usually uninteresting, boring, uninformative, and not worth the writer's or the reader's time.

Hieu shows in his essay that he understands the narrative form. Despite some of the simple sentences, the way he tells his story touches us. As time goes by and he continues to develop his understanding of the English language, Hieu should have little difficulty writing the way he wants. His sincere desire to learn to write better and his willingness to spend time revising are starting to show results.

Viewpoints on Some Social Concerns

"My proposal is for the revival or reassertion of personal responsibility in all human acts, good and bad."
Karl Menninger

BEIJING, CHINA A farmer who stole the head of a 3rd-century B.C. terra cotta warrior and tried to sell it for $81,000 has been sentenced to death, an official Chinese newspaper reported Saturday.

SAN FRANCISCO A man convicted and sentenced to prison for raping a young girl, then cutting off her arms and leaving her to die, was released today after serving three years of a twenty-year sentence.

*I*N OUR SOCIETY most of us proba-
bly feel that a death sentence for stealing the head of a statue is too severe, while letting a man free after serving only a three-year term for rape and mutilation of a child seems an outrage. But regardless of our reactions, the newspaper items reflect the social values of two different cultures.

As we live and grow, we learn the culture of the society in which we live. Sociologist Rodney Stark, in his book *Sociology*, tells us that the most significant elements of culture that we must learn are values, norms, and roles. Stark defines **values** thus: "The values of a culture identify its ideals—its ultimate aims and most general standards for assessing good and bad or desirable and undesirable. When we say people need self-respect, dignity, and freedom . . . we are invoking values." While values are rather general, **norms** are quite specific. "They are rules of governing behavior," Stark says. "Norms define what behavior is required, acceptable, or prohibited in particular circumstances. Norms indicate that a person should, ought, or must act (or not act) in a certain way." A collection of these norms connected with a particular position in a society is called a **role**. For instance, each of us has "a relatively clearly defined role to fulfill: student, friend, woman, husband, shopper, pedestrian, cop, nun, bartender, wife, and so on." Thus, values, norms, and roles are connected.

How we think and act in the various roles we play is based on our society's values and norms. For instance, we generally expect a minister's behavior to follow certain norms: no smoking, no sexually deviant behavior, no using bad language, no wearing swim trunks while delivering a Sunday sermon. At the same time, your role while attending a church service is composed of certain norms: no playing your Walkman during the service, no shouting at friends across the aisle, no removing money from the collection plate.

History shows us that Americans have always been concerned with moral values. Chapters in textbooks are devoted to issues of right and wrong. Today we wonder how belief systems could ever have permitted the hanging of people as witches in Salem, the once widespread acceptance of slavery, the disregard for the rights of the native American, the long denial of voting rights and working privileges for women, the overt discrimination toward Jews and other religious groups, the racial segregation from drinking fountains to schoolrooms, and the "blacklisting" and labeling as communists those who spoke out against government policies in the 1950s. Yet, at various times in our society such norms were considered acceptable social behavior.

More recently, our society has had to deal with the social clashes caused by our involvement in Vietnam, the Watergate and Iran-contra scandals, our presence in the Persian Gulf and Central America, attitudes toward gay rights, prayer in the public schools, AIDS, abortion, and definitions of pornography and censorship, just to name a few. Disagreements over such issues as these create conflicts within our society which force us to re-examine our social values, norms, and roles. Doing so often brings about a change in attitudes and values from generation to generation. What was acceptable and valued in society yesterday may not be today. What is acceptable today may not be tomorrow. And vice versa.

The following reading selections reflect some viewpoints and reactions to some current social concerns. Use them to practice your critical reading skills and to stimulate your own thinking regarding social issues and values.

📖 *Preparing to Read*

Take a minute or two to look over the following reading selection. Note the title and author, read the opening paragraph, and check the length. Make certain you have the time now to read it carefully and to do the exercises that follow it. Then, in the spaces provided, answer the following questions.

1. What do you think will be the author's viewpoint regarding value

   judgments? _____

   _____

2. What might you learn from reading this selection? _____

   _____

   _____

Vocabulary

Good comprehension of what you are about to read depends upon your understanding of the words below. The number following each word refers to the paragraph where it is used.

muddled (1) confused, jumbled

ethics (1) the study of the nature of morals and specific moral choices

accord (4) give or grant

medieval (6) pertaining to a historical period known as the Middle Ages, from around 476 to 1453

excommunicated (6) excluded or dropped from membership

penetrate (6) to force a way into

reprehensible (6) worthy of blame

perspective (8) point of view, way of seeing things

condoned (8) forgave, overlooked

wanton (9) excessive

Now read the essay.

Debating Moral Questions

VINCENT RYAN RUGGIERO

1   Nowhere is modern thinking more muddled than over the question of whether it is proper to debate moral issues. Many argue it is not, saying it is wrong to make "value judgments." This view is shallow. If such judgments were wrong, then ethics, philosophy, and theology would be unacceptable in a college curriculum—an idea that is obviously silly. As the following cases illustrate, it is impossible to avoid making value judgments.

2   Raoul Wallenberg was a young Swedish aristocrat. In 1944 he left the safety of his country and entered Budapest. Over the next year he outwitted the Nazis and saved as many as 100,000 Jews (he was not himself Jewish) from the death camps. In 1945 he was arrested by the Russians, charged with spying, and imprisoned in a Russian labor camp. He may still be alive there.[1] Now, if we regard him as a hero—as there is excellent reason to do—we are making a value judgment. Yet if we regard him neutrally, as no different from anyone else, we are also making a value judgment. We are judging him to be neither hero nor villain, but average.

3   Consider another case. In late 1981 a 20-year-old mother left her three infant sons unattended in a garbage-strewn tenement in New York City.[2] Police found them there, starving, the youngest child lodged between a mattress and a wall, covered with flies and cockroaches, the eldest playing on the second-floor window ledge. The police judged the mother negligent, and the court agreed. Was it wrong for them to judge? And if we refuse to judge, won't that refusal itself be a judgment in the mother's favor?

4   No matter how difficult it may be to judge such moral issues, we *must* judge them. Value judgment is the basis not only of our social code, but of our legal system. The quality of our laws is directly affected by the quality of our moral judgments. A society that judges blacks inferior is not likely to accord blacks equal treatment. A society that believes a woman's place is in the home is not likely to guarantee women equal employment opportunity.

5   Other people accept value judgments as long as they are made *within* a culture, and not about other cultures. Right and wrong, they believe, vary from one culture to another. It is true that an act frowned

---

[1] The story of Raoul Wallenberg is detailed in John Bierman, *Righteous Gentile* (New York: Viking, 1982).

[2] "Starving Children Saved by NYC Police," *Oneonta Star*, 13 October 1981, p. 13.

upon in one culture may be tolerated in another, but the degree of difference has often been grossly exaggerated. When we first encounter an unfamiliar moral view, we are inclined to focus on the difference so much that we miss the similarity.

6   For example, in medieval Europe animals were tried for crimes and often formally executed. In fact, cockroaches and other bugs were sometimes excommunicated from the church.[3] Sounds absurd, doesn't it? But when we penetrate beneath the absurdity, we realize that the basic view—that some actions are reprehensible and ought to be punished—is not so strange. The core idea that a person bitten by, say, a dog, has been wronged and requires justice is very much the same. The only difference is our rejection of the idea that animals are responsible for their behavior.

7   Is it legitimate, then, for us to pass judgment on the moral standards of another culture? Yes, if we do so thoughtfully, and not just conclude that whatever differs from our view is necessarily wrong. We can judge, for example, a culture that treats women as property, or places less value on their lives than on the lives of men. Moreover, we can say a society is acting immorally by denying women their human rights. Consider the following cases.

8   In nineteenth-century Rio de Janeiro, Brazil, a theatrical producer shot and killed his wife because she insisted on taking a walk in the botanical gardens against his wishes. He was formally charged with her murder, but the judge dismissed the charge. The producer was carried through the streets in triumph. The moral perspective of his culture condoned the taking of a woman's life if she disobeyed her husband, even in a relatively small matter. A century later that perspective had changed little. In the same city, in 1976, a wealthy playboy, angry at his lover for flirting with others, fired four shots into her face at point-blank range, killing her. He was given a two-year suspended sentence in light of the fact that he had been "defending his honor."[4]

9   Surely it is irresponsible for us to withhold judgment on the morality of these cases merely because they occurred in a different culture. It is obvious that in both cases the men's response, murder, was out of all proportion to the women's "offenses," and therefore demonstrated a wanton disregard for the women's human rights. Their response is thus properly judged immoral. And this judgment implies another—that the culture condoning such behavior is guilty of moral insensitivity.

---

[3]Joseph Jastrow, *Effective Thinking* (New York: Simon and Schuster, 1931), p. 121.
[4]Warren Hoge, "Machismo 'Absolved' in Notorious Brazilian Trial," *New York Times*, 28 October 1979, p. 24.

Understanding the Content

Feel free to reread all or parts of the selection to answer the following questions.

1. What, accoding to Ruggiero, are value judgments?

2. How does Ruggiero feel about people who accept value judgments as long as they are made *within* a culture, but not those made *about* other cultures?

3. What connection does the author make between the quality of our laws and the quality of our moral judgments?

4. Why does the author believe that it is important to debate moral issues?

5. Circle the letter of the following statements from the essay that are facts:
   a. "Many argue it is…wrong to make 'value judgments.' This view is shallow." (1)
   b. "…In medieval Europe animals were tried for crimes and often formally executed." (6)
   c. "In late 1981 a 20-year-old mother left her three infant sons unattended in a garbage-strewn tenement in New York City." (3)
   d. "Nowhere is modern thinking more muddled than over the question of whether it is proper to debate moral issues." (1)

6. Explain in your own words the meaning of the last two sentences in paragraph 9.

7. What can we infer from this piece about Ruggiero's position on teaching or debating moral issues in schools?

8. Can we infer from what the author says that he feels our moral judgments and values should be based on what the majority of the people in the society believe?

Looking at Structure and Style

1. How does Ruggiero use paragraphs 2 and 3 to support paragraph 1? Is this a productive method to use here? Why?

2. Where else in the essay does Ruggiero use this same method of development? Are they suitable examples?

3. Ruggiero documents four sources to help support his views. Are they valid sources? Of what value is documentation?

4. Rewrite the following passages from the essay in your own words:
   a. "This view is shallow." (1)
   b. "…He outwitted the Nazis…" (2)
   c. "…not likely to accord blacks equal treatment." (4)
   d. "…penetrate beneath the absurdity…" (6)

e. "...His culture condoned the taking of a woman's life...." (8)

f. "...a wanton disregard for..." (9)

5. What is Ruggiero's attitude toward his subject and the tone of his writing? To what audience is he probably writing?

6. Is this essay written mostly from an objective or subjective viewpoint? Explain.

7. Discuss your response to the writer's writing style. What techniques does he use that you like or dislike? What suggestions, if any, might you offer him for revision?

Evaluating the Author's Viewpoints

1. Explain why you agree or disagree with what the author asserts in paragraph 1. Is this his thesis? Explain.

2. In paragraph 4, Ruggiero says, "Value judgment is the basis not only of our social code, but of our legal system." Explain what he means and whether or not you agree.

3. Ruggiero feels that the examples in paragraph 8 reflect the thinking and actions of an immoral—or morally insensitive—society. Explain why you agree or disagree.

4. In some societies, when a person is caught stealing, that person's hand is cut off. If the thief is caught twice, the other hand is removed. What do you think Ruggiero might say about such a law? Why?

5. Has reading Ruggiero's essay caused you to think about issues you never thought about before? Explain.

Pursuing Possible Essay Topics

1. Make a list of Ruggiero's main points, then think of reasons to disagree with each of them, even if you really don't.

2. Brainstorm or freewrite on one or more of the following:

   a. morality   d. culture
   b. social codes   e. human rights
   c. social values   f. immorality

3. Reread the opening question in paragraph 7. Write your own answer by supplying your own reasons and examples. Try to find examples from current events to support your views. If possible, document your sources as Ruggiero does. (See Appendix B for documentation information.)

4. Write about a custom or law in the United States that you feel reflects what Ruggiero calls "moral insensitivity" and that you feel should be changed.

5. Argue for or against Ruggiero's statement, "The quality of our laws is directly affected by the quality of our moral judgments" (4).

6. Write an essay that deals with a current social value that seems to be undergoing change. Show both the pros and cons of the issue but take a stand for one side.

7. Look for current articles in newspapers or magazines that would serve as examples to support Ruggiero's viewpoints (see examples in paragraph 3). Then use them to write your own essay patterned after Ruggiero's essay. Use recent issues of the *Reader's Guide to Periodical Literature* in your library.

8. Ignore all of these and come up with your own topic that deals with some aspect of changing social values.

📖 Preparing to Read

Take a minute or two to look over the following reading selection. Note the title and author, read the opening paragraph, and check the length of the essay. Make certain you have the time now to read it carefully and to do the exercises that follow it. Then, in the spaces provided, answer the following questions.

1. What do you think the essay will be about? _____

_____

_____

2. What do you think the title means? _____

_____

_____

Vocabulary

Good comprehension of what you are about to read depends upon your understanding of the words below. The number following each word refers to the paragraph where it is used.

coming up (1) growing up

plight (1) difficult situation or condition

civics (2) the study of the rights/duties of a citizen

submissive (4) meek, tame, docile, subdued

segregated (4) separated, isolated

disillusionment (6) the experience of having your hopes shattered and learning the truth

endear (7) to make beloved, to cause a feeling of affection

boycott (9) a blocking or stopping of the use of something as a means of protest

awe (13) wonder, strong respect

Now read the essay.

A Long Way to Go

ROSA PARKS

1   When I was coming up, I went to a one-room country school in Pine Level, Ala., where all the pupils and the teachers were black. In the sixth grade, my mother sent me to Montgomery, where I went to the Montgomery Industrial School, which was run by Miss Alice White. She was a very proper older woman who ran the school with a group of Northern white ladies who were sympathetic to the plight of Negroes. That's what they called us back then.

2   In school, we learned all of the civics lessons that children were supposed to learn. We had to memorize Abraham Lincoln's Gettysburg Address and portions of the Constitution. We recited the Pledge of Allegiance. We studied all of the Presidents—Washington, Jefferson, Lincoln—and we knew about all the wars.

3   I guess for most of us children, the Statue of Liberty was just something we read about in a civics book. We learned that poem about the statue, but it was just another lesson we had to recite, just like the Civil War poem about the Blue and the Gray, or the Gettysburg Address.

4   The Africans who came over on the slave ships never saw the statue. Of course, they didn't mention that in the history books. The studies we did in our books were based on freedom and equality and the pursuit of happiness and all. But in reality we had to face the fact that we were not as free as the books said. What they taught us in school didn't apply to us as a race. We were being told to be as submissive and as useful as possible to white people, to do their work

and see to their comforts and be segregated from them when they saw fit for us not to be around.

5   Even Miss Alice White, who had all the best intentions in the world, was part of the system. In her lectures, she would tell us how horrible slavery was, but then she would say that at least it brought the Negro out of savagery in Africa. Of course, none of those slave traders ever asked the Africans whether they wanted to come to America. I imagine that if the Africans had come around after the statue was built, they would have had some terrible ideas about what it meant to them. I don't think they would have written any poems.

6   My family knew the brutality and disillusionment of not being treated like human beings. My grandfather was a slave. He was the son of the plantation owner, so he was very white in appearance. My grandfather used to say that the overseer took an instant dislike to him because he looked so white. He would always tell me how he had to dodge and hide to keep out of trouble with the overseer. Until the day he died, my grandfather had a fierce hatred of white people.

7   My mother had a mind of her own. She always held to the belief that none of us should be mistreated because of our race. She was pretty outspoken, and of course that didn't endear her to too many whites. It didn't endear her to too many blacks, either, because in those days the general attitude among our people was to go along in silence. If you differed with that, you had to stand pretty much alone.

8   I remember that one of the first books I read, back when I was 8 years old, was called *Is the Negro a Beast?* That was the kind of attitude that white people had in Alabama in those days. It was so different from what we were reading about in our American history and civics lessons, with all the positive messages about life in this country, and I could see that what we were being taught wasn't so, at least as far as black people were concerned.

9   It didn't change much when I was working. I encountered all kinds of discrimination. If you were black in the South, it was just something you lived with all the time. I would just meet it in silence, bite my lip, go on. I saw it a lot with the bus drivers. If they thought you were about to make trouble, they would just shut the door on you and drive on off. In fact, the same red-headed driver who arrested me in 1955 [starting the Montgomery bus boycott led by Martin Luther King] had evicted me from a bus in 1943. He didn't want me to walk through the white section of the bus to get to the section for blacks, and I told him I wasn't going to get off the bus while I was already on. He took me by the sleeve of my winter coat and led me off. When I got on his bus again 12 years later, I remembered him very well, but I didn't expect him to disturb me a second time.

10   I didn't actually get to see the Statue of Liberty until about a year after the boycott. By that time, my attitude was a little different. I thought that saying—"Give me your tired, your poor..."—was impressive, that we should help people who come to the United States. This was a better place than where they had been.

11   I was invited to come to New York by Dr. Ralph Bunche and met him at the United Nations. I stayed with a Quaker couple, Mr. and Mrs. Stuart Meacham, who lived on Franklin D. Roosevelt Drive in Manhattan, right on the East River. Mr. Meacham asked me what was the first thing I wanted to do in New York. I told him, to see the Statue of Liberty. I had always been fascinated by tall buildings and monuments.

12   We went across the water by ferry about noon. It was just the way I thought it would be, that big arm waving the torch high above everything. We walked up all those stairs to the very top, right in the crown. We looked out from the windows in the crown, and we could see for miles. When we went back down, Mr. Meacham took my picture at the foot of the statue.

13   I guess the statue should be a symbol of freedom. I would not want our young people to be so disillusioned that they couldn't feel a sense of awe about it. But I can't find myself getting overwhelmed. We are supposed to be loyal and dedicated and committed to what America stands for. But we are still being denied complete equality. We have to struggle to gain a little bit, and as soon as it seems we make some gains for all our sacrifices, there are new obstacles, and people trying to take away what little we have.

14   Certainly there is a degree of freedom in America that we can celebrate, but as long as a difference in your complexion or your background can be used against you, we still have a long way to go.

Understanding the Content

Feel free to reread all or parts of the selection to answer the following questions.

1. Explain what the essay has to do with social values and roles.

2. Describe the type of education Rosa Parks received.

3. What can we infer about social values during Rosa Parks's childhood from the title of the book she read, *Is the Negro a Beast?*

4. What attitude toward the Statue of Liberty does the author believe Africans would have had if it had been around when they were first brought to America? How is this contradictory to the symbolic meaning of the Statue of Liberty?

5. What can we infer was the historical significance of her arrest by a Montgomery, Alabama, bus driver in 1955? (See paragraph 9.)

6. How does Rosa Parks feel about the Statue of Liberty?

7. What do we learn in paragraph 6 about "acceptable" social attitudes of whites during Parks's grandfather's time?

8. What attitude did the author's mother have that went against the social values held in that day by both whites and blacks?

9. What is the significance of her title, "A Long Way to Go"?

Looking at Structure and Style

1. In what paragraph is the thesis best stated? Is it implied or directly stated?

2. Select some passages that reveal the author's attitude and tone.

3. To what audience is Parks probably writing? What makes you think so?

4. The author spends the first several paragraphs narrating events of her early schooling. What is their purpose and function?

5. What is the point of paragraphs 6 and 7?

6. What is the value of the several references to the Statue of Liberty? How do they help support the author's point?

7. Discuss what you like or dislike about the author's style. What suggestions, if any, might you offer for revision?

Evaluating the Author's Viewpoints

1. Explain why you agree or disagree with the viewpoint expressed in the last paragraph.

2. What present social values do you think the author wants to see changed?

3. Mrs. Parks was arrested twice, once in 1943 and again in 1955, for not giving up her seat to a white man, even though she was sitting in the section designated for blacks! In effect, she broke the law established by accepted social values of the time. What does this tell you about her? Should she have done this? Explain.

4. In paragraph 13, Parks says blacks are still being denied complete equality. Can you offer some examples to support this?

5. How has Parks's heritage, early education, and treatment by society influenced her viewpoints?

Pursuing Possible Essay Topics

1. Brainstorm or freewrite on one or more the following:

   a. civil rights   d. Martin Luther King, Jr.
   b. civil disobedience   e. boycott
   c. racial prejudice   f. apartheid

2. Use the title "A Long Way to Go" and write an essay about social values that you feel need to change and have a long way to go.

3. Look for recent information that would support Rosa Parks's statement in paragraph 13 that blacks are still being denied complete equality, or look for support to show that gains by blacks are being made. Use the evidence as support for your own thesis.

4. Rosa Parks was willing to go to jail rather than give up her seat on a bus to a white man. Her trial was the beginning of the civil rights movement. For what cause would you be willing to go to jail? Explain the cause and support your viewpoints with reason.

5. In his book *Stride Toward Freedom*, Martin Luther King, Jr., considered by many the greatest leader in the history of the civil rights movement in America, wrote the following:

   > There was to be much speculation about why Mrs. Parks did not obey the driver. Many people in the white community argued that she had been "planted" by the NAACP [National Association for the Advancement of Colored People] in order to lay the groundwork for a test case.... But the accusation was totally unwarranted, as the testimony of both Mrs. Parks and the officials of the NAACP revealed. Actually no one can understand the action of Mrs. Parks unless he realizes that eventually the cup of endurance runs over, and the human personality cries out, "I can take it no longer." Mrs. Parks's refusal to move back was her intrepid affirmation that she had had enough. It was an individual expression of a timeless longing for human dignity and freedom. She was not "planted" there by the NAACP, or any other organization; she was planted there by her personal sense of dignity and self-respect. She was anchored to that seat by the accumulated indignities of days gone by and by boundless aspirations of generations yet unborn.

   Use this and any other information you can discover through research and write an essay about your views of Mrs. Parks or about other people in history who have changed social values regarding race.

6. Write an essay that reflects various racist views. Show why these views are wrong.

7. Boycott these ideas and find your own topic on some aspect of changing social values.

Preparing to Read

Take a minute or two to look over the following reading selection. Note the title and authors, read the opening *two* paragraphs and check the length. Make certain you have the time now to read it carefully and to do the exercises that follow it. Then, in the spaces provided, answer the following questions.

1. What questions does the title raise in your mind? _____

_____

_____

2. What is an "ethnic stereotype"? _____

_____

_____

3. What is an "overachiever"? _____

_____

_____

Vocabulary

Good comprehension of what you are about to read depends upon your understanding of the words below. The number following each word refers to the paragraph where it is used.

basking (4) enjoying, thriving on the pleasure of something

limelight (4) the focus of public attention

condescending (5) snobbish, arrogant, haughty

elitist (6) a member of a small and privileged group

abounds (9) multiplies, appears everywhere

culinary (11) pertaining to the kitchen or cooking

metamorphose (12) change, transform, alter

bigotry (14) intolerance of others' beliefs, race, or politics

Now read the essay.

Eggs, Twinkies and Ethnic Stereotypes

JEANNE PARK

1   Who am I?

2   For Asian-American students, the answer is a diligent, hard-working and intelligent young person. But living up to this reputation has secretly haunted me.

3   The labeling starts in elementary school. It's not uncommon for a teacher to remark, "You're Asian, you're supposed to do well in math." The underlying message is, "You're Asian and you're supposed to be smarter."

4   Not to say being labeled intelligent isn't flattering, because it is, or not to deny that basking in the limelight of being top of my class isn't ego-boosting, because frankly it is. But at a certain point, the pressure became crushing. I felt as if doing poorly on my next spelling quiz would stain the exalted reputation of all Asian students forever.

5   So I continued to be an academic overachiever, as were my friends. By junior high school I started to believe I was indeed smarter. I became condescending toward non-Asians. I was a bigot; all my friends were Asians. The thought of intermingling occurred rarely if ever.

6   My elitist opinion of Asian students changed, however, in high school. As a student at what is considered one of the nation's most competitive science and math schools, I found that being on top is no longer an easy feat.

7   I quickly learned that Asian students were not smarter. How could I ever have believed such a thing? All around me are intelligent, ambitious people who are not only Asian but white, black and Hispanic.

8   Superiority complexes aside, the problem of social segregation still exists in the schools. With few exceptions, each race socializes only with its "own kind." Students see one another in the classroom, but outside the classroom there remains distinct segregation.

9   Racist lingo abounds. An Asian student who socializes only with other Asians is believed to be an Asian Supremacist or, at the very least, arrogant and closed off. Yet an Asian student who socializes only with whites is called a "twinkie," one who is yellow on the outside but white on the inside.

10   A white teen-ager who socializes only with whites is thought of as prejudiced, yet one who socializes with Asians is considered an "egg," white on the outside and yellow on the inside.

11   These culinary classifications go on endlessly, needless to say, leaving many confused, and leaving many more fearful than ever of social experimentation. Because the stereotypes are accepted almost unanimously, they are rarely challenged. Many develop harmful stereotypes of entire races. We label people before we even know them.

12   Labels learned at a young age later metamorphose into more visible acts of racism. For example, my parents once accused and ultimately fired a Puerto Rican cashier, believing she had stolen $200 from the register at their grocery store. They later learned it was a mistake. An Asian shopkeeper nearby once beat a young Hispanic youth who worked there with a baseball bat because he believed the boy to be lazy and dishonest.

13   We all hold misleading stereotypes of people that limit us as individuals in that we cheat ourselves out of the benefits different cultures can contribute. We can grow and learn from each culture whether it be Chinese, Korean or African-American.

14   Just recently some Asian boys in my neighborhood were attacked by a group of young white boys who have christened themselves the Master Race. Rather than being angered by this act, I feel pity for this generation that lives in a state of bigotry.

15   It may be too late for our parents' generation to accept that each person can only be judged for the characteristics that set him or her apart as an individual. We, however, can do better.

Understanding the Content

Feel free to reread all or parts of the selection to answer the following questions.

1. Explain what the title means.

2. Why did Park become an overachiever?

3. What has Park's becoming an overachiever to do with her thesis? What is her thesis?

4. Why is the author against what she calls "culinary classifications"?

5. Does Park believe that Asian students are smarter than most others? Why?

6. Explain Park's comment, "Labels learned at a young age later metamorphose into more visible acts of racism" (12).

Looking at Structure and Style

1. How effective is the one-sentence opening paragraph? Does the author answer her own question?

2. What is the function of paragraphs 3 through 5?

3. What is the function of paragraphs 6 and 7?

4. In what paragraph does Park move from discussing her dilemma to discussing a larger problem? Is the transition smooth? Explain.

5. How does Park support her statement that begins paragraph 9, "Racist lingo abounds"?

6. Explain how Park supports her topic sentence in paragraph 12.

7. To what audience does Park seem to be writing? Explain why you think so.

Evaluating the Author's Viewpoints

1. Park believes that learning ethnic stereotypes at a young age can create "more visible acts of racism." What does she mean? Do you agree? Why?

2. Do you agree with the author that we all hold misleading stereotypes of people that limit us from learning about other cultures? What stereotypes of other cultures do you have?

3. Reread the last paragraph. Is Park being too idealistic? Why?

4. What advice, if any, would you give the author if she asked for your help in revising this essay?

Pursuing Possible Essay Topics

1. Discuss any stereotypes you have of others. Where did you get these opinions? What would it take to change your mind?

2. Write an essay revealing some of the current ethnic slurs and name calling ("racist lingo") that you have heard, similar to what Park calls "culinary classifications."

3. Pick one foreign culture, such as Chinese or Mexican, and discuss what immigrants from that culture have brought to this country that we now take for granted as "American."

4. Discuss your own social circle and explain why it is composed of the people in it.

5. Begin an essay as Park does with the question, "Who am I?" and answer your question.

6. Write an essay about the stereotype most people have of your ethnic background.

7. Brainstorm or freewrite on one or more of the following:
   a. prejudice   d. skinheads
   b. stereotypes   e. intolerance
   c. bigotry   f. your neighborhood

8. If you are prejudiced against these suggestions, come up with one of your own that deals with a social issue you want to explore.

Preparing to Read

Take a minute or two to look over the following reading selection. Note the title and author, read the opening paragraph, and check the length. Make certain you have the time now to read it carefully and to do the exercises that follow it. Then, in the spaces provided, answer the following questions.

1. What do you think is the point of this reading selection? _____

   _____

   _____

2. What do you already know about the topic? _____

   _____

3. What might you learn from reading this? _____

   _____

   _____

   _____

Vocabulary

Good comprehension of what you are about to read depends upon your understanding of the words below. The number following each word refers to the paragraph where it is used.

volatile (1) prone to violence, unstable

boycotting (1) avoiding, blocking

compounded (3) combined, in this case made worse

intervene (3) step in to settle

brusque (4) abrupt, blunt, harsh, testy

sporadic (4) infrequent, not regular

demeanor (8) attitude, behavior

gregarious (9) friendly, outgoing

chided (10) scolded, looked upon with disapproval

prestigious (12) distinguished, well known for quality

Confucian ethos (16) rules of conduct as taught by Confucius, a Chinese philosopher and educator (551–479 B.C.)

Now read the essay.

A Battle of Cultures

K. CONNIE KANG

1   A volatile inner-city drama is taking place in New York where blacks have been boycotting Korean groceries for four months.

2   The recent attack on three Vietnamese men by a group of blacks who mistook them for Koreans has brought this long-simmering tension between two minority groups to the world's attention. Korean newspapers from San Francisco to Seoul have been running front-page stories. Non-Asian commentators around the country, whose knowledge of Korea may not be much more than images from the Korean war and the ridiculous television series "M.A.S.H.," are making all sorts of comments.

3   As I see it, the problem in the Flatbush area of Brooklyn started with cultural misunderstanding and was compounded by a lack of bilingual and bicultural community leaders to intervene quickly.

4   Frictions between Korean store owners in New York and blacks had been building for years. Korean merchants have been complaining about thefts. On the other hand, their black customers have been accusing immigrant store owners of making money in their neighborhoods without putting anything back into the community. They have also complained about store owners being brusque. Over the past eight years, there have been sporadic boycotts but none has lasted as long as the current one, which stemmed from an accusation by a black customer in January that she had been attacked by a store

employee. In defense, the store owner has said the employee caught the woman stealing.

5   The attack on the Vietnamese on May 13 wasn't the first time one group of Asians has been mistaken for another in America. But the publicity surrounding the case has made this unfortunate situation a case study in inter-ethnic tension.

6   What's missing in this inner-city drama is cultural insight.

7   What struck me more than anything was a recent remark by a black resident: "The Koreans are a very, very rude people. They don't understand you have to smile."

8   I wondered whether her reaction would have been the same, had she known that Koreans don't smile at Koreans either without a reason. To a Korean, a smile is not a facial expression he can turn on and off mechanically. Koreans have a word for it—mu-ttuk-ttuk-hada" (stiff). In other words, the Korean demeanor is "myu-po-jung"—lack of expression.

9   It would be an easy thing for blacks who are naturally friendly and gregarious to misunderstand Korean ways.

10   As a Korean American I've experienced this many times. Whenever I'm in Korea, which is often, I'm chided for smiling too much. "Why do you smile so easily? You act like a Westerner," people tell me. My inclination is to retort: "Why do you always have to look like you've got indigestion?" But I restrain myself because I know better.

11   In our culture, a smile is reserved for people we know and for a proper occasion. Herein lies a big problem when newcomers from Korea begin doing business in America's poor inner-city neighborhoods.

12   Culturally and socially, many newcomers from Korea, like other Asian immigrants, are ill-equipped to run businesses in America's inner-cities. But because they are denied entry into mainstream job markets, they pool resources and open mom-and-pop operations in the only places where they can afford it. They work 14 and 15 hours a day, seven days a week, dreaming of the day when their children will graduate from prestigious schools and make their sacrifices worthwhile.

13   From the other side, inner-city African Americans must wonder how these new immigrants find the money to run their own businesses, when they themselves can't even get a small loan from a bank. Their hope of getting out of the poverty cycle is grim, yet they see newcomers living in better neighborhoods and driving new cars.

14   "They ask me, 'Where do you people get the money to buy a business?' " Bong-jae Jang, owner of one of the grocery stores being boycotted, told me, "How can I explain to my neighbors in my poor

English the concept of our family system, the idea of 'kye' (uniquely Korean private money-lending system), our way of life?"

15   I think a little learning is in order on both sides. Korean immigrants, like other newcomers, need orientation before they leave their country as well as when they arrive in the United States. It's also important for Korean immigrants, like other Asians who live in the United States, to realize that they are indebted to blacks for the social gains won by their civil rights struggle. They face less discrimination today because blacks have paved the way. Instead of looking down on their culture, it would be constructive to learn their history, literature, music and values and see our African American brothers and sisters in their full humanity.

16   I think it is also important to remind ourselves that while the Confucian culture has taught us how to be good parents, sons and daughters and how to behave with people we know, it has not prepared us for living in a democracy. The Confucian ethos lacks the value of social conscience, which makes democracy work.

17   It isn't enough that we think of educating our children and send them to the best schools. We need to think of other peoples' children, too. Most of all, we need to be more tolerant of other peoples' cultures. We need to celebrate our similarities as well as our differences.

18   Jang, the grocer, told me this experience has been painful but he has learned an important lesson. "We Koreans must learn to participate in this society," he said. "When this is over, I'm going to reach out. I want to give part-time work to black youths."

19   He also told me that he has been keeping a journal. "I'm not a writer but I've been keeping a journal," he said. "I want to write about this experience someday. It may help someone."

20   By reaching out, we can make a difference. The Korean grocer's lesson is a reminder to us all that making democracy work in a multicultural society is difficult but we have no choice but to strive for it.

Understanding the Content

1. What is the specific "battle of cultures" named in the title? What cultures are discussed?

2. Kang presents the positions of both the Korean store owners and the blacks who boycotted the Korean store. What are the two positions?

3. What does Kang think is at the root of cultural misunderstanding?

4. Why don't Koreans smile as readily as Westerners? How does this affect the ways Westerners view Koreans?

5. Why do many Asians open their own small businesses when they immigrate to this country?

6. What does Kang propose as a step toward solving multicultural misunderstandings?

Looking at Structure and Style

1. Is Kang's thesis stated or implied? If stated, where?

2. What is the function of paragraph 3?

3. In paragraph 4, Kang attempts to show both sides of the conflict. How does she do this?

4. What is the function of paragraphs 6 through 11?

5. How does Kang use paragraphs 12–14 to support her views?

6. In what paragraphs does Kang begin to offer a possible step toward solving cultural misunderstandings?

7. Why do you think Kang quotes the Korean grocer in paragraph 18?

8. Does the author, a Korean, seem biased toward her culture? Explain.

Evaluating the Author's Viewpoints

1. Reread paragraph 3. Explain why you agree or disagree with Kang.

2. Kang says "cultural insight" is missing in the boycotting of the Korean grocery store by blacks. What does she mean? Do you agree? Explain.

3. Reread paragraph 9. Does Kang reveal any "cultural misunderstandings" of her own in remarking that blacks are "naturally friendly and gregarious"? How might African Americans respond?

4. Kang believes that Asian immigrants need orientation before they leave their home countries. What kind of orientation do you think she would recommend?

5. Do you agree with Kang that Asian immigrants need to learn the "history, literature, music and values" of African Americans? Explain.

6. Kang says "that making a democracy work in a multicultural society is difficult but we have no choice but to strive for it" (20). Discuss your views on this statement.

Pursuing Possible Essay Topics

1. Write an essay discussing ways multicultural communities can live in harmony.

2. If you were in charge of an immigrant orientation program, what would it contain?

3. Research "Confucian ethos." Why does it lack "the value of social conscience, which makes democracy work" (16)?

4. Write an essay on "the American Dream." What is it? Is it possible to achieve? Does it mean the same thing to native-born Americans as it does to immigrants?

5. Write an essay on inter-ethnic tension. What causes it? What are some possible solutions?

6. What can American citizens do to help recent immigrants adjust better to life in the United States? What can the government do?

7. Interview someone new to this country. What are his or her impressions? hardships? concerns? problems? needs?

8. Suppose you were forced to leave this country for good. What country would you pick to live in? Why? What would you have to do to adjust?

9. If you have foreign students in any of your classes, write an essay explaining why you do or do not interact with them.

10. Brainstorm or freewrite on one or more of the following:
    a. intercultural conflicts   d. our changing society
    b. responsible citizenship   e. social values
    c. cultural customs   f. personal changes

11. If you don't care for these, find your own topic for an essay on some social problem that concerns you.

Preparing to Read

Take a minute or two to look over the following reading selection. Note the title and author, read the opening paragraph, and check the length. Make certain you have the time now to read it carefully and to do the exercises that follow it. Then, in the spaces provided, answer the following questions.

1. Judging by the title, what do you think will be the subject of the essay?

_____

_____

2. Why do you think the author opens his essay with the incident he

describes? _____

_____

3. What connection do you make between the title and the opening para-

graph? _____

_____

Vocabulary

Good comprehension of what you are about to read depends upon your understanding of the words below. The number following each word refers to the paragraph where it is used.

severing (title) cutting, removing from

sullen (1) gloomy, showing no humor

skulk (1) creep around, move sneakily

striped overalls ... pocket (1) prisoner's uniform

John Dillinger (3) bank robber declared by the FBI as one of the ten most wanted criminals, shot to death by G-men in 1934

deadbeat (3) a person who doesn't pay his or her debts

Mace (4) an irritating aerosol spray used to ward off an attacker

12-gauges (4) shotguns

Armageddon (4) in the Bible, the place where the end of the world will occur in a battle between good and evil

impenetrable (4) not capable of being entered or invaded

depleting (4) using up

surveillance devices (4) equipment, such as closed-circuit TV cameras and electronic sensors, that observes your actions while you shop

gas chiselers (4) those who drive away without paying for their gasoline

incorrigibly (5) in the manner of one who cannot be corrected or changed

integrity (5) personal honesty

collective paranoia (5) society's developing fear that no one can be trusted and "everyone is out to get me"

.38 (6) pistol

habitable (7) suitable for living in

punitive (7) punishing

Now read the essay.

Severing the Human Connection

H. BRUCE MILLER

1   Went down to the local self-serve gas station the other morning to fill up. The sullen cashier was sitting inside a dark, glassed-in, burglar-proof, bullet-proof, probably grenade-proof cubicle covered with cheerful notices. "NO CHECKS." "NO CREDIT." "NO BILLS OVER $50 ACCEPTED." "CASHIER HAS NO SMALL CHANGE." And the biggest one of all: "PAY BEFORE PUMPING GAS." A gleaming steel box slid out of the wall and gaped open. I dropped in a $20 bill. "Going to fill 'er up with no-lead on Number 6," I said. The cashier nodded. The steel box swallowed my money and retracted into the cubicle. I walked back to the car to pump the gas, trying not to slink or skulk. I felt like I ought to be wearing striped overalls with a number on the breast pocket.

2   The pay-before-you-pump gas station (those in the trade call it a "pre-pay") is a response to a real problem in these days of expensive gas and cut-rate ethics: people who fill their tanks and then tear out of the station without paying. Those in the business call them "drive-offs." The head of one area gasoline dealers' association says drive-offs cost some dealers $500 to $600 a month. With a profit margin of only about a nickel a gallon, a dealer has to sell a lot of gallons to make up that kind of loss. The police aren't much help. Even if the attendant manages to get a license plate number and description of the car, the cops have better things to do than tracking down a guy who stole $15 worth of gas. So the dealers adopt the pre-pay system.

3   Intellectually, I understand all of this, yet I am angry and resentful. Emotionally I cannot accept the situation. I understand the dealers' position, I understand the cops' position. But I cannot understand why I should be made to feel like John Dillinger every time I buy a tank of gasoline. It's the same story everywhere. You go to a department store and try to pay for a $10.99 item with a check and you have to pull out a driver's license, two or three credit cards and a character reference from the pope—and then stand around for 15 minutes to get the manager's approval. Try to pay with a credit card and you have to wait while the cashier phones the central computer bank to make sure you're not a deadbeat or the Son of Sam or something. It's not that we don't trust you, they smile. It's just that we have to protect ourselves.

4   Right. We all have to protect ourselves these days. Little old ladies with attack dogs and Mace and 12-gauges, shopkeepers with closed-circuit TVs and electronic sensors to nab shoplifters, survivalists storing up ammo and dehydrated foods in hope of riding out Armageddon, gas station owners with pay-before-you-pump signs and impenetrable cashiers' cages—all protecting themselves. From what? From each other. It strikes me that we are expending so much time, energy and anguish on protecting ourselves that we are depleting our stock of mental and emotional capital for living. It also strikes me that the harder we try to protect ourselves, the less we succeed. With all the home burglar alarms and guard dogs and heavy armament, the crime rate keeps going up. With all the electronic surveillance devices, the shoplifters' take keeps climbing. The gas chiselers haven't figured out a way to beat the pre-pay system yet, but they will.

5   Is it that the people are simply incorrigibly dishonest, that the glue of integrity and mutual respect that holds society together is finally dissolving? I don't know, but I suspect that if something like this really is going on, our collective paranoia contributes to the process. People, after all, tend to behave pretty much the way other people expect them to behave. If the prevailing assumption of a society is that people are honest, by and large they will be honest. If the prevailing assumption is that people are crooks, more and more of them will be crooks.

6   What kind of message does a kid get from an environment where uniformed guards stand at the entrance of every store, where every piece of merchandise has an anti-shoplifting tag stapled to it, where every house has a burglar alarm and a .38, where the gas station cashiers huddle in glass cages and pass your change out through a metal chute? What can he conclude but that thievery and violence are normal, common, expected behaviors?

7   A society which assumes its members are honest is humane, comfortable, habitable. A society which treats everyone like a criminal becomes harsh, unfeeling, punitive, paranoid. The human connection is severed; fear of detection and punishment becomes the only deterrent to crime, and it's a very ineffective one. Somehow, sometime— I don't know when, but it was within my lifetime—we changed from the first type of society to the second. Maybe it's too late to go back again, but the road we are now on is a dark and descending one.

Understanding the Content

Feel free to reread all or parts of the selection to answer the following questions.

1. What does Miller mean by his title, "Severing the Human Connection"? How does it relate to his thesis?

2. What is a "pre-pay" station and why, according to the author, were they started?

3. Circle the letters of the following statements from the essay that are facts:

    a. "...The cops have better things to do than tracking down a guy who stole $15 worth of gas." (2)

    b. "The gas chiselers haven't figured out a way to beat the pre-pay system yet, but they will." (4)

    c. "People, after all, tend to behave pretty much the way other people expect them to behave." (5)

    d. "The head of one area gasoline dealers' association says drive-offs cost some dealers $500 to $600 a month." (2)

    e. "A society which assumes its members are honest is humane, comfortable, habitable." (7)

4. In paragraph 3, Miller mentions the Son of Sam. Even if you don't know to whom this refers, what conclusions can you draw about the character of the Son of Sam, based on this reference?

5. Can we infer that the author believes our society was more honest and humane when he was younger than it is today?

6. Can we infer that Miller believes that the more we surround ourselves with devices to protect us from crime, the more young people will assume that crime is a common way of life?

7. Do you think Miller himself has succumbed to "our collective paranoia"? Why?

8. Does Miller conclude his essay with any hope for a better society?

Looking at Structure and Style

1. What experience caused Miller to think about the subject of his essay? How does he use that experience in his introduction?

2. What other examples besides the pre-pay gas station does the author use to help support his viewpoint?

3. What image does the author want us to see in the last sentence of paragraph 1?

4. Rewrite or explain the following passages from the essay in your own words:

    a. "The steel box swallowed my money and retracted into the cubicle." (1)

b. "It strikes me that we are expending so much time, energy and anguish on protecting ourselves that we are depleting our stock of mental and emotional capital for living." (4)

c. "...The road we are now on is a dark and descending one." (7)

d. "...survivalists storing up ammo and dehydrated foods in hope of riding out Armageddon..." (4)

5. Reread the opening paragraph. How would you describe Miller's tone? What particular words or phrases help establish this tone?

6. Is this essay written mostly from an objective or subjective viewpoint? Explain.

7. Discuss your response to Miller's writing style. What techniques does he use that you like or dislike? What suggestions would you offer him for revision?

Pursuing Possible Essay Topics

1. Agree or disagree with Miller's statement in question 4b above.

2. Write an essay describing a time in your life when you were treated or made to feel like a criminal.

3. Write an essay that answers the opening question in paragraph 5.

4. Do some research in the library on crime statistics over the last few years to see if Miller's statement that "...crime keeps going up" is true. Use the statistics to support or refute Miller. You might begin your research by using the *Reader's Guide to Periodical Literature* or the card catalog. Look for current publication dates.

5. Miller suggests that the effect of seemingly everyone protecting themselves with "attack dogs and Mace and 12-gauges...closed- circuit TVs ...enclosed cashier cages...burglar alarms...and shoplifting tags in stores" is causing young people to get the message that thievery and violence are normal behaviors. Argue for or against his viewpoint.

6. Look through your local newspapers for some stories that show not the severing of the human connection, but a "linking of the human connection." Write about them.

7. Brainstorm or freewrite on one or more of the following:

   a. crime   d. collective paranoia
   b. "pay before you pump"   e. honesty is the best policy
   c. mutual respect   f. expected social behaviors

8. Ignore these and come up with your own topic on some aspect of a social issue that concerns you.

📖 *Preparing to Read*

Take a minute or two to look over the following reading selection. Note the title and author, read the two opening paragraphs, and check the length. Make certain you have the time now to read it carefully and to do the exercises that follow it. Then, in the spaces provided, answer the following questions.

1. What do you know about the AIDS virus? _____

   _____

   _____

2. Do you believe AIDS should be treated as a personal problem or a social

   problem? Explain. _____

   _____

   _____

3. What do you think the author will say about AIDS? _____

   _____

   _____

Vocabulary

Good comprehension of what you are about to read depends upon your understanding of the words below. The number following each word refers to the paragraph where it is used.

AIDS (title) acquired immune deficiency syndrome

poise (2) self-confidence, assurance

candor (2) honesty, truth, frankness

consign (2) to give over to another

pieties (3) devout, moral, or commendable statements

transvestite (5) a person who dresses in the clothing of the opposite sex for psychological reasons

Brownings (7) reference to Robert and Elizabeth Browning, nineteenth-century English poets

abstraction (15) hypothetical ideal or example

Now read the essay.

America Discovers AIDS Is Real

RICHARD RODRIGUEZ

1   Will you weep now, America?

2   Magic Johnson is infected with the AIDS virus. A celebrity, a graceful god from the sports pages, is infected with the AIDS virus. Magic Johnson tells us of his infection with poise and dignity. He speaks with candor of the disease that many in this country have chosen to deny or consign to some other part of town where queers or addicts live and die.

3   The newscasters with their orange hair and blue sports jackets are full of pieties now. The politicians rush forward with their lament. It is as if AIDS has come, at last, to their side of town.

4   I know many men like Magic Johnson, men infected with the AIDS virus. Men of poise and dignity. But they cannot gather press conferences to announce the news of their infection. They fear telling their employers; they fear telling their landlords; they fear confessing to their priests; they fear, most of all, telling their families.

5   The spotted transvestite lies on his mattress on the floor in a single room. His companion, most days, most hours, is the TV that is never turned off. Doubtless, the TV was jabbering the news last Thursday of Magic Johnson's infection.

6   But, of course, you will say Magic Johnson is famous and a great athlete and a role model for millions of young people who never guessed that heroes can die. What do I expect? Magic Johnson is a television hero.

7   But let me tell you about some other heroes I know. I know two men in their 20s—lovers—each infected with the AIDS virus, each dying. One is closer to death than the other. Recently, I saw them— two skeletal figures, inching from their bedroom to the toilet. The healthier of the two was propping up his lover with a thin shoulder. Nothing I have ever read in Shakespearean sonnets, nothing I have heard from the Courtier poets or from the Brownings, could have prepared me for this vision of love.

8   A high school kid I know came running into a store last Thursday night with the news. It was like Pearl Harbor. Magic Johnson has the AIDS virus.

9   A generation that has been raised with multimillion-dollar rock stars, multimillion-dollar running-shoe contracts and mega-sports heroes is in shock. The newspaper shows a photo of high school jocks weeping. Suddenly, we hear, Americans of all ages are phoning their local AIDS hotline. Suddenly, the thought occurs to millions that maybe AIDS is not just something happening in some other part of the city.

10   "How do I get tested?"

11   "How can a person contract the virus?"

12   Where have these Americans been for the last 10 years? How is it possible that, after 10 years, they still need to be told about condoms and dirty needles and body fluids? The young, certainly, are innocent of death and are startled to discover its possibility. But America has, regarding AIDS, been in a determined state of denial. So, of course, health officials are pleased by the sudden interest, the anxious questions.

13   America will learn from Magic Johnson—and this is the piety—that even "normal" people get AIDS. And America will learn that even celebrities get AIDS. Magic Johnson is Rock Hudson and Perry Ellis and Brad Davis all rolled into one. But he is more. He exists in the manly world of professional sports, a world as far away from the AIDS ward as it is possible, we imagine, to get.

14   Ten years into the AIDS epidemic, Americans pretend to be surprised that AIDS is real and that it implicates all of us. Americans learn from the man who flies across the TV screen that thousands and thousands and thousands of people have been dying for 10 years. Why do we need a celebrity to tell us such a thing?

15   Why do we need someone who lives on a television screen—an image in million-dollar running shoes, a beautiful abstraction, to remind us that men and women are dying with tough purple scabs on their bodies, that people are dying with little flesh on their bodies, that people are dying in terror or in madness or blind or, in the end, singing of God in a morphine dream?

16   America learns from Magic Johnson, the celebrity, that AIDS is real.

Understanding the Content

1. Explain Rodriguez's title and its connection to his thesis.

2. Who is Magic Johnson? What is Rodriguez's attitude toward him?

3. How does Rodriguez feel toward other victims of AIDS? Who are the people he describes?

4. According to Rodriguez, how did people react to Magic Johnson's announcement that he has the AIDS virus? What, in turn, is the author's reaction to how people reacted to Johnson's announcement?

5. How does Rodriguez portray the majority of Americans' attitude toward the AIDS virus before Magic Johnson's announcement?

6. Why does the author feel that America will learn more from Magic Johnson than from other celebrities who have died of AIDS?

Looking at Structure and Style

1. Is the thesis stated or implied? If stated, where? If implied, how?

2. What is the point of paragraph 1? How is it related to the thesis?

3. What is the point of paragraph 3? What is the tone? How does Rodriguez create that tone?

4. What effect does Rodriguez create in paragraphs 3–7? Do these comments help support his thesis? If so, how? If not, why not?

5. How does Rodriguez prepare us for paragraph 12?

6. Paragraph 15 is one long question. What is the author comparing and contrasting? Is the contrast effective? Explain.

7. Find some examples of graphic description used by the author. Is it appropriately used? How does the language help develop a tone and attitude?

Evaluating the Author's Viewpoints

1. Rodriguez says, "Ten years into the AIDS epidemic, Americans pretend to be surprised that AIDS is real and that it implicates all of us" (14). Then he asks, "Why do we need a celebrity to tell us [about AIDS]?" Is this a valid question? How would you answer it?

2. In paragraph 7, Rodriguez describes what he calls "some other heroes" he knows. Why does he call them heroes? Do you agree?

3. In his opening paragraph, Rodriguez asks, "Will you weep now, America?" What do you think he wants people to weep about?

4. Rodriguez concludes, "America learns from Magic Johnson, the celebrity, that AIDS is real." You are reading this essay long after Magic Johnson's televised announcement was made in November 1991. Do you think Americans *are* doing more about AIDS education and spending more on research than before? Explain.

Pursuing Possible Essay Topics

1. Read up on AIDS and then write an essay that defines and explains it.

2. Write an essay that argues for or against mandatory testing of AIDS under selected circumstances.

3. Find out what research reveals about America's sexual habits since the spread of the AIDS virus and compare-contrast any changes that have occurred.

4. Define the term "hero."

5. Discuss what moral responsibility for AIDS education falls to the media, the schools and/or the family.

6. Answer Rodriguez's question in paragraph 15.

7. Brainstorm or freewrite on one or more of the following:
   a. overpopulation   d. sex education in schools
   b. the homeless   e. drug addiction
   c. homosexuality   f. pollution

8. Come up with your own topic that deals with a social problem that concerns you.

Student Essay

Read the following student essay dealing with a social concern. As you read it, look for answers to these questions:

1. Does the essay deal with a social conern?

2. Does the student have a thesis? Is so what is it?

3. Is the thesis stated or implied? If stated, where?

4. Does the author sound genuinely concerned with the issue discussed? Why?

Can Magic Breach the Wall of Denial?

Tatiana Litvin

1   University students too often behave as if they are invincible to the HIV virus.

2   When conversations turn to sex, as they frequently do on college campuses, the risks of contracting AIDS are seldom mentioned. University health officials at USC have, from time to time,

tried to remind students about these risks. Safe-sex information and condoms are made available at AIDS-awareness promotions. And there are lectures on the virtues of abstinence, which are not taken very seriously. Generally, though, students remain dangerously passive in the face of the AIDS risk.

3   Magic Johnson's disclosure that he has the HIV virus has helped to change that. The subject of AIDS is no longer ignored in sex talk at USC. Yet, it is still not regarded as the real threat it is. After Magic's press conference, for example, I overhead students say, "I never would have imagined HIM to be a fag" or—my favorite—"We all gotta go sometime." Such flippant remarks sadly mirror the responses of the Reagan and Bush administrations to the AIDS epidemic.

4   I suppose it follows that when our nation's political leaders deal half-haphazardly with the AIDS menace, our concerns about the disease would reflect their attitude. Is there any excuse, for example, why funding for AIDS research was limited while two Republican administrations spent nearly a billion dollars in military aid to prop up a corrupt, authoritarian government in El Salvador? Is there any justification for bailing out a greed-driven savings-and-loan industry with taxpayer money, to the tune of $500 billion, while thousands and thousands and thousands of people have died of AIDS. These victims languished with little hope of any help from our political leaders—the people who were capable of providing financial support for better health care and research.

5   Without a doubt, such moral contradictions have undermined the public's confidence in its national leaders and its desire to tackle the AIDS issue. We are daily bombarded with fears: of

AIDS, of ecological destruction, of crime, of economic calamity. But politicians do little to alleviate our fears.

6   As a result, young people are maturing in a political environment that leads them to believe that this is the way it has always been; therefore, it is the way it must always be. Why should we bother getting mad when no one listens? In so doing, we have permitted AIDS to overtake us.

7   Magic's announcement has helped to slow this process. It again brought the AIDS issue into public view, though it seems odd that the only way to get our country's—and our universities'—attention was to have a world-renowned athlete go public about his contracting the AIDS virus. Do I dare raise the question of what would have happened if the celebrity were a woman who had contracted the HIV virus from promiscuity, as Magic claims to have?

8   Yet, Magic did bring it all home to us. He has, once and for all, broken the stereotype of AIDS being a disease that exclusively strikes drug addicts and homosexuals. If even a hero of Magic's stature is not immune, we—including college and university students—must acknowledge that we are vulnerable to the disease as well.

9   In paving the way for further debate and discussion on AIDS, Magic's disclosure should also lead to a greater self-understanding of why our society seems to quickly forget and disregard such pressing issues as AIDS.

10   Still, with all the renewed media attention on AIDS, it would seem to follow that contributions, private and public, to AIDS-related research would dramatically increase. But let's not bet on it. Let's demand it.

Reaction

In the space below, write your reaction to the essay.

Commentary

Obviously this essay was written in response to Magic Johnson's announcement that he had contracted the HIV virus, which virtually always leads to AIDS. Her opening paragraph gives us a clue as to what slant she will take on the connection between Magic Johnson's announcement and the problem of AIDS itself: students too often behave as though they are immune to the HIV virus. Her title becomes clear at this point. Can Magic Johnson's public declaration make students more aware that they, too, can become victims of the disease? Will his being a victim of the disease cause more money to be directed toward research?

The function of paragraph 2 is to show some of the nonchalance or naive attitudes some students have about the HIV virus, a sort of "well-it-can't-happen-to-me; I'm-not-a-homosexual," or "we-all-gotta-go-some-time" attitude. She then explains why she thinks such student attitudes are prevalent, blaming the Bush and Reagan administrations for not doing more to promote education, health care, and research on the problem. Paragraphs 5 and 6 deal with a cause-effect reaction: Why should we get upset over social problems when nobody in charge seems to care or pay attention?

Paragraphs 7 and 8 speculate that Magic's announcement may bring about a change in such attitudes, but not without a little jab at us: "Do I dare raise the question of what would have happened if the celebrity were a woman who had contracted the HIV virus from promiscuity, as Magic claims to have?" A good question to raise, I think. It makes me wonder.

Her conclusion is strong. Her last two sentences make us aware that we can't just hope that Magic's announcement will increase AIDS-related research, but that we should demand it.

Not every instructor will agree with me, but I think this is a thought-provoking essay, well written and arguing a sound point.

Viewpoints on Family Relationships

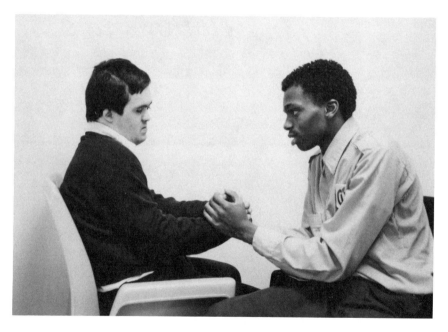

*"Treat people as if they were what they
ought to be and you help them become
what they are capable of being."*
Johann Goethe

*A*MERICA IS MADE UP of family groups of many diverse cultures: the Asian-American family, the Hispanic family, the black family, the European family, the Middle Eastern family, and so on. Still, despite this wide range of backgrounds, some recent research* suggests there are six major qualities shared by healthy families of all races and cultures:

1. a high degree of commitment to the family group and to promoting each other's happiness and welfare

2. an appreciation of one another; making each other feel good about himself or herself

3. good communication patterns developed through spending time talking with and listening to each other

4. a desire to spend time together in active interaction

5. a strong value system, such as that found in religious orientation

6. an ability to deal with crises and stress in a positive manner

Few families can live up to these ideals all of the time. Just as an individual must work to keep mentally and physically fit, so must family members work to keep the family mentally and physically fit. Like individuals, even strong families have problems. Sometimes families break up. And just as there are no perfect parents, there are no perfect children. But we have the option of changing our imperfect

---

*N. Stinnet and J. DeFrain, *Secrets of Strong Families* (Boston: Little, Brown, 1985).

271

family relationships by working to develop those six characteristics of a strong family.

The subject of family relationships is one we all share no matter what our backgrounds. The following essays reveal some varied viewpoints on this broad subject, covering such aspects as wedding preparations, "house-fathering," gender differences, mother love, and the effects family breakups can have. Read them to understand how others feel about family and relationships, as well as to stimulate ideas for an essay of your own.

📖 Preparing to Read

Take a minute or two to look over the following reading selection. Note the title and author, read the opening paragraph, and check the length. Make certain you have the time now to read it carefully and to do the exercises that follow it. Then, in the spaces provided, answer the following questions.

1. What do you think the author means by "pre-wedding syndrome"? ____

    _____

    _____

2. What does she mean by "registering for silver at Bloomingdale's"? What

   has this to do with "pre-wedding" activities? _____

    _____

    _____

3. What do you think the tone (serious, humorous, sarcastic) of this essay

   will be? Explain. _____

    _____

Vocabulary

Good comprehension of what you are about to read depends upon your understanding of the words below. The number following each word refers to the paragraph where it is used.

euphoria (2) a state of ecstasy, a high rush

Retin-A (2) a prescription medication for skin problems frequently used to remove or lessen facial wrinkles caused by aging

syndrome (3) a complex of symptoms or characteristic patterns of behavior

confabs (3) informal talks

intact (4) complete, undamaged, whole

incorrigible (5) incapable of changing, firmly rooted

choreographing (5) arranging dance or ballet movements

damask (8) a rich, fine, patterned fabric used for table linens

fray (10) argument, commotion, dispute

brouhaha (10) uproar; noisy excitement

litany (16) a repetitive list or supply

oxymoron (21) a statement of contradictory terms, such as "a deafening silence"

ecumenical (23) universal, worldwide

Now read the essay.

Pre-Wedding Syndrome

JANE WHITNEY

1   I'd reached that certain age when some studies said I had a better chance of being attacked by nuclear terrorists than registering for silver at Bloomingdale's.

2   Then I became engaged and proved the doomsayers wrong. But even as I reveled in the euphoria of shedding my terminally single Retin-A'ed skin, I developed symptoms of a different disorder.

3   No one had ever warned me about the pitfalls of "Pre-Wedding Syndrome." Not Oprah nor Phil nor Geraldo in any of their consciousness-raising television confabs—and, certainly not *Bride's* magazine.

4   Now, I know the truth. Anyone who survives planning a wedding with sense of humor intact and new spouse in tow could take a respectable crack at negotiating peace in the Middle East.

5   Before being ambushed by "P.W.S.," I was exhilarated by the thought of planning my wedding. For years I had been an incorrigible wedding fanatic, choreographing my fantasy, recasting the key players—especially the groom—and revising details to reflect passages in my life.

6   Since planning a wedding is lumped in with what's billed as the happiest day of your life, I always assumed it would be a blissful part of the package.

7   Instead, it is not unlike clicking back into that 22-year-old mind-set you joyfully left behind—a nether world of insecurity, shaky self-esteem and vying for first place in a no-win popularity contest.

8   I never suspected that as an independent, self-confident over-35-year-old, I could agonize over rental flatware patterns or suffer recurring out-of-body experiences debating the merits of poached versus mesquite-grilled salmon. I never imagined I'd embark on an investigative search for ivory damask napkins that would rival the travails of a Pulitzer Prize contender. Or that I would become physically attached to a heavyweight coffee-table book called "Weddings," dragging it hither and yon like a security blanket.

9   My future husband, Lindsey Gruson, a correspondent for *The Times*, kicked off the proceedings with his Christmas Eve proposal. In a charming variation on a romantic De Beers diamond commercial, he dropped a ring from my dog Max's collar into my glass of champagne. When I gently hinted he had missed the point of the ad, he said not at all, we could register for the real thing.

10   Then his family, my family and our friends got into the act. The ornate china pattern I chose set off such a controversy in his family that I half expected to tune in and see Tom Brokaw delivering nightly updates on the fray. (In the end, I decided to switch rather than fight. The brouhaha had effectively tarnished my fondness for gold-rimmed Haviland Limoges. Who wants good china with bad karma?)

11   Meanwhile, my father turned into Monty Hall playing "Let's Make a Deal" long distance from Florida. One night I told my parents that we had to supply musicians, a dance floor and piano at the reception. There was silence. Then my father started ticking off each name on my parents' guest list.

12   "Uncle Jim is older, he can't dance."

13   "Mrs. Klein has been sick. She probably won't dance."

14   "And cousin Mary has an artificial leg. She doesn't dance. You see, all that's a waste of money. No one on our side will dance," he concluded triumphantly. (It was the same song, different verse on the subject of serving spirits at the reception. No one on their side would drink, either.)

15   Even longtime friends tested my diplomatic skill. One urged us to book the new-wave reggae band that played at her wedding; another requested we serve sushi for dinner; a third lobbied for a nuptial date out of high-humidity season so her hair wouldn't frizz.

16   Thanks to these well-intentioned souls, I learned quickly that any well-wisher who coos, "It's your day; do whatever you want," inev-

itably launches into a litany of unsolicited advice guaranteed to shatter whatever certainty you have left.

17   Then there was the guest list. Why is it that some people assume a "Best Wishes!" when they hear the news translates into an engraved invitation? Even as I demurred about our small wedding with only family and closest friends in attendance, those best described as "Christmas card acquaintances" would whisk out their calendars, circle the date and snap the book shut with a jaunty "we'll be there!"

18   Equally endearing were those solo entities who accorded their invitation "two-fer" status. In one case, when subtlety failed to convey the message that our wedding was not analogous to a senior prom, we caved in on our "no guests" rule. (After all, he was my fiancé's boss.)

19   Even the ballyhooed fairy tale of finding the perfect wedding dress is so much "P.W.S." mythology. Amid a gaggle of bare-shouldered postadolescent brides-to-be floating past triple-view mirrors, I dreaded the approach of the saleswoman who would chirp, "Something for the mother of the bride?"

20   The memory of standing stripped-down in a fluorescent-lit cubicle wearing what looked like a pink mesh beekeeper's mask over my head, listening to seed pearls pop off the too-small floor-sample dress while the saleswoman soothed, "Don't worry, every bride loses weight," is forever etched in my mind. I didn't feel like a vision of loveliness. I felt like a nurse on steroids.

21   I also learned that the term "wedding budget" is an oxymoron. Even though our heartfelt desires coincided with the bare-bones event—no open bar, no video-camera crew, no Rockettes—we actually considered staging a benefit to underwrite the festivities.

22   A wedding budget abhors a vacuum. For nearly two months, my calculator remained embedded in my right palm while I stared dolefully at the line-item estimates, willing them to change. Sometimes they did. But the victory of "saving" on discount drugstore aspirin for the women's-room emergency basket was short-lived. For instance, considering what Crane & Company charges to engrave stationery, they should have written our thank-you notes for us.

23   No bona fide bout of Pre-Wedding Syndrome is complete without the traditional top-of-the-lungs shouting match punctuated by shrill cries of "Let's call the whole thing off." Ours came during the final 48 hours, while we were haggling over the ecumenical ceremony we'd written. Navigating a sensitive stage in the negotiations, we'd compromised on the number of times we'd mention God vis-à-vis Moses. (Final count: 6 to 5.)

24   But when my fiancé quipped that a snippet of prose I'd selected sounded like a badly written Hallmark card, I snapped. A battle born

of prenuptial jitters ensued. My panicking thoughts zig-zagged from wondering if I could actually marry someone whose hips are smaller than mine to whether Miss Manners would approve of serving defrosted wedding cake at a disengagement dinner party.

25   Only on the day of the wedding did the Pre-Wedding Syndrome stop. Yet even as I shakily inched up the aisle, the nagging conviction that we should have seated his mother and stepmother in separate states skittered across my reverie.

26   One of my married friends had said that planning a wedding is a lot like childbirth—you remember the joy, not the pain. Don't believe it. Once is enough.

Understanding the Content

1. Explain "P.W.S."

2. Describe the way Whitney's husband proposed.

3. What are some of the pre-wedding details the author agonized over?

4. What was her own family's reaction to her request for musicians at the wedding reception?

5. What pre-wedding problems did her friends create?

6. Why does she call the term "wedding budget" an oxymoron?

7. Explain Whitney's response to a friend's comparison of planning a wedding to childbirth.

Looking at Structure and Style

1. Is the thesis stated or implied? If stated, where?

2. How effective is the opening paragraph? Explain your reaction.

3. Describe the tone of the essay and locate some words or phrases that help develop that tone.

4. How effectively does Whitney move from one point to the next? Are the transitions smooth? Explain.

5. To what audience do you think the author writes? Why do you think so?

6. What advice, if any, would you give the author for revision?

Evaluating the Author's Viewpoints

1. Does Whitney cover most of the details involved in planning a wedding? Is there anything else she might have included?

2. What does Whitney mean in paragraph 22 when she says, "A wedding budget abhors a vacuum"?

3. Do you think planning a wedding can be as much of an ordeal as Whitney makes it sound? Explain.

4. To what degree did Whitney's age affect her pre-wedding syndrome?

Pursuing Possible Essay Topics

1. Describe an event or ritual you have gone through that involved a lot of pre-planning. Was it worth it? What effect did it have on the event itself?

2. Argue for or against marriage as a legal necessity in our society.

2. Argue for or against the tradition of making weddings "big events."

3. Argue for or against spending money on honeymoons.

4. Write about a time when you had to give up a long-time dream to the reality of dealing with other people's wishes or logic.

5. Pretend you are a marriage counselor. What advice would you have given Whitney if she had come to you during her "P.W.S."? What advice would you have given her then fiancé?

6. Brainstorm or freewrite on one or more of the following:
   a. marriage rituals   d. making marriage work
   b. engagements   e. marriage counseling
   c. P.W.S.   f. elopement

7. Divorce yourself from these ideas and find a topic of your own on personal relationships.

Preparing to Read

Take a minute or two to look over the following reading selection. Note the title and author, read the opening paragraph, and check the length. Make certain you have the time now to read it carefully and to do the exercises that follow it. Then, in the spaces provided, answer the following questions.

1. What attitude toward family do you think the author has? _____

_____

_____

2. Do you think you will agree with him? Why? _____

_____

3. What might you learn from reading this essay? _____

_____

Vocabulary

Good comprehension of what you are about to read depends upon your understanding of the words below. The number following each word refers to the paragraph where it is used.

   crucial (1) important, vital, necessary

   tyrants (1, 3) dictators, fascists

   utopians (1) believers in an idealistic, dream state of perfection

   commonwealth (1) the people of a nation or state

   antipathy (1) a feeling of intense dislike

   dehumanization (2) to take away human qualities

   visceral (2) instinctive, innate

   slavish (3) slave-like

   usurped (4) overthrew, took over power

   degradation (4) shame

   dysfunctional (6) not working correctly

   profusion (7) growing quantity

   disintegration (9) collapse, destruction

Now read the essay.

*The Importance of Family**

SAM KEEN

1   To understand how crucial the existence of strong families is to the cultivation of free spirits we might meditate on the odd fact that the first target of tyrants and utopians of the political right and left is always the family. From Plato to Marx to Mao, all those thinkers who want society organized so individuals will fit into some overarching five-year plan for the ideal republic, the ideal socialist or

_____

*Editor's title.

religious state, inevitably try to replace the family and place the education of the young in the hands of state-run institutions. Under the banner of freeing women for productive work, or liberating the young from the prejudices of the old, or instilling the values necessary for an ideal commonwealth, parents and children are separated or allowed minimal contact. The motive behind this antipathy toward the family is not difficult to find. So long as men's and women's prime loyalty is to family and kin, they cannot be controlled by the state or any other institution. But if they can be convinced to switch their loyalty to some "higher" cause or institution, they will obey the dictates of their leaders.

2   For better and for worse, the family is the first line of defense against dehumanization and misplaced loyalty. Within the privacy of the home, we may think, speak, and worship as we please. We may educate our children in the values we cherish and teach them respect for the traditions we uphold. Because it is easiest to love our own children unconditionally, the family is the natural school of love. Loving our kin, we may gradually learn to extend kindness to strangers. And because children incarnate our hopes, they are our visceral evidence of the wisdom of investing our time and care in the lives of others.

3   Almost without noticing it, we are voluntarily eroding the freedoms and surrendering the loyalties that no tyrant could take from us without a fight. By our increasingly slavish devotion to the economic order, we are destroying the cradle of freedom. The iron law of profit is best served by those who are willing to depersonalize themselves by valuing efficiency above compassion, and devotion to the competitive goals of the corporation over loyalty to family.

4   A history of the word "economics" contains a parable that illuminates our present dilemma and offers a challenge to men and women. Originally "economics" meant "the art of managing a household" and it contained the notion of thrift and voluntary simplicity. Later, under the impact of the industrial revolution, "economics" came to mean the system of production, distribution, and consumption of commodities. When factory, store, office, and bank usurped the loyalties of men and replaced the home as the center of economic activity, women who chose to give serious attention to homemaking were given the condescending title of "home economists." And the final transformation, which is to say degradation, of the dignity of the home, is symbolized by a recent change made at the University of Iowa. What was once the College of Home Economics has now been renamed the College of Consumer Sciences.

5   The only revolution that will heal us is one in which men and women come together and place the creation of a rich family life back

in the center of the horizon of our values. A letter I got recently from a woman makes the point: "Perhaps the real shift will come when men fully realize, in the gut and not just in the head, that they are equally responsible, with women, for the creation, nurturing, and protection of children—that children are not simple sex objects, ego trips, or nuisances, but their first responsibility—before war, money, power, and status."

6   You may object: "All of this is well enough in theory, but unfortunate in fact, for many people the family was a vicious trap and a cruel destiny. The place that should have been a sanctuary was often a torture house. The arms that should have held us often pushed us away. Many flee the family because it was the place of injury, captivity, disappointment, abuse. The children of alcoholics and abusive parents fear marriage and family and find their solace in becoming solitary. There are so many bad marriages and dysfunctional families it sometimes seems only reasonable to junk the institution or invent a replacement." True enough, but hopes of replacing the family with some more perfect institution, like hi-tech pipe dreams of creating space colonies into which we can escape when we have polluted the earth, have proven to be both dangerous and deluded. It is within the bonds of what is familial that we must live or perish.

7   Fortunately, the profusion of dysfunctional families does not necessarily predict a grim future for the family. One of the standard themes in mythology is the promise of the wounded healer. In our hurt lies the source of our healing. The bird with the broken and mended wing soars the highest. Where you stumble and fall, there you find the treasure.

8   One of men's greatest resources for change is our wound and our longing for the missing father. We can heal ourselves by becoming the kind of fathers we wanted but did not have. Create out of the void, out of the absence. Our best map for parenting is outlined like a photographic negative in the shadow side of our psyches. Get in touch with your disappointment, your rage, your grief, your loneliness for the father, the intimate touching family you did not have, and you will find a blueprint for parenting. Become the father you longed for. We heal ourselves by learning to give to our children what we did not receive.

9   If you are not married, do not have children, or are gay, find a friend's child who needs nurturing and become a part-time substitute parent. It strikes me that the lack of substantial manliness one finds in some gay communities is a result not of a homoerotic expression of sexuality, but of the lack of a relationship of nurturance to the young. To be involved in creating a wholesome future, men, gay or straight, need an active caring relationship to children. A man who takes no care of and is not involved in the process of caring for and

initiating the young remains a boy no matter what his achievements. This generation of men knows by its longing for fathers who were absent that nothing fills the void that is created when men abandon their families, whether out of selfishness, dedication to work, or devotion to "important" causes. When anything becomes more important to a society than the welfare of its children, it is a sure sign of spiritual disintegration.

Understanding the Content

1. Why are philosopher-writers such as Plato, Karl Marx, and Mao Zedong mentioned in connection with the subject of family? If you are unfamiliar with them, can you infer what their writings teach?

2. Why does Keen believe that "the family is the first line of defense against dehumanization and misplaced loyalty" (2)? What does he mean by "misplaced loyalty"?

3. In paragraph 4, Keen gives a short history of the word "economics" as used in our society. What's the connection with family?

4. What is the "only revolution" (5) that will heal our society's ills, according to Keen?

5. What can someone learn from having grown up in a dysfunctional family?

6. What advice does Keen give to unmarried or gay men?

Looking at Structure and Style

1. If you have read the previous essay, "Pre-Wedding Syndrome," compare its tone and style with Keen's. How are they different?

2. Is Keen's thesis implied or stated? If stated, where?

3. Explain the function of paragraphs 1 and 2. How does Keen tie them together?

4. How would you describe Keen's use of language? Give some examples.

5. What is the point of paragraph 4? What does its contents have to do with his thesis?

6. Explain Keen's use of quotation marks in paragraph 6.

7. How well developed is Keen's thesis? Explain.

Evaluating the Author's Viewpoints

1. Keen says, "For better or for worse, the family is the first line of defense against dehumanization and misplaced loyalty" (2). Do you agree? Why does he say, "For better *or for worse*..."?

2. Keen sees our "slavish devotion to the economic order" (3) as having a negative effect on family. He views this devotion as "misplaced," equally as bad as being controlled by the state. Do you agree? Explain.

3. Do you believe, as Keen does, that someone "wounded" by a dysfunctional family environment can become a healthy parent? Explain his views and then yours.

4. Keen says, "We heal ourselves by learning to give to our children what we did not receive" (8). What does he mean? Do you agree? Explain.

5. React to Keen's viewpoints in the first three sentences of paragraph 9.

6. In what ways, according to Keen, do men "abandon" their families without actually leaving home? Do you agree or disagree with his definition of "abandon"? Explain.

Pursuing Possible Essay Topics

1. Explain in an essay why you do or do not want to have children.

2. Find a statement in Keen's essay that you strongly agree or disagree with and write about your reaction.

3. Reread Keen's last sentence. What "signs" of spiritual disintegration do you see in our society? What can be done to slow or halt the disintegration?

4. Do some research on dysfunctional families and write an essay describing some of the causes of this phenomenon.

5. React to these words spoken a traditional wedding vow: " . . . for better or for worse, 'til death us do part."

6. Brainstorm or freewrite on one or more of the following:
   a. home economics   d. fatherly love
   b. company man   e. child abuse
   c. my family   f. being a parent

7. If you don't like the family of questions above, find your own topic on family relationships.

Preparing to Read

Take a minute or two to look over the following reading selection. Note the title and author, read the first *four* paragraphs, and check the length. Make certain you have the time now to read it carefully and to do the exercises that follow it. Then, in the spaces provided, answer the following questions.

1. What do you think the essay is about? _____

   _____

2. How do you feel about fathers who stay home to watch the children while

   the mothers work? Why? _____

   _____

Vocabulary

Good comprehension of what you are about to read depends upon your understanding of the words below. The number following each word refers to the paragraph where it is used.

euphemism (4) a term used to replace one that might offend or upset someone (for example, *passed away* instead of *kicked the bucket* or *died*)

rhapsodized (4) expressed in an overly enthusiastic way

interminably (5) endlessly

ambivalent (7) having two conflicting feelings at the same time

treadmill (8) metaphor for a monotonous routine

lethargy (8) passiveness, indifference

taboos (9) behaviors prohibited by social custom

mitigated (10) made less intense

therapeutic (11) having healing powers

chronic (11) constant, lingering

subside (11) lessen, decrease

obnoxious (11) highly disagreeable or offensive

heresy (11) a controversial, almost unacceptable opinion

benchmark (12) a standard by which others can be compared

typified (14) were typical examples of

proxy (14) authorization for another person to act on one's behalf

incredulously (17) disbelievingly

violated (18) broke (a law, for example), didn't follow

succumbing (18) yielding, giving in to

claustrophobics (22) people afraid of being in confined spaces

idyll (23) a carefree experience

apprehension (25) dread

tangible (25) real, concrete, touchable

contingent (26) a representative group

mundane (28) ordinary, common

anathema (28) something or someone shunned or avoided

resurrecting (28) bringing back to life, bringing back into practice

shtick (30) entertainment routine

Now read the essay.

Escaping the Daily Grind for Life as a House Father

RICK GREENBERG

1   "You on vacation?" my neighbor asked.

2   My 15-month-old son and I were passing her yard on our daily hike through the neighborhood. It was a weekday afternoon and I was the only working-age male in sight.

3   "I'm uh...working out of my house now," I told her.

4   Thus was born my favorite euphemism for house fatherhood, one of those new life-style occupations that is never merely mentioned. Explained, yes. Defended. Even rhapsodized about. I was tongue-tied then, but no longer. People are curious and I've learned to oblige.

5   I joined up earlier this year when I quit my job—a dead-end, ulcer-producing affair that had dragged on interminably. I left to be with my son until something better came along. And if nothing did, I'd be with him indefinitely.

6   This was no simple transition. I had never known a house father, never met one. I'd only read about them. They were another news magazine trend. Being a traditionalist, I never dreamed I'd take the plunge.

7   But as the job got worse, I gave it serious thought. And more thought. And in the end, I still felt ambivalent. This was a radical change that seemed to carry as many drawbacks as benefits. My dislike for work finally pushed me over the edge. That, and the fact that we had enough money to get by.

8   Escaping the treadmill was a bold stroke. I had shattered my lethargy and stopped whining, and for that I was proud.

9   Some friends said they were envious. Of course they weren't quitting one job without one waiting—the ultimate in middle-class taboos. That ran through my mind as I triumphantly, and without notice, tossed the letter of resignation on my boss's desk. Then I walked away wobbly-kneed.

10   The initial trauma of quitting, however, was mitigated by my eagerness to raise our son. Mine was the classic father's lament. I felt excluded. I had become "the man who got home after dark," that other person besides Mama. It hurt when I couldn't quiet his crying.

11   I sensed that staying home would be therapeutic. The chronic competitiveness and aggressiveness that had served me well as a daily journalist would subside. Something better would emerge, something less obnoxious. My ulcer would heal. Instead of beating deadlines, I'd be doing something important for a change. This was heresy coming from a newspaper gypsy, but it rang true.

12   There was unease, too. I'd be adrift, stripped of the home-office-home routine that had defined my existence for more than a decade. No more earning a living. No benchmarks. Time would be seamless. Would Friday afternoons feel the same?

13   The newness of it was scary.

14   Until my resignation, my wife and I typified today's baby-boomer couples, the want-it-all generation. We had two salaries, a full-time nanny and guilt pangs over practicing parenthood by proxy.

15   Now, my wife brings home the paychecks, the office problems and thanks for good work on the domestic front. With me at home, her work hours are more flexible. Nanny-less, I change diapers, prepare meals and do all the rest. And I wonder what comes next.

16   What if I don't find another job? My field is tight. At 34, I'm not getting any more marketable and being out of work doesn't help.

17   As my father asked incredulously: "Is this going to be what you do?"

18   Perhaps. I don't know. I wonder myself. It's even more baffling to my father, the veteran of a long and traditional 9-to-5 career. For most of it, my mother stayed home. My father doesn't believe in trends. All he knows is that his only son—with whom he shares so many traits—has violated the natural order of men providing and women raising children. In his view, I've shown weakness and immaturity by succumbing to a bad job.

19   But he's trying to understand, and I think he will.

20   I'm trying to understand it myself. House fatherhood has been humbling, rewarding and unnerving.

21   "It's different," I tell friends. "Different."

22   Imagine never having to leave home for the office in the morning. That's how different. No dress-up, no commute. Just tumble out of bed and you're there. House fathering is not for claustrophobics.

23   I find myself enjoying early morning shopping. My son and I arrive right after the supermarket opens. The place is almost empty. For the next hour we glide dreamily, cruising the aisles to a Muzak accompaniment. This is my idyll. My son likes it, too; he's fascinated by the spectacle.

24   Housekeeping still doesn't seem like work, and that's by design. I've mastered the art of doing just enough chores to get by. This leaves me enough free time. Time to read and write and daydream. Time with my son. Time to think about the structure.

25   So much time, and so little traditional structure, that the days sometimes blur together. I remember on Sunday nights literally dreading the approaching work week, the grind. Today, the close of the weekend still triggers a shiver of apprehension; I now face the prospect of a week without tangible accomplishments, a void.

26   On our hikes to the playground, I can feel my old identity fading. All around are people with a mission, a sense of purpose. Workers. And then there's the rest of us—the stroller and backpack contingent. The moms, the nannies, and me. I wonder if I've crossed over a line never to return.

27   Still, the ulcer seems to be healing. I take pride in laying out a good dinner for the family and in pampering my wife after a tough day at the office. I love reading to my son. Running errands isn't even so bad. A lot of what had been drudgery or trivia is taking on new meaning; maybe I'm mellowing.

28   Which is ironic. To be a truly committed and effective at-home parent, there must be this change—a softening, a contentment with small pleasures, the outwardly mundane. This is a time of reduced demands and lowered expectations. Progress is gradual, often agonizingly so. Patience is essential. Ambition and competitiveness are anathema. Yet eliminating these last two qualities—losing the edge— could ruin my chances of resurrecting my career. I can't have it both ways.

29   The conflict has yet to be resolved. And it won't be unless I make a firm commitment and choose one life-style over the other. I'm not yet ready for that decision.

30   In the meantime, a wonderful change is taking place in our home. Amid all the uncertainties, my son and I have gotten to know each other. He can't put a phrase together, but he confides in me. It can be nothing more than a grin or a devilish look. He tries new words on me, new shtick. We roll around a lot; we crack each other up. I'm no longer the third wheel, the man who gets home after dark. Now, I'm as much a part of his life as his mother is. I, too, can stop his crying. So far, that has made the experiment worthwhile.

Understanding the Content

Feel free to reread all or parts of the selection to answer the following questions.

  1. What was Greenberg's job before he quit? What reasons does Greenberg give for quitting?

2. What are some of the things Greenberg mentions that were difficult to get used to as a house father? What advantages to his new role does he mention?

3. Being a traditionalist, how difficult was it for Greenberg's father to accept his son's new "job"? Why?

4. What special qualities does Greenberg believe a "truly committed and effective at-home parent" (28) must have?

5. How would you describe Greenberg's attitude about being a house father?

6. What is Greenberg's thesis? Is it implied or stated?

Looking at Structure and Style

1. What function do paragraphs 1–4 serve?

2. What is the purpose of the first sentence in paragraph 6?

3. Why do paragraphs 7–9 work well in that order? What do they reveal about the author himself?

4. How do paragraphs 10 and 11 contrast with paragraphs 7–9?

5. Explain or rewrite the following passages from the essay:
   a. "I was tongue-tied then, . . ." (4)
   b. "Escaping the treadmill was a bold stroke." (8)
   c. "Time would be seamless." (12)
   d. "I'm not getting any more marketable. . . ." (16)
   e. "And then there's the rest of us—the stroller and backpack contingent." (26)

Evaluating the Author's Viewpoints

1. In paragraph 22, Greenberg says, "House fathering is not for claustrophobics." What does he mean? Do you agree?

2. Reread paragraph 28. Do you agree with his statement about what it takes to be an effective at-home parent? What does Greenberg mean when he says he can't have it both ways?

3. The author ends his essay by saying that what he has done so far has been worthwhile. Do you infer otherwise? Explain.

4. Do you think Greenberg will remain a house father? Why?

Pursuing Possible Essay Topics

1. Write an essay that tries to convince Greenberg to go back to work. Be sure to give counterarguments for some of his points.

2. Write an essay that supports the role of house father. Direct your arguments to those who feel as Greenberg's traditionalist father does.

3. Interview some older people to discover what a "traditional" family life-style was like forty years ago. Compare it to today's.

4. Talk to some recent immigrants to this country to discover what their traditional family life-style was like before and after coming to this country. How much, if any, has it changed?

5. In many families both parents must now work for economic reasons. What effect will that have on the way the children of those families perceive family life, particularly parenting? Show how being a parent today is different from your grandparents' day.

6. What other trends in our society are changing the traditional family unit as many people have known it? Write an essay on the forces in society that are changing the family unit.

7. Brainstorm or freewrite on one or more of the following:

   a. family life
   b. family traditions
   c. the changing family

   d. single parenting
   e. house fathers
   f. working mothers

8. Ignore these and come up with an idea of your own that deals with some aspect of family relationships.

📖 Preparing to Read

Take a minute or two to look over the following reading selection. Note the title and author, read the opening paragraph, and check the length. Make certain you have the time now to read it carefully and to do the exercises that follow it. Then, in the spaces provided, answer the following questions.

1. What is your reaction to the title? _____

_____

2. What do you think the subject of this essay is? _____

_____

3. What do you think is going to happen? _____

_____

Vocabulary

Good comprehension of what you are about to read depends upon your understanding of the words below. The number following each word refers to the paragraph where it is used.

ironically (2) oppositely or differently from what is expected

traumas (4) severe shocks to the mind or body

trounced (4) beaten, defeated

relinquishing (7) giving up to another, surrendering

quavering (8) quivering, trembling

taken aback (11) surprised, caught off guard

Now read the essay.

One Son, Three Fathers

STEVEN O'BRIEN

1   The first time I met him, he fell asleep in his spaghetti. It didn't matter. I was in love. Not with him, but with his mother. She had kept Sebastian from napping so that we wouldn't be interrupted after dinner. He was only 18 months old, a tiny little body topped off by a big head covered with blond hair.

2   His divorced mother and I, both 25, dated for a month, lived together nine more, and then married. It was Karen I wanted, not Sebastian, but they were a package deal. Ironically, he turned out to be the best part of the bargain.

3   Because my teaching schedule matched Sebastian's preschool schedule, I spent more time with him than his mother did. On the way home after school in the afternoon, he loved to sit on his Scooby-Doo lunch box in the back seat of my car and sing hit pop tunes like "Fly, Robin, Fly" and "SOS."

4   His biological father wasn't as available as I was to deal with the unscheduled traumas of childhood. I slowly began to fill his role. Seb turned to me for comfort the night before he had to face a bully who had promised to hurt him. At age 4, he didn't understand, and I couldn't explain, why the world needed bullies. I could only repeat what my father had said: fight back as best you can and don't let anyone know that he can push you around, or it will never end. He cried at breakfast, regained his composure before school, stood up for his rights and got thoroughly trounced. When he couldn't fall

asleep that night, he asked to borrow my wool knit sailor cap. "To-morrow," he said, "with this on, I won't be afraid. I'll be 100 times stronger." The bully ignored him the next day, in order to torment someone else.

5   Brian, Sebastian's father, and I had been trained as teachers. Perhaps this was why both of us wanted to help the boy. Then, too, I had been raised with a stepsister and had seen the psychological damage that loss of contact with a parent could cause. In any case, Seb continued to spend time with me and with his father even after Brian remarried. Seb never had any problem distinguishing between the two of us, although other people were often confused because he referred to us as Daddy Steve and Daddy Brian. We all benefited from the arrangement. Sebastian shared things with Brian that I couldn't give him. For instance, I never followed sports, but Brian had studied to be a sports announcer.

6   After eight years of marriage, my wife and I separated. At first, Seb stayed with me and visited his mother, but after her remarriage, she missed him too much. He was moved to her new home nearby. Legally, of course, I had no rights. A child counselor I consulted suggested that I fade out of the picture as soon as possible. Instead, I maintained my home, with a bedroom for Seb, within walking distance of his. With his mother's consent, he started spending one night a week at my place. He loved to show off his second home to his friends by bringing them around, unannounced, for snacks.

7   Seb's grandparents had died years before. My place in his life gradually changed to resemble the role my favorite uncle and grand-parents played in mine. It was hard at first, relinquishing my old relationship with him, but I grew to like the new one. I had the fun of seeing him without the frustration of trying to live with and dis-cipline him.

8   Although we talked about it, and he understood after the divorce that we were no longer legally connected, Seb insisted on continuing to call me dad and using my last name as his own. I asked, "What's in a name, anyway?" He responded, "It says whose son I am." I told him that wasn't the issue. That I didn't have any choice. Neither biology nor law gave me the right to claim such a role; but he shat-tered my logic in a quavering voice with the question, "Don't you want to be my father anymore?" We hugged; I said: "Of course I want to. As long as you want me to be your father, I will be." That was five years ago.

9   Because Sebastian and I live in the same community, I often learn details about him I would otherwise miss. My neighbor, Sebastian's eighth-grade social-studies teacher, told me that he was going up and

down the aisles asking each student at the end of the year if they had any brothers or sisters who would be going to the junior high the next fall. When he got to Seb, he said, "Oh, that's O.K. Seb, I used to live next door to you, and I know that you are an only child." Sebastian answered with a smile, "That's right, Mr. Tulley, there are so many parents in my family that there isn't room for any more kids."

10   After the laughter died down, several fellow students asked Seb how many parents he had. He said three fathers and two mothers. Another said, "Wow, Christmas must be great." Seb hesitated and then explained, "Christmas is about a 7, but birthdays are a definite 10."

11   Still, I wonder how he and his generation will view marriage. One night, we were talking about girls, the next-most-important issue on his mind, after driving. I said, "Well, someday, you'll find the right young woman and you won't be satisfied until you marry her." I wasn't prepared for his reply: "No, dad, I don't think so. It never works for long, and divorce hurts too much." Taken aback, I assured him that marriage did work, and that just because his parents' marriages hadn't, it was no reason to give up on the institution. He looked at me patiently and said: "Dad, none of my friends' parents are still together. Everybody gets divorced sooner or later. Don't worry, I'm all right. I can take care of myself. Love 'em and leave 'em. Right?"

12   I don't think I had realized until that moment that, since my divorce from Sebastian's mother, "love 'em and leave 'em" exactly described the way I had been living and handling my own relationships with women. What could I say to Seb?

Understanding the Content

Feel free to reread all or parts of the selection to answer the following questions.

1. What is the exact relationship between O'Brien and Sebastian? Who are Sebastian's three fathers?

2. Why was O'Brien able to spend more time with Seb than Seb's mother was? What effect did this have on O'Brien's and Seb's relationship?

3. What advice did a child counselor give O'Brien when he and Seb's mother divorced? Did he follow this advice? Why?

4. What can you infer about the way O'Brien and Seb feel about each other now? Why do you think so?

5. What can you infer about the effects of divorce on Seb's views of marriage?

6. What revelation strikes O'Brien at the end of the essay?

7. What is the point of this selection?

Looking at Structure and Style

1. How effective is the opening paragraph in getting your attention? Why?

2. What is the main idea of paragraph 2? What would be the effect if O'Brien had put his last sentence first?

3. For what purpose does O'Brien quote dialogue in paragraphs 4, 8, 9, 10, and 11?

4. How much time is covered in this essay? How does O'Brien move us from one time period to the next?

5. While most of the essay deals with his relationship with Seb, the last paragraph shifts to O'Brien's relationships with women. Is this appropriate? Explain.

Evaluating the Author's Viewpoints

1. What are O'Brien's feelings about Seb's biological father, Brian? Seb's mother, Karen?

2. What does O'Brien mean in paragraph 4 when he refers to "the unscheduled traumas of childhood"? Why does he feel he was better prepared to help Sebastian deal with them than Brian was? Do you think he was?

3. In paragraph 5, O'Brien says that one of the reasons he may have wanted to help Seb after the divorce was because he was trained as a teacher, but he adds, "Then, too, I had been raised with a stepsister and had seen the psychological damage that loss of contact with a parent could cause." What can we infer from this statement about the author? Do you think O'Brien sees himself in Seb?

4. O'Brien says he had "the fun of seeing him [Seb] without the frustration of trying to live with and discipline him" (7). If you were one of Sebastian's biological parents living with and disciplining him, how would you feel about O'Brien's relationship with Seb? Why?

5. O'Brien chose not to take the child counselor's advice to "fade out of the picture as soon as possible" (6). Do you think he made the right choice? Why?

6. What do you think is O'Brien's attitude toward marriage? Why?

Pursuing Possible Essay Topics

1. Reread the last paragraph in the essay. Write an essay that answers the question, "What could I say to Seb?"

2. Assume that you have a four-year-old son and that he tells you he has to face a bully at school tomorrow. Discuss how you might handle the situation. What would you do? What would you say to your son? Would you try to explain why there are bullies in the world, or as O'Brien puts it, why the world needs bullies? How?

3. Reread what Seb tells O'Brien in paragraph 11. Write an essay that argues against the conclusion Seb has come to.

4. Brainstorm or freewrite on one or more the following:

   a. divorce   d. stepparents
   b. marriage   e. "love 'em and leave 'em"
   c. stepchildren   f. loss of contact with a parent

5. Do some research on marriage and divorce. What are the latest trends? Is Seb right? (In addition to the card catalog and the *Reader's Guide to Periodical Literature*, you might want to see what you can find in the latest *Facts on File* and the latest *World Almanac and Book of Facts*.)

6. Write about your views on marriage or divorce.

7. Divorce yourself from these and pick your own topic.

Preparing to Read

Take a minute or two to look over the following reading selection. Note the title and author, read the first paragraph, and check the length. Make certain you have the time now to read it carefully and to do the exercises that follow it. Then, in the spaces provided, answer the following questions.

1. What do you think the title means? _____

_____

2. What do you think will be the subject of this selection? _____

_____

3. What do you expect to learn from this reading? _____

_____

Vocabulary

Good comprehension of what you are about to read depends upon your understanding of the words below. The number following each word refers to the paragraph where it is used.

hollow (8) valley, basin, indentation in the earth

Mon-o-lah (9) Cherokee Indian word for *Earth Mother*

'coon (28) abbreviation for raccoon

Cherokee (28) a tribe of North American Indians, formerly inhabiting North Carolina and northern Georgia, forcibly relocated in the 1830s to Oklahoma

Now read the following selection..

The Way

FORREST CARTER

1   It had taken Granma, sitting in the rocker that creaked with her slight weight as she worked and hummed, while the pine knots spluttered in the fireplace, a week of evenings to make the boot moccasins. With a hook knife, she had cut the deer leather and made the strips that she wove around the edges. When she had finished, she soaked the moccasins in water and I put them on wet and walked them dry, back and forth across the floor, until they fitted soft and giving, light as air.

2   This morning I slipped the moccasins on last, after I had jumped into my overalls and buttoned my jacket. It was dark and cold—too early even for the morning whisper wind to stir the trees.

3   Granpa had said I could go with him on the high trail, if I got up, and he had said he would not wake me.

4   "A man rises of his own will in the morning," he had spoken down to me and he did not smile. But Granpa had made many noises in his rising, bumping the wall of my room and talking uncommonly loud to Granma, and so I had heard, and I was first out, waiting with the hounds in the darkness.

5   "So. Ye're here," Granpa sounded surprised.

6   "Yes, sir," I said, and kept the proud out of my voice.

7   Granpa pointed his finger at the hounds jumping and prancing around us. "Ye'll stay," he ordered, and they tucked in their tails and whined and begged and ol' Maud set up a howl. But they didn't follow us. They stood, all together in a hopeless little bunch, and watched us leave the clearing.

8   I had been up the low trail that followed the bank of the spring branch, twisting and turning with the hollow until it broke out into a meadow where Granpa had his barn and kept his mule and cow. But this was the high trail that forked off to the right and took to the side of the mountain, sloping always upward as it traveled along the

hollow. I trotted behind Granpa and I could feel the upward slant of the trail.

9   I could feel something more, as Granma said I would. Mon-o-lah, the earth mother, came to me through my moccasins. I could feel her push and swell here, and sway and give there . . . and the roots that veined her body and the life of the water-blood, deep inside her. She was warm and springy and bounced me on her breast, as Granma said she would.

10   The cold air steamed my breath in clouds and the spring branch fell far below us. Bare tree branches dripped water from ice prongs that teethed their sides, and as we walked higher there was ice on the trail. Gray light eased the darkness away.

11   Granpa stopped and pointed by the side of the trail. "There she is—turkey run—see?" I dropped to my hands and knees and saw the tracks: little sticklike impressions coming out from a center hub.

12   "Now," Granpa said, "we'll fix the trap." And he moved off the trail until he found a stump hole.

13   We cleaned it out, first the leaves, and then Granpa pulled out his long knife and cut into the spongy ground and we scooped up the dirt, scattering it among the leaves. When the hole was deep, so that I couldn't see over the rim, Granpa pulled me out and we dragged tree branches to cover it and, over these, spread armfuls of leaves. Then, with his long knife, Granpa dug a trail sloping downward into the hole and back toward the turkey run. He took the grains of red Indian corn from his pocket and scattered them down the trail, and threw a handful into the hole.

14   "Now we will go," he said, and set off again up the high trail. Ice, spewed from the earth like frosting, crackled under our feet. The mountain opposite us moved closer as the hollow far below became a narrow slit, showing the spring branch like the edge of a steel knife, sunk in the bottom of its cleavage.

15   We sat down in the leaves, off the trail, just as the first sun touched the top of the mountain across the hollow. From his pocket, Granpa pulled out a sour biscuit and deer meat for me, and we watched the mountain while we ate.

16   The sun hit the top like an explosion, sending showers of glitter and sparkle into the air. The sparkling of the icy trees hurt the eyes to look, and it moved down the mountain like a wave as the sun backed the night shadow down and down. A crow scout sent three hard calls through the air, warning we were there.

17   And now the mountain popped and gave breathing sighs that sent little puffs of steam into the air. She pinged and murmured as the sun released the trees from their death armor of ice.

18   Granpa watched, same as me, and listened as the sounds grew with the morning wind that set up a low whistle in the trees.

19   "She's coming alive," he said, soft and low, without taking his eyes from the mountain.

20   "Yes, sir," I said, "she's coming alive." And I knew right then that me and Granpa had us an understanding that most folks didn't know.

21   The night shadow backed down and across a little meadow, heavy with grass and shining in the sun bath. The meadow was set into the side of the mountain. Granpa pointed. There was quail fluttering and jumping in the grass, feeding on the seeds. Then he pointed up toward the icy blue sky.

22   There were no clouds but at first I didn't see the speck that came over the rim. It grew larger. Facing into the sun, so that the shadow did not go before him, the bird sped down the side of the mountain; a skier on the treetops, wings half-folded...like a brown bullet... faster and faster, toward the quail.

23   Granpa chuckled. "It's ol' Tal-con, the hawk."

24   The quail rose in a rush and sped into the trees—but one was slow. The hawk hit. Feathers flew into the air and then the birds were on the ground; the hawk's head rising and falling with the death blows. In a moment he rose with the dead quail clutched in his claws, back up the side of the mountain and over the rim.

25   I didn't cry, but I know I looked sad, because Granpa said, "Don't feel sad, Little Tree. It is The Way. Tal-con caught the slow and so the slow will raise no children who are also slow. Tal-con eats a thousand ground rats who eat the eggs of the quail—both the quick and the slow eggs—and so Tal-con lives by The Way. He helps the quail."

26   Granpa dug a sweet root from the ground with his knife and peeled it so that it dripped with its juicy winter cache of life. He cut it in half and handed me the heavy end.

27   "It is The Way," he said softly. "Take only what ye need. When ye take the deer, do not take the best. Take the smaller and the slower and then the deer will grow stronger and always give you meat. Pa-koh, the panther, knows and so must ye."

28   And he laughed, "Only Ti-bi, the bee, stores more than he can use ...and so he is robbed by the bear, and the 'coon...and the Cherokee. It is so with people who store and fat themselves with more than their share. They will have it taken from them. And there will be wars over it...and they will make long talks, trying to hold more than their share. They will say a flag stands for their right to do this ...and men will die because of the words and the flag...but they will not change the rules of The Way."

29   We went back down the trail, and the sun was high over us when we reached the turkey trap. We could hear them before we saw the trap. They were in there, gobbling and making loud whistles of alarm.

30   "Ain't no closing over the door, Granpa," I said. "Why don't they just lower their heads and come out?"

31   Granpa stretched full length into the hole and pulled out a big squawking turkey, tied his legs with a throng and grinned up at me.

32   "Ol' Tel-qui is like some people. Since he knows everything, he won't never look down to see what's around him. Got his head stuck up in the air too high to learn anything."...

33   Granpa laid them out on the ground, legs tied. There were six of them, and now he pointed down at them. "They're all about the same age...ye can tell by the thickness of the combs. We only need three so now ye choose, Little Tree."

34   I walked around them, flopping on the ground. I squatted and studied them, and walked around them again. I had to be careful. I got down on my hands and knees and crawled among them, until I had pulled out the three smallest I could find.

35   Granpa said nothing. He pulled the throngs from the legs of the others and they took to wing, beating down the side of the mountain. He slung two of the turkeys over his shoulder.

36   "Can ye carry the other?" he asked.

37   "Yes, sir," I said, not sure that I had done right. A slow grin broke Granpa's bony face. "If ye was not Little Tree...I would call ye Little Hawk."

38   I followed Granpa down the trail. The turkey was heavy, but it felt good over my shoulder. The sun had tilted toward the farther mountain and drifted through the branches of the trees beside the trail, making burnt gold patterns where we walked. The wind had died in that late afternoon of winter, and I heard Granpa, ahead of me, humming a tune. I would have liked to live that time forever... for I knew I had pleased Granpa. I had learned The Way.

Understanding the Content

Feel free to reread all or parts of the selection to answer the following questions.

1. Describe the relationship between Little Tree and his grandfather.

2. We are not told, but how old would you guess Little Tree was when these events occurred? What makes you think so?

3. Explain how Little Tree and his grandfather trapped the turkeys.

4. What does Little Tree's grandfather tell him about animals and people who take more than they can use?

5. Why does Granpa say in paragraph 37, "If ye was not Little Tree...I would call ye Little Hawk"?

6. What does Little Tree mean when he says, "I had learned 'The Way' "? What is "The Way"?

Looking at Structure and Style

1. While there is no stated thesis, how does Little Tree use narration to define "The Way"? Would the traditional essay form work just as well? Explain.

2. How do paragraphs 3–5 give us an insight into Granpa's character? What other paragraphs also develop the grandfather's character?

3. How do paragraphs 9 and 17, for example, reveal the author's feelings toward nature? What other paragraphs help develop this feeling?

4. Most of the narration is about Little Tree and his grandfather, but the author also tells us about his grandmother's character. What image of her does he present?

Evaluating the Author's Viewpoints

1. Reread paragraph 9. Do most people feel this way about the earth? Explain.

2. Why do you believe "The Way," as explained in the selection, does or does not makes sense?

3. Reread paragraph 28. Is the grandfather correct? Can you give any examples in history to support or refute his viewpoint?

4. In paragraph 32, Granpa makes an analogy between the squawking turkey and "some people." Is this a valid analogy? Explain it.

5. Is it possible to follow "The Way" in today's society? Explain.

Pursuing Possible Essay Topics

1. Explore in an essay how this country does or does not live by "The Way."

2. Write an essay about your relationship with one of your grandparents.

3. Have you ever experienced a moment, as Little Tree says (38), that you "would have liked to live...forever"? Write about it.

4. Write about a time when you pleased one of your parents but neither of you made a fuss about it.

5. Describe similarities or differences between the way you see things and the way your parents or grandparents do. What causes this difference?

6. Read the book from which this selection was taken, *The Education of Little Tree*, and write an essay reacting to a different passage from it.

7. Brainstorm or freewrite on one or more of the following:
   a. "The Way"
   b. TV families vs. real families
   c. parental teachings
   d. the perfect parent
   e. man's place/woman's place
   f. Earth Mother

8. If you don't like these, hunt up a topic of your own on family relationships.

Preparing to Read

Take a minute or two to look over the following reading selection. Note the title and author, read the first *two* paragraphs, and check the length. Make certain you have the time now to read it carefully and to do the exercises that follow it. Then, in the spaces provided, answer the following questions.

1. What do you think is the subject of this essay? _____

_____

2. What will the author probably say about mother love? _____

_____

_____

3. Do you think mother love is different from other types of love? Explain.

_____

_____

Vocabulary

Good comprehension of what you are about to read depends upon your understanding of the words below. The number following each word refers to the paragraph where it is used.

ambivalence (1) the state of having two conflicting feelings at the same time

infinite (3) endless

entrenches (3) fixes firmly and securely

stance (3) position

hailed (3) acclaimed, saluted

enigmatic (4) puzzling, confusing

articulate (4) express, make known

thwarted (4) prevented from taking place

matronly (7) motherly

invincible (8) not able to be conquered

inherent (8) existing as an essential characteristic

impaired (9) lessened the quality and intensity of

will-o'-the-wisp (9) a deceptive or misleading goal

touchstone (10) a test of value

pretense (10) a false appearance intended to deceive

Now read the essay.

Mother Love

NANCY FRIDAY

1   We are raised to believe that mother love is different from other kinds of love. It is not open to error, doubt, or the ambivalence of ordinary affections. This is an illusion.

2   Mothers may love their children, but they sometimes do not like them. The same woman who may be willing to put her body between her child and a runaway truck will often resent the day-by-day sacrifice the child unknowingly demands of her time, sexuality, and self-development.

3   A woman without a daughter may try to explore life's infinite possibilities. Her own mother left out so much. But when a daughter is born, fears she thought she had conquered long ago are re-aroused. Now there is another person, not simply dependent on her, but *like* her, and therefore subject to all the dangers she has fought all her life. The mother's progress into a larger sexuality is halted. Ground gained that she could have held alone is abandoned. She retreats and entrenches herself in the cramped female stance of security and defense. The position is fondly hailed as mother protector. It is the position of fear. She may be only half alive but she is safe, and so is her daughter. She now defines herself not as a woman but primarily as a mother. Sex is left out, hidden from the girl who must never think of her mother in danger: in sex. It is only with the greatest effort that the girl will be able to think of herself that way.

4   When women's lives were more predictable, we could more easily afford this enigmatic picture of womanhood. When we had no alter-

native but to repeat our mother's life, our mistakes and disappointments were pretty much confined to her space, her margin of error and unhappiness. I do believe our grandmothers, even our mothers, were happier; not knowing as much as we do and not having our options, there was less to be unhappy about. A woman might give up her sexuality, hate being a housewife, not like children, but if every woman was doing it, how could she articulate her frustration? She could feel it certainly, but you can't want what you don't know about. Television, for instance, gave them no sense of thwarted expectations. Today women's lives are changing at a rate and by a necessity we couldn't control if we wanted to; we need all the energy that suppression consumes. If we are going to fill more than women's traditional role, we can't afford the exhaustion that goes with constant emotional denial. There are pressures on women other than the "maternal instinct." They are the new economic and social demands. Even if we decide to lead our mothers' lives, the fact is that our daughter may not. We may continue, through denial and repression, to keep alive the idealization of motherhood for another generation, but where will that leave her?

5   If women are going to be lawyers as well as mothers, they must differentiate between the two, and then differentiate once again about their sexuality. That is the third—and *not* mutually exclusive—option. As the world changes, and women's place in it, mothers must consciously present this choice to their daughters. A woman may incorporate all three choices within herself—and even more—but at any given moment she must be able to say to herself and her daughter, "I chose to have you because I wanted to be a mother. I chose to work—to have a career, to be in politics, to play the piano—because that gives me a different feeling of value about myself, a value that is not greater nor lesser than motherhood, only different. Whether you choose to work or not, to be a mother or not, it will have nothing to do with your sexuality. Sexuality is the third option—as meaningful as either of the other two."

6   The truth is that the woman and the mother are often at war with one another—in the same body. Like so many women since the world began, my mother could not believe in this opposition of the two desires. Tradition, society, her parents, religion itself told her that there was no conflict; that motherhood was the logical and natural end product of sex. Instead of believing what every woman's body tells every woman's mind, that sexuality and eroticism are a fundamentally different and opposite drive to motherhood, my mother accepted the lie. She took as her act of faith the proposition that if she were a real woman, she would be a good mother and I would grow up the same. If I repeated her path and pattern of motherhood,

it would justify and place the final stamp of value on what she had done. It would say her attitude, behavior, and deepest feelings were not split, but were in fact in harmony, a woman in unison with nature.

7   Some women do make this choice gladly. They may be the majority, but my mother was not one of them. As I am not—her daughter in this too. Even in a good marriage, many women resent the matronly, nonsexual role their children force them to play. My mother didn't even have a good marriage; she was a young widow.

8   Frightened as she was, as much in need of my father as my sister and I were of her, mother had no choice but to pretend that my sister and I were the most important part of her life; that neither fear, youth and inexperience, loss, loneliness or her own needs could shake the unqualified and invincible love she felt for us. My mother had no body of woman-to-woman honesty and shared experience to use in her fight against the folk wisdom that said just being a woman carried all the inherent wisdom needed to be a mother—that it was either "natural" to her, or she was a failure as a woman.

9   In all the years we lived together, it is a shame we never talked honestly about our feelings. What neither of us knew then was that I could have stood honesty, no matter how frightening. Her angers, disillusionments, fears of failure, rage—emotions I seldom saw—I could have come to terms with them if she had been able to speak to me. I would have grown used to the idea that while mother loved me, at times other emotions impaired that love, and developed trust that in time her love for me would always return. Instead, I was left trying to believe in some perfect love she said she had for me, but in which I could not believe. I did not understand why I couldn't feel it no matter what her words said. I grew to believe that love itself, from her or anybody else, was a will-o'-the-wisp, coming or going for reasons I could not control. Never knowing when or why I was loved, I grew afraid to depend on it.

10   The older I get, the more of my mother I see in myself. The more opposite my life and my thinking grow from hers, the more of her I hear in my voice, see in my facial expression, feel in the emotional reactions I have come to recognize as my own. It is almost as if in extending myself, the circle closes in to completion. She was my first and most lasting model. To say her image is not still a touchstone in my life—and mine in hers—would be another lie. I am tired of lies. They have stood in the way of my understanding myself all my life. I have always known that what my husband loves most in me is that I have my own life. I have always felt that I had partially deceived him in this; I am very clever at pretense. My work, my marriage, and my new relationships with other women are beginning to make his assumptions about me true—that I am an independent, separate in-

dividual. They have allowed me to respect myself, and admire my own sex. What still stands between me and the person I would like to be is this illusion of perfect love between my mother and me. It is a lie I can no longer afford.

Understanding the Content

Feel free to reread all or parts off the selection to answer the following questions.

1. How does Friday define mother love? How is it different from or like other kinds of love?

2. What are the three options Friday says women have?

3. Friday says that "through denial and repression" women may "keep alive the idealization of motherhood" (4). What is this ideal she discusses? What is being denied and repressed?

4. What does Friday mean when she says that "the woman and the mother are often at war with one another—in the same body" (6)? What reasons for this does she give?

5. What "lie" does the author say she can no longer afford?

Looking at Structure and Style

1. How effective in getting your attention is Friday's opening paragraph? Why?

2. In paragraph 3, Friday discusses what often happens to a woman when she has a daughter. What is the function of paragraph 4?

3. Look carefully at paragraph 5. What writing method is used? Is it effective as structured?

4. Friday mentions her relationship with her own mother at times even though she is writing objectively about mother love. Are her subjective comments out of place or do they fit here? Explain.

5. What can you infer about the author's mother-daughter relationship?

6. Is Friday's intended audience only women? Explain.

Evaluating the Author's Viewpoints

1. Reread paragraph 1. Do you agree? Explain.

2. Friday discusses changes that women go through when they become mothers, changes that halt their growth as individuals. Which of these changes do you or don't you agree happen?

3. The author says that when women's lives were more predictable, a woman had "no alternative but to repeat [her] mother's life" (4). What does she mean? When were women's lives more predictable?

4. In paragraph 4, Friday says she believes "our grandmothers, even our mothers, were happier." What do you think?

5. How does Friday's view of mother love differ from that of her mother's?

Pursuing Possible Essay Topics

1. Use this line from Friday's essay to get you started: "The older I get, the more of my mother [father] I see in myself" (10).

2. Compare and contrast the way you and your mother might view mother love.

3. Write your own extended definition of mother love.

4. Write about a time in your life when you felt your father or mother didn't love you because he or she didn't live up to your image of a parent. Looking back, were you right or wrong? What did you learn from the incident?

5. Write about your relationship with your mother or father. How close are you? What have you experienced together? Can you be honest about your feelings and ideas with one another?

6. Have your feelings toward your mother [father] changed as you've gotten older? In what way? Why?

7. Brainstorm or freewrite on one or more of the following:

   a. motherhood/fatherhood   d. perfect love
   b. the perfect mom/dad   e. maternal instinct
   c. discussing sex with parents f. stereotyped parents

8. Forget these and come up with your own topic on some aspect of family relationships.

Student Essay

As you read the following student essay, look for answers to these questions:

1. Does the essay fit the assignment to write on some aspect of family and relationships?

2. Is there a thesis? If so, is it well supported?

3. How well written is the essay? Does it hold your interest?

In Defense of Motherhood

Rosa Avolio

1   In Nancy Friday's essay "Mother Love," she states:

> We are raised to believe that mother love is different from other kinds of love. It is not open to error, doubt, or the ambivalence of ordinary affections. This is an illusion.

Perhaps this is what Ms. Friday was raised to believe, but I wasn't. While I agree with her that women should not have babies just because "women are supposed to," Friday seems to think that women in general give up a part of their individuality when they become mothers in order to become some standard of motherhood set by society. Her comments make me wonder if she is a mother herself.

2   As a daughter as well as a mother of two, I know that mother love _is_ different from other kinds of love. Yes, I may have given up some things in expectation of others, but that happens to both men and women when certain life choices are made. We can't have it all in life. My choice to become a mother wasn't made because it was expected of me. My husband and I wanted to have a family. And our decision was worth it.

3   Certainly, motherhood sometimes has its down side. Staying up all night with a sick child is no fun. Preparing the meals and doing the dishes for a family of four is not always easy. Staying home with the kids instead of going out when you'd like sometimes feels confining. Worrying about finances for a decent house, clothes, and health care can be draining. But I expected those things when I decided to have a family.

4   What I've gained from being a mother far outweighs the negative. Motherhood is something very special. My pleasure comes

from watching my children take the first steps or say "momma" for the first time with recognition. I enjoy watching them learn anything new. To see their eyes widen with excitement on Christmas morning or to hold them and help soothe the hurt from a fall is all part of the joy of being a mother.

5   No one can explain truly what it is like to get up twice a night to nurse a crying baby, but neither can they describe the wonderful feeling of holding that baby in your arms and nourishing it from your own body. Watching that baby grow and develop daily, I sometimes wanted to stop the clock to be able to savor a special time.

6   I have never felt that my children intruded on a happy marriage, rather, they enhanced it. We're a family now instead of a couple. I'm not saying all couples should have children. But if you decide to, don't feel that you have to be a super mom. You only have to enjoy your children and help them grow and develop.

Reaction

In the space below, write your reaction to the essay. What would you tell the student about her essay?

Commentary

Avolio's essay begins very well. She correctly identifies the author and the essay to which she is reacting. She also correctly uses a block quotation because of the length of the passage from Friday's essay. However, although her sentence structure and paragraphing are acceptable, her thesis and support need some help.

Notice that Avolio's essay really has little to do with the passage she quotes. She says she agrees with Friday about not having children unless you want to, but disagrees that women give up part of their individuality in order to meet some social standard. Then she ends her paragraph by wondering if Friday is a mother herself. The problem here is that Avolio has drifted away from responding to the quote she cites. If you look at that quotation, you will see that her essay has little to do with Friday's comments about the illusion of mother love.

In paragraph 2, Avolio starts to discuss mother love by disagreeing with Friday's excerpt. But again Avolio drifts away with remarks that have nothing to do with mother love—at least not as she states them.

Avolio's paragraph 3 is a good, tight paragraph showing the examples of the "down side" of motherhood. Alone the paragraph is acceptable, but again she does not relate any of this to Friday's comments about mother love.

In paragraphs 4 and 5, we get examples of the positive side of having children. But what has this to do with the illusion of mother love that Nancy Friday discusses?

Rosa's last paragraph has three unrelated points: that her children have enhanced her marriage; that she doesn't recommend that all couples have children; and that if you do have children, don't feel you have to be a "super mom." (This last comment limits her audience to women.) In addition, each of these three points needs more development than she gives here. If Avolio wanted, she could write an essay based on those three points. But that would make it an entirely different essay, since none of the points has any direct bearing on the Friday quotation used in the opening. Also, her last sentence makes a difficult task sound rather simple.

Avolio no doubt dislikes some of what Nancy Friday has to say about mothers and mother love. Reacting to what she read is a good place to start. But Avolio never develops what she starts out to say and ends up writing about other things. Thus we are left with an unclear thesis.

The essay was returned to Avolio for revision with the suggestion that she either clarify what she disagrees with in the Nancy Friday quote and then support her own position better, or that she use the three points in her last paragraph as a basis for a different essay altogether.

Viewpoints on Work

*"Every man's work,
whether it be literature or
music or picture or
architecture or
anything else, is always
a portrait of himself."*
Samuel Butler

*F*OR MANY PEOPLE the real reason for working is not the work itself but the money or the status or the power the work may bring. Sociologists claim that the average person more or less puts up with a job because of personal and family needs that are considered to be more important, such as food, clothing, and shelter.

The style of our lives is often based on the type of work we do. Some jobs allow for flexible schedules, which mean we can take advantage of convenient times to meet personal or family needs; on the other hand, flexible schedules can be a disadvantage if we decide to take our work home with us. Other jobs are inflexible, even requiring us to punch time clocks. Such work means we cannot easily take time off to tend to personal or family needs, leaving only evenings and weekends. Yet, in those cases work can be left behind at the job site. The time that we have for ourselves and family, then, is determined by the type of job we have.

The work we do not only determines the quality of our lives by shaping our time, our leisure, our buying power, our ability to travel; it even shapes our identities. When we meet someone for the first time, we generally ask, "What do you do?" The meaning behind the question is understood: "What do you do for a living?" And when the answer is waitress, police officer, doctor, writer, sales clerk, or whatever, we generally categorize that person to fit our stereotype of that particular jobholder.

As our economy changes, so do our jobs. Many of us find we must move from community to community to keep up with jobs that require our skills or to find new ones when laid off. Many of us attend college in preparation for a particular line of work only to discover that there are no positions available, or to realize that what we've prepared for is not what we really want to do. Many of us who have been in the same job for years suddenly find we must go back to school to retrain in order to meet the advancements made in our field.

Changes in traditional family roles are also changing over work habits. Some men are discovering they would rather stay home and raise their children while their wives go off to work. Many women are realizing they prefer a career to the traditional mother or housewife role. Such changes are redefining the term *homemaker*.

The reading selections in this unit supply a wide range of viewpoints toward work, from how to go for a job interview to attempts at defining what "real work" is. Use them to discover and to stimulate your own view on work.

Preparing to Read

Take a minute or two to look over the following reading selection. Note the title and author, read the opening paragraph, and check the length. Make certain you have the time now to read it carefully and to do the exercises that follow it. Then, in the spaces provided, answer the following questions.

1. What is the subject of the essay? _____

   _____

2. What do you think you will learn from reading this selection? _____

   _____

   _____

Vocabulary

Good comprehension of what you are about to read depends upon your understanding of the words below. The number following each word refers to the paragraph where it is used.

recruiter (1) a person who seeks out new employees (or members or students)

corporate headquarters (1) the main offices of a large corporation

cubicle (3) a small room or partitioned-off area

branch office (3) a smaller office set up away from the main corporate headquarters, usually in another city or country

deteriorates (10) declines, worsens

Laurel and Hardy (10) a famous comedy team in the '30s and '40s

résumé (13) a summary of work qualifications and experience

screening (15) separating out unsuitable candidates

sidewinderlike (21) like a rattlesnake, moving in sideways loops

strenuously (30) forcefully, vigorously

adamant (35) inflexible, firm of mind, unyielding

Now read the essay.

How to Take a Job Interview

KIRBY W. STANAT

1   To succeed in campus job interviews, you have to know where that recruiter is coming from. The simple answer is that he is coming from corporate headquarters.

2   That may sound obvious, but it is a significant point that too many students do not consider. The recruiter is not a free spirit as he flies from Berkeley to New Haven, from Chapel Hill to Boulder. He's on an invisible leash to the office, and if he is worth his salary, he is mentally in corporate headquarters all the time he's on the road.

3   If you can fix that in your mind—that when you walk into that bare-walled cubicle in the placement center you are walking into a branch office of Sears, Bendix or General Motors—you can avoid a lot of little mistakes and maybe some big ones.

4   If, for example, you assume that because the interview is on campus the recruiter expects you to look and act like a student, you're in for a shock. A student is somebody who drinks beer, wears blue jeans and throws a Frisbee. No recruiter has jobs for student Frisbee whizzes.

5   A cool spring day in late March, Sam Davis, a good recruiter who has been on the college circuit for years, is on my campus talking to candidates. He comes out to the waiting area to meet the student who signed up for an 11 o'clock interview. I'm standing in the doorway of my office taking in the scene.

6   Sam calls the candidate: "Sidney Student." There sits Sidney. He's at a 45 degree angle, his feet are in the aisle, and he's almost lying down. He's wearing well-polished brown shoes, a tasteful pair of brown pants, a light brown shirt, and a good looking tie. Unfor-

tunately, he tops off this well-coordinated outfit with his Joe's Tavern Class A Softball Championship jacket, which has a big woven emblem over the heart.

7   If that isn't bad enough, in his left hand is a cigarette and in his right hand is a half-eaten apple.

8   When Sam calls his name, the kid is caught off guard. He ditches the cigarette in an ashtray, struggles to his feet, and transfers the apple from the right to the left hand. Apple juice is everywhere, so Sid wipes his hand on the seat of his pants and shakes hands with Sam.

9   Sam, who by now is close to having a stroke, gives me that what-do-I-have-here look and has the young man follow him into the interviewing room.

10   The situation deteriorates even further—into pure Laurel and Hardy. The kid is stuck with the half-eaten apple, doesn't know what to do with it, and obviously is suffering some discomfort. He carries the apple into the interviewing room with him and places it in the ashtray on the desk—right on top of Sam's freshly lit cigarette.

11   The interview lasts five minutes. . . .

12   Let us move in for a closer look at how the campus recruiter operates.

13   Let's say you have a 10 o'clock appointment with the recruiter from the XYZ Corporation. The recruiter gets rid of the candidate in front of you at about 5 minutes to 10, jots down a few notes about what he is going to do with him or her, then picks up your résumé or data sheet (which you have submitted in advance). . . .

14   Although the recruiter is still in the interview room and you are still in the lobby, your interview is under way. You're on. The recruiter will look over your sheet pretty carefully before he goes out to call you. He develops a mental picture of you.

15   He thinks, "I'm going to enjoy talking with this kid," or "This one's going to be a turkey." The recruiter has already begun to make a screening decision about you.

16   His first impression of you, from reading the sheet, could come from your grade point. It could come from misspelled words. It could come from poor erasures or from the fact that necessary information is missing. By the time the recruiter has finished reading your sheet, you've already hit the plus or minus column.

17   Let's assume the recruiter got a fairly good impression from your sheet.

18   Now the recruiter goes out to the lobby to meet you. He almost shuffles along, and his mind is somewhere else. Then he calls your name, and at that instant he visibly clicks into gear. He just went to work.

19   As he calls your name he looks quickly around the room, waiting for somebody to move. If you are sitting on the middle of your back, with a book open and a cigarette going, and if you have to rebuild yourself to stand up, the interest will run right out of the recruiter's face. You, not the recruiter, made the appointment for 10 o'clock, and the recruiter expects to see a young professional come popping out of that chair like today is a good day and you're anxious to meet him.

20   At this point, the recruiter does something rude. He doesn't walk across the room to meet you halfway. He waits for you to come to him. Something very important is happening. He wants to see you move. He wants to get an impression about your posture, your stride, and your briskness.

21   If you slouch over him, sidewinderlike, he is not going to be impressed. He'll figure you would probably slouch your way through your workdays. He wants you to come at him with lots of good things going for you. If you watch the recruiter's eyes, you can see the inspection. He glances quickly at shoes, pants, coat, shirt; dress, blouse, hose—the whole works.

22   After introducing himself, the recruiter will probably say, "Okay, please follow me," and he'll lead you into his interviewing room.

23   When you get to the room, you may find that the recruiter will open the door and gesture you in—with him blocking part of the doorway. There's enough room for you to get past him, but it's a near thing.

24   As you scrape past, he gives you a closeup inspection. He looks at your hair; if it's greasy, that will bother him. He looks at your collar; if it's dirty, that will bother him. He looks at your shoulders; if they're covered with dandruff, that will bother him. If you're a man, he looks at your chin. If you didn't get a close shave, that will irritate him. If you're a woman, he checks your makeup. If it's too heavy, he won't like it.

25   Then he smells you. An amazing number of people smell bad. Occasionally a recruiter meets a student who smells like a canal horse. That student can expect an interview of about four or five minutes.

26   Next the recruiter inspects the back side of you. He checks your hair (is it combed in front but not in back?), he checks your heels (are they run down?), your pants (are they baggy?), your slip (is it showing?), your stockings (do they have runs?).

27   Then he invites you to sit down.

28   At this point, I submit, the recruiter's decision on you is 75 to 80 percent made.

29   Think about it. The recruiter has read your résumé. He knows who you are and where you are from. He knows your marital status,

your major and your grade point. And he knows what you have done with your summers. He has inspected you, exchanged greetings with you and smelled you. There is very little additional hard information that he must gather on you. From now on it's mostly body chemistry.

30   Many recruiters have argued strenuously with me that they don't make such hasty decisions. So I tried an experiment. I told several recruiters that I would hang around in the hall outside the interview room when they took candidates in.

31   I told them that as soon as they had definitely decided not to recommend (to department managers in their companies) the candidate they were interviewing, they should snap their fingers loud enough for me to hear. It went like this.

32   First candidate: 38 seconds after the candidate sat down: Snap!

33   Second candidate: 1 minute, 42 seconds: Snap!

34   Third candidate: 45 seconds: Snap!

35   One recruiter was particularly adamant, insisting that he didn't rush to judgment on candidates. I asked him to participate in the snapping experiment. He went out in the lobby, picked up his first candidate of the day, and headed for an interview room.

36   As he passed me in the hall, he glared at me. And his fingers went "Snap!"

Understanding the Content

Feel free to reread all or parts of the selection to answer the following questions.

1. According to Stanat, how should you dress for an interview on a college campus? Why?

2. Where and how do some recruiters technically begin the interview?

3. Why won't some interviewers walk across the waiting room to meet you halfway when it's your turn for an interview?

4. Why do some recruiters seem to block the doorway when you are called into the interviewing room?

5. According to Stanat, what percent of a recruiter's mind is made up by the time you sit down for your interview?

6. What is Stanat's thesis? Is is implied or stated?

Looking at Structure and Style

1. How do paragraphs 5–11 help Stanat develop his thesis? What advice regarding job interview techniques is being implied in these paragraphs?

2. What is the function of paragraph 12?

3. Paragraphs 13–28 reveal the way a recruiter works. What are each of the steps? Why do you think Stanat uses the point of view of the recruiter rather than the person being interviewed?

4. What transitional devices does Stanat use to move us smoothly through the essay?

5. The author uses short sentences and paragraphs on the whole. Is such writing effective in this case? Explain.

6. How would you describe Stanat's tone? What are some examples of words or phrases that establish his tone?

7. To what specific audience is Stanat writing? Does the tone fit?

Evaluating the Author's Viewpoints

1. Stanat states that college students often don't consider the way they dress for interviews. Do you feel that dress and appearance are important job screening criteria? Explain.

2. Look at each of the steps you listed in question 3 above. Does Stanat exaggerate each step's importance? Explain.

3. Stanat says that by the time you are invited to sit down, a "recruiter's decision on you is 75 to 80 percent made" (28). Do you think this is true? Why?

4. The author implies that the actual interview itself may not be as important as your body language and chemistry. How do you react to this? Does Stanat provide enough evidence to make his implication factual?

Pursuing Possible Essay Topics

1. Think about a time when you wanted to make a good appearance but botched it up. Try writing an essay that uses some of the devices Stanat uses in paragraphs 5–11 to relate your experience comically. Try to imply your thesis rather than state it.

2. Write an essay that reflects all of the qualifications and experience you have for a job you are interested in. Your audience is your potential employer.

3. Using all the steps Stanat provides but with a more formal tone than Stanat uses, write an essay that deals with how to take a job interview.

4. Write about a time when you didn't get a job you applied for. Why do you think you didn't get it? How did you feel? What did you learn that will help you in the future?

5. If you are already working, write an essay directed to someone new on the job. Provide advice on how best to get the work done, how to get along with the boss and fellow employees, or how to do a specific task.

6. Write an essay that begins where Stanat stops: the interview itself. Provide practical advice for the actual interview. Try matching his tone and writing style.

7. Brainstorm or freewrite on one or more of the following:

   a. résumé   d. your dream job
   b. job interview   e. school vs. work
   c. job preparation f. your first job

8. Ignore these and recruit your own topic that deals with some aspect of work.

Preparing to Read

Take a minute or two to look over the following reading selection. Note the title and author, read the opening paragraph, and check the length. Make certain you have the time now to read it carefully and to do the exercises that follow it. Then, in the spaces provided, answer the following questions.

1. What is the difference between harassment and sexual harassment? ___

_____

_____

2. What do you think the essay will say about sexual harassment at work?

_____

_____

3. What might you learn from reading this essay? _____

_____

_____

Vocabulary

Good comprehension of what you are about to read depends upon your understanding of the words below. The number following each word refers to the paragraph where it is used.

hostile (1) warlike, combative, dangerous

intimidating (1) threatening, discouraging

EEOC (3) Equal Employment Opportunity Commission

subordinate (4) one with a lesser position

insinuation (9) hint, suggestion

chic (15) fashionable, stylish

snide (18) nasty, insulting

CEOs (22) chief executive officers of a company

Now read the essay.

A Primary Lesson in Sexual Harassment

KATHLEEN NEVILLE

1   There are two main types of sexual harassment: *quid pro quo* (you give me this, I'll give you that) and *hostile work environment* (an intimidating, hostile, or offensive atmosphere). It is not always necessary that the employer or supervisor be specifically aware that he or she is inflicting one of these types of sexual harassment upon an employee. For example: Someone said to me once that he couldn't have possibly committed an act of quid pro quo sexual harassment because he didn't know what it meant. And even others have attempted to convince themselves that they are not guilty of contributing to a hostile work environment because they are very quiet and not at all hostile about the way they bother and annoy the same person day-after-day.

2   Once individuals understand what these two types of behaviors are, they must also understand all the different faces they may have in the workplace. Many specific types of acts fall between these two broad categories—and it is between those wide cracks that the confusion begins and remains.

A Closer Look at Definitions

3   To simplify what the EEOC guidelines are is to put the definition of sexual harassment in another way.

The Power Threat

4   Quid pro quo is all about using the power one individual has over another for the sake of personal gain or enjoyment. You simply can't ask a subordinate or coworker to sleep with you in order for him or

her to receive a raise, or perk, get a promotion, or have better working conditions than other employees. Nor can you ask that person to sleep with you to avoid losing his/her job. That's a threat and a form of sexual blackmail.

The Polluter

5   Those individuals who help create a workplace environment that is unsuitable for other people to work in because such individuals are continually and repeatedly exposing others to sexual remarks, gestures, suggestive pictures or pornography are polluters of the workplace atmosphere and guilty of sexual harassment.

6   You can't bother others at work continuously by saying or doing things of a sexual nature so that you annoy, upset, or offend them to the point of interfering with their job or the jobs of those around them. That's why this second type of sexual harassment is appropriately termed "hostile work environment"—because it causes great anxiety and ultimately a good deal of antagonism within the workplace environment. And people can't work effectively if they feel as though a "sexual war" is going on all around them. They certainly can't be productive if they happen to be targets of such abusive behavior.

Some Ground Rules

7   Because the two types of sexual harassment are general behavior patterns, there are specific kinds of behavior which should not take place in the workplace.

8   **Inappropriate Remarks/Shades of Implication.** You should not refer to a coworker or a subordinate as a sexual human being or refer to his/her physical looks in a sexual manner. Telling a coworker she has nice legs is out of place at work. Telling a coworker you had a dream about him last night is also out of place. Any thoughts of a sexual nature should be kept to yourself.

9   **Sexual Generalizations/Sexual Put-downs.** You should not make any insinuation that others at work are of less quality or ability because of their sex. Although the issue of discrimination has been discussed widely and is strongly discouraged in today's companies, it still is going on—and sometimes is coupled with shades of sexual harassment.

10   **Terms of Endearment.** Calling any coworker or subordinate such names as "cutie," "blondie," "honey," "dear," or "sweetie," should be avoided in the working environment. Sometimes they are harmless expressions of affection for a subordinate, but they are just not acceptable for addressing another employee. They are intimate terms, not workplace names.

11   **By Any Other Name Is Just Not the Same.** No nicknames for coworkers or subordinates that you or anyone else thought of—are allowed at work. Nicknames are acceptable only when an employee insists that you call him or her by his or her own chosen nickname and the self-chosen name is appropriate for the workplace.

12   **Danger Zones and Out-of-Bound Compliments.** You may tell someone how nice he or she looks—if you say exactly that. But if you dare to get creative or specific in your compliment, you may cross the border of good taste and sexual harassment. Remember that you need to be concerned with what the other individual's own personal definition of sexual harassment is. For example, if you tell someone else you like the way her dress fits rather than just complimenting her on how nice she looks, you are knowingly or unknowingly implying something to her. Keep your compliments general and sincere—and safe.

13   **The Body Snatchers.** These people are the body adjusters or the fashion police of the workplace. They pick at lint, adjust hair ornaments, snap men's suspenders, touch and pull on men's ties, play with jewelry, adjust belts, smooth shoulder pads, straighten hemlines, and generally touch other people at work. It is an invasion of the person being "pulled at and pawed" and can sometimes be very unwelcome. It's a kindergarten rule for sure, but keep your hands to yourself.

14   **Corporate Kissing.** The general rule in the workplace is NO KISSING. I disagree with those who loosely say that kissing at work is okay. Kissing is defined as a caress or a salutation. In the corporate world it can also mean either—and that is where the trouble starts. Unless your relationship with the person is an established and comfortable friendship that has been built and developed beyond and outside your professional relationship, I don't recommend kissing as a form of greeting a business associate. A good rule to follow is to ask yourself if the person you are leaning over to kiss gingerly is someone who has authority or power to alter or change any short- or long-term aspects of your job.

15   Chances are, most people can get by just fine without kissing coworkers, clients, or bosses. Although some people believe it is very chic to spring a light kiss on someone before getting down to business, many others insist that it says a lot more about the person's genuine character, not to mention professionalism, when they don't kiss you hello but rather offer a warm and sincere handshake, instead of a kiss.

16   **Rubbing Others the Wrong Way.** These forms of physical contact don't really need any explanation. They simply don't belong in the workplace:

back rubbing
leg rubbing
knee touching
leaning
embracing
handholding
bumping or brushing up against another person

17   **Guilty Eyes**. Prolonged staring at a coworker or subordinate can be termed sexual harassment if it begins to interfere with the person's work. It is another nonverbal form of sexual harassment.

18   **Dr. Heckle and Mr. Snide**. Taunting and teasing another employee amounts to something called "heckling," which can easily amount to sexual harassment. "But I was just teasing" is the common defense of those who step over the line of friendly chiding. On the not-so-friendly side is the continuous act of delivering snide remarks to another employee that come in the form of "sexual snides." This type of behavior falls well within the category of hostile work environment.

19   **Blaming It on Uncle Guido**. One of the most common excuses for unacceptable behavior on the job is the one used by the person who insists that he or she can't stop his or her own behavior. "Hey, what can I say, it's in my blood. I'm Italian; we just naturally act this way." Blaming your behavior on your ethnic background probably would not please your ancestors or relatives in the least.

Sexual Harassment Outside the Workplace

20   Sexual harassment can and does take place outside the workplace. Often, someone harassing someone at work will continue to do it in other places and in other ways. Such behavior may include making unwanted visits to someone's home, calling the person repeatedly, sending the person letters—and sexually harassing the person while traveling together on business. Many victims of sexual harassment have told me about their discomfort and fear of being sexually harassed on a business trip.

21   Just because it doesn't happen in the office doesn't mean the offender isn't liable for his or her actions. It's still sexual harassment of another employee.

WHO'S HARASSING WHOM—AND WHERE?

22   There is no stereotype when it comes to sexual harassment. Those who engage in it range from men and women suffering from serious mental illness to those who are merely unaware or culturally and socially ignorant of their inappropriate behavior. And harassers can

take any form. They can be a line supervisor in a factory, CEOs of a Fortune 500 firm, artists, doctors, human resource specialists, accountants, film producers, repairmen, sales managers, lawyers, teachers, bankers or dispatchers. They can be extremely powerful and highly educated people or people without professional degrees; the person can be someone who is quiet or someone who is outgoing. The person could be married or single; rich or poor, good-looking or unattractive, well dressed or slovenly. It could be anyone.

23   And sexual harassment is found in large corporations, small businesses, factories, hospitals, human resource offices, government offices, military services, retail stores, art departments, shoe departments, law firms, real estate offices, construction sites, insurance offices, schools, television repair shops; in banks, network television offices; in coal mines, out on utility poles, inside operating rooms, on ships and in restaurants. It exists everywhere in the working world and no particular industry can claim that it is free of the behavior.

Understanding the Content

Feel free to reread all or parts of the selection in order to answer the following questions.

1. What are the two main types of sexual harassment? How do they differ?

2. Name at least six different kinds of behavior that should not take place at work. Why are they considered sexual harassment?

3. Why does Neville disagree with those who feel kissing on the workplace is okay?

4. What types of sexual harassment can take place outside the workplace?

5. What does Neville mean when she says, "There is no stereotype when it comes to sexual harassment" (22)?

6. Where is sexual harassment found?

Looking at Structure and Style

1. Why does Neville use the words "primary lesson" in her title? What is the implication regarding what she doesn't say in the essay?

2. How well does Neville define and differentiate the two types of sexual harassment? By what means does she define her terms?

3. Neville begins some of her paragraphs with bold faced words and phrases, some of them "a play on words," such as **The Body Snatchers**, a play on the title of a movie by that name. What are some other examples of her playing on words?

4. To what audience does Neville write: men, women, or both? Explain.

5. In the last paragraph, the author lists many workplaces where sexual harassment occurs. Why does she do this? Is it effective? Explain.

6. How well does Neville establish a thesis? Is it stated or implied? If stated, where?

Evaluating the Author's Viewpoints

1. In paragraph 1, Neville states, "Someone said to me once that he couldn't have possibly committed an act of quid pro quo sexual harassment because he didn't know what it meant." Why doesn't she accept this excuse? Is she justified?

2. Neville lists many different types of sexual harassment. Has she mentioned any that you do *not* believe should be so labeled? Explain.

3. Neville says that those people who engage in sexual harassment range from the mentally ill to the culturally or socially ignorant. Do you agree? Explain.

4. Reread the last sentence. Do you agree? Why?

Pursuing Possible Essay Topics

1. In the May 1991 issue of *Mademoiselle*, an article dealing with sexual harassment says at one point, "Sexual harassment in all its wondrous forms is still a fact of life. But try to avoid charging your superiors with sexism—it is the most dangerous of weapons." Is this good advice? Write an essay on the perils of charging your boss with sexual harassment.

2. In the October 1991, media in the United States were filled with stories about Professor Anita Hill's charges of sexual harassment brought against Clarence Thomas, a nominee to be a U.S. Supreme Court Justice. The country was divided over who to believe, but after a televised hearing, the Senate voted 52–48 to confirm Thomas's appointment. Look through the *Reader's Guide to Periodical Literature* for that month and the next, and find some sources that recount statements of those who believed Hill's charges and those who believed Thomas's denials. Then use the sources to write an essay that expresses your reaction to the results. How would you have voted? Why?

3. Write an essay about your own experiences with sexual harassment on or off the job.

4. Explain in an essay why proven sexual harassment should or should not involve punitive damages.

5. Brainstorm or freewrite on one or more of the following:
   a. working relationships   d. verbal abuse

b. unequal pay for women   e. sexual arrogance
c. gender relationships   f. hostile working environment

6. Sever yourself from these ideas and search for a topic on your own that deals with some aspect of work relationships.

📖 Preparing to Read

Take a minute or two to look over the following reading selection. Note the title and author, read the opening paragraph, and check the length. Make certain you have the time now to read it carefully and to do the exercises that follow it. Then, in the spaces provided, answer the following questions.

1. What does the title lead you to think is the subject of the essay? _____

_____

2. To what audience do you think the essay is aimed? Why? _____

_____

3. What might you learn from reading this selection? _____

_____

Vocabulary

Good comprehension of what you are about to read depends upon your understanding of the words below. The number following each word refers to the paragraph where it is used.

detriment (2) harm, injury

spate (3) a sudden rush or outpouring

inevitable (4) definite, unavoidable

statutory right (7) a privilege guaranteed by law

workaholism (9) addiction to work

innovative (10) new, original

sabbaticals (10) leaves of absence, often with some pay, usually granted every seventh year

deleterious (15) harmful, detrimental

docile (17) pliable, yielding, meek

pits (21) puts one against another

Now read the essay.

Less Is More: A Call for Shorter Work Hours

BARBARA BRANDT

1   America is suffering from overwork. Too many of us are too busy, trying to squeeze more into each day while having less to show for it. Although our growing time crunch is often portrayed as a personal dilemma, it is in fact a major social problem that has reached crisis proportions over the past 20 years.

2   The simple fact is that Americans today—both women and men— are spending too much time at work, to the detriment of their homes, their families, their personal lives, and their communities. The American Dream promised that our individual hard work paired with the advances of modern technology would bring about the good life for all. Glorious visions of the leisure society were touted throughout the '50s and '60s. But now most people are working more than ever before, while still struggling to meet their economic commitments. Ironically, the many advances in technology, such as computers and fax machines, rather than reducing our workload, seem to have speeded up our lives at work. At the same time, technology has equipped us with "conveniences" like microwave ovens and frozen dinners that merely enable us to adopt a similar frantic pace in our home lives so we can cope with more hours at paid work.

3   A recent spate of articles in the mainstream media has focused on the new problems of overwork and lack of time. Unfortunately, overwork is often portrayed as a special problem of yuppies and professionals on the fast track. In reality, the unequal distribution of work and time in America today reflects the decline in both standard of living and quality of life for most Americans. Families whose members never see each other, women who work a double shift (first on the job, then at home), workers who need more flexible work schedules, and unemployed and underemployed people who need more work are all casualties of the crisis of overwork.

4   Americans often assume that overwork is an inevitable fact of life—like death and taxes. Yet a closer look at other times and other nations offers some startling surprises.

5   Anthropologists have observed that in pre-industrial (particularly hunting and gathering) societies, people generally spend 3 to 4 hours a day, 15 to 20 hours a week, doing the work necessary to maintain life. The rest of the time is spent in socializing, partying, playing, storytelling, and artistic or religious activities. The ancient Romans

celebrated 175 public festivals a year in which everyone participated, and people in the Middle Ages had at least 115.

6   In our era, almost every other industrialized nation (except Japan) has fewer annual working hours and longer vacations than the United States. This includes all of Western Europe, where many nations enjoy thriving economies and standards of living equal to or higher than ours. Jeremy Brecher and Tim Costello, writing in *Z Magazine* (Oct. 1990), note that "European unions during the 1980s made a powerful and largely successful push to cut working hours. In 1987 German metalworkers struck and won a 37.5-hour week; many are now winning a 35-hour week. In 1990, hundreds of thousands of British workers have won a 37-hour week."

7   In an article about work-time in the *Boston Globe*, Suzanne Gordon notes that workers in other industrialized countries "enjoy—as a statutory right—longer vacations [than in the U.S.] from the moment they enter the work force. In Canada, workers are legally entitled to two weeks off their first year on the job. . . . After two or three years of employment, most get three weeks of vacation. After 10 years, it's up to four, and by 20 years, Canadian workers are off for five weeks. In Germany, statutes guarantee 18 days minimum for everyone, but most workers get five or six weeks. The same is true in Scandinavian countries, and in France."

8   In contrast to the extreme American emphasis on productivity and commitment, which results in many workers, especially in professional-level jobs, not taking the vacations coming to them, Gordon notes that "In countries that are America's most successful competitors in the global marketplace, all working people, whether lawyers or teachers, CEOs or janitors, take the vacations to which they are entitled by law. 'No one in West Germany,' a West German embassy's officer explains, 'no matter how high up they are, would ever say they couldn't afford to take a vacation. Everyone takes their vacation.' "

9   And in Japan, where dedication to the job is legendary, Gordon notes that the Japanese themselves are beginning to consider their national workaholism a serious social problem leading to stress-related illnesses and even death. As a result, the Japanese government recently established a commission whose goal is to promote shorter working hours and more leisure time.

10   Most other industrialized nations also have better family-leave policies than the United States, and in a number of other countries workers benefit from innovative time-scheduling opportunities such as sabbaticals.

11   While the idea of a shorter workweek and longer vacations sounds appealing to most people, any movement to enact shorter work-time

as a public policy will encounter surprising pockets of resistance, not just from business leaders but even from some workers. Perhaps the most formidable barrier to more free time for Americans is the widespread mind-set that the 40-hour workweek, 8 hours a day, 5 days a week, 50 weeks a year, is a natural rhythm of the universe. This view is reinforced by the media's complete silence regarding the shorter work-time and more favorable vacation and family-leave policies of other countries. This lack of information, and our leaders' reluctance to suggest that the United States can learn from any other nation (except workaholic Japan) is one reason why more Americans don't identify overwork as a major problem or clamor for fewer hours and more vacation. Monika Bauerlein, a journalist originally from Germany now living in Minneapolis, exclaims, "I can't believe that people here aren't rioting in the streets over having only two weeks of vacation a year."

12   A second obstacle to launching a powerful shorter work-time movement is America's deeply ingrained work ethic, or its modern incarnation, the workaholic syndrome. The work ethic fosters the widely held belief that people's work is their most important activity and that people who do not work long and hard are lazy, unproductive, and worthless.

13   For many Americans today, paid work is not just a way to make money but is a crucial source of their self-worth. Many of us identify ourselves almost entirely by the kind of work we do. Work still has a powerful psychological and spiritual hold over our lives—and talk of shorter work-time may seem somehow morally suspicious.

14   Because we are so deeply a work-oriented society, leisure-time activities—such as play, relaxation, engaging in cultural and artistic pursuits, or just quiet contemplation and "doing nothing"—are not looked on as essential and worthwhile components of life. Of course, for the majority of working women who must work a second shift at home, much of the time spent outside of paid work is not leisure anyway. Also much of our non-work time is spent not just in personal renewal, but in building and maintaining essential social ties—with family, friends, and the larger community.

15   Today, as mothers and fathers spend more and more time on the job, we are beginning to recognize the deleterious effects—especially on our young people—of the breakdown of social ties and community in American life. But unfortunately, our nation reacts to these problems by calling for more paid professionals—more police, more psychiatrists, more experts—without recognizing the possibility that shorter work hours and more free time could enable us to do much of the necessary rebuilding and healing, with much more gratifying and longer-lasting results.

16   Of course, the stiffest opposition to cutting work hours comes not from citizens but from business. Employers are reluctant to alter the 8-hour day, 40-hour workweek, 50 weeks a year because it seems easier and more profitable for employers to hire fewer employees for longer hours rather than more employees—each of whom would also require health insurance and other benefits—with flexible schedules and work arrangements.

17   Harvard University economist Juliet B. Schor, who has been studying issues of work and leisure in America, reminds us that we cannot ignore the larger relationship between unemployment and overwork: While many of us work too much, others are unable to find paid work at all. Schor points out that "workers who work longer hours lose more income when they lose their jobs. The threat of job loss is an important determinant of management's power on the shop floor." A system that offers only two options—long work hours or unemployment—serves as both a carrot and a stick. Those lucky enough to get full-time jobs are bribed into docile compliance with the boss, while the spectre of unemployment always looms as the ultimate punishment for the unruly.

18   Some observers suggest that keeping people divided into "the employed" and "the unemployed" creates feelings of resentment and inferiority/superiority between the two groups, thus focusing their discontent and blame on each other rather than on the corporations and political figures who actually dictate our nation's economic policies.

19   Our role as consumers contributes to keeping the average work week from falling. In an economic system in which addictive buying is the basis of corporate profits, working a full 40 hours or more each week for 50 weeks a year gives us just enough time to stumble home and dazedly—almost automatically—shop; but not enough time to think about deeper issues or to work effectively for social change. From the point of view of corporations and policymakers, shorter worktime may be bad for the economy, because people with enhanced free time may begin to find other things to do with it besides mindlessly buying products. It takes more free time to grow vegetables, cook meals from scratch, sew clothes, or repair broken items than it does to just buy these things at the mall.

20   Any serious proposal to give employed Americans a break by cutting into the eight-hour work day is certain to be met with anguished cries about international competitiveness. The United States seems gripped by the fear that our nation has lost its economic dominance, and pundits, policymakers, and business leaders tell us that no sacrifice is too great if it puts America on top again.

21   As arguments like this are put forward (and we can expect them

to increase in the years to come), we need to remember two things. First, even if America maintained its dominance (whatever that means) and the economy were booming again, this would be no guarantee that the gains—be they in wages, in employment opportunities, or in leisure—would be distributed equitably between upper management and everyone else. Second, the entire issue of competitiveness is suspect when it pits poorly treated workers in one country against poorly treated workers in another; and when the vast majority of economic power, anyway, is in the control of enormous multinational corporations that have no loyalty to the people of any land.

Understanding the Content

Feel free to reread all or parts of the selection in order to answer the following questions.

1. The author believes that America is suffering from overwork. Explain that position.

2. What reasons does Brandt give to support her viewpoint?

3. How does American vacation time compare with time off in most other industrialized nations?

4. What does the author mean by the term "workaholic syndrome" (12)?

5. What are some of the traditional arguments used to refute a shorter worktime for American workers? Whose arguments are these? What arguments do Brandt and others use in rebuttal?

Looking at Structure and Style

1. Is the thesis stated or implied? If stated, where?

2. Explain how paragraphs 4–6 function together. What point is being made?

3. How does the Gordon quote in paragraph 7 help support the author's views?

4. How do paragraphs 8–10 function together? What point is being made?

5. What transitional words and devices are used in paragraphs 11–12?

6. How does the Schor quote in paragraph 17 help support the main point of paragraph 16?

7. Explain whether or not paragraph 21 is effective.

Evaluating the Author's Viewpoints

1. The author says that America is suffering from overwork and that our time crunch has become "a major social problem that has reached crisis proportions" (1). Explain why you agree or disagree.

2. The author argues against the traditional "8-hour day, 40-hour week, 50 weeks a year" work place. Do you agree? Why?

3. The author says, "The work ethic fosters the widely held belief that people's work is their most important activity and that people who do not work long and hard are lazy, unproductive, and worthless" (12). Is this true in your social circle? Explain.

4. According to the author, more free time is the best way to nurture our families and rebuild our communities. Explain why you agree or disagree.

5. Explain whether you agree or disagree with the last sentence in the essay.

Pursuing Possible Essay Topics

1. Write a plan for a better work week (and/or work day, work year) than the traditional one mentioned in the essay.

2. Assume that you are on a committee to come up with a better work week and vacation plan for the company you work for. Give arguments for your positions. Or, be a company person and defend the status quo.

3. Argue the need for hard work and long hours.

4. Show how our role as consumers of a large portion of the world's natural resources contributes to our need to work long hours.

5. Discuss how the effects of advertising have or have not forced people to work harder.

6. What would you do with your life if you did not have to work?

7. Define the term "workaholic" and give some examples.

8. Brainstorm or freewrite on one or more of the following:

   a. workaholism   d. free time
   b. work conditions e. working overtime
   c. the ideal job   f. minimum wages

9. Lay off these ideas, and fire away at one of your own ideas for an essay on work.

Preparing to Read

Take a minute or two to look over the following reading selection. Note the title and author, read the opening paragraph, and check the length. Make certain you have the time now to read it carefully and to do the exercises that follow it. Then, in the spaces provided, answer the following questions.

1. What does the title mean to you at this point? _____

2. Do you agree with the opening sentence? Why? _____

_____

_____

3. What do you think will be the point of this essay? _____

_____

Vocabulary

Good comprehension of what you are about to read depends upon your understanding of the words below. The number following each word refers to the paragraph where it is used.

validate (1) verify, make acceptable

limbo (1) a place or condition of neglect and stagnation

cast in bronze (2) permanent or fixed (like a statue)

discounted (3, 7) having undervalued significance

titled nobility (4) refers to such titles as Lord and Lady So-and-So, or the Duke and Duchess of Whatever

dynastic privilege (4) special favors to those powerful families or groups that have held their positions for several generations

deference (6) courteous respect, submission to others out of respect

entrepreneur (7) one who undertakes and assumes the risk of a new business venture

phenomenon (7) a perceivable, often unusual, occurrence or fact

fawn (7) to seek favor or attention by flattery

Now read the essay.

What You Do Is What You Are

NICKIE McWHIRTER

1   Americans, unlike people almost everywhere else in the world, tend to define and judge everybody in terms of the work they do, especially work performed for pay. Charlie is a doctor; Sam is a carpenter; Mary Ellen is a copywriter at a small ad agency. It is as if by defining how a person earns his or her rent money, we validate

or reject that person's existence. Through the work and job title, we evaluate the worth of the life attached. Larry is a laid-off auto worker; Tony is a retired teacher; Sally is a former showgirl and blackjack dealer from Vegas. It is as if by learning that a person currently earns no money at a job—and maybe hasn't earned any money at a job for years—we assign that person to limbo, at least for the present. We define such non-employed persons in terms of their past job history.

2   This seems peculiar to me. People aren't cast in bronze because of the jobs they hold or once held. A retired teacher, for example, may spend a lot of volunteer time working with handicapped children or raising money for the Loyal Order of Hibernating Hibiscus. That apparently doesn't count. Who's Tony? A retired teacher. A laid-off auto worker may pump gas at his cousin's gas station or sell encyclopedias on weekends. But who's Larry? Until and unless he begins to work steadily again, he's a laid-off auto worker. This is the same as saying he's nothing now, but he used to be something: an auto worker.

3   There is a whole category of other people who are "just" something. To be "just" anything is the worst. It is not to be recognized by society as having much value at all, not now and probably not in the past either. To be "just" anything is to be totally discounted, at least for the present. There are lots of people who are "just" something. "Just" a housewife immediately and painfully comes to mind. We still hear it all the time. Sometimes women who have kept a house and reared six children refer to themselves as " 'just' a housewife." "Just" a bum, "just" a kid, "just" a drunk, bag lady, old man, student, punk are some others. You can probably add to the list. The "just" category contains present non-earners, people who have no past job history highly valued by society and people whose present jobs are on the low-end of pay and prestige scales. A person can be "just" a cab driver, for example, or "just" a janitor. No one is ever "just" a vice-president, however.

4   We're supposed to be a classless society, but we are not. We don't recognize a titled nobility. We refuse to acknowledge dynastic privilege. But we certainly separate the valued from the valueless, and it has a lot to do with jobs and the importance or prestige we attach to them.

5   It is no use arguing whether any of this is correct or proper. Rationally it is silly. That's our system, however, and we should not only keep it in mind, we should teach our children how it works. It is perfectly swell to want to grow up to be a cowboy or a nurse. Kids should know, however, that quite apart from earnings potential, the cattle breeder is much more respected than the hired hand. The doctor gets a lot more respect and privilege than the nurse.

6   I think some anthropologist ought to study our uncataloged system of awarding respect and deference to each other based on jobs we hold. Where does a vice-president–product planning fit in? Is that better than vice-president–sales in the public consciousness, or unconsciousness? Writers earn diddly dot, but I suspect they are held in higher esteem than wealthy rock musicians—that is, if everybody older than 40 gets to vote.

7   How do we decide which jobs have great value and, therefore, the job-holders are wonderful people? Why is someone who builds shopping centers called an entrepreneur while someone who builds freeways is called a contractor? I have no answers to any of this, but we might think about the phenomenon the next time we are tempted to fawn over some stranger because we find out he happens to be a judge, or the next time we catch ourselves discounting the personal worth of the garbage collector.

Understanding the Content

Feel free to reread all or parts of the selection to answer the following questions.

1. How does McWhirter claim we define and judge others? Is it common worldwide or just an American trait?

2. According to McWhirter, how do we regard unemployed people?

3. The author states, "There is a whole category of other people who are 'just' something" (3). Name some people who fit into this category. Name some people who are never put there.

4. Does McWhirter think we are a classless society? Explain.

5. What does she say we should warn our children about certain occupations?

6. What is the thesis of the essay? Is it stated or implied?

Looking at Structure and Style

1. How does McWhirter support her topic sentence in paragraph 1?

2. What is the function of paragraph 3? How does it relate to the thesis?

3. Explain or rewrite the following statements from the essay:
   a. "People aren't cast in bronze because of the jobs they hold or once held." (2)
   b. "But we certainly separate the valued from the valueless, ..." (4)
   c. "Writers earn diddly dot, but I suspect they are held in higher esteem

than wealthy rock musicians—that is, if everybody older than 40 gets to vote." (6)

4. What is McWhirter's tone? What words or phrases establish the tone?

5. To what audience is McWhirter writing? What makes you think so?

6. What advice, if any, would you give the author for revision?

Evaluating the Author's Viewpoints

1. McWhirter says we define and judge ourselves according to the jobs we do. Do you agree? Explain.

2. Is defining ourselves according to jobs a distinctly American trait as McWhirter says? How do you know?

3. Do we "separate the valued from the valueless" (4)? Give some examples of your own if you agree with her.

4. In general, do people "fawn over some stranger because [they] find out he happens to be a judge" and discount "the personal worth of a garbage collector" (7)? What qualities in particular make a job or career esteemed?

5. What can you infer about the author based on what she says here?

Pursuing Possible Essay Topics

1. Explain why you want to become a doctor, lawyer, teacher, mechanic, electrician, computer programmer, or whatever. How much of your desire has to do with what McWhirter discusses in her essay? How much of your desire has to do with earning money?

2. Compare/contrast a job with an occupation.

3. Write a rebuttal to McWhirter.

4. Write an essay that classifies our social structure as you see it. How much do job positions and money earned have to do with the way we classify people?

5. Write an essay that shows which positions are most/least respected in our society and why. Here are some suggestions to get you started; feel free to add job positions to the list.

    a. police officer   f. lawyer
    b. minister   g. elementary teacher
    c. taxi driver   h. university professor
    d. car salesman   i. writer
    e. surgeon   j. garbage collector

6. Answer one of the questions McWhirter raises in her last paragraph. Turn the question into your thesis statement.

7. Brainstorm or freewrite on one or more of the following:

a. job   d. nobility
b. housework   e. entertainers
c. retirement   f. "just a bum"

8. These are not cast in bronze; try your own idea on some aspect of work.

📖 Preparing to Read

Take a minute or two to look over the following reading selection. Note the title and author, read the opening paragraph, and check the length. Make certain you have the time now to read it carefully and to do the exercises that follow it. Then, in the spaces provided, answer the following questions.

1. What work-related subject will this essay discuss? _____

_____

2. What do you think will happen? _____

_____

_____

Vocabulary

Good comprehension of what you are about to read depends upon your understanding of the words below. The number following each word refers to the paragraph where it is used.

menial (1) servile, describing work regarded as lower class

skepticism (4) doubt, disbelief

tedious (5) boring, tiresome

ember (5) a piece of live coal from a fire

exotics (9) those from another part of the world; in this case, those new to his personal world

diversity (9) variety

aliens (10) unnaturalized residents of another country

debris (10) scattered remains of something destroyed

fatalistic (10) pertaining to the belief that all events are predetermined by fate

vulnerability (16, 19) open to being taken advantage of

ludicrous (16) laughable, ridiculous

profoundly (18) deeply, absolutely

uncanny (19) inexplicable

compliance (19) obedience to a request or command

pathos (19) a quality in someone or something that arouses feelings of sympathy, sadness, sorrow, pity

Now read the essay.

Workers

RICHARD RODRIGUEZ

1   It was at Stanford, one day near the end of my senior year, that a friend told me about a summer construction job he knew was available. I was quickly alert. Desire uncoiled within me. My friend said that he knew I had been looking for summer employment. He knew I needed some money. Almost apologetically he explained: It was something I probably wouldn't be interested in, but a friend of his, a contractor, needed someone for the summer to do menial jobs. There would be lots of shoveling and raking and sweeping. Nothing too hard. But nothing more interesting either. Still, the pay would be good. Did I want it? Or did I know someone who did?

2   I did. Yes, I said, surprised to hear myself say it.

3   In the weeks following, friends cautioned that I had no idea how hard physical labor really is. ("You only *think* you know what it is like to shovel for eight hours straight.") Their objections seemed to me challenges. They resolved the issue. I became happy with my plan. I decided, however, not to tell my parents. I wouldn't tell my mother because I could guess her worried reaction. I would tell my father only after the summer was over, when I could announce that, after all, I did know what "real work" is like.

4   The day I met the contractor (a Princeton graduate, it turned out), he asked me whether I had done any physical labor before. "In high school, during the summer," I lied. And although he seemed to regard me with skepticism, he decided to give me a try. Several days later, expectant, I arrived at my first construction site. I would take off my shirt to the sun. And at last grasp desired sensation. No longer afraid. At last become like a *bracero*. "We need those tree stumps out of here by tomorrow," the contractor said. I started to work.

5   I labored with excitement that first morning—and all the days after. The work was harder than I could have expected. But it was never as tedious as my friends had warned me it would be. There was too much physical pleasure in the labor. Especially early in the

day, I would be most alert to the sensations of movement and straining. Beginning around seven each morning (when the air was still damp but the scent of weeds and dry earth anticipated the heat of the sun), I would feel my body resist the first thrusts of the shovel. My arms, tightened by sleep, would gradually loosen; after only several minutes, sweat would gather in beads on my forehead and then— a short while later—I would feel my chest silky with sweat in the breeze. I would return to my work. A nervous spark of pain would fly up my arm and settle to burn like an ember in the thick of my shoulder. An hour, two passed. Three. My whole body would assume regular movements. Even later in the day, my enthusiasm for primitive sensation would survive the heat and the dust and the insects pricking my back. I would strain wildly for sensation as the day came to a close. At three-thirty, quitting time, I would stand upright and slowly let my head fall back, luxuriating in the feeling of tightness relieved.

6   Some of the men working nearby would watch me and laugh. Two or three of the older men took the trouble to teach me the right way to use a pick, the correct way to shovel. "You're doing it wrong, too fucking hard," one man scolded. Then proceeded to show me— what persons who work with their bodies all their lives quickly learn—the most economical way to use one's body in labor.

7   "Don't make your back do so much work," he instructed. I stood impatiently listening, half listening, vaguely watching, then noticed his work-thickened fingers clutching the shovel. I was annoyed. I wanted to tell him that I enjoyed shoveling the wrong way. And I didn't want to learn the right way. I wasn't afraid of back pain. I liked the way my body felt sore at the end of the day.

8   I was about to, but, as it turned out, I didn't say a thing. Rather it was at that moment I realized that I was fooling myself if I expected a few weeks of labor to gain me admission to the world of the laborer. I would not learn in three months what my father had meant by "real work." I was not bound to this job; I could imagine its rapid conclusion. For me the sensations of exertion and fatigue could be savored. For my father or uncle, working at comparable jobs when they were my age, such sensations were to be feared. Fatigue took a different toll on their bodies—and minds.

9   It was, I know, a simple insight. But it was with this realization that I took my first step that summer toward realizing something even more important about the "worker." In the company of carpenters, electricians, plumbers, and painters at lunch, I would often sit quietly, observant. I was not shy in such company. I felt easy, pleased by the knowledge that I was casually accepted, my presence taken for granted by men (exotics) who worked with their hands. Some

days the younger men would talk and talk about sex, and they would howl at women who drove by in cars. Other days the talk at lunchtime was subdued; men gathered in separate groups. It depended on who was around. There were rough, good-natured workers. Others were quiet. The more I remember that summer, the more I realize that there was no single *type* of worker. I am embarrassed to say I had not expected such diversity. I certainly had not expected to meet, for example, a plumber who was an abstract painter in his off hours and admired the work of Mark Rothko. Nor did I expect to meet so many workers with college diplomas. (They were the ones who were not surprised that I intended to enter graduate school in the fall.) I suppose what I really want to say here is painfully obvious, but I must say it nevertheless: The men of that summer were middle-class Americans. They certainly didn't constitute an oppressed society. Carefully completing their work sheets; talking about the fortunes of local football teams; planning Las Vegas vacations; comparing the gas mileage of various makes of campers—they were not *los pobres* my mother had spoken about.

10   On two occasions, the contractor hired a group of Mexican aliens. They were employed to cut down some trees and haul off debris. In all, there were six men of varying age. The youngest in his late twenties; the oldest (his father?) perhaps sixty years old. They came and they left in a single old truck. Anonymous men. They were never introduced to the other men at the site. Immediately upon their arrival, they would follow the contractor's directions, start working— rarely resting—seemingly driven by a fatalistic sense that work which had to be done was best done as quickly as possible.

11   I watched them sometimes. Perhaps they watched me. The only time I saw them pay me much notice was one day at lunchtime when I was laughing with the other men. The Mexicans sat apart when they ate, just as they worked by themselves. Quiet. I rarely heard them say much to each other. All I could hear were their voices calling out sharply to one another, giving directions. Otherwise, when they stood briefly resting, they talked among themselves in voices too hard to overhear.

12   The contractor knew enough Spanish, and the Mexicans—or at least the oldest of them, their spokesman—seemed to know enough English to communicate. But because I was around, the contractor decided one day to make me his translator. (He assumed I could speak Spanish.) I did what I was told. Shyly I went over to tell the Mexicans that the *patrón* wanted them to do something else before they left for the day. As I started to speak, I was afraid with my old fear that I would be unable to pronounce the Spanish words. But it was a simple instruction I had to convey. I could say it in phrases.

13   The dark sweating faces turned toward me as I spoke. They stopped their work to hear me. Each nodded in response. I stood there. I wanted to say something more. But what could I say in Spanish, even if I could have pronounced the words right? Perhaps I just wanted to engage in small talk, to be assured of their confidence, our familiarity. I thought for a moment to ask them where in Mexico they were from. Something like that. And maybe I wanted to tell them (a lie, if need be) that my parents were from the same part of Mexico.

14   I stood there.

15   Their faces watched me. The eyes of the man directly in front of me moved slowly over my shoulder, and I turned to follow his glance toward *el patrón* some distance away. For a moment I felt swept up by that glance into the Mexicans' company. But then I heard one of them returning to work. And then the others went back to work. I left them without saying anything more.

16   When they had finished, the contractor went over to pay them in cash. (He later told me that he paid them collectively—"for the job," though he wouldn't tell me their wages. He said something quickly about the good rate of exchange "in their own country.") I can still hear the loudly confident voice he used with the Mexicans. It was the sound of the *gringo* I had heard as a very young boy. And I can still hear the quiet, indistinct sounds of the Mexican, the oldest who replied. At hearing that voice I was sad for the Mexicans. Depressed by their vulnerability. Angry at myself. The adventure of the summer seemed suddenly ludicrous. I would not shorten the distance I felt from *los pobres* with a few weeks of physical labor. I would not become like them. They were different from me....

17   In the end, my father was right—though perhaps he did not know how right or why—to say that I would never know what real work is. I will never know what he felt at his last factory job. If tomorrow I worked at some kind of factory, it would go differently for me. My long education would favor me. I could act as a public person—able to defend my interests, to unionize, to petition, to speak up—to challenge and demand. (I will never know what real work is.) I will never know what the Mexicans knew, gathering their shovels and ladders and saws.

18   Their silence stays with me now. The wages those Mexicans received for their labor were only a measure of their disadvantaged condition. Their silence is more telling. They lack a public identity. They remain profoundly alien. Persons apart. People lacking a union obviously, people without grounds. They depend upon the relative good will or fairness of their employers each day. For such people, lacking a better alternative, it is not such an unreasonable risk.

19   Their silence stays with me. I have taken these many words to

describe its impact. Only: the quiet. Something uncanny about it. Its compliance. Vulnerability. Pathos. As I heard their truck rumbling away, I shuddered, my face mirrored with sweat. I had finally come face to face with *los pobres*.

Understanding the Content

Feel free to reread all or parts of the essay in order to answer the following questions.

1. At what point in Rodriguez's life did the incidents in the essay occur?

2. For what reasons did Rodriguez take the summer job? Why didn't he want to tell his parents?

3. How did Rodriguez react to the work? Why was he reluctant to accept advice from the older workers?

4. What revelation about "real work" did Rodriguez have? How did this insight cause him to better understand the construction workers? What surprised him about the construction workers?

5. What did Rodriguez learn from the group of Mexican aliens hired by the construction boss? Why did his summer suddenly seem ludicrous after this encounter?

6. How does Rodriguez's definition of "real work" change over the course of the summer?

7. What is the point of the essay?

Looking at Structure and Style

1. Rodriguez compares/contrasts the American construction workers with the Mexican aliens. What is the advantage of discussing the Mexicans second? With which group does he identify more closely? How can you tell?

2. Much of the essay is told narratively. Which passages are not narrative? At what points in the essay do they occur? Why?

3. Rodriguez frequently uses Spanish words in a context that allows us to infer their meanings. Why does he use these words? How does their use add to the point he is making? What do you infer about the meaning of *el patrón*, *gringo*, and *los pobres*?

4. What is the effect of making paragraph 14 consist of only one sentence, when most of the other paragraphs are rather long?

5. Select some passages that reflect the author's ability to use descriptive language. What are some lifelike images he creates?

6. Explain or rewrite the following passages from the essay:
   a. "I would feel my body resist the first thrusts of the shovel." (5)
   b. "I was fooling myself if I expected a few weeks of labor to gain me admission to the world of the laborer." (8)
   c. "I felt easy, pleased by the knowledge that I was casually accepted, my presence taken for granted by men (exotics) who worked with their hands." (9)
   d. "My long education would favor me. I could act as a public person— able to defend my interests, to unionize, to petition, to speak up—to challenge and demand." (17)

Evaluating the Author's Viewpoints

1. What stereotyped attitude toward laborers did Rodriguez have before he took the summer job? Is your attitude similar?

2. Rodriguez did not want to accept advice on how to shovel correctly. At this point just before his insight, why is it important to him to feel the pain? How does this need connect Rodriguez to his father and uncle?

3. Do you agree with Rodriguez that he will probably never know what real work is? Is it because of his college education? Explain.

4. In paragraph 16, Rodriguez says he got angry with himself. Why? Should he have been?

5. In paragraphs 17 and 18, Rodriquez compares his advantages to those of *los pobres*. How does he view this group? What is he saying about cultural identity? about education?

Pursuing Possible Essay Topics

1. Describe vividly your first job experience. What did you expect? What insights did you gain?

2. Think about other jobs or occupations that are stereotyped. Pick one and show why the image is or isn't correct.

3. Describe the type of job one of your parents has. Analyze why you would or would not want to have that job.

4. Discuss a job you wouldn't take even if you were desperate.

5. Write your own definition of "real work." Depending upon your viewpoint regarding real work, you may want to begin your essay by reacting to the way Rodriguez defines it in his essay.

6. Reread paragraph 18. Write an essay that attempts to show how such conditions might be changed. Is it possible? What would have to be done?

7. Do some research on famous minority leaders involved in the labor prob-

lems of aliens, such as Cesar Chávez. See if anything you read triggers some ideas. Don't just write a report unless your assignment allows for it.

8. Brainstorm or freewrite on one or more of the following:

   a. menial jobs   d. blue-collar workers
   b. demeaning jobs   e. white-collar workers
   c. construction work   f. the perfect job

9. If these topics are too "menial" or not "real" enough, find your own topic on some aspect of work.

📖 *Preparing to Read*

Take a minute or two to look over the following reading selection. Note the title and author, read the first *ten* paragraphs of dialogue, and check the length. Make certain you have the time now to read it carefully and to do the exercises that follow it. Then, in the spaces provided, answer the following questions.

1. What do you think the essay is about? _____

   _____

2. What do you think the social security worker will say when she gets back

   on the line? _____

   _____

Vocabulary

Good comprehension of what you are about to read depends upon your understanding of the words below. The number following each word refers to the paragraph where it is used.

dispensed (11) handed out, distributed

wooed (11) sought to marry, courted

reciprocated (11) gave in return

capital (13) any form of material wealth

to set hens (13) to put hens on eggs in order to hatch them

scrounge (13) obtain by salvaging or foraging

shuck (13) remove the shell or husk

threshers (13) people who remove the grain from the plant

shock (13) gather into sheaves for drying

rutted (13) full of grooves made by wheels

reclaimed (14) made suitable for cultivation or habitation

Canadian thistles (14) prickly weeds

flax (14) a plant from which textile fibers are taken

spaded (14) dug

cholera (15) an infectious disease

sustenance (21) livelihood, that which provides nourishment and supports life

Now read the essay.

My Mother Never Worked

BONNIE SMITH-YACKEL

1   "Social Security Office." (The voice answering the telephone sounds very self-assured.)

2   "I'm calling about...I...my mother just died...I was told to call you and see about a...death-benefit check, I think they call it...."

3   "I see. Was your mother on Social Security? How old was she?"

4   "Yes...she was seventy-eight...."

5   "Do you know her number?"

6   "No...I ah...don't you have a record?"

7   "Certainly. I'll look it up. Her name?"

8   "Smith, Martha Smith. Or maybe she used Martha Ruth Smith. ...Sometimes she used her maiden name...Martha Jerabeck Smith."

9   "If you'd care to hold on, I'll check our records—it'll be a few minutes."

10   "Yes...."

11   Her love letters—to and from Daddy—were in an old box, tied with ribbons and stiff, rigid-with-age leather thongs: 1918 through 1920; hers written on stationery from the general store she had worked in full-time and managed, single-handed, after her graduation from high school in 1913; and his, at first, on YMCA or Soldiers and Sailors Club stationery dispensed to the fighting men of World War I. He wooed her thoroughly and persistently by mail, and though she reciprocated all his feeling for her, she dreaded marriage....

12   "It's so hard for me to decide when to have my wedding day—that's all I've thought about these last two days. I have told you dozens of times that I won't be afraid of married life, but when it comes down to setting the date and then picturing myself a married woman with half a dozen or more kids to look after, it just makes me sick. ...I am weeping right now—I hope that some day I can look back and say how foolish I was to dread it all."

13   They married in February, 1921, and began farming. Their first baby, a daughter, was born in January, 1922, when my mother was 26 years old. The second baby, a son, was born in March, 1923. They were renting farms; my father, besides working his own fields, also was a hired man for two other farmers. They had no capital initially, and had to gain it slowly, working from dawn until midnight every day. My town-bred mother learned to set hens and raise chickens, feed pigs, milk cows, plant and harvest a garden, and can every fruit and vegetable she could scrounge. She carried water nearly a quarter of a mile from the well to fill her wash boilers in order to do her laundry on a scrub board. She learned to shuck grain, feed threshers, shock and husk corn, feed corn pickers. In September, 1925, the third baby came, and in June, 1927, the fourth child—both daughters. In 1930, my parents had enough money to buy their own farm, and that March they moved all their livestock and belongings themselves, 55 miles over rutted, muddy roads.

14   In the summer of 1930 my mother and her two eldest children reclaimed a 40-acre field from Canadian thistles, by chopping them all out with a hoe. In the other fields, when the oats and flax began to head out, the green and blue of the crops were hidden by the bright yellow of wild mustard. My mother walked the fields day after day, pulling each mustard plant. She raised a new flock of baby chicks—500—and she spaded up, planted, hoed, and harvested a half-acre garden.

15   During the next spring their hogs caught cholera and died. No cash that fall.

16   And in the next year the drought hit. My mother and father trudged from the well to the chickens, the well to the calf pasture, the well to the barn, and from the well to the garden. The sun came out hot and bright, endlessly, day after day. The crops shriveled and died. They harvested half the corn, and ground the other half, stalks and all, and fed it to the cattle as fodder. With the price at four cents a bushel for the harvested crop, they couldn't afford to haul it into town. They burned it in the furnace for fuel that winter.

17   In 1934, in February, when the dust was still so thick in the Minnesota air that my parents couldn't always see from the house to the barn, their fifth child—a fourth daughter—was born. My father

hunted rabbits daily, and my mother stewed them, fried them, canned them, and wished out loud that she could taste hamburger once more. In the fall the shotgun brought prairie chickens, ducks, pheasant, and grouse. My mother plucked each bird, carefully reserving the breast feathers for pillows.

18   In the winter she sewed night after night, endlessly, begging cast-off clothing from relatives, ripping apart coats, dresses, blouses, and trousers to make them to fit her four daughters and son. Every morning and every evening she milked cows, fed pigs and calves, cared for chickens, picked eggs, cooked meals, washed dishes, scrubbed floors, and tended and loved her children. In the spring she planted a garden once more, dragging pails of water to nourish and sustain the vegetables for the family. In 1936 she lost a baby in her sixth month.

19   In 1937 her fifth daughter was born. She was 42 years old. In 1939 a second son, and in 1941 her eighth child—and third son.

20   But the war had come, and prosperity of a sort. The herd of cattle had grown to 30 head; she still milked morning and evening. Her garden was more than a half acre—the rains had come, and by now the Rural Electricity Administration and indoor plumbing. Still she sewed—dresses and jackets for the children, housedresses and aprons for herself, weekly patching of jeans, overalls, and denim shirts. She still made pillows, using the feathers she had plucked, and quilts every year—intricate patterns as well as patchwork, stitched as well as tied—all necessary bedding for her family. Every scrap of cloth too small to be used in quilts was carefully saved and painstakingly sewed together in strips to make rugs. She still went out in the fields to help with the haying whenever there was a threat of rain.

21   In 1959 my mother's last child graduated from high school. A year later the cows were sold. She still raised chickens and ducks, plucked feathers, made pillows, baked her own bread, and every year made a new quilt—now for a married child or for a grandchild. And her garden, that huge, undying symbol of sustenance, was as large and cared for as in all the years before. The canning, and now freezing, continued.

22   In 1969, on a June afternoon, mother and father started out for town so that she could buy sugar to make rhubarb jam for a daughter who lived in Texas. The car crashed into a ditch. She was paralyzed from the waist down.

23   In 1970 her husband, my father, died. My mother struggled to regain some competence and dignity and order in her life. At the rehabilitation institute, where they gave her physical therapy and trained her to live usefully in a wheelchair, the therapist told me: "She did fifteen pushups today—fifteen! She's almost seventy-five years old! I've never known a woman so strong!"

24   From her wheelchair she canned pickles, baked bread, ironed clothes, wrote dozens of letters weekly to her friends and her "half dozen or more kids," and made three patchwork housecoats and one quilt. She made balls and balls of carpet rags—enough for five rugs. And kept all her love letters.

25   "I think I've found your mother's records—Martha Ruth Smith; married to Ben F. Smith?"

26   "Yes, that's right."

27   "Well, I see that she was getting a widow's pension. . . ."

28   "Yes, that's right."

29   "Well, your mother isn't entitled to our $255 death benefit."

30   "Not entitled? But why?"

31   The voice on the telephone explains patiently:

32   "Well, you see—your mother never worked."

Understanding the Content

Feel free to reread all or parts of the selection in order to answer the following questions.

1. Why was the author's mother afraid to marry, according to one of her letters? Were her fears realized?

2. How old was her mother when she had her last child? How many children did she have? How old was she when she died?

3. Describe the kind of life her mother led. Would you call what she did work? How does it differ from what the government defines as "work"?

4. Apparently the author's mother was eligible for a death benefit and Social Security pension when her husband died. Why wasn't the author's family eligible for a death-benefit check when her mother died?

5. What is the thesis? Is it implied or stated?

Looking at Structure and Style

1. How does Smith-Yackel use the narrative dialogue at the beginning and end of the essay to tell her story? How effective is this in capturing our interest? Would the story have been as effective in making its point if we knew at the beginning that the family was not entitled to a death-benefit check?

2. What is the function of paragraph 12? Aside from being a bit ironic, what can we infer from the paragraph about the mother's character?

3. Smith-Yackel tells her story in a chronological fashion between para-

graphs 11 through 25. What transitional devices does she use to help us follow along over so many years?

4. Why does the author spend so much time providing specific details, such as dates, number of farm animals, chores, the amount the death-benefit check would be, and so on? Do such details help the author make her point? Explain.

5. What attitude do you see revealed in the opening and closing dialogue passages with the voice from the Social Security office? Look carefully at the words used to describe the voice.

6. Search the essay for words the author uses to help us feel and imagine the difficulties her mother experienced. How do such words and phrases help us understand the author's definition of "work"?

Evaluating the Author's Viewpoints

1. The author apparently felt the need to write this essay after being told that her mother "never worked." How would you describe Smith-Yackel's attitude toward this statement? toward the voice on the telephone?

2. Do you think the author has negative or positive feelings toward the Social Security system? Explain why you do or don't agree with her.

3. Does the author imply that families of people like her mother should receive a death-benefit check? If so, do you agree? If she doesn't imply this, then what is her point?

4. What adjectives do you think the author might use to describe her mother to us? Why?

5. Why do you think the author says so little about her father? Would a discussion of him help make her point stronger?

Pursuing Possible Essay Topics

1. Compare/contrast working conditions you have known with those your parents or grandparents have known. What changes have occurred? Would you want to have lived their work lives?

2. It is a fact that women in general receive less pay than men on most jobs, even when they perform the same tasks. Why does this policy seem to continue? Why did it begin?

3. Defend housework as "real work."

4. Research information on the Social Security system. Does it favor men over women? Are there inequities that need to be remedied? You might

begin by asking the research librarian if the library has any current government pamphlets on the Social Security system.

5. Define and classify "a man's job" and "a woman's job."

6. Brainstorm or freewrite on one or more of the following:

   a. definition of "work"
   b. sexual harrassment at work
   c. "A woman's place is in the home."
   d. "A woman's work is never done."
   e. workaholics
   f. classifications of work

7. If none of these work for you, come up with your own topic on some aspect of work.

Student Essay

Read the following student essay. As you read, look for the answers to these questions:

1. Does the essay fit the assignment to write on some aspect of work?

2. Does the essay have a thesis and adequate support?

3. Does the essay hold your interest?

"Oh, I'm Just a Housewife"

Roy Wilson

1   After watching my mother deal with our family of five, I can't understand why her answer to the question, "What do you do?" is always, "Oh, I'm just a housewife." JUST a housewife? Anyone who spends most of her time in meal preparation and cleanup, washing and drying clothes, keeping the house clean, attending PTA meetings, leading a cub scout troop, playing taxi driver to us kids when it's time for school, music lessons or the dentist, doing volunteer work for her favorite charity, and making sure that all our family needs are met is not JUST a housewife. She's the real Wonder Woman.

2   Why is it that so many mothers like mine think of themselves as second-class citizens or something similar? Where has
this notion come from? Have we males made them feel this way?
Has our society made "going to work" outside the home seem
more important than what a housewife must face each day?

3   I would be very curious to see what would happen if a housewife went on strike. Dishes would pile up. Food in the house
would run out. No meals would appear on the table. There would
be no clean clothes when needed. Hobbed-nailed boots would be
required just to make it through the cluttered house. Walking
and bus riding would increase. Those scout troops would have to
disband. Charities would suffer.

4   I doubt if the man of the house would be able to take over.
Oh, he might start out with the attitude that he can do just as
good a job, but how long would that last? Not long, once he had
to come home each night after work to more chores. There would
be no more coming home to a prepared meal; he'd have to fix it
himself. The kids would all be screaming for something to eat,
clean clothes and more bus fare money. Once he quieted the kids,
he'd have to clean the house (yes, housewives do windows), go
shopping (either take the kids or get a baby sitter), make sure
that kids got a bath (after cleaning out all the dog hairs from the
bathtub), and fix lunches for the next day. Once the kids were
down for the night, he might be able to crawl into an unmade
bed and try to read the morning newspaper.

5   No, I don't think many males are going to volunteer for the
job. I know I don't want it. So, thanks, mom! I'll do what I can to
create a national holiday for housewives. It could be appropriately called Wonder Woman Day.

Reaction

In the space below, write your reaction to the essay. What would you tell the student?

Commentary

Wilson says the idea for his essay came from reading Bonnie Smith-Yackel's piece, "My Mother Never Worked." It made him take another look at his mother's typical day. While he had always appreciated everything his mother had done for him and his family, Wilson says the Smith-Yackel essay caused him to get more in touch with his own mother and the work she does every day.

The short essay is a tribute of sorts to housewives like his mother. His title attracts our attention and his opening paragraph makes his viewpoint clear. His paragraphs are coherent and he supports them with specifics.

Some students, however, had trouble focusing on Wilson's actual thesis statement when he shared his essay in class. Some students pointed out that the opening paragraph raises the question of why so many housewives think of themselves as "just" housewives. But the second paragraph, they said, raises a whole series of questions of "why?" Has the male caused this? Has society? Who is to blame for this?

In the next paragraph, a few students felt that Wilson forgot his own questions as he began to wonder what would happen if housewives went on strike. They liked the way the paragraph describes what would happen, but felt that the questions in paragraph 2 still hadn't been addressed.

In paragraph 4, Wilson shows us what would happen if the male tried to assume the housewife's role. While his descriptions of the chaos are clear and humorous, Wilson's critics felt he still had not addressed his own questions.

Wilson ends by saying he doesn't think males will take over, in essence because they couldn't handle the job. Then he calls for a national holiday for housewives.

While everything Wilson says certainly centers around his subject, the essay seems loose and disjointed to some. They couldn't understand what specific point Wilson wants to make. If his point is to develop the idea that housewives are "Wonder Women," then they felt he needs to provide more examples of why housewives deserve such praise and give less attention to the male's attempts at housework.

Other students in the class, however, felt that although Wilson's essay was not tightly held together, he does imply that a housewife should be considered a Wonder Woman by showing the male's awareness that he wouldn't want the job. They felt his critics were being too picky for the type of essay Wilson wrote.

What do you think? What advice did you give to Wilson in the space above?

Viewpoints on the Media

*"Reality has come to seem more and more like
what we are shown by cameras."*
Susan Sontag

GETTING THROUGH A DAY without being touched by the media would be difficult. We have daily morning and evening newspapers. We have weekly news magazines to recap what we might have missed in the daily papers. We have digest magazines that gather articles and even books from a variety of sources and condense them for us so that we can keep up with what's new without straining ourselves. We have how-to books and magazines on everything from sex to bomb-making. We stand in line for hours to be among the first to see the latest Star Wars movie; we wouldn't think of owning a car without a radio (AM *and* FM, of course) and cassette player. We can't seem to get enough music as stores and elevators numb us with Muzak; the streets pulse with sounds from "boom boxes" on strollers' shoulders; parks fill up with runners wired to their headsets. More than 87 million homes in the United States alone have television sets, each one turned on for an average of more than seven hours a day. According to one study done by the Roper Organization, 64 percent of the American public turns to television for most of its news. And 53 percent rank TV as the most believable news source.

Collectively, the power the media have on us is worth examining. Both directly and indirectly, the media have a profound effect on our lives. What we eat, what we buy, what we do, even what we think is influenced by the media.

Recent concern for the direction the media are taking us has prompted such books as Marie Winn's *The Plug-In Drug* and *Unplugging the Plug-In Drug*, which deal with the negative effects of television; David Halberstam's *The Powers That Be,* an account of the people who create, control, and use the media to shape American policy and politics; Norman Corwin's *Trivializing America: The Triumph of Mediocrity,* a look at the way the media have contributed to a lowering of our cultural standards; Ben Bagdikian's *The Media Monopoly,* in which it is revealed that only 26 corporations control half or more of all media, including book publishers, television and radio stations, newspapers, and movie companies; Mark Hertsgaard's *On Bended Knee: The Press and the Reagan Presidency,* which reveals how the press gets conned by the candidates and ignores election issues; and Patricia Greenfield's *Mind and the Media,* which shows the media's effects on us.

How believable, how revealing, how comprehensive, how good is what the media provide us? How much influence do advertising sponsors have on the media? Should we become more concerned with its effects than we are? Just what effects *do* the media have on our lives? These are questions that the reading selections in this unit may prompt you to ask. It is hoped that reading them will stimulate both your thinking and your writing.

📖 Preparing to Read

Take a minute or two to look over the following reading selection. Note the title and author, read the opening paragraph, and check the length. Make certain you have the time now to read it carefully and to do the exercises that follow it. Then, in the spaces provided, answer the following questions.

1. What viewpoint about the media does the title indicate the essay will

   hold? _____

   _____

2. What do you think you will learn from reading this essay? _____

   _____

Vocabulary

Good comprehension of what you are about to read depends upon your understanding of the words below. The number following each word refers to the paragraph where it is used.

ubiquitous (1) widespread, common, seemingly everywhere

smoking gun (6) used to mean actual evidence, proof

myriad (7) many, too numerous to count

begets (8) breeds, produces

lurid (11) grisly, shocking, gruesome

mitigates (12) eases, lessens

cognitive (15) mental, psychological

Now read the essay.

Murder on the Dial: Does Television Set the Killers Loose?

NEAL R. PEIRCE

1   The latest rap on American television is a killer—that it's responsible for half the 20,000 murders in this country each year. That means the now ubiquitous tube may have doubled our homicide rate since it first invaded our living rooms in the early 1950s.

2   The man behind this shocker is Brandon Centerwall, a professor of psychiatry and behavioral science at the University of Washington. In his research, made public a few weeks ago, Centerwall analyzes the murder rates in three countries—the United States, Canada and South Africa.

3   His discovery: Almost like clockwork, 10 to 15 years after television is introduced, a country's murder rate shoots up dramatically. That's just enough time, he notes, for the first generation of children weaned on television to reach adulthood and move into their most crime-prone years.

4   Because the politically dominant Afrikaners resisted, television wasn't introduced in South Africa until 1974. The murder rate had held steady for decades.

5   Then, in the early 1980s, a decade after television's arrival, South Africa saw its murder rate soar 56%. Racial conflict wasn't the cause: In all three nations, Centerwall chose to measure murder rates among whites only.

6   Has Centerwall produced the smoking gun that definitely links television and dangerous, violent—even killing—behavior? Critics will no doubt challenge his numbers, his choice of countries. Scientifically, you can't call the evidence conclusive.

7   But sometime in the 21st Century we may well conclude that television, in myriad subtle and psychological ways, is as dangerous to a nation's behavioral norms as smoking has been proven injurious to our bodies. Centerwall's research may then compare to early reports by the Surgeon General linking smoking with cancer.

8   The first congressional hearings on television violence and its potential link to aggressive behavior were held 37 years ago, in 1952. Hundreds of successive studies have said violent television begets violent personal behavior.

9   There have even been sensational "TV-made-me-do-it" crimes, among them a 1977 robbery-murder by a 15-year-old Miami boy whose attorney claimed he'd been "involuntarily intoxicated" by television.

10   At the very least, children become anesthetized to human suffering when they sit for hours a day watching television portray hundreds of acts of zero civility and maximum brutality. In television's twisted world, notes Norman Cousins in the *Christian Science Monitor*, ordinary conversation escalates suddenly into verbal abuse and violent attacks. Youngsters easily "develop a warped view of human relationships."

11   The average child at 16, it is claimed, has witnessed 18,000 televised murders. In the last few years, violence has dropped on network television. But it abounds on local channels and cable. Now we have "trash TV," including supposed crime-busting programs that feed lurid tastes with slow-motion reenactment of gruesome crimes.

12   Censorship raises serious First Amendment issues. But we ought at least look into strict licensing standards to force commercial television station owners to make better use of the public's airwaves with more varied and intellectually stimulating fare. Don't hold your breath, though: Television's economic and political clout mitigates against a licensing cure.

13   How then shall we cope? Perhaps by dealing with television the only way we've been mildly successful dealing with other addictions such as smoking, liquor and drugs—by reducing demand.

14   The critical first step is parents (hopefully not hooked on television themselves) determining to pick, choose and cut back on what their children watch. Communities can organize counseling for parents, to let them know of television's perils. It can follow up with quality day care, Head Start-like education programs. With parents so often working, all-day schools could offer stimulating sports and cultural programs that would replace television as the late-afternoon baby-sitter.

15   All this means a major investment of community energies and government monies. Have we the will? One has to be skeptical. But

until we do, we remain at the mercy of a powerful medium that can reasonably be held responsible for cutting children's cognitive powers to letting them think it's acceptable to be violent.

16   So it's expensive to tend for kids well? Yes. But if you buy the Centerwall argument, it may be murder if we don't.

Understanding the Content

Feel free to reread all or parts of the selection to answer the following questions.

1. Who is Brandon Centerwall? Why is he mentioned in the essay?

2. How many murders per year does Centerwall's research blame on television? On what does he base this figure?

3. Explain why Centerwall's research can or cannot be considered conclusive. Why does the author base his essay on the research?

4. What analogy does the author draw between television viewing and smoking?

5. What effect does watching television for hours a day have on children?

6. What does the author mean by "trash TV"?

7. Why does the author think we should look more closely at television licensing standards? Why will stricter licensing probably not happen?

8. What alternatives to many hours of television viewing does the author suggest?

Looking at Structure and Style

1. How does the author attempt to get your attention in his opening paragraph? Does his strategy work?

2. Explain how well paragraphs 2 and 3 follow the first one.

3. In what paragraph does the author shift from discussing Centerwall's research to stating his own opinions?

4. What seems to be the main function of paragraphs 8–11?

5. Discuss whether or not the essay is mostly fact or mostly opinion.

6. Explain or rewrite the following passages from the essay:
   a. "The latest rap on American television is a killer...." (1)
   b. "That's just enough time ... for the first generation of children weaned on television to reach adulthood and move into their most crime-prone years." (3)
   c. "...children become anesthetized to human suffering when they sit

for hours a day watching television portray hundreds of acts of zero civility and maximum brutality." (10)

d. "Television's economic and political clout mitigates against a licensing cure." (12)

Evaluating the Author's Viewpoints

1. Do you agree or disagree with Peirce's thesis? Explain.

2. Do you think Brandon Centerwall's research has validity? Why?

3. Peirce says that by the twenty-first century, television may well be "as dangerous to a nation's behavioral norms as smoking has proven to be injurious to our bodies." Do you think this is possible? Why?

4. Reread paragraph 12. Do you agree that we ought to demand stricter television licensing standards? Explain.

5. React to Peirce's statement that "...we remain at the mercy of a powerful medium that can reasonably be held responsible for cutting children's cognitive powers to letting them think it's acceptable to be violent" (15).

Pursuing Possible Essay Topics

1. Look through the listings in a television guide for one week. How many of the programs deal with crime or "crime busting"? What crimes are featured most? Watch one of the programs and then write your opinion of its value.

2. Write an essay arguing for or against Peirce's thesis.

3. Write an essay directed to parents suggesting what their children might do instead of watching television.

4. Write an essay about your own television viewing habits. What do you watch? How many hours a week do you watch television? What do you get from it? Are you addicted to television?

5. Do some research on the negative influences of television viewing. Try one of Marie Winn's two books, *The Plug-In Drug* or *Unplugging the Plug-In Drug*; Jeffrey Schrank's *Snap, Crackle and Popular Taste in America*; Norman Corwin's *Trivializing America*; Mark Hertsgaard's *On Bended Knee*; or any other current book or article on the subject. These sources should provide you with many ideas for an essay.

6. Brainstorm or freewrite on one or more of the following:
   a. TV crime shows   d. TV addiction
   b. your favorite TV show e. the worst TV program
   c. reading vs. television f. television violence

7. Censor the above ideas and think of your own topic related to some aspect of the media.

📖 Preparing to Read

Take a minute or two to look over the following reading selection. Note the title and authors, read the opening paragraph, and check the length. Make certain you have the time now to read it carefully and to do the exercises that follow it. Then, in the spaces below, answer the following questions.

1. What is MTV? Do you ever watch it? _____

   _____

2. What do you think the authors will say about MTV? _____

   _____

   _____

3. What do you think you will learn from reading this essay? _____

   _____

   _____

Vocabulary

Good comprehension of what you are about to read depends upon your understanding of the words below. The number following each word refers to the paragraph where it is used.

scantily (1) barely, scarcely

libidinal (1) having to do with lustful desires

hype (1) overstatement, exaggeration, often false claims

lothario (2) a seducer

Milli Vanilli (2) a singing duo that won musical acclaim and awards only to be discovered later to have lip-synched songs actually sung by others

heretical (3) irreverent, sacrilegious

avant-garde conceptualists (5) those active in invention and applying new techniques, especially in the arts

fetish (5, 6) obsession, fixation

pretensions (7) false or showy mannerisms or affectations

juxtapositions (7) side-by-side placements for comparison or contrast

Now read the essay.

Do You Still Want Your MTV?

JOHN LELAND with MARC PEYSER

1   An image of the heavy-metal band Warrant, hosing down a scantily clad woman, appears on a video screen as a professorial man looks on. "Confused libidinal orientation," he says. Critics have been making such complaints about music videos for years. But this time, the knock comes from MTV itself. It's a station ID. This is something new: a network so steeped in hype that it can turn even the insults of its detractors into a hip sales pitch.

2   MTV, or Music Television, turns 10 years old this week. It has been a stormy decade. From the start, the network drew charges of racism: of the first 750 videos played, fewer than 25 were by black acts. Videos like lothario Robert Palmer's "Addicted to Love," in which identically rouged models slink anonymously, provoked complaints of routine sexism. MTV has also been accused of shrinking young people's attention spans and killing rock and roll. Todd Gitlin, a professor of sociology at the University of California, Berkeley, thinks that MTV has "accelerated the process by which people are more likely to think in images than in logic....That's bad news for those who believe in democratic discussion." And clearly, the network is to blame for Milli Vanilli.

3   In the face of protest, MTV has integrated its programming, adding segments devoted to rap and dance music, and embraced new acts like the Black Crowes or M. C. Hammer before pop radio. But to its critics, that's just damage control. Like rock and roll in the old days, MTV has driven a wedge between generations. Music videos are essentially commercials for songs, ads posing as programming. To people who grew up with rock as the voice of unfulfilled desire— "I can't get no satisfaction" or "There ain't no cure for the summertime blues"—this pact with advertising seems heretical. To others it's progress.

4   Yes, progress. MTV has changed the way we talk, dress, dance, make and consume music, and how we process information. It created a new breed of *visual* pop star: Cyndi Lauper, Boy George, Janet Jackson, Madonna. And its reach is growing. In 1985, the network launched VH-1, a sop for older rockers. In the next two years, MTV itself plans to divide into three channels running simultaneously, each catering to a different taste. Already, MTV extends to 40 countries. In September, when Asia gets wired, the network will add 33 more countries. That's a lot of people watching Madonna grab her crotch.

5   In many ways, MTV is the rock revolution all over again—alienating the grown-ups, alarming the alarmists, impressing the impressionable to adopt silly hairstyles. Like parents horrified by Elvis's pelvis in the 1950s, an older generation worries that MTV will seduce their children with its hypnotic sexuality, though the network rejects explicit sexual material. Arguably the first television format not adapted from radio, theater or the movies, MTV brings new visual ideas to light faster than any other medium, embracing high art and trash—selections from Kafka and biker sluts—with equal zest. Artists like Robert Longo and Andy Warhol have made music videos, and avant-garde conceptualists like Survival Research Laboratories and Jenny Holzer have worked for the network. Rock video even rehashes the transgressions of rock music, only for the tube: instead of coming on too loud, MTV is too fast and jumpy; instead of venting raw libido, it makes all of life a cool sexual fetish.

6   **Mesh of messages:** And it pitches those fetishes—along with messages flogging the environment, voter registration, the newest hit record, clothes and a hip lifestyle—in an undifferentiated mesh of hype. Part of the appeal of MTV is that anything can happen next. This is a world without perspective: Paula Abdul dances with a cartoon cat; a clay hammer spurts from Peter Gabriel's clay head; David Byrne of Talking Heads is a child one minute, a face projected on a house the next. For 16 minutes—the network's estimate of the average viewer visit—logic takes a break.

7   MTV is the most electrifying bore on television. Its furious pace and hard sell make near-instant clichés of even the most jarring images. But the mess is intriguing. MTV is a swarm of contradictions—it sells sexism and feminism, environmentalism and conspicuous consumption, arty pretensions and tripe—that are never reconciled. It gives you impossible juxtapositions every time you turn it on. That's as exciting as rock and roll has been in a long time.

Understanding the Content

Feel free to reread all or parts of the selection to answer the following questions.

1. What do critics have against MTV? What have been some past and present complaints?

2. How has MTV changed since its beginnings over ten years ago?

3. The authors claim that MTV has created a new breed of visual pop star. What do they mean? Who are some examples they give?

4. In what ways is MTV "the rock revolution all over again" (5)? What are some parallels the authors make between the rock revolution and MTV?

5. How do the authors define "music videos"?

6. Do the authors like or dislike MTV? What is their thesis? Is it stated or implied?

Looking at Structure and Style

1. How well does the opening paragraph work in drawing your attention to the subject of MTV? Explain your reaction to the introduction.

2. How do the authors support the point of paragraph 2?

3. What is the function of paragraph 3?

4. Explain how *and* how well the authors support the topic sentence of paragraph 5.

5. Explain or rewrite the following passages from the essay:
   a. " ...a network so steeped in hype that it can turn even the insults of its detractors into a hip sales pitch." (1)
   b. " ...MTV has 'accelerated the process by which people are more likely to think in images than in logic.... That's bad news for those who believe in democratic discussion.' " (2)
   c. " ...MTV brings new visual ideas to light faster than any other medium, embracing high art and trash.... " (5)

6. Find some passages that you think are well-written and some that you think need revision. Explain your choices.

Evaluating the Authors' Viewpoints

1. Why do you think the authors say, "And clearly, the network [MTV] is to blame for Milli Vanilli" (2)? What is the implication? Do you agree?

2. If you are unfamiliar with MTV, watch it for 16 minutes ("the network's estimate of the average viewer visit" [6]) and explain why you do or do not agree that "Music videos are essentially commercials for songs, ads posing as programming" (3).

3. Based on the examples given in paragraph 6, why do the authors say "logic takes a break" when you watch MTV? Are they correct? Explain.

4. The authors claim that "MTV has changed the way we talk, dress, dance, make and consume music, and how we process information" (4) Give your own views of agreement or disagreement about MTV's influence on each subject mentioned.

5. What personal feelings toward MTV do the authors reveal? What passages give you that sense? Explain why you agree or disagree with them.

Pursuing Possible Essay Topics

1. Answer the question posed by the title of the essay: "Do You Still Want Your MTV?"

2. Watch MTV for fifteen minutes or so for three or four consecutive days, then write an essay evaluating or describing what you saw. To what audience does MTV cater? Are the videos essentially commercials posing as programming? Are they worth watching? Is MTV "a swarm of contradictions"? Why?

3. Would you rather "watch" music as seen on MTV or listen without the video? Explain your preference in a comparison and contrast essay.

4. Take the part of a parent and explain why you would or would not want your adolescent son or daughter to watch MTV.

5. Brainstorm or freewrite on one or more of the following:
   a. heavy-metal music lyrics   d. rap music
   b. Madonna's influence   e. sex as portrayed in the media
   c. VH-1 vs. MTV   f. your favorite rock star

6. Tune out these ideas and create a topic of your own dealing with some aspect of the media.

📖 *Preparing to Read*

Take a minute or two to look over the following reading selection. Note the title and author, read the opening paragraph, and check the length. Make certain you have the time now to read it carefully and to do the exercises that follow it. Then, in the spaces provided, answer the following questions.

1. What do you think the title means? _____

_____

2. What subject does the essay discuss? _____

_____

3. What do you think is the author's viewpoint on the subject? _____

_____

Vocabulary

Good comprehension of what you are about to read depends upon your understanding of the words below. The number following each word refers to the paragraph where it is used.

grisly (1) gruesome, horrible

allegedly (2) supposedly

Mrs. Grundy (3) an extremely conservative, prudish person

garroting (3) strangling

desecrating (4) abusing something sacred

prestigious (5) highly respected

denunciations (5) formal condemnations or accusations

advocates (7) recommends, supports

purveyors (7) distributors

lepers (7) outcasts

proffers (7) offers

Walter Cronkite (8) a popular TV news announcer, now retired

sanction (9) authorize, approve

trivial (10) insignificant

cerebral (10) intellectual, theoretical

propagandists (11) advocates, those who spread their doctrines and beliefs

rampant (13) widespread

endemic (14) prevalent, common in our society

forum (15) a medium for open discussion

bluenoses (15) puritanical people

Now read the essay.

The Issue Isn't Sex, It's Violence

CARYL RIVERS

1   After a grisly series of murders in California, possibly inspired by the lyrics of a rock song, we are hearing a familiar chorus: Don't blame rock and roll. Kids will be kids. They love to rebel, and the more shocking the stuff, the better they like it.

2   There's some truth in this, of course. I loved to watch Elvis shake

his torso when I was a teen-ager, and it was even more fun when Ed Sullivan wouldn't let the cameras show him below the waist. I snickered at the forbidden "Rock with Me, Annie" lyrics by a black Rhythm and Blues group, which were deliciously naughty. But I am sorry, rock fans, that is not the same thing as hearing lyrics about how a man is going to force a woman to perform oral sex on him at gunpoint in a little number called "Eat Me Alive." It is not in the same league with a song about the delights of slipping into a woman's room while she is sleeping and murdering her, the theme of an AC/DC ballad that allegedly inspired the California slayer.

3   Make no mistake, it is not sex we are talking about here, but violence. Violence against women. Most rock songs are not violent— they are funky, sexy, rebellious, and sometimes witty. Please do not mistake me for a Mrs. Grundy. If Prince wants to leap about wearing only a purple jock strap, fine. Let Mick Jagger unzip his fly as he gyrates, if he wants to. But when either one of them starts garroting, beating, or sodomizing a woman in their number, that is another story.

4   I always find myself annoyed when "intellectual" men dismiss violence against women with a yawn, as if it were beneath their dignity to notice. I wonder if the reaction would be the same if the violence were directed against someone other than women. How many people would yawn and say, "Oh, kids will be kids," if a rock group did a nifty little number called "Lynchin," in which stringing up and stomping on black people were set to music? Who would chuckle and say, "Oh, just a little adolescent rebellion" if a group of rockers went on MTV dressed as Nazis, desecrating synagogues and beating up Jews to the beat of twanging guitars?

5   I'll tell you what would happen. Prestigious dailies would thunder on editorial pages; senators would fall over each other to get denunciations into the Congressional Record. The president would appoint a commission to clean up the music business.

6   But violence against women is greeted by silence. It shouldn't be.

7   This does not mean censorship, or book (or record) burning. In a society that protects free expression, we understand a lot of stuff will float up out of the sewer. Usually, we recognize the ugly stuff that advocates violence against any group as the garbage it is, and we consider its purveyors as moral lepers. We hold our nose and tolerate it, but we speak out against the values it proffers.

8   But images of violence against women are not staying on the fringes of society. No longer are they found only in tattered, paper-covered books or in movie houses where winos snooze and the scent of urine fills the air. They are entering the mainstream at a rapid rate. This is happening at a time when the media, more and more,

set the agenda for the public debate. It is a powerful legitimizing force—especially television. Many people regard what they see on TV as the truth; Walter Cronkite once topped a poll as the most trusted man in America.

9   Now, with the advent of rock videos and all-music channels, rock music has grabbed a big chunk of legitimacy. American teen-agers have instant access, in their living rooms, to the messages of rock, on the same vehicle that brought them Sesame Street. Who can blame them if they believe that the images they see are accurate reflections of adult reality, approved by adults? After all, Big Bird used to give them lessons on the same little box. Adults, by their silence, sanction the images. Do we really want our kids to think that rape and violence are what sexuality is all about?

10   This is not a trivial issue. Violence against women is a major social problem, one that's more than a cerebral issue to me. I teach at Boston University, and one of my most promising young journalism students was raped and murdered. Two others told me of being raped. Recently, one female student was assaulted and beaten so badly she had $5,000 worth of medical bills and permanent damage to her back and eyes.

11   It's nearly impossible, of course, to make a cause-and-effect link between lyrics and images and acts of violence. But images have a tremendous power to create an atmosphere in which violence against certain people is sanctioned. Nazi propagandists knew that full well when they portrayed Jews as ugly, greedy, and powerful.

12   The outcry over violence against women, particularly in a sexual context, is being legitimized in two ways: by the increasing movement of these images into the mainstream of the media in TV, films, magazines, albums, videos, and by the silence about it.

13   Violence, of course, is rampant in the media. But it is usually set in some kind of moral context. It's usually only the bad guys who commit violent acts against the innocent. When the good guys get violent, it's against those who deserve it. Dirty Harry blows away the scum, he doesn't walk up to a toddler and say, "Make my day." The A Team does not shoot up suburban shopping malls.

14   But in some rock songs, it's the "heroes" who commit the acts. The people we are programmed to identify with are the ones being violent, with women on the receiving end. In a society where rape and assaults on women are endemic, this is no small problem, with millions of young boys watching on their TV screens and listening on their Walkmans.

15   I think something needs to be done. I'd like to see people in the industry respond to the problem. I'd love to see some women rock stars speak out against violence against women. I would like to see

disc jockeys refuse air play to records and videos that contain such violence. At the very least, I want to see the end of the silence. I want journalists and parents and critics and performing artists to keep this issue alive in the public forum. I don't want people who are concerned about this issue labeled as bluenoses and bookburners and ignored.

16   And I wish it wasn't always just women who were speaking out. Men have as large a stake in the quality of our civilization as women do in the long run. Violence is a contagion that infects at random. Let's hear something, please, from the men.

Understanding the Content

Feel free to reread all or parts of the selection to answer the following questions.

1. What does Rivers mean by her title, "The Issue Isn't Sex, It's Violence"? Violence against whom?

2. Why is Rivers concerned that teenagers who were raised on "Sesame Street" might be misled by some rock videos and all-music channels?

3. Rivers says that violence is rampant in the media, mentioning the Dirty Harry movies and the now-cancelled television show, "The A Team." Why does she consider this type of violence less harmful than some of the rock lyrics and rock videos? How do the heroes in these shows differ from the "heroes" in the rock videos?

4. What examples from her personal life does Rivers offer to support her view that violence against women "is not a trivial issue"? Are they persuasive examples?

5. What suggestions does Rivers offer to people in the music industry as a way to combat violence against women? Who else does she wish would speak out? Why?

Looking at the Structure and Style

1. In paragraph 2, Rivers mentions that she "loved to watch Elvis shake his torso," and "snickered" at certain rock lyrics that were "deliciously naughty." What function does this serve?

2. What function does paragraph 3 serve?

3. How do paragraphs 4–6 work together to make Rivers's point? Why does she make paragraph 6 a single sentence?

4. How do paragraphs 7 and 8 work together? Why does she make it clear she is not talking about censoring rock lyrics or videos?

5. What is the function of paragraphs 13 and 14? How do they work together to help support her thesis?

6. Concluding paragraphs 15 and 16 present Rivers's suggestions for curtailing the problem. Would it make much difference if she reversed the order of the two paragraphs? Explain.

7. Explain or rewrite the following passages from the essay:
   a. "I always find myself annoyed when 'intellectual' men dismiss violence against women with a yawn, as if it were beneath their dignity to notice." (4)
   b. "Usually, we recognize the ugly stuff that advocates violence against any group as the garbage it is, and we consider its purveyors as moral lepers." (7)
   c. "It [the media] is a powerful legitimizing force...." (8)
   d. "I don't want people who are concerned about this issue labeled as bluenoses and bookburners and ignored." (15)

Evaluating the Author's Viewpoints

1. Rivers believes that some rock lyrics and music videos express a violence toward women, frequently a sexual violence. Do you agree? Have you listened to enough rock lyrics or seen enough MTV to speak from knowledge?

2. Look at each of the suggestions Rivers offers in paragraph 15. Do you think each suggestion is worth considering? Would implementing her suggestions be better than applying censorship laws? Explain.

3. In paragraphs 4 and 16, Rivers implies that men are not doing enough, that they are too silent about the problem. Do you agree? On what do you base your answer?

4. What is your response to paragraph 12? Is this a fairly good statement of her thesis?

Pursuing Possible Essay Topics

1. If you are not familiar with some recent rock lyrics or music videos, turn on the radio or MTV. Do you see or hear any violence toward women? Write an essay that agrees or disagrees with Rivers's thesis.

2. Analyze the lyrics of a "top-ten" rock song. What is being said? What is being implied? Do the words have any merit?

3. Write an essay that describes a rock video that appears on MTV (or some other all-music channel). What is happening? Do the images fit the lyrics? Are the images suggestive? What values are being portrayed that young viewers might accept simply because they admire the musician or singer?

4. Defend or refute the need for some type of censorship in the music in-

dustry as a way to protect young children and teenagers from exposure to sexual looseness or violence in songs and videos.

5. Brainstorm or freewrite on one or more of the following:

   a. MTV   d. rock-and-roll
   b. punk rock   e. your favorite music group
   c. the Top Forty   f. influence of music

6. Come up with your own topic on some aspect of the media.

Preparing to Read

Take a minute or two to look over the following reading selection. Note the title and author, read the opening paragraph, and check the length. Make certain you have the time now to read it carefully and to do the exercises that follow it. Then, in the spaces provided, answer the following questions.

1. What will you be reading about? _____

   _____

2. What can you tell about the author's attitude and tone from the title and

   first paragraph? _____

   _____

   _____

Vocabulary

Good comprehension of what you are about to read depends upon your understanding of the words below. The number following each word refers to the paragraph where it is used.

permeated (1) spread throughout

petrochemical (1) a chemical derived from petroleum or natural gas

saunter (4) to stroll at a leisurely pace

mince (4) chop, hash up

somber (9) solemn, serious

Now read the essay.

TV or Not TV

DAVE BARRY

1   The turning point, in terms of my giving in to the concept of being a Television Personality, was when I let them put the styling mousse on my hair. Hair has always been my dividing line between television personalities and us newspaper guys. We newspaper guys generally have hair that looks like we trim it by burning the ends with Bic lighters. We like to stand around and snicker at the TV guys, whose hair all goes in the same direction and looks as though it's full-bodied and soft, but which in fact has been permeated with hardened petrochemical substances to the point where it could deflect small-caliber bullets. We newspaper guys think these substances have actually penetrated the skulls and attacked the brain cells of the TV guys, which we believe explains why their concept of a really major journalistic achievement is to interview Mr. T.

2   So I need to explain how I became a Television Personality. A while back, a public-television station asked me to be the host of a new TV series they want to start for parents of young children, and I said, sure, what the heck. I remember saying, "Sounds like fun." And thus I became a talent. That's what TV people call you if you go in front of the camera: a "talent." They call you that right to your face. Only after a while you realize they don't mean that you have any actual *talent*. In fact, it's sort of an insult. In the TV business, "talent" means "not the camera, lighting, or sound people, all of whom will do exactly what they're supposed to do every single time, but the bonehead with the pancake makeup who will make us all stay in the studio for two extra hours because he cannot remember that he is supposed to say 'See you next *time*' instead of 'See you next *week*.'" It reminds me of the way people in the computer industry use the word "user," which to them means "idiot."

3   When you are a TV talent, you are meat. People are always straightening your collar, smearing things on your face, and talking about you in the third person, saying things like: "What if we had him sitting down?" and "Can we make his face look less round?" and "Can we do anything about his nose?" This is how my hair came to contain several vats of styling mousse, which is this gunk that looks like shaving cream and which you can just tell was invented by a French hair professional whom, if you met him, you would want to punch directly in the mouth. The TV people felt it made me look older. I felt it made me look like a water bed salesman, but hey, I'm just a talent.

4   Still, I thought I'd be all right, once we got into the studio. What I pictured was, I would saunter in front of the camera, and say something like, "Hi! Welcome to our show! Here's an expert psychological authority to tell you what it means when your child puts the cat in the Cuisinart! And sets it on 'mince'!" Then I would just sit back and listen to the expert, nodding my head and frowning with concern from time to time. And every now and then I might say something spontaneous and riotously funny.

5   As it turns out, *nothing* happens spontaneously in a television studio. Before anything can happen, they have to spend several hours shining extremely bright lights on it from different angles, then they have to stand around frowning at it, then they have to smear it and dust it with various substances to get it to stop the glare from those bright lights that they are shining on it, and then they have to decide that it has to be moved to a completely different place so they can start all over.

6   Once they get all set up, once they're satisfied that the lights are as bright and as hot as they can possibly get them, it's time for the talent to come in and make a fool out of itself. On a typical day, I would have to do something like walk up to a table, lean on it casually, say some witty remarks to one camera, turn to the right and say some more witty remarks to another camera, and walk off. This sounds very easy, right? Well, here's what would happen. I would do my little performance, and there would be a lengthy pause while the director and the producer and the executive producer and all the assistant producers back in the control room discussed, out of my hearing, what I had done wrong.

7   Now I can take criticism. I'm a writer and my editor is always very direct with me. "Dave, this column bites the big one," is the kind of thing he'll say by way of criticism. And I can handle it. But in the TV world, they never talk to you like that. They talk to you as though you're a small child, and they're not sure whether you're just emotionally unbalanced or actually retarded. They take tremendous pains not to hurt your feelings. First of all, they *always* tell you it was great.

8   "That was great, Dave. We're going to try it again, with just a little more energy, OK? Also, when you walk in, try not to shuffle your feet, OK? Also, when you turn right, dip your eyes a bit, then come up to the next camera, because otherwise it looks odd, OK? Also, don't bob your head so much, OK? And try not to smack your lips, OK? Also, remember you're supposed to say next *time*, not next *week*, OK? So just try to be natural, and have some fun with it, OK? I think we're almost there."

9   So I had to do everything a great many times, and of course all

my jokes, which I thought were absolute killers when I wrote them in the privacy of my home, soon seemed, in this studio where I was telling them over and over to camera persons who hadn't even laughed the first time, remarkably stupid, or even the opposite of jokes, antihumor, somber remarks that you might make to somebody who had just lost his whole family in a boat explosion. But I kept at it, and finally after God knows how many attempts, would come the voice from the control room: "That was perfect, Dave. Let's try it again with a little more energy. Also you forgot to say your name."

Understanding the Content

Feel free to reread all or parts of the selection to answer the following questions.

1. What was the turning point, "in terms of [Barry's] giving in to the concept of being a Television Personality"? How did his views of television personalities and newspaper journalists differ?

2. What, according to Barry, is a "talent"?

3. How does being a "talent" differ from what he thought it would be? Give some examples he uses to explain.

4. Why does Barry say that nothing happens spontaneously in a television studio?

5. What is the difference between the way his newspaper editor criticizes him and the way his television directors and producers do? Which does he prefer?

6. What is Barry's thesis? Is it implied or stated?

Looking at Structure and Style

1. How would you describe the tone (sad, serious, sarcastic, bitter, whatever) of the essay? What words or phrases help establish the tone?

2. What is Barry's attitude toward his subject? How can you tell?

3. How does Barry establish his views of television personalities in the first paragraph? Why does he do it at this point?

4. Who is Barry actually making fun of in paragraphs 2 and 3? in paragraph 8?

5. What is the function of the first sentence in paragraph 4?

6. How do paragraphs 7 and 8 work together?

7. How effective is the final paragraph?

Evaluating the Author's Viewpoints

1. What do you think is Barry's opinion of television journalists? Why?

2. To what audience do you think Barry is writing? Why do you think so?

3. Does Barry sound like he enjoys being a "talent"? How serious do you think he is?

4. How does Barry portray himself as a television personality? Should we believe him? Why?

Pursuing Possible Essay Topics

1. Write an essay describing how one of the major network news anchors, such as Tom Brokaw, Peter Jennings, or Dan Rather, presents the news.

2. Compare a major news story as it is reported in the newspaper with the way the story is presented on television. Which medium gives more detail, focus, or coverage? Which way do you prefer to get your news?

3. Analyze some television commercials, looking carefully at what, besides the product, is being "sold." What suggestions are made or implied regarding the use of the product? At whom is the commercial aimed? What values, if any, are implied that have nothing to do with the product itself? What effect do you think each ad has on viewers?

4. Brainstorm or freewrite on one or more the the following:
   a. frequency of TV ads
   b. the funniest TV commercial
   c. the worst TV commercial
   d. TV beer commercials
   e. the funniest TV program
   f. the worst TV program

5. Compare and contrast newspaper advertising with television advertising.

6. Ignore these and think of your own topic on some aspect of the media.

Preparing to Read

Take a minute or two to look over the following reading selection. Note the title and author, read the opening paragraph, and check the length. Make certain you have the time now to read it carefully and to do the exercises that follow it. Then, in the spaces provided, answer the following questions.

1. What do you think the title means? _____

2. What subject does the essay discuss? _____

_____

_____

3. What do think is the author's viewpoint on the subject? _____

_____

_____

Vocabulary

Good comprehension of what you are about to read depends upon your understanding of the words below. The number following each word refers to the paragraph where it is used.

Operation Desert Storm (1) the name given to the 1991 U.S.-led military operation against Iraq after that country's invasion of Kuwait

lulled (1) deceived into trustfulness, calmed

symposium (2) a meeting to discuss a particular topic

military spin (3) a term used to suggest the military provided only the information they wanted people to have, as in "to spin a tale"

Baghdad (3) capital of Iraq

briefers (6) those who handed out the latest war news information

monitoring (13) checking, screening, keeping track of

ominous (15) prophetic or predictive of something foreboding

annihilation (15) total destruction

Now read the selection.

Did the Media Buy a Military Spin on the Gulf War?

TERRY PRISTIN

1   CBS News correspondent Betsy Aaron has covered conflicts for 27 years, but it was not until she reported on Operation Desert Storm that she felt so cut off from the realities of war. So skillful were the military briefings and so impressive the images of pinpoint bombing,

she said, that it was easy to be lulled into forgetting that multitudes of Iraqis were actually dying.

2   "We got into bed with the military," Aaron declared Friday at a Women, Men and Media symposium on war coverage. "There's a price to pay when you climb into bed with someone."

3   The military's spin on the war was "bought by our bosses" and affected what she and most other network reporters were later able to broadcast from Baghdad, she said, adding that it was deemed "not good business" to raise questions about the conflict.

4   In an interview after the panel discussion, Aaron declined to specifically enumerate her complaints against CBS. Instead, stressing that she was referring to all the networks except CNN, she said: "There was a sensitivity about what you could and could not put on the air from Baghdad. And I think it was an oversensitivity."

5   Speaking to a largely female audience of about 180 at the Bel Age Hotel in West Hollywood, Aaron and syndicated columnist Richard Reeves agreed that the news media by and large allowed themselves to be manipulated by the U.S. military into presenting a sanitized, one-sided version of the war. The panel, sponsored by USC's School of Journalism and Institute for the Study of Women and Men, was entitled "Macho and Media Coverage of the Gulf War."

6   "We have simply ignored the moral dimension," said Reeves, who referred to the military news briefers as "PNN—Pentagon News Network" and the news media as "defense contractors." As he traveled around the country during the war, he noticed that many papers were running virtually identical stories that seemed to come straight from military handouts, he said.

7   "They [the military] did their job," he said. "We didn't do ours." The Pentagon has learned that if news can be tightly controlled for a day or two, the American people will become psychologically committed to the government's position, he added.

8   Taking issue with Reeves, Capt. Michael Sherman, who created the first combat reporting pools in the Gulf, said, "People who say I was out there to put a spin on the news are either stupid or ignorant."

9   Sherman, director of the Navy's Office of Information and the officer who set up the Joint Information Bureau in Dhahran, Saudi Arabia, blamed the complaints of manipulation on "wounded egos" and "whining." He said many reporters were more motivated by competition with one another than by a desire to inform the public.

10   "The American public seems to be quite satisfied ... as to what they saw," he said.

11   While also finding fault with the news media for the "constant blathering by people from think tanks" and "too much reliance on technology," Howard Rosenberg, *The Times*' television critic, noted that the war yielded some benefits for women.

12   It became routine to see "powerful symbols" of women as military officers and war correspondents, and certain other stereotypes were also shattered, Rosenberg said. "The only person among reporters I saw really panic on television was not a woman—it was Charles Jaco of CNN," he noted.

13   Women, Men and Media, a research and monitoring project dealing with gender issues, also released a study showing that at the height of the Gulf War in February, more than 85% of the front-page news and 70% of the local section first-page news in 20 selected newspapers was devoted to men. Military officials said that 10% of the U.S. forces in the Gulf were women.

14   When stories about military women appeared, they tended to center on their problems as parents, according to the study based on a tally of the number of times women's names appeared in the coverage, either as sources or subjects of the articles.

15   Betty Friedan, the author of "The Feminist Mystique" and co-chair of Women, Men and Media, portrayed the study results as "ominous danger signals for women." She told the gathering that there has been a "symbolic annihilation of women" in the media, as progress is being eroded.

Understanding the Content

1. What was the name of the symposium mentioned in the essay, and with what issues did it deal?

2. Who is Betsy Aaron and why is she quoted in this essay?

3. Who is Richard Reeves and why does he refer to the military news briefers as "PNN"?

4. What was the name of the symposium panel in which Aaron and Reeves participated? What does the title imply?

5. How did Captain Sherman, director of the Navy's Office of Information, respond to the accusations of Aaron, Reeves, and other reporters?

6. What benefit of the TV war coverage for women was mentioned by Howard Rosenberg, a television critic?

7. How much attention did the newspapers give women involved in the war? What was co-chair of the symposium Betty Friedan's response to the statistics given?

Looking at Structure and Style

1. Why do you think the author begins with the comments of reporter Betsy Aaron? Would it have been better to begin by mentioning the symposium he is reporting about? Explain.

2. How do paragraphs 6 and 7 work together? How do these paragraphs fit in with the first four paragraphs? What do all these paragraphs have in common?

3. What is the point of paragraphs 8–10? What do the ellipses in paragraph 10 indicate?

4. How does the author use paragraph 11 to turn to another aspect of the symposium?

5. How do paragraphs 13 and 14 lead into the last paragraph?

6. Is there a thesis, stated or implied? Is this selection really an essay? Explain.

Evaluating Various Viewpoints

1. Before the U.S. invasion of Grenada in 1983 and Iraq in 1991, news correspondents were generally permitted freedom to go where they wished and print what they wanted. During these two military engagements, however, restrictions were placed on the media as to where they could travel and what information they could publish without government clearance. A "pool" of reporters was selected by the Pentagon to receive information to be shared with those not in the pool. According to correspondent Betsy Aaron and others, the military spin on the war "was bought by our bosses" [publishers and broadcasting executives] and affected what she and other reporters could get into the media. How do you feel about this? Should the military have the authority to control access to information during times of war?

2. The Pentagon spokesperson, Captain Michael Sherman, says, "The American public seems to be quite satisfied ... as to what they saw" during the conflict known as Operation Desert Storm. What is your reaction to this statement?

3. Betty Friedan regards the study results as "ominous danger signals for women" (15) and that there has been a "symbolic annihilation of women" in the media. Do you think she is right? Explain.

Pursuing Possible Essay Topics

1. Write a definition of "freedom of the press." Then show why you think we do or do not have a truly free press in the United States.

2. Compare or contrast television reporting with newspaper reporting.

3. Is your local newspaper really a *news*paper? How much of it is devoted to advertisements, horoscope predictions, advice columns, comics, and the like? How do you rate it in terms of fairness and balanced coverage?

4. Write an extended definition of "journalism." What makes good journalism? What is its importance in our society?

5. Frequently people complain that the media seem to report only "bad news," such as airplane crashes, freeway accidents, murders, riots, fires, wars, and so on. What "good news" should be emphasized instead? What if only "good news" was reported? Describe the difference in the way the news might affect us.

6. Brainstorm or freewrite on one or more of the following:

   a. news censorship   d. slanted news coverage
   b. news "sound bites"   e. a day without news
   c. weekly news magazines   f. the media

7. Find your own newsworthy topic on some aspect of the media.

📖 Preparing to Read

Take a minute or two to look over the following reading selection. Note the title and author, read the opening paragraph, and check the length. Make certain you have the time now to read it carefully and to do the exercises that follow it. Then, in the spaces provided, answer the following questions.

1. What do you think the essay will discuss? _____

   _____

   _____

2. What does the author feel the media are doing that is wrong? _____

   _____

   _____

Vocabulary

Good comprehension of what you are about to read depends upon your understanding of the words below. The number following each word refers to the paragraph where it is used.

Time Warner (1) the corporation that owns *TIME*, *People*, Warner books, movie studios, and other holdings involving the media

elite (2, 8) the upper class, nobility, the best

mock (2) fake, artificial, pretend

Druid (2) a member of an order of priests in ancient Gaul and Britain who appear in myths as prophets and sorcerers

infiltrate (6) sneak in

mega-corporate (10) refers to many corporations or businesses being under the control of one group

Now read the essay.

Bohemian Grove: Off-Limits to News Coverage*

JEFF COHEN

1   It was pure luck that a Time Warner journalist ran into a Time Warner executive this summer at a redwood retreat 70 miles north of San Francisco. It was also bad luck, at least for the journalist. The Time Warner executive threw him out.

2   You see, it wasn't just any retreat. The chance meeting occurred at the exclusive, super-secret Bohemian Grove, where the old boys (no women, ever) of America's government and corporate elite gather each summer for two weeks of laid-back schmoozing and speech-making, not to mention the club's mock-Druid fire rituals.

3   And it wasn't just any journalist. Dirk Mathison was, until recently, the enterprising San Francisco bureau chief of *People* magazine, owned by Time Warner. Since reporters are banned from Bohemian Grove, Mathison hiked over back-country trails to sneak into the July "encampment" three different times. The third time, he ran into the Time Warner executive who recognized him and tossed him out.

4   Mathison had already learned a lot. Contrary to the claims of the grove, Mathison saw more than just summertime relaxation. Former Secretary of the Navy John Lehman, for example, gave a lecture in which he stated that the Pentagon estimated 200,000 Iraqis were killed during the six weeks of the Gulf War. The Pentagon never gave the rest of us an official count. Other speakers included Defense Secretary Dick Cheney and former Health, Education and Welfare Secretary Joseph A. Califano, speaking on "America's Health Revolution—Who Lives, Who Dies, Who Pays."

5   Expecting to read all about it in *People?* It won't happen. Even though Mathison embarked on the Bohemian Grove story with his editor's approval, and even though Mathison says his article was so

---

*Editor's title.

well received that extra space was allotted for it, the story was mysteriously killed.

6   *People's* managing editor told my researchers that although he had authorized Mathison to infiltrate the grove, he later killed the piece after realizing that he had authorized "trespassing." He denied any pressure from Time Warner higher-ups.

7   Mathison said a full explanation would be elusive: "It's easier to penetrate the Bohemian Grove than the Time-Life building."

8   But one need not penetrate Time-Life to realize what this episode says about journalism today: It can be difficult for journalists to report fully on America's political and economic elite when their bosses are loyal members of that elite.

9   Every year at Bohemian Grove, media executives hobnob with news makers. Walter Cronkite, for example, resides at the same lodge at the grove as George Bush. But the grove—whose membership includes every Republican President since Coolidge, and on whose premises presidential campaigns have been fueled and the Manhattan (A-bomb) Project conceived—is off-limits to news coverage.

10   Since the grove is such a closed institution, it is admittedly difficult for journalists to cover. But what about other issues that affect reporters' new mega-corporate masters? How tough can the public expect major media to be in covering mergers, buyouts and executive greed in an era of middle-class downturn and layoffs?

11   Well, working journalists are part of that middle class, with reason to be cautious. After Time merged with Warner to form the biggest media firm in the world, Time Warner Chairman Steve Ross told *Variety* that journalists "cannot afford to be anywhere but part of a strong, diverse company with global reach and responsibility.... A diverse, financially strong media company makes it possible for managers to attract and nurture talented journalists."

12   Instead of nurturing journalists, Time Warner—thanks largely to debt incurred during the merger—recently laid off 600 magazine employees, including 19 of *Time's* 75 correspondents, to achieve a savings of $30 million (this after Ross, the nation's most highly compensated chief executive, made $78 million last year in salary and stock profits).

13   And what about Dirk Mathison, the enterprising journalist who tried to cover the lords of free enterprise? He's one of the 600. He's been notified that his San Francisco bureau will be shut down Dec. 31 in a cost-cutting measure.

Understanding the Content

Feel free to reread all or parts of the selection in order to answer the following questions.

1. What and where is Bohemian Grove? Why are no journalist allowed?

2. Who were some of the people at the Bohemian Grove retreat mentioned in the essay?

3. Who is Dirk Mathison? Why was he thrown out of Bohemian Grove? by whom?

4. What did Mathison learn at Bohemian Grove before he was "tossed out"? Why will we not read about it in *People* magazine?

5. How much did Time Warner save by laying off 600 magazine employees, including 19 of *TIME*'s 75 correspondents, when Time merged with Warner? How much did Time Warner Chairman Steve Ross earn in salary and stock profits that same year?

6. What is ironic about the comment of Time Warner's Chairman Ross to *Variety* and what happened to Dirk Mathison? What is Cohen implying about the way the business elite are affecting news coverage?

Looking at Structure and Style

1. How effective is Cohen's opening paragraph? What information does it contain?

2. Reread paragraph 2. What tone is conveyed here? What words help create that tone?

3. Explain Cohen's use of the phrase "the club's mock-Druid fire rituals" in paragraph 2. How does this let you know Cohen's attitude toward the "elite" news executives? What are some other words Cohen uses to describe corporate news executives in his essay?

4. What is the function of paragraph 4? How does this information relate to some of the comments made in Terry Pristin's "Did the Media Buy a Military Spin on the Gulf War"?

5. What is the function of paragraphs 8 and 9?

6. Discuss the effectiveness of the last paragraph.

Evaluating the Author's Viewpoints

1. Cohen says, "It can be difficult for journalists to report fully on America's political and economic elite when their bosses are loyal members of that elite" (8). Is Cohen right? Should we be concerned? Explain.

2. In paragraph 6, *People*'s editor explains why the magazine did not print Mathison's story about Bohemian Grove. Does Cohen accept this reason? Do you? Explain.

3. Cohen asks, "How tough can the public expect major media to be in covering mergers, buyouts and executive greed in an era of middle-class

downturn and layoffs?'' (10). Based on the comments made in the essay, what is Cohen's answer to this rhetorical question? Do you agree? Explain.

Pursuing Possible Essay Topics

1. When *TIME* magazine discovered that one of its readers' favorite features was the "People" section, Time, Inc., started a spinoff magazine, *People*. Examine an issue or two of *People* and evaluate it and/or the people who are interested in reading it. What does its popularity tell you about our society?

2. Discuss why it is important for a democratic society to keep its people well informed. Are we a well-informed people? Do most people really care or want to know about what goes on at Bohemian Grove?

3. As of 1988, ten large companies own the majority of the 2,500 publishing houses in this country, and most of those corporations also own banking, insurance, industrial, and defense-related subsidiaries. Is there a danger in this? Does it matter that there is a "media monopoly" in this country?

4. Pick a magazine you like to read. Write an essay explaining why you like to read it. What do you learn from it? What values does it impart? What companies advertise in it? What do these ads tell you about the magazine's readers?

5. Jeff Cohen, author of the essay, is executive director of FAIR (Fairness and Accuracy in Reporting), which publishes the journal *Extra!* Read an issue or two and react to one of the stories in it.

6. Toss these and find your own topic on some aspect of the media.

📖 Preparing to Read

Take a minute or two to look over the following reading selection. Note the title and author, read the opening paragraph, and check the length. Make certain you have the time now to read it carefully and to do the exercises that follow it. Then, in the spaces provided, answer the following questions.

1. What do you think the essay will be about? _____

_____

_____

2. What do you think you will learn from reading this essay? _____

_____

_____

Vocabulary

Good comprehension of what you are about to read depends upon your understanding of the words below. The number following each word refers to the paragraph where it is used.

barbiturate (1) any sedative or hypnotic-type drug

credible (2) believable

quantum (3) a specified quantity, usually a significant amount

non-partisan (9, 10) not favoring any political party

Now read the essay.

TV + Telephone = Electronic Democracy

DUANE ELGIN

1   Although television has been called a "vast wasteland," a "boob tube," an "idiot box," and a "cultural barbiturate," the fact remains that it is now the primary source of information for a majority of citizens: Roughly two-thirds of the people in the United States get most of their news about the world from TV, and nearly half get all of their news from TV. By any measure, television has become the "social brain" of modern democracy.

2   Television dominates the social imagination of democracy in the United States: 98 percent of all homes have a TV set, and the average person watches more than four hours per day. If an issue or concern does not appear on television, then, for all practical purposes, it does not exist in the mass social consciousness. Television determines which issues will dominate the public agenda, which spokespersons will be credible, and which trends will be considered critical.

3   In describing democracy in the United States in the early 1800s, Alexis de Tocqueville said that newspapers were vital because they could put a single idea into 10,000 minds all on the same day. Tele-

vision has a similar but magnified power—it can deliver a single idea to 100 million minds at the same instant. We now have tools that can make a quantum leap forward in our communication as a conscious democracy.

4   A conscious democracy pays attention to what is going on. A conscious democracy is awake and watches the trends and events that shape the short-term and long-term future. Citizens of a conscious democracy "know their own mind"—they are in touch with changing thoughts and sentiments of the larger communities through regular dialogue and feedback.

5   Despite the power of television, it is not currently being used to serve the urgent needs of democracy. In the United States, roughly 97 percent of prime-time, broadcast TV is devoted to entertainment programming. American citizens are entertainment rich and knowledge poor. Therefore, one requirement for giving television a role in promoting a more conscious democracy is a dramatic increase in the level and quality of television-based learning (accompanied by supporting learning in many other media).

6   Further, a conscious democracy depends on public discussion of the major issues of the day and publicly building working agreements for appropriate courses of action. If democracy is "the art of the possible," then we don't know what's possible (or desired) until citizens have an accurate sense of how the overall community thinks and feels about different issues and priorities.

7   There is a way to obtain rapid and representative feedback, and that is by obtaining responses (via telephone voting) from a preselected, scientific sample of citizens to get a reliable sense of overall community views.

8   Because representative approaches are already used to run democracies, and because scientific procedures for assuring fair representation are well developed, obtaining feedback from a random sample represents an excellent solution. By relying upon a scientific sample, a community or nation can rapidly obtain input from a trustworthy cross section of citizens and know its own mind on the vital issues of the day.

9   How could this work? Imagine that a random sample of a thousand or more citizens in a community (or country) is called several weeks in advance of a televised "town meeting" and asked to participate. Those who agree are sent a list of phone numbers to dial in and register their views the night of the electronic town meeting. By dialing a particular number, they can show their agreement or disagreement with various options or their intensity of sentiment. This kind of telephone-based, scientific feedback can be obtained in the TV studio in three minutes or less and displayed for everyone to see. By combining representative feedback with an informational docu-

mentary program and non-partisan dialogue, a community can know its own mind with a high degree of accuracy on the key issues of the day.

10   A representative approach to mass community dialogue and feedback was successfully tested in the San Francisco Bay area in 1987 with a prime-time electronic town meeting. This pioneering experiment was developed through the cooperative efforts of a non-partisan media reform organization (Choosing Our Future), the local ABC-TV station, and the League of Women Voters. The program was viewed by more than 300,000 persons, and six "votes" were taken during the hour. The meeting began with a documentary overview and was followed by a live studio dialogue among persons representing differing viewpoints. As questions came into focus, the preselected random sample of citizens was invited to dial in their vote on an issue. Because feedback was so fast, the community was able to ask itself a half-dozen questions during the course of the hour-long program.

11   With weekly or monthly electronic town meetings in major metropolitan areas across the nation as well as regular national ones, a new level of communication and accountability could be established between the public and decision makers. Because this feedback would be strictly advisory, it respects both the responsibility of the decision maker to make decisions and the responsibility of the citizen to give feedback to those who govern.

Understanding the Content

Feel free to reread all or parts of the selection to answer the following question.

1. How many people in the United States get most of their news about the world from television? How many U.S. homes have a TV? How many hours a day does the average person watch television? What power does this give to television?

2. What does Elgin mean when he says that television has become the "social brain" of modern democracy? Why has television become more vital to democracy than the newspaper?

3. What does the author mean by a "conscious democracy" (4)?

4. Why does Elgin feel that despite the power of television, it is not presently serving the needs of democracy?

5. Explain Elgin's plan to make television more than a "cultural barbiturate." Why does Elgin think his plan would work?

6. Upon whom does Elgin place the responsibility for making democracy work?

Looking at Structure and Style

1. What is the function of the first two paragraphs?

2. What is the point of mentioning Alexis de Tocqueville in paragraph 3? Who is Alexis de Tocqueville?

3. Explain the point of paragraph 4.

4. How does paragraph 6 connect with paragraph 5? What transition words or phrases are used?

5. Why does Elgin place the information in paragraph 10 after paragraphs 7–9?

6. How effective is the concluding paragraph? Explain.

7. Is Elgin's thesis stated or implied? If stated, where? What is his thesis?

Evaluating the Author's Viewpoints

1. Do you agree with Elgin that television has become the "social brain" of democracy? Explain your views.

2. Elgin says that Americans are "entertainment rich and knowledge poor" (5). Do you agree? What important knowledge have you learned from watching television?

3. If television stations in your town offered you an opportunity to telephone your views to a televised town meeting, would you participate? Explain your reaction to Elgin's "telecommunication" proposal.

4. Do you feel you are a citizen of a "conscious democracy"? Explain.

5. Do you agree with the last sentence in paragraph 11? Why?

Pursuing Possible Essay Topics

1. Write an essay that discusses what is right or wrong with television as you view it.

2. Write about your own television habits.

3. Support or refute Elgin's claim that television is a "cultural barbiturate."

4. Provide some ideas for television producers that you think would help develop a "conscious democracy."

5. Pretend you own a major television network and have complete control over programming. What types of programs will your network provide?

6. Discuss why it is important for a democratic society to keep its people well informed. Are we a well-informed nation? Are we given access to the kind of information we need?

7. Brainstorm or freewrite on one or more of the following:
   a. the *National Enquirer*   d. *People* magazine
   b. responsibility of the press e. CNN
   c. TV talk shows   f. influence of the media

8. Cast your vote against the above and find your own topic on some aspect of the media.

Student Essay

Read the following student essay, looking for answers to the following questions:

1. Does the essay fit the assignment to write on some aspect of the media?

2. Does the essay have a clear thesis and good support?

3. Does the essay follow the writing guidelines suggested in Unit 2, "Viewpoints on Writing Essays"?

TV News: Journalism or Propaganda?

Jim Stone

1   Not all television news organizations report the news fairly or completely. They all may begin covering stories with the basic idea of truthfulness in reporting, but by air time this has fallen by the wayside. All news organizations face pressures from many different angles. Each sponsor has its wishes, special interest groups have theirs, the network and local station executives have theirs, and finally, the censors and "old man time" limit what can be shown. These pressures, as well as manipulation on the part of government, can all act on a news story and, in many cases, slant it by the time we get it.

2   Here's how it typically works. A news crew, usually consisting of a reporter and a cameraman, is sent to the scene of an incident or press conference. Today's story is about a leaking toxic waste dump. A state spokesman is holding a press conference at

the site of the dump. The conference is attended by most major newspapers, the major wire services (AP, UPI, etc.), and the local TV networks. The state spokesman presents the problem to the press in a prepared statement, and then our illustrious reporter faces the camera and paraphrases what the state spokesman just said. The crew then gets some camera shots of leaking chemical drums and proceeds to tour the neighborhood.

3   They are, of course, looking for "the man in the street" for a "salt of the earth" impression of this latest item of gloom and doom. The first person being interviewed, someone who wants the dump removed from his neighborhood anyway, begins to see some fairly lucrative lawsuits on the horizon. When asked to describe any recurrent or frequent health problems, the interviewee rattles off a lengthy list including but not limited to gout, ulcers, arthritis, hemorrhoids and many other common ailments that he feels sure are caused by the leaking dump next door. The news crew repeats this scene two or three times with other disgruntled neighbors and gets almost identical answers from each respondent. The news crew then returns to the studio and proceeds to review the fruits of their labors in the video editing room.

4   The editor then begins to "make" the story. This is where the potential for propaganda comes in; the editor is the person who bears the brunt of the pressures from special interest groups. At this point he can downplay the story by stressing the state's official assertion that they do not know the extent of the hazard, while dropping the spokesman's later comment that damage appears extensive. Or, at the request of another interest group, such as an environmental one, the editor can stress that damage

is believed to be extensive and may even be irreversible. He drops the spokesman's comment that damage assessments cannot be made at this time. Or, the editor can stress the cost of the cleanup in order to help the state environmental protection agency secure a larger budget by the use of public furor that will no doubt occur from an incident of this sort. In this instance, he would probably tie in footage of all the other leaking waste dumps around the state as well as total cleanup costs. To add the human element, he can put in some of the footage of the neighborhood people with their assorted illnesses, or just the portion of the interview in which the people express their shock and outrage over the dump spill.

5   In most cases, if not all, the editor is trying to do us, the viewer, a favor. He is creating a news story that is digestible in the short time allotted for each news story. If time allows, and the story is really important, the network can do an in-depth story which might include history, background, further ramifications, and future dump site plans. Most of us would not want to sit and sift through the daily deluge of news items. This would quickly become a full-time job and is best left to the professionals.

6   But in a few instances, the editor does the viewing public a disservice by slanting the story in order to influence public opinion. This can be done either through omission or through emphasis of key points, as is often done in political campaigns. The editor favoring a candidate can downplay or ignore negative items while stressing the good ones. In contrast, if the editor dislikes a candidate, he can emphasize the negative items and downplay the positive ones.

7   In today's political world, television plays a huge role in who will get elected. Most of us don't take the time to really deal with the issues. A 1988 <u>TV Guide</u> poll shows that most of us vote for the candidate who makes the most favorable impression on us. The politician knows this as well as news editors.

8   All of this leads to the conclusion that we still can't believe everything we see in print or on television. That old warning about buyer beware, caveat emptor, should be changed to include television news.

Reaction

In the space below, write your reaction to the essay. What would you tell the student about his essay?

Commentary

This final revision of Stone's essay shows his attention to some basic composition guidelines: a clear thesis, strong support, good paragraph control, sentence variety, helpful transitions, and attention to word choices. Let's look at some of these elements.

Notice in the first paragraph that Stone makes it clear what his subject and thesis are. Although television stations may begin with the intention of truthfully covering news stories, pressures from various sources, including time itself, may all serve to slant a story by the time we see it on television.

His second paragraph begins, "Here's how it typically works." From there through paragraph 4, Stone takes us from the step-by-step process of reporters covering a news story to the editorial room where the selection of what will be finally shown is decided. As he describes the process, he is also supporting his thesis by showing how and why a story may become slanted by the time we view it on television.

Paragraphs 5 and 6 deal with the editor. Paragraph 5 gives the editor credit for the job he must perform. It recognizes the service the editor provides for us and lets us know that Stone is not accusing all editors of slanting news stories. Paragraph 6, in contrast, shows the disservice an editor can perform when his biases interfere with a story.

It could be argued that paragraph 7 is not needed because it begins to raise a different issue. Stone's topic sentence (that television plays a huge role in who will get elected) is certainly true, but that in itself seems a thesis of its own needing further development and discussion. The previous paragraph (6) ends with a commentary on how editors may slant stories to favor or downplay a political candidate. No doubt that statement brought up the ideas Stone expresses in paragraph 7. But as written, the paragraph takes us away from the process involved in developing a television news story. It doesn't support Stone's thesis.

The last paragraph draws a logical conclusion: we shouldn't believe everything we see and hear on television news. The body of his essay shows us why.

Despite the question of the appropriateness of paragraph 7, Stone's essay shows he applied what he has learned about composition. He began writing with the idea he would compare/contrast the way newspapers report a story with the way television does. As you can see, he narrowed the topic down to something more manageable. After several false starts and many revisions, this student finished with an acceptable essay that fits the assignment.

*V*iewpoints on

Two Controversial Issues

"When a thing ceases to be a subject of controversy,
it ceases to be a subject of interest."
William Hazlitt

SOMEONE once said that there are three sides to every questionable issue: your side, my side, and the "right" side. In truth, there may be many sides, depending upon the issue itself. For instance, the reactions to the issue of abortion are usually divided into two basic viewpoints: for or against. But the issue is not that simple. Other questions begin to surface. For instance, do women have the right to decide for themselves whether or not they wish to remain pregnant? Does the government have the right to involve itself in such an issue, or is it meddling in private lives? Are abortion laws, whether pro or con, constitutional? Is abortion really a legal question or a moral and religious one? When should a fetus be considered a "person"? Are a potential mother's rights and a fetus's rights equal? Can aborting a fetus be considered murder, as some say? If a fetus is not human life, as some say, what kind of life is it? Are there times when an abortion is more humane than the alternative? What if an abortion under certain circumstances would save an endangered mother's life? Is it better to have an unwanted child who can't or won't be cared for than to have an abortion? Should pregnant junior and senior high schoolers be forced to have unwanted children? Should parents of a 16-year-old be notified if their daughter makes an appointment for an abortion? These are just a few of the kinds of questions that create controversy on touchy issues, making it difficult for any thinking person to make quick decisions.

According to psychologists, numerous studies have been done that show the urge to conform to group thinking is too powerful for most people to resist. Unknowingly, we become conditioned to ways of thinking. This usually happens because we are molded at an early age by our parents, relatives, teachers, and friends. We tend to honor their value systems because we love them and trust their judgments. If our families vote Republican, we usually vote Republican. If our families go to a particular church, we tend to continue in that church. If our parents and church leaders speak out against abortion, we tend to accept such views as "right." Their beliefs become our beliefs without much questioning or thought on our part.

As we mature, our beliefs are also molded both directly and indirectly by the media. What we wear, what we eat, what music we accept, even what media we enjoy become tied in with our desire to be accepted as part of a group. Even when we think we are acting as individuals by rejecting the ideas of one group, we are often just accepting the ideas of another. We become self-deceptive. Our thinking process becomes overruled by others' opinions that we think are truly our own thoughtful reactions because we have heard them for so long. We become biased and forget to weigh our opinions by looking at facts or reasoning that goes against our belief system. And even when we do try to see "facts," we often don't have the experience needed to evaluate the information. In such cases, it is better to suspend our decision on which "side" to take until we do some more investigating.

This unit contains essays on two controversial subjects: capital punishment and multicultural education. You will read essays on both topics expressing various viewpoints. At this point you may not have a particular viewpoint of your own on either topic. Once you have finished the readings, you will at least know more about the issues involved and will be better able to form an opinion. If you already have a viewpoint on one or both of the topics, try to suspend your opinions as you read the selections. Avoid letting your own biases cloud any opinions that are opposite yours, not always an easy task. We sometimes have a tendency to view ourselves as superior to another person's race, religion, or culture even though we may not think we are doing so. Such views limit our objectivity and keep us from learning from others.

As you read each selection, ask yourself these questions regarding the strengths and weaknesses of the arguments being made:

1. Is the **problem** being expressed too simplistically?
2. Does the author use mostly **facts** or mostly **opinions**?
3. Is the author trying to reach my **emotions** or my **mind**?
4. Are the judgments being made based on solid **reasoning** and **verifiable information**?

5. Is the **evidence** convincing and provable, or deceptive and distracting?
6. What **sources** are cited? Are they reliable?
7. Is the author an **authority** on the subject?

Use these questions to let go of your own feelings long enough to understand the author's position, especially if it is different from your own.

Even after reading the selections, you may discover you need more information than is provided here in order to take a stand of your own. That's a healthy sign you are not being easily swayed. You will probably want to read more and discuss these subjects with others. That, of course, is why you are being asked to read these selections.

One final word. New information on these and other controversial issues continues to come out. What you think today, may not be what you think tomorrow. That's healthy, too, as long as you are truly making sound judgments and critically weighing the evidence. A changing mind is better than a closed one.

ISSUE I: VIEWPOINTS ON THE DEATH PENALTY

Most of us do not like to think about the subject of capital punishment—the death penalty. It disturbs us, makes us feel uneasy; it's something we would rather let other people deal with. Still, whether we like it or not, it is an issue we all should think about and must take responsibility for. Polls conducted in the late 1980s showed that a majority thought capital punishment was justified. However, the pendulum swings back and forth, sometimes with more people in favor and at other times, less.

The death penalty laws vary from state to state. A few prohibit it altogether, most permit it. But other questions are involved beyond the question of whether or not capital punishment should be available to the courts. Is capital punishment a leftover from more barbaric times? When should the death penalty be administered? If it is allowed, is there a "humane" way to do it? Should the guilty be gassed, electrocuted, hanged, given lethal injections? Can we be sure the person is guilty? Do we as a society have a right to take someone's life? Does the Bible say capital punishment is permissible? These and other questions make it obvious that the issue is a complicated one requiring more than emotional responses.

All the essays in this unit deal with this subject. Hold your own opinions until you have read each piece. See if they help you understand the issue any better. You will then be asked to write an essay on your viewpoints regarding capital punishment.

📖 *Preparing to Read*

Before reading this selection, make certain you have read the introduction to this unit, pages 397–399.

Take a minute or two to look over the following reading selection. Note the title and author, read the first *two* paragraphs, and check the length. Make certain you have the time now to read it carefully and to do the exercises that follow it. Then, in the spaces provided, answer the following questions.

1. What is the subject of the essay? _____

   _____

2. What is the author's viewpoint on the subject? _____

   _____

3. Do you already have views on the death penalty that might make you

   biased as you read this essay? Explain. _____

   _____

Vocabulary

Good comprehension of what you are about to read depends upon your understanding of the words below. The number following each word refers to the paragraph where it is used.

dispatching (2) killing

abundance (6) great number or amount

retribution (7) punishment, something demanded in return for harm having been done

Cook County (8) the county in Illinois that includes the city of Chicago

delegate (9) authorize, entrust someone

deter (10) prevent, discourage

decomposed (12) rotted, falling apart

befriended (18) was friendly toward

Now read the essay.

Death to the Killers

MIKE ROYKO

1   Some recent columns on the death penalty have brought some interesting responses from readers all over the country.

2   There were, of course, expressions of horror and disgust that I would favor the quick dispatching of convicted murderers.

3   I really don't like to make fun of people who oppose the death penalty because they are so sincere. But I wish they would come up with some new arguments to replace the worn-out ones.

4   For example, many said something like this: "Wouldn't it be better to keep the killers alive so psychiatrists can study them in order to find out what makes them the way they are?"

5   It takes the average psychiatrist about five years to figure why a guy wants to stop for two drinks after work and won't quit smoking. So how long do you think it will take him to determine why somebody with an IQ of 92 decided to rape and murder the little old lady who lives next door?

6   Besides, we have an abundance of killers in our prisons—more than enough to keep all the nation's shrinks busy for the next 20 years. But shrinks aren't stupid. Why would they want to spend all that time listening to Willie the Wolfman describe his ax murders when they can get $75 an hour for listening to an executive's fantasies about the secretarial pool?

7   Another standard is: "The purpose of the law should be to protect society, not to inflict cruel retribution, such as the death penalty."

8   In that case, we should tear down all the prisons and let all the criminals go because most people would consider a long imprisonment to be cruel retribution—especially those who are locked up. Even 30 days in the Cook County Jail is no picnic.

9   And: "What gives society the right to take a life if an individual can't?" The individuals who make up society give it that right. Societies perform many functions that individuals can't. We can't carry guns and shoot people, but we delegate that right to police.

10   Finally: "The death penalty doesn't deter crime." I heard from a number of people who have a less detached view of the death penalty than many of the sensitive souls who oppose it.

11   For instance, Doris Porch wrote me about a man on Death Row in Tennessee. He hired men to murder his wife. One threw in a rape, free of charge.

12   Porch wrote: "My family had the misfortune of knowing this man [the husband] intimately. The victim was my niece. After her decomposed body was found in the trunk of her car, I made the trip to Homicide with my sister."

13   Sharon Rosenfeldt of Canada wrote: "We know exactly what you are talking about because our son was brutally murdered and sexually abused by mass murderer Clifford Olson in Vancouver.

14   "Words can't explain the suffering the families of murder victims are left to live with. After two years, we're still trying to piece our lives back together mentally and spiritually."

15   Eleanor Lulenski of Cleveland said: "I'm the mother of one of the innocent victims. My son was a registered nurse on duty in an emergency room. A man walked in demanding a shot of penicillin. When he was told he would have to be evaluated by a physician, he stomped out, went to his car, came back with a shotgun and killed my son.

16   "He was sentenced to life, but after several years the sentence was reversed on a technicality—it being that at the time of his trial it was mentioned that this was his second murder."

17   And Susie James of Greenville, Miss.: "My tax dollars are putting bread into the mouth of at least one murderer from Mississippi who showed no mercy to his innocent victim.

18   "He caught a ride with her one cold February night. She was returning to her home from her job in a nursing home. She was a widow. The murderer, whom she had befriended, struck her on the head with a can of oil. Ignoring her pleas, he forced her through a barbed-wire fence into the woods at knifepoint. He stabbed her repeatedly, raped her and left her for dead.

19   "When the victim's son walked down the stairs to leave the courthouse after the guilty sentence had been uttered, he happened to look at the killer's mother.

20   "She said: 'You buzzard, watching me.'

21   "The murder victim was my mother."

22   There are many others. The mother of the boy who angered some drunken street thugs. They shot him and then ran him over repeatedly with a car. The mother whose son and daughter were beaten to death. The brother who remembers how his little sister would laugh as they played—until she was butchered.

23   They have many things in common. They suffered a terrible loss, and they live with terrible memories.

24   One other thing they share: The knowledge that the killers are alive and will probably remain alive and cared for by society.

25   Opponents of the death penalty should try explaining to these people just how cruel it is to kill someone.

Understanding the Content

Feel free to reread all or parts of the selection to answer the following questions.

1. What is Royko's viewpoint on the death penalty?

2. Royko says that he wishes people who oppose his views would come up with some new arguments. What are the "worn-out" ones he cites? What are his responses to each one?

3. Royko quotes from several letters written to him by relatives of murder victims. What does he say they all have in common?

4. What is the thesis? Is it implied or stated?

Looking at Structure and Style

1. Royko's essay originally appeared as a newspaper column, which is why there are so many short paragraphs. Are there any sentences you would combine into one paragraph if you were to edit this essay? Which ones? Why?

2. How would you describe the tone of this selection? What words or phrases contribute to this tone?

3. What is Royko's attitude toward people who oppose capital punishment? toward psychiatrists? How can you tell?

4. What is the basic writing method Royko uses in paragraphs 11–21? Is this effective?

5. Explain or rewrite the following passages from the essay:
   a. "...the quick dispatching of convicted murderers." (2)
   b. "Why would they ["shrinks"] want to spend all that time listening to Willie the Wolfman describe his ax murders when they can get $75 an hour for listening to an executive's fantasies about the secretarial pool?" (6)
   c. "Even 30 days in the Cook County Jail is no picnic." (8)
   d. "I heard from a number of people who have a less detached view of the death penalty than many of the sensitive souls who oppose it." (10)

6. To what audience is Royko writing? Explain.

Evaluating the Author's Viewpoints

1. Does Royko convince you that there should be laws allowing for "the quick dispatching of convicted murderers"? Why?

2. In paragraphs 4, 7, 9, and 10, Royko provides four "worn-out" arguments of those who oppose the death penalty. Are they worn-out? Comment on the reasoning he uses to disagree with them. Are they logical rebuttals? Is he convincing in his counterarguments for each one?

3. How effective is Royko's use of quotes from letters in paragraphs 11–21? Do they gain your sympathy? Is this "stacking the deck" in favor of his views?

4. What is the function of paragraph 22?

5. Do you agree with Royko's conclusion? Explain.

Pursuing Possible Essay Topics

Unless you already have an idea for an essay, wait until you have read all the selections on this issue and have studied the list of ideas at the end before deciding on your own topic related to capital punishment.

Preparing to Read

Before reading this selection, make certain you have read the introduction to this unit, pages 397–399.

Take a minute or two to look over the following reading selection. Note the title and author, read the opening paragraph, and check the length. Make certain you have time now to read it carefully and to do the exercises that follow it. Then, in the spaces provided, answer the following questions.

1. What does the title tell you about the author's viewpoint? _____

   _____

   _____

2. What do you think you will learn about capital punishment from reading

   this selection? _____

   _____

   _____

3. Do you think you will agree with the author's viewpoints? Why? _____

   _____

   _____

Vocabulary

Good comprehension of what you are about to read depends upon your understanding of the words below. The number following each word refers to the paragraph where it is used.

voir dire (4) a preliminary examination to decide if someone is eligible to serve on a jury

cerebral (4, 5) having to do with intellect, using the mind

inherently (4) basically, native, inborn

hypocritical (5) saying one thing but meaning or acting the opposite

retribution (6) revenge, payment in return for a wrong

deterrent (6) something that stops an occurrence

recidivism (6) a tendency to relapse into a former pattern of behavior, especially criminal habits

Now read the essay.

Death Penalty's False Promise

ANNA QUINDLEN

1   Ted Bundy and I go back a long way, to a time when there was a series of unsolved murders in Washington State known only as the Ted murders. Like a lot of reporters, I'm something of a crime buff. But the Washington Ted murders—and the ones that followed in Utah, Colorado and finally in Florida, where Ted Bundy was convicted and sentenced to die—fascinated me because I could see myself as one of the victims. I looked at the studio photographs of young women with long hair, pierced ears, easy smiles, and I read the descriptions: polite, friendly, quick to help, eager to please. I thought about being approached by a handsome young man asking for help, and I knew if I had been in the wrong place at the wrong time I would have been a goner.

2   By the time Ted finished up in Florida, law enforcement authorities suspected he had murdered dozens of young women. He and the death penalty seemed made for each other.

3   The death penalty and I, on the other hand, seem to have nothing in common. But Ted Bundy has made me think about it all over again, now that the outlines of my '60s liberalism have been filled in with a decade as a reporter covering some of the worst back alleys in New York City and three years as a mother who, like most, would lay down her life for her kids.

4   Simply put, I am opposed to the death penalty. I would tell that to any judge or lawyer undertaking the voir dire of jury candidates in a state in which the death penalty can be imposed. That is why I would be excused from such a jury. In a rational, completely cerebral way, I think the killing of one human being as punishment for the killing of another makes no sense and is inherently immoral.

5   But whenever my response to an important subject is rational and completely cerebral, I know there is something wrong with it— and so it is here. I have always been governed by my gut, and my gut says I am hypocritical about the death penalty. That is, I do not in theory think that Ted Bundy, or others like him, should be put to death. But if my daughter had been the one clubbed to death as she slept in a Tallahassee sorority house, and if the bite mark left in her buttocks had been one of the prime pieces of evidence against the young man charged with her murder, I would with the greatest plea- sure kill him myself.

6   The State of Florida will not permit the parents of Bundy's victims to do that, and, in a way, that is the problem with an emotional response to capital punishment. The only reason for a death penalty is to exact retribution. Is there anyone who really thinks that it is a deterrent, that there are considerable numbers of criminals out there who think twice about committing crimes because of the sentence involved? The ones I have met in the course of my professional duties have either sneered at the justice system, where they can exchange one charge for another with more ease than they could return a shirt to clothing store, or they have simply believed that it is the other guy who will get caught, get convicted, get the stiffest sentence. Of course, the death penalty would act as a deterrent by eliminating recidivism, but then so would life without parole, albeit at greater taxpayer expense.

7   I don't believe deterrence is what most proponents seek from the death penalty anyhow. Our most profound emotional response is to want criminals to suffer as their victims did. When a man is accused of throwing a child from a high-rise terrace, my emotional—some might say hysterical—response is that he should be given an oppor- tunity to see how endless the seconds are from the 31st story to the ground. In a civilized society that will never happen. And so what many people want from the death penalty, they will never get.

8   Death is death, you may say, and you would be right. But anyone

who has seen someone die suddenly of a heart attack and someone else slip slowly into the clutches of cancer knows that there are gradations of dying.

9   I watched a television re-enactment one night of an execution by lethal injection. It was well done; it was horrible. The methodical approach, people standing around the gurney waiting, made it more awful. One moment there was a man in a prone position; the next moment that man was gone. On another night I watched a television movie about a little boy named Adam Walsh, who disappeared from a shopping center in Florida. There was a re-enactment of Adam's parents coming to New York, where they appeared on morning talk shows begging for their son's return, and in their hotel room, where they received a call from the police saying that Adam had been found: not all of Adam, actually, just his severed head, discovered in the waters of a Florida canal. There is nothing anyone could do that is bad enough for an adult who took a 6-year-old boy away from his parents, perhaps tortured, then murdered, him and cut off his head. Nothing at all. Lethal injection? The electric chair? Bah.

10   And so I come back to the position that the death penalty is wrong, not only because it consists of stooping to the level of the killers, but also because it is not what it seems. Just before Ted Bundy's most recent execution date was postponed, pending further appeals, the father of his last known victim, a 12-year-old girl, said what almost every father in his situation must feel. "I wish they'd bring him back to Lake City," said Tom Leach of the town where Kimberly Leach lived and died, "and let us all have at him." But the death penalty does not let us all have at him in the way Mr. Leach seems to mean. What he wants is for something as horrifying as what happened to his child to happen to Ted Bundy. And that is impossible.

Understanding the Content

Feel free to reread all or parts of the essay in order to answer the following questions.

1. Based on what you read, who is Ted Bundy? What have you learned about him? Why does the author refer to him?

2. What arguments against the death penalty does Quindlen provide?

3. What does she claim is "the only argument" (6) for the death penalty?

4. What does Quindlen mean when she says the death penalty is "not what it seems" (10)?

Looking at Structure and Style

1. In the opening paragraph, Quindlen sees herself as a possible victim of Ted Bundy. What is her purpose in doing so?

2. Quindlen tells us quite a lot about herself. Why? What has the personal information to do with the death penalty?

3. To what audience do you think the author is writing? Why?

4. Look again at her arguments for opposing the death penalty. Are they based on facts?

5. Reread paragraph 9. Why does Quindlen write so graphically here? Does this style help support her thesis? Explain.

6. Is the thesis stated or implied? If stated, where?

Evaluating the Author's Viewpoints

1. Quindlen says that she does not believe Ted Bundy should be put to death, yet she says that had it been her daughter he murdered, she would "with the greatest pleasure kill him myself." Is this contradictory? Does this statement help or hurt her thesis? Explain.

2. Quindlen says that she does not believe deterrence is what most proponents of the death penalty seek; instead, they want revenge. Is she right? With what evidence does she support this view?

3. Quindlen believes that nothing is a bad enough punishment for someone who commits fiendish murders, including the death penalty. Is she right? Is this a sound argument against the death penalty?

4. Look through the essay for the following:
    a. Factual statements that support Quinden's thesis.
    b. Opinions or emotional appeals that support the thesis.
    c. The most convincing argument for her thesis.
    d. The weakest argument for her thesis.

Pursuing Possible Essay Topics

Unless you already have an idea for an essay, wait until you have read all the selections on this issue and have studied the list of ideas at the end before deciding on your own topic related to capital punishment.

 ## Preparing to Read

Before reading this selection, make certain you have read the introduction to this unit, pages 397–399.

Take a minute or two to look over the following reading selection. Note the title and author, read the first paragraph or two, and check the length. Make certain you have time now to read it carefully and to do the exercises that follow it. Then, in the spaces provided, answer the following questions.

1. What does the title tell you about the author's viewpoint? _____

_____

_____

2. What do you think you will learn about capital punishment from reading

this selection? _____

_____

_____

3. Do you think you will agree with the author's viewpoints? Why? _____

_____

_____

Vocabulary

Good comprehension of what you are about to read depends upon your understanding of the words below. The number following each word refers to the paragraph where it is used.

clemency (1) mercy, leniency
constituencies (4) those voters represented by an elected official
heinous (4) dreadful, wicked
flagrant (6) obvious, conspicuous
sophistic (10) an argument that sounds possible but is false
ambivalent (12) uncertain, mixed
paramount (15) primary, foremost, top of the list

Now read the essay.

Death and Justice

EDWARD I. KOCH

1   Last December a man named Robert Lee Willie, who had been convicted of raping and murdering an 18-year-old woman, was executed in the Louisiana state prison. In a statement issued several minutes before his death, Mr. Willie said: "Killing people is wrong.

...It makes no difference whether it's citizens, countries, or governments. Killing is wrong." Two weeks later in South Carolina, an admitted killer named Joseph Carl Shaw was put to death for murdering two teenagers. In an appeal to the governor for clemency, Mr. Shaw wrote: "Killing is wrong when I did it. Killing is wrong when you do it. I hope you have the courage and moral strength to stop the killing."

2   It is a curiosity of modern life that we find ourselves being lectured on morality by cold-blooded killers. Mr. Willie previously had been convicted of aggravated rape, aggravated kidnapping, and the murders of a Louisiana deputy and a man from Missouri. Mr. Shaw committed another murder a week before the two for which he was executed, and admitted mutilating the body of the 14-year-old girl he killed. I can't help wondering what prompted these murderers to speak out against killing as they entered the death-house door. Did their newfound reverence for life stem from the realization that they were about to lose their own?

3   Life is indeed precious, and I believe the death penalty helps to affirm this fact. Had the death penalty been a real possibility in the minds of these murderers, they might well have stayed their hand. They might have shown moral awareness before their victims died, and not after. Consider the tragic death of Rosa Velez, who happened to be home when a man named Luis Vera burglarized her apartment in Brooklyn. "Yeah, I shot her," Vera admitted. "She knew me, and I knew I wouldn't go to the chair."

4   During my 22 years in public service, I have heard the pros and cons of capital punishment expressed with special intensity. As a district leader, councilman, congressman, and mayor, I have represented constituencies generally thought of as liberal. Because I support the death penalty for heinous crimes of murder, I have sometimes been the subject of emotional and outraged attacks by voters who find my position reprehensible or worse. I have listened to their ideas. I have weighed their objections carefully. I still support the death penalty. The reasons I maintain my position can be best understood by examining the arguments most frequently heard in opposition.

5   (1) *The death penalty is "barbaric."* Sometimes opponents of capital punishment horrify with tales of lingering death on the gallows, of faulty electric chairs, or of agony in the gas chamber. Partly in response to such protests, several states such as North Carolina and Texas switched to execution by lethal injection. The condemned person is put to death painlessly, without ropes, voltage, bullets, or gas. Did this answer the objections of death penalty opponents. Of course not. On June 22, 1984, *The New York Times* published an editorial that sarcastically attacked the new "hygienic" method of death by

injection, and stated that "execution can never be made humane through science." So it's not the method that really troubles opponents. It's the death itself they consider barbaric.

6   Admittedly, capital punishment is not a pleasant topic. However, one does not have to like the death penalty in order to support it any more than one must like radical surgery, radiation, or chemotherapy in order to find necessary these attempts at curing cancer. Ultimately we may learn how to cure cancer with a simple pill. Unfortunately, that day has not yet arrived. Today we are faced with the choice of letting the cancer spread or trying to cure it with the methods available, methods that one day will almost certainly be considered barbaric. But to give up and do nothing would be far more barbaric and would certainly delay the discovery of an eventual cure. The analogy between cancer and murder is imperfect, because murder is not the "disease" we are trying to cure. The disease is injustice. We may not like the death penalty, but it must be available to punish crimes of cold-blooded murder, cases in which any other form of punishment would be inadequate and, therefore, unjust. If we create a society in which injustice is not tolerated, incidents of murder—the most flagrant form of injustice—will diminish.

7   (2) *No other major democracy uses the death penalty.* No other major democracy—in fact, few other countries of any description—is plagued by a murder rate such as that in the United States. Fewer and fewer Americans can remember the days when unlocked doors were the norm and murder was a rare and terrible offense. In America the murder rate climbed 122 percent between 1963 and 1980. During that same period, the murder rate in New York City increased by almost 400 percent, and the statistics are even worse in many other cities. A study at M.I.T. showed that based on 1970 homicide rates a person who lived in a large American city ran a greater risk of being murdered than an American soldier in World War II ran of being killed in combat. It is not surprising that the laws of each country differ according to differing conditions and traditions. If other countries had our murder problem, the cry for capital punishment would be just as loud as it is here. And I daresay that any other major democracy where 75 percent of the people supported the death penalty would soon enact it into law.

8   (3) *An innocent person might be executed by mistake.* Consider the work of Adam Bedau, one of the most implacable foes of capital punishment in this country. According to Mr. Bedau, it is "false sentimentality to argue that the death penalty should be abolished because of the abstract possibility that an innocent person might be executed." He cites a study of the 7,000 executions in this country from 1893 to 1971, and concludes that the record fails to show that

such cases occur. The main point, however, is this. If government functioned only when the possibility of error didn't exist, government wouldn't function at all. Human life deserves special protection, and one of the best ways to guarantee that protection is to assure that convicted murderers do not kill again. Only the death penalty can accomplish this end. In a recent case in New Jersey, a man named Richard Biegenwald was freed from prison after serving 18 years for murder; since his release he has been convicted of committing four murders. A prisoner named Lemuel Smith, who, while serving four life sentences for murder (plus two life sentences for kidnapping and robbery) in New York's Green Haven Prison, lured a woman corrections officer into the chaplain's office and strangled her. He then mutilated and dismembered her body. An additional life sentence for Smith is meaningless. Because New York has no death penalty statute, Smith has effectively been given a license to kill.

9 But the problem of multiple murder is not confined to the nation's penitentiaries. In 1981, 91 police officers were killed in the line of duty in this country. Seven percent of those arrested in the cases that have been solved had a previous arrest for murder. In New York City in 1976 and 1977, 85 persons arrested for homicide had a previous arrest for murder. Six of these individuals had two previous arrests for murder, and one had four previous murder arrests. During those two years the New York police were arresting for murder persons with a previous arrest for murder on the average of one every 8.5 days. This is not surprising when we learn that in 1975, for example, the median time served in Massachusetts for homicide was less than two-and-a-half years. In 1976 a study sponsored by the Twentieth Century Fund found that the average time served in the United States for first-degree murder is ten years. The median time served may be considerably lower.

10 (4) *Capital punishment cheapens the value of human life.* On the contrary, it can be easily demonstrated that the death penalty strengthens the value of human life. If the penalty for rape were lowered, clearly it would signal a lessened regard for the victims' suffering, humiliation, and personal integrity. It would cheapen their horrible experience, and expose them to an increased danger of recurrence. When we lower the penalty for murder, it signals a lessened regard for the value of the victim's life. Some critics of capital punishment, such as columnist Jimmy Breslin, have suggested that a life sentence is actually a harsher penalty for murder than death. This is sophistic nonsense. A few killers may decide not to appeal a death sentence, but the overwhelming majority make every effort to stay alive. It is by exacting the highest penalty for the taking of human life that we affirm the highest value of human life.

11   (5) *The death penalty is applied in a discriminatory manner.* This factor no longer seems to be the problem it once was. The appeals process for a condemned prisoner is lengthy and painstaking. Every effort is made to see that the verdict and sentence were fairly arrived at. However, assertions of discrimination are not an argument for ending the death penalty but for extending it. It is not justice to exclude everyone from the penalty of the law if a few are found to be so favored. Justice requires that the law be applied equally to all.

12   (6) *Thou Shalt Not Kill.* The Bible is our greatest source of moral inspiration. Opponents of the death penalty frequently cite the sixth of the Ten Commandments in an attempt to prove that capital punishment is divinely proscribed. In the original Hebrew, however, the Sixth Commandment reads, "Thou Shalt Not Commit Murder," and the Torah specifies capital punishment for a variety of offenses. The biblical viewpoint has been upheld by philosophers throughout history. The greatest thinkers of the 19th century—Kant, Locke, Hobbes, Rousseau, Montesquieu, and Mill—agreed that natural law properly authorizes the sovereign to take life in order to vindicate justice. Only Jeremy Bentham was ambivalent. Washington, Jefferson, and Franklin endorsed it. Abraham Lincoln authorized executions for deserters in wartime. Alexis de Tocqueville, who expressed profound respect for American institutions, believed that the death penalty was indispensable to the support of social order. The United States Constitution, widely admired as one of the seminal achievements in the history of humanity, condemns cruel and inhuman punishment, but does not condemn capital punishment.

13   (7) *The death penalty is state-sanctioned murder.* This is the defense with which Messrs. Willie and Shaw hoped to soften the resolve of those who sentenced them to death. By saying in effect, "You're no better than I am," the murderer seeks to bring his accusers down to his own level. It is also a popular argument among opponents of capital punishment, but a transparently false one. Simply put, the state has rights that the private individual does not. In a democracy, those rights are given to the state by the electorate. The execution of a lawfully condemned killer is no more an act of murder than is legal imprisonment an act of kidnapping. If an individual forces a neighbor to pay him money under threat of punishment, it's called extortion. If the state does it, it's called taxation. Rights and responsibilities surrendered by the individual are what give the state its power to govern. This contract is the foundation of civilization itself.

14   Everyone wants his or her rights, and will defend them jealously. Not everyone, however, wants responsibilities, especially the painful responsibilities that come with law enforcement. Twenty-one years ago a woman named Kitty Genovese was assaulted and murdered on

a street in New York. Dozens of neighbors heard her cries for help but did nothing to assist her. They didn't even call the police. In such a climate the criminal understandably grows bolder. In the presence of moral cowardice, he lectures us on our supposed failings and tries to equate his crimes with our quest for justice.

15 The death of anyone—even a convicted killer—diminishes us all. But we are diminished even more by a justice system that fails to function. It is an illusion to let ourselves believe that doing away with capital punishment removes the murderer's deed from our conscience. The rights of society are paramount. When we protect guilty lives, we give up innocent lives in exchange. When opponents of capital punishment say to the state: "I will not let you kill in my name," they are also saying to murderers: "You can kill in your *own* name as long as I have an excuse for not getting involved."

16 It is hard to imagine anything worse than being murdered while neighbors do nothing. But something worse exists. When those same neighbors shrink back from justly punishing the murderer, the victim dies twice.

Understanding the Content

1. What argument *for* the death penalty does Koch give for each of the following arguments against?
   a. The death penalty is "barbaric."
   b. No other major democracy uses the death penalty.
   c. An innocent person might be executed by mistake.
   d. Capital punishment cheapens the value of human life.
   e. The death penalty is applied in a discriminatory manner.
   f. Thou Shalt Not Kill.

2. What do you learn about the author in the essay? Why does he tell you about himself?

3. Is Koch's argument based mostly on fact or on opinion? Explain.

4. What does Koch mean when he says, "the victim dies twice" (16) if the murder isn't justly punished?

Looking at Structure and Style

1. Is the thesis stated or implied? If stated, where?

2. What is the point of quoting the two convicted murders on death row in paragraph 1? Is this an effective technique? Explain.

3. Koch chooses to defend capital punishment by refuting what he says are the most prevalent arguments of those who oppose the death penalty. Is this a good method? Does it make him seem more knowledgeable on the subject? Explain.

4. What is the function of paragraph 4?

5. How well does the author use outside sources to reinforce his arguments? What are some of his sources?

Evaluating the Author's Viewpoints

1. Koch says, "If we create a society in which injustice is not tolerated, incidents of murder—the most flagrant for of injustice—will diminish." Do you agree? Why?

2. Do you agree with Koch's distinction between murder and capital punishment? Why?

3. Do you agree with the analogies he draws in paragraph 13 about imprisonment vs. kidnapping and taxation vs. extortion (blackmail)? Are these good analogies? Explain.

4. How well does Koch conclude his essay? Is it convincing? Explain.

5. Look through the essay for the following:
   a. Factual statements that support the author's thesis.
   b. Opinions or emotional appeals that support the thesis.
   c. The most convincing argument for the thesis.
   d. The weakest argument for the thesis.

Pursuing Possible Essay Topics

Unless you already have an idea for an essay, wait until you have read all the selections on this issue and have studied the list of ideas at the end before deciding on your own topic related to capital punishment.

Preparing to Read

Before reading this selection, make certain you have read the introduction to this unit, pages 397–399.

Take a minute or two to look over the following reading selection. Note the title and author, read the first *two* paragraphs, and check the length. Make certain you have the time now to read it carefully and to do the exercises that follow it. Then, in the spaces provided, answer the following questions.

1. What do the title and the opening paragraph tell you about the subject

of the essay? _____

2. What is King's view of capital punishment? _____

_____

3. Having read Royko's and Koch's views in the earlier essays, what should

   you look for in this essay? _____

_____

_____

4. Have you heard of the author? What do you know about her? _____

_____

_____

Vocabulary

Good comprehension of what you are about to read depends upon your understanding of the words below. The number following each refers to the paragraph where it is used.

backlash (3) angry reaction

abhor (3) strongly hate

sanctioned (3) permitted

deterrent (3) prevention, a discouraging force

unequivocally (4) clearly, without doubt

capital offenses (4) crimes involving death

redeemed (5) made up for

retaliation (5) revenge, paying back evil with evil

irrevocable (7) irreversible

miscarriage (7) mismanagement, bad administration

specter (7) haunting possibility

unwarranted (8) not supported by facts

inequitable (9) unfair

credibility (10) believability

proponents (11) supporters, those in favor of

defies (11) challenges

Now read the essay.

The Death Penalty Is a Step Back

CORETTA SCOTT KING

1   When Steven Judy was executed in Indiana [in 1981], America took another step backwards towards legitimizing murder as a way of dealing with evil in our society.

2   Although Judy was convicted of four of the most horrible and brutal murders imaginable, and his case is probably the worst in recent memory for opponents of the death penalty, we still have to face the real issue squarely: Can we expect a decent society if the state is allowed to kill its own people?

3   In recent years, an increase of violence in America, both individual and political, has prompted a backlash of public opinion on capital punishment. But however much we abhor violence, legally sanctioned executions are no deterrent and are, in fact, immoral and unconstitutional.

4   Although I have suffered the loss of two family members by assassination, I remain firmly and unequivocally opposed to the death penalty for those convicted of capital offenses.

5   An evil deed is not redeemed by an evil deed of retaliation. Justice is never advanced in the taking of a human life.

6   Morality is never upheld by legalized murder. Morality apart, there are a number of practical reasons which form a powerful argument against capital punishment.

7   First, capital punishment makes irrevocable any possible miscarriage of justice. Time and again we have witnessed the specter of mistakenly convicted people being put to death in the name of American criminal justice. To those who say that, after all, this doesn't occur too often, I can only reply that if it happens just once, that is too often. And it has occurred many times.

8   Second, the death penalty reflects an unwarranted assumption that the wrongdoer is beyond rehabilitation. Perhaps some individuals cannot be rehabilitated; but who shall make that determination? Is any amount of academic training sufficient to entitle one person to judge another incapable of rehabilitation?

9   Third, the death penalty is inequitable. Approximately half of the 711 persons now on death row are black. From 1930 through 1968, 53.5% of those executed were black Americans, all too many of whom were represented by court-appointed attorneys and convicted after hasty trials.

10   The argument that this may be an accurate reflection of guilt, and homicide trends, instead of a racist application of laws lacks credibility in light of a recent Florida survey which showed that persons convicted of killing whites were four times more likely to receive a death sentence than those convicted of killing blacks.

11   Proponents of capital punishment often cite a "deterrent effect" as the main benefit of the death penalty. Not only is there no hard evidence that murdering murderers will deter other potential killers, but even the "logic" of this argument defies comprehension.

12   Numerous studies show that the majority of homicides committed in this country are the acts of the victim's relatives, friends and acquaintances in the "heat of passion."

13   What this strongly suggests is that rational consideration of future consequences is seldom a part of the killer's attitude at the time he commits a crime.

14   The only way to break the chain of violent reaction is to practice nonviolence as individuals and collectively through our laws and institutions.

Understanding the Content

Feel free to reread all or parts of the selection in order to answer the following questions.

1. What is King's viewpoint toward the death penalty?

2. Aside from her feeling that capital punishment is immoral, what "practical reasons" does she present as arguments against it?

3. King says that proponents of the death penalty often cite it as a "deterrent effect." What argument does she present against this claim?

4. King cites a recent Florida survey which showed that persons convicted of killing whites were four times more likely to receive a death sentence than those convicted of killing blacks. How does she interpret this statistic?

5. Does King suggest an alternative to the death penalty? Explain.

Looking at Structure and Style

1. What is the function of the first two paragraphs?

2. In paragraph 4, King refers to the assassination of two family members, including her husband, Martin Luther King, Jr. What effect might this experience have on her credibility to discuss capital punishment?

3. What transitional devices does King use in paragraphs 6–9?

4. Paragraphs 7–9 state what King calls "practical reasons which form a powerful argument against capital punishment." What is the function of paragraphs 10–11? What arguments in favor of the death penalty does King dispute?

5. What is the point being made in paragraphs 12–13? How do they relate to her thesis?

6. How effective is King's concluding paragraph?

7. Explain or rewrite the following passages from the essay:
   a. "An evil deed is not redeemed by an evil deed of retaliation." (5)
   b. "...Capital punishment makes irrevocable any possible miscarriage of justice." (7)
   c. "Time and again we have witnessed the specter of mistakenly convicted people being put to death in the name of...justice." (7)
   d. "The only way to break the chain of violent reaction is to practice nonviolence as individuals and collectively through our laws and institutions." (14)

Evaluating the Author's Viewpoints

1. Reread the rhetorical question King asks in paragraph 2. Based on what Royko says in his essay, how would he answer the question? (See Royko, paragraph 9.) What is your response?

2. One of King's arguments against the death penalty is that it "makes irrevocable any possible miscarriage of justice." What does she mean? Do you agree that even if it only happens once it is too often? Why? What do you think Koch's response would be? (See Koch, paragraph 8.)

3. Another of her arguments is that no one can say whether or not a person can be rehabilitated, implying that efforts toward rehabilitation should always be made. Reread paragraphs 4–6 in Royko's essay. How does his discussion of rehabilitation differ from King's? Which one presents the better argument? Why?

4. King says that the death penalty does not deter crime (paragraphs 3 and 11); Royko implies it does (paragraphs 10+). Who provides the better argument? How and why?

5. King calls the death penalty "inequitable." What does she mean? Is her support valid?

6. Reread paragraph 14. Is King correct? Explain.

Pursuing Possible Essay Topics

Unless you already have an idea for an essay, wait until you have read all the selections on this issue and have studied the ideas at the end before deciding on your own topic related to capital punishment.

📖 *Preparing to Read*

Before reading this selection, make certain you have read the introduction to this unit, pages 397–399.

Take a minute or two to look over the following reading selection. Note the title and author, read the opening paragraph, and check the length. Make certain you have time now to read it carefully and to do the exercises that follow it. Then, in the spaces provided, answer the following questions.

1. The title tells you something about the subject of the essay, but what do

   you think the author will say about it? _____

   _____

   _____

2. Based on the opening paragraph, what might make this essay different

   from the others on capital punishment? _____

   _____

   _____

3. What do you think you will learn about capital punishment from reading

   this selection? _____

   _____

   _____

4. What do you think the author's viewpoint on capital punishment might

   be? _____

   _____

Vocabulary

Good comprehension of what you are about to read depends upon your understanding of the words below. The number following each word refers to the paragraph where it is used.

sodden (1) soaking wet
warders (2) guards, watchmen

desolately (3) weakly, mutely, sounding thin and isolated

Dravidian (4) a member of a native tribe of southern India whose native tongue is Dravidian

magistrates (6) judges, justices

pariah (6) a social outcast

gambolled (8) behaved playfully

incuriously (8) with no curiosity or interest

servile (11) groveling, lowly, slave-like

Ram (12) probably a reference to Rama, a god-like hero in Hinduism

timorously (15) shyly

Now read the essay.

A Hanging

GEORGE ORWELL

1   It was in Burma, a sodden morning of the rains. A sickly light, like yellow tinfoil, was slanting over the high walls into the jail yard. We were waiting outside the condemned cells, a row of sheds fronted with double bars, like small animal cages. Each cell measured about ten feet by ten and was quite bare within except for a plank bed and a pot for drinking water. In some of them brown, silent men were squatting at the inner bars, with their blankets draped round them. These were the condemned men, due to be hanged within the next week or two.

2   One prisoner had been brought out of his cell. He was a Hindu, a puny wisp of a man, with a shaven head and vague liquid eyes. He had a thick, sprouting mustache, absurdly too big for his body, rather like the mustache of a comic man on the films. Six tall Indian warders were guarding him and getting him ready for the gallows. Two of them stood by with rifles and fixed bayonets, while the others handcuffed him, passed a chain through his handcuffs and fixed it to their belts, and lashed his arms tight to his sides. They crowded very close about him, with their hands always on him in a careful, caressing grip, as though all the while feeling him to make sure he was there. It was like men handling a fish which is still alive and may jump back into the water. But he stood quite unresisting, yielding his arms limply to the ropes, as though he hardly noticed what was happening.

3   Eight o'clock struck and a bugle call, desolately thin in the wet air, floated from the distant barracks. The superintendent of the jail, who was standing apart from the rest of us, moodily prodding the

gravel with his stick, raised his head at the sound. He was an army doctor, with a grey toothbrush mustache and a gruff voice. "For God's sake, hurry up, Francis," he said irritably. "The man ought to have been dead by this time. Aren't you ready yet?"

4   Francis, the head jailer, a fat Dravidian in a white drill suit and gold spectacles, waved his black hand. "Yes sir, yes sir," he bubbled. "All iss satisfactorily prepared. The hangman iss waiting. We shall proceed."

5   "Well, quick march, then. The prisoners can't get their breakfast till this job's over."

6   We set out for the gallows. Two warders marched on either side of the prisoner, with their rifles at the slope; two others marched close against him, gripping him by arm and shoulder, as though at once pushing and supporting him. The rest of us, magistrates and the like, followed behind. Suddenly, when we had gone ten yards, the procession stopped short without any order or warning. A dreadful thing had happened—a dog, come goodness knows whence, had appeared in the yard. It came bounding among us with a loud volley of barks and leapt round us wagging its whole body, wild with glee at finding so many human beings together. It was a large woolly dog, half Airedale, half pariah. For a moment it pranced around us, and then, before anyone could stop it, it had made a dash for the prisoner, and jumping up tried to lick his face. Everybody stood aghast, too taken aback even to grab the dog.

7   "Who let that bloody brute in here?" said the superintendent angrily. "Catch it, someone!"

8   A warder detached from the escort, charged clumsily after the dog, but it danced and gambolled just out of his reach, taking everything as part of the game. A young Eurasian jailer picked up a handful of gravel and tried to stone the dog away, but it dodged the stones and came after us again. Its yaps echoed from the jail walls. The prisoner, in the grasp of the two warders, looked on incuriously, as though this was another formality of the hanging. It was several minutes before someone managed to catch the dog. Then we put my handkerchief through its collar and moved off once more, with the dog still straining and whimpering.

9   It was about forty yards to the gallows. I watched the bare brown back of the prisoner marching in front of me. He walked clumsily with his bound arms, but quite steadily, with that bobbing gait of the Indian who never straightens his knees. At each step his muscles slid neatly into place, the lock of hair on his scalp danced up and down, his feet printed themselves on the wet gravel. And once, in spite of the men who gripped him by each shoulder, he stepped lightly aside to avoid a puddle on the path.

10   It is curious; but till that moment I had never realized what it

means to destroy a healthy, conscious man. When I saw the prisoner step aside to avoid the puddle, I saw the mystery, the unspeakable wrongness, of cutting a life short when it is in full tide. This man was not dying, he was alive just as we are alive. All the organs of his body were working—bowels digesting food, skin renewing itself, nails growing, tissues forming—all toiling away in solemn foolery. His nails would still be growing when he stood on the drop, when he was falling through the air with a tenth-of-a-second to live. His eyes saw the yellow gravel and the grey walls, and his brain still remembered, foresaw, reasoned—even about puddles. He and we were a party of men walking together, seeing, hearing, feeling, understanding the same world; and in two minutes, with a sudden snap, one of us would be gone—one mind less, one world less.

11   The gallows stood in a small yard, separate from the main grounds of the prison, and overgrown with tall prickly weeds. It was a brick erection like three sides of a shed, with planking on top, and above that two beams and a crossbar with the rope dangling. The hangman, a greyhaired convict in the white uniform of the prison, was waiting beside his machine. He greeted us with a servile crouch as we entered. At a word from Francis the two warders, gripping the prisoner more closely than ever, half led, half pushed him to the gallows and helped him clumsily up the ladder. Then the hangman climbed up and fixed the rope round the prisoner's neck.

12   We stood waiting, five yards away. The warders had formed in a rough circle round the gallows. And then, when the noose was fixed, the prisoner began crying out to his god. It was a high, reiterated cry of "Ram! Ram! Ram! Ram!" not urgent and fearful like a prayer or cry for help, but steady, rhythmical, almost like the tolling of a bell. The dog answered the sound with a whine. The hangman, still standing on the gallows, produced a small cotton bag like a flour bag and drew it down over the prisoner's face. But the sound, muffled by the cloth, still persisted, over and over again: "Ram! Ram! Ram! Ram! Ram!"

13   The hangman climbed down and stood ready, holding the lever. Minutes seemed to pass. The steady, muffled crying from the prisoner went on and on, "Ram! Ram! Ram!" never faltering for an instant. The superintendent, his head on his chest, was slowly poking the ground with his stick; perhaps he was counting the cries, allowing the prisoner a fixed number—fifty, perhaps, or a hundred. Everyone had changed colour. The Indians had gone grey like bad coffee, and one or two of the bayonets were wavering. We looked at the lashed, hooded man on the drop, and listened to his cries—each cry another second of life; the same thought was in all our minds; oh, kill him quickly, get it over, stop that abominable noise!

14   Suddenly the superintendent made up his mind. Throwing up his

head he made a swift motion with his stick. "Chalo!" he shouted almost fiercely.

15   There was a clanking noise, and then dead silence. The prisoner had vanished, and the rope was twisting on itself. I let go of the dog, and it galloped immediately to the back of the gallows; but when it got there it stopped short, barked, and then retreated into a corner of the yard, where it stood among the weeds, looking timorously out at us. We went round the gallows to inspect the prisoner's body. He was dangling with his toes pointed straight downwards, very slowly revolving, as dead as a stone.

16   The superintendent reached out with his stick and poked the bare brown body; it oscillated slightly. *"He's* all right," said the superintendent. He backed out from under the gallows, and blew out a deep breath. The moody look had gone out of his face quite suddenly. He glanced at his wrist-watch. "Eight minutes past eight. Well, that's all for this morning, thank God."

17   The warders unfixed bayonets and marched away. The dog, sobered and conscious of having misbehaved itself, slipped after them. We walked out of the gallows yard, past the condemned cells with their waiting prisoners, into the big central yard of the prison. The convicts, under the command of warders armed with lathis, were already receiving their breakfast. They squatted in long rows, each man holding a tin pannikin, while two warders with buckets marched around ladling out rice; it seemed quite a homely, jolly scene, after the hanging. An enormous relief had come upon us now that the job was done. One felt an impulse to sing, to break into a run, to snigger. All at once everyone began chattering gaily.

Understanding the Content

1. Where did the hanging take place? Who was being hanged? Are we told why? Does it make any difference to the point of the essay?

2. Why is the superintendent in charge of the hanging in such a hurry?

3. When a dog came into the hanging yard, Orwell calls it a "dreadful thing." Why? Why do you think Orwell included the episode in his account of the hanging?

4. Orwell's attitude about the hanging seems to change when the prisoner, walking to the gallows, steps aside to avoid a puddle. Why the change?

5. How did the crowd watching the hanging act once the execution was over? Why do you think they reacted as they did?

6. What is Orwell's attitude toward capital punishment?

Looking at Structure and Style

1. Orwell includes a good deal of description in his essay. Find some examples of figurative language, such as metaphors and similes, that you feel are effectively used. What do they add to the feeling of the hanging?

2. Why does the author provide such detailed descriptions of the prisoners' cells? the Hindu about to be hanged? the preparations for the execution?

3. Discuss Orwell's description of the following: the superintendent; Francis; the prisoner; the dog; the crowd; the hangman; the hanging itself.

4. How does the episode with the dog, especially its joyous licking of the prisoner's face, add or detract to the picture of the hanging?

5. How effective is the ending? Do such actions of the author and the crowd seem appropriate? Explain.

6. How would you describe Orwell's tone and attitude?

7. What is Orwell's thesis? Is it implied or stated? If stated, where?

Evaluating the Author's Viewpoints

1. Orwell says, "It was curious; but till that moment I had never realized what it means to destroy a healthy, conscious man." Is this abnormal? Could he be speaking for most of us? Explain.

2. As the prisoner was crying, "Ram," Orwell says "the same thought was in all our minds; oh, kill him quickly, get it over, stop that abominable noise!" What is your reaction to this statement?

3. After such an experience, do you think you might react as Orwell and the crowd did? Explain.

Pursuing Possible Essay Topics

1. Pick one of the essays on capital punishment and write an argument against the author's viewpoint. Show the fallacies (examples of false or incorrect reasoning) in the argument. Or agree with one of the authors, but provide your own arguments. Use quotations from the essay you are reacting to.

2. King claims that the death penalty is "unconstitutional." Read the Constitution and its Amendments (found in the appendix of most United States history books) and write an essay that supports or refutes King's position.

3. Write an essay that outlines your opinion of when the death penalty is and is not appropriate.

4. Write an essay on your views of the death penalty using arguments that none of the essays in the unit discuss.

5. Between 1930–1967, 3,859 people were legally executed. Of this number a slight majority were blacks, a proportion that is far above blacks' share of the population. This supports King's statistics in paragraph 9. But what do current statistics show? Do some research on the number of legal executions since 1977. Does King's implication that there is racial discrimination when applying the death penalty seem plausible?

6. In a 1986 Gallup Poll, 70 percent of the people polled were in favor of the death penalty. Between 1977 and 1987, 37 states passed new death-penalty laws. Twenty years earlier, a slight majority opposed the death penalty. Should laws regarding the death penalty change based on popular opinion? Are most people well informed enough to make intelligent decisions on the subject? How important are emotions in making such a decision?

7. Research information on the death penalty that has been published since 1981. Use the sources to take a stand on capital punishment. In addition to your library's card catalog and the *Reader's Guide to Periodical Literature*, you might want to look in the *Criminology and Penology Abstracts*.

8. Brainstorm or freewrite on one or more of the following:
   a. death row
   b. degrees of murder
   c. death penalty as deterrent
   d. "an eye for an eye"
   e. punishment for crimes
   f. legal loopholes

9. If you don't like any of these ideas, write an essay on some other aspect of capital punishment.

ISSUE II: VIEWPOINTS ON MULTICULTURAL EDUCATION

At the time this book goes to press, the term "multiculturalism" is being argued in academic circles as well as in the popular media. The argument, basically over what should be taught in the humanities and the social sciences, has even filtered down into disputes about what should be taught in grades K–12.

Educators are questioning the place of the classics, which are basically European in thought, in our literature classrooms. Do the Great Books, which deal with such ancient Greek philosophers as Aristotle and Plato and their heritage, and classical literature, like Shakespeare and Tolstoy, still have a place in the school's curriculum? Should history classes continue to be taught with an emphasis on European discovery? Yes, say the traditionalists. Or, should they be replaced with multicultural writings, introducing students to African-American, Asian, and third world literature and thought? Yes, say the multiculturalists. Some multiculturalists, for example, those labeled "Afrocentric," want African and African-American history and literature to be at the core of schools for African-Americans.

The essays in this section present you with various viewpoints on this controversy. Some of the courses you are presently taking may even be in the process of change or flux because of this issue. Carefully read each of the following essays. If you can, avoid taking sides until you have understood and evaluated each author's argument. You will then be asked to write an argumentative essay of your own on this topic.

📖 Preparing to Read

Before reading this selection, make certain you have read the introduction to Unit 10, pages 397–399.

Take a minute or two to look over the following reading selection. Note the title and author, read the opening paragraph, and check the length. It is longer than most other essays in this unit. Make certain you have time now to read it carefully and to do the exercises that follow it. Then, in the spaces provided, answer the following questions.

1. How do you define "multiculturalism"? _____

    _____

    _____

2. What does the title tell you about the author's viewpoint on his subject?

    _____

    _____

3. What do you think you will learn about multiculturalism from reading

    this selection? _____

    _____

    _____

4. Do you think you will agree or disagree with the author's viewpoints?

    Why? _____

    _____

Vocabulary

Good comprehension of what you are about to read depends upon your understanding of the words below. The number following each word refers to the paragraph where it is used.

syllabi (1, 7, 18) outlines or summaries of courses taught (plural of *syllabus*)

multiculturalism (1) in education, the belief that all cultural backgrounds be given equal recognition

misnomer (2) a name wrongly used or applied

derives (4) comes from, begins with

Afrocentrism (5) the belief that African and Afro-American studies should be at the core of the curriculum

the Holocaust (7) the term applied to the Nazis' attempt to exterminate the Jews during World War II

vouchers (9) tickets, passes, permits

nuanced (11, 14) shaded, subtly touched up

inculcation (11) conversion, teaching, instilling

acquiescence (13) submission, compliance

lineaments (19) characteristic features

polity (20) form of political organization

congeries (21) collection

Serbia, Croatia, Quebec (23) three countries that, at the time of this writing, wanted to be independent from their present government

Now read the essay.

In Defense of Multiculturalism

NATHAN GLAZER

1   I served as a member of the committee appointed by New York's commissioner of education, Thomas Sobol, to review the social studies syllabi in the state's elementary and high schools. Our committee, composed of academics and teachers, was not particularly biased toward strong advocates of multiculturalism. It included critics of the multicultural trend—Arthur Schlesinger, Kenneth Jackson, Paul

Gagnon, and myself. Nevertheless, the report that emerged, "One Nation, Many Peoples: A Declaration of Cultural Interdependence," called for further acknowledgment of American diversity, and was severely attacked by some members of the committee, and in many editorials, for further dissolving the common bonds that make us a nation. I also appended critical remarks to the report, yet had reservations in joining in a frontal attack. The report needs its sharp critics.... But we also need to see why the demand for something called multiculturalism is now so widespread, and why American education will have to respond to it.

2   Multiculturalism can mean many things, and no one argues with a curriculum that gives proper weight to the role of American Indians, blacks, Asians, and European immigrant and ethnic groups in American history. But as currently used, the word "multiculturalism" is something of a misnomer. It suggests a general desire or need for students to have something in the curriculum that relates to their own ethnic traits, if these exist, or to those of their parents or ancestors. I don't think this desire is particularly widespread among many ethnic groups. "We are all immigrants" is nice rhetoric, but in fact we are not all immigrants. Some of us came in the last decade, some of our parents came long before that, many millions of us have only the haziest idea of how many ancestors came from where. Since 1980 the census has included a new question, "What is your ancestry?" The great majority of respondents report two, three, or more ancestries. Tens of millions simply insist on being "American," and nothing else.

3   Nor does multiculturalism reflect the increased immigration of recent decades, particularly to some of our largest cities, such as New York, Los Angeles, San Francisco, and Miami. It is not the new immigrants who are arguing for multiculturalism. Most of them would be content with the education provided to the previous waves of European immigrants, which paid not a whit of attention to their ethnic or racial background, or to their distinct culture or language. A product of that kind of education, I was also quite content with it.

4   But if it is not the new immigration that is driving the multicultural demands, what is? Multiculturalism in its present form derives basically from black educators. It is one of the longest settled elements in the American population that makes the sharpest case for multiculturalism. Asians, who make up half of current immigrants, are not much concerned. Nor are Spanish-speaking immigrants from Central and South America. Puerto Ricans and Mexican-Americans do tend to support bilingual education and the mainte-

nance of the Spanish language. But they are definitely junior partners in the fight for multiculturalism.

5   I'm convinced that were it not for the pattern of poor achievement among blacks in the schools, the multicultural movement would lose much of its force. Even taking into account recent progress among blacks, shown in NAEP (National Assessment of Educational Progress) scores, SAT scores, and high school graduation rates, blacks still regularly score below whites, often below Hispanics and Native Americans, and far below Asians. Multiculturalism, and one of its variants, Afrocentrism, is presented to us by black educators and leaders as one of the means whereby this deficiency may be overcome.

6   It is not a new proposal, though it has achieved greater force and notoriety in the past few years. Many of us are simply not aware how far advanced our schools already are on the road to a black-oriented version of multiculturalism. The SATs, according to David Reich in *The New York Times*, are now thoroughly multicultural, the questions requiring knowledge of Zora Neale Hurston, Ralph Ellison, Richard Wright, Gwendolyn Brooks, Lorraine Hansberry, and Jackie Robinson (he comes up twice). The fiction reading is from Maya Angelou. Diane Ravitch and Chester Finn, in *What Do Our 17-Year-Olds Know?*, report that in a national sample of 17-year-olds more could identify Harriet Tubman than Winston Churchill or Joseph Stalin, more knew Tubman than knew that George Washington commanded the American Army during the Revolution, or that Lincoln wrote the Emancipation Proclamation.

7   The mass of materials that flowed in on us as we worked on our report showed how established multiculturalism was in New York state. One of the documents listed teachers' guides available from the State Education Department, in addition to the social studies syllabi. Of the seven publications available, four dealt with minorities and women. One of them, the most substantial, was a three-volume publication on the teaching of the Holocaust. A survey of in-service workshops completed by New York state teachers in 1990–91 showed that far more had taken workshops on African history, black studies, ethnic studies, multicultural education, and cultural diversity than on American and European history.

8   One of the reasons all this is so agitating to so many is historical. After all, when Jewish and Italian American students dominated the public schools of New York City, George Washington and Abraham Lincoln were still on the walls, not Herzl and Garibaldi, and students were told that the Anglo-American forefathers of the American commonwealth were their forefathers. The students and their parents did not object, and most embraced the new identity. This background dominates much of the argument over multiculturalism. "We didn't

get it, why should they? We didn't need it, why do they? We didn't want it, why do they?" But things change. They—and by that I mean primarily American blacks—may need it. I say "may" because we don't know. Nor are we clear on how many want it, but there are certainly a good number.

9　　Multiculturalism today is in the same class as the proposals for schools for black boys, another desperate try to help black high school achievement. Or vouchers to permit black students to attend private black schools. In view of the extensive failure among low-income blacks, it is not easy to stand four-square against these proposals, particularly when advanced by black advocates aiming to overcome black school failure.

10　　I do not see how school systems with a majority of black and Latino students, with black or Latino leadership at the top, as is true of almost all our big-city school systems, can stand firmly against the multicultural thrust. The new president of the New York City Board of Education, H. Carl McCall, is reported by *The New York Times* as saying he could support a school "focusing primarily, but not exclusively, on black male students" and that "an Afrocentric curriculum . . . can be positive." One could add other testimonials, from members of other big-city school boards, and from school superintendents. In the big cities, in many schools, an unbalanced, indeed distorted view of American and world history and culture is prevailing. We should fight its excesses. Yet when set against the reality of majorities of black and Latino students in these schools, the political dominance of black and Latino administrators, the weak preparation of teachers and administrators in history, and the responsiveness of textbook publishers to organized pressure, the weight of the truth of history, as determined by the best scholars, is reduced to only one interest.

11　　This may appear shocking, but it is not an entirely new phenomenon. In the elementary and high schools, a properly nuanced historical truth based on the best available evidence has always been only one interest among many. History in the schools has always played a socializing, nationalizing function (sometimes a regional pride function, as in the Southern versions of some texts). That function was the inculcation of patriotism in immigrants, and their assimilation to a culture deriving from England, and the experience of English-speaking colonists.

12　　Some recent trends, even without the pressure of multiculturalists, are already changing that pattern. The most important is the general challenge to an unquestioning, simple, and direct American patriotism. After the past twenty years, with the relative decline of American power and the doubts about an unblemished American virtue, we will not have the triumphalist history that prevailed until a few decades ago. Our little war in Iraq will not turn around this tendency to be skeptical about the American past and present. (The worst of all histories, except for all the others, we might say.)

13   What does one do in the face of these trends? One thing is to fight the errors, distortions, untruths, imbalances. Some of the comments attached to the report did that, and the report fortunately did not add further weight to the more extreme claims. But the sharper critics of the report, I believe, have failed to recognize that demographic and political pressures change the history that is to be taught. They direct us to look for things we could not have noticed before. Assertions that are at first glance fantastic may have to be given some modest acquiescence. Yes, it seems that there were some Egyptian pharaohs who were racially black. (What one makes of it is another matter.) Yes, it seems that some ancient Greeks believed that they got their gods, myths, mystical knowledge from ancient Egypt. Martin Bernal's *Black Athena* will eventually leave some deposit in textbook accounts. (It will be ironic if one consequence of Afrocentrism is that our students, who know nothing of ancient Greece and less of ancient Egypt, will now be forced to learn something in order to accommodate the argument of African influences!) Yes, there is another side to the story of the expansion of Europe and imperialism. Yes, it is possible that, as the economic historian Barbara Solow argues, the weight of slave-produced plantation products was much greater in shaping the economy of the American colonies than is generally understood. Yes, there is a Mexican perspective on the Mexican-American War, and when one deals with classes that are dominantly Latin American it would be best to know it. And so on.

14   Black and Hispanic advocates will call for these new perspectives; historians, attracted by new ideas, politicized by new trends, looking for new topics, will explore them, and their researches will over time change weight and nuance in the treatment of various issues in the textbooks. It's happened before; it will happen again.

15   Yet another development bears on the multicultural problem. This is the push for more choice in the public school system. That effort, supported by conservatives today, was first introduced as a policy alternative in American education in the late 1960s by liberals and radicals. Choice bears upon this debate because it implies diversity of curricula, because there should be something to choose among. It implies that quite a range of emphases may be offered, from Afrocentrism to Eurocentrism—perhaps, some have noted in alarm, the spectrum will run all the way from black Muslims to white racists.

16   In Milwaukee today hundreds of low-income black students attend, with state grants, inner-city black private schools, some of which emphasize Afrocentrism or black nationalism in their curricula. This program, under strong attack by the local teachers' union and others, has been adopted less because Milwaukee black leaders want to promote Afrocentrism than because they are fed up with the poor education their children receive in the public schools and hope that private schools, whatever their orientation, will do better—a view bolstered by the researches of James Coleman, John Chubb, and Terry Moe.

17   The movement for choice means the acceptance of more diversity in school curricula. At the margin, this diversity can be limited, if public funds are to be provided to assist choice. But there seems to me a kind of contradiction in simultaneously insisting on a strong, common, assimilationist curriculum in the public schools and accepting a wide range of diversity in the non-public school system. The line between the two systems and the two functions will not be easily maintained.

18   Inevitably, the current debate is focused on high-profile reports, large statements. But much of it ignores the reality of what goes on in American schooling. While multiculturalism and Afrocentrism race ahead in some schools and systems, others may happily continue to be the schools many of us remember and approve of, with only some modest modifications to prepare students for tests with a surprisingly high content of questions dealing with blacks and women, and particularly black women. The New York state report is only one step in a process that is far from concluded. The syllabi we reviewed are not required or imposed. The specific curricula of the classrooms are developed by hundreds of school districts, thousands of schools, many thousands of administrators and teachers. The syllabi are themselves broad outlines with examples. Many schools in the state already do more in the way of "multiculturalism" than the syllabi call for, many do less, and this ragged pattern will continue.

19   Whatever the strength of the multicultural thrust, I believe that American history in its main lineaments will have to be what it has been, and will not become completely alien to those of us educated in another time. We will find the story of the settlement by the English, but students will also be told that the Spaniards got to New Mexico and Florida first. The description of colonial America will place more emphasis on blacks, slave and free. The War for Independence will still play a large role, but we will now certainly find the blacks who fought in the war, along with Pulaski, von Steuben, Lafayette, and Haym Solomon. The Constitution will maintain its

centrality, but we will now emphasize the argument over slavery, the references to the Indians. The expansion westward will emphasize how nasty we were to the Indians and the Mexicans. The struggle over slavery leading to the Civil War will emphasize even more strongly the criminal failure of Reconstruction and the importance of the postwar amendments and their role. The story of industrialization and the rise of the city will include more about the immigrants and the black migration north. And so on.

20   The skeletal structure will remain, because we still live under the polity established by the Constitution, and it is in that polity, under that Constitution, that racial and ethnic and minority groups and women seek to expand their rights. It will be quite a job to keep nonsense and exaggeration and mindless ethnic and racial celebration out of the schools, but the basic structure of instruction in history will survive.

21   In my own comments, attached to the report, I took issue with the attempt to turn the United States into a congeries of ethnic and racial groups, and nothing more. Assimilation is a reality; scores of millions of unhyphenated Americans, who owe no allegiance to any identity other than American, are evidence of that. And assimilation continues to work its way, through the processes of work and of entertainment, with less help from the schools than before.

22   In this respect, present-day immigrants will not be very different from previous immigrants. They will assimilate. But one group, because of its experience of cruel, centuries-long ill treatment, is not yet fully incorporated in this generally successful process of nation-building. Present-day multiculturalism is a product of the apartness. Most of those who embrace it, I believe, do so in the hope that it will overcome that apartness. They want, in some key respects, to become more like other Americans—for example, in educational achievement—not different from them, and believe that the way to becoming more like them is to take more account of difference, and yes, of ill-treatment, of past and current achievement, even if exaggerated.

23   That is where we stand, and while some parts of this phenomenon are alarming enough, the proper parallel is not with Serbia and Croatia, or even Quebec. It is with our own American past, and the varying ways over time in which people of different race, religion, and ethnic background have become one nation.

Understanding the Content

Feel free to reread all or parts of the selection to answer the following questions.

1. What committee did Glazer serve on? Is it important that he include this information in his essay? Explain.

2. How does Glazer define "multiculturalism"? To what does he attribute the rise of interest in multicultural education?

3. How have the questions on the SATs changed in the past few years?

4. Based on available teacher's guides, how established is multicultural education in New York state? in Milwaukee?

5. Why are some students receiving vouchers to attend private black schools? How does Glazer feel about this procedure?

6. List some arguments raised by critics of multicultural education. How does Glazer answer some of those criticisms?

7. Is multicultural education a new phenomenon, according to Glazer? Explain.

8. Based on the current thrust for multiculturalism in education, what end result does Glazer see? What does he believe will be the effect of this debate on future curricula?

9. Why does Glazer think that "American education will have to respond" (1) to the present emphasis on multiculturalism?

Looking at Structure and Style

1. Why, in the first paragraph, does Glazer establish his membership on the committee appointed by New York's commissioner of education? Is this a good way to begin an essay? Explain.

2. How well does Glazer define "multiculturalism" in paragraph 2?

3. What is the importance of the question that begins paragraph 4? How does it serve as a transition device?

4. What can we infer about all the names mentioned in paragraph 6? Why does the author list them? How does this support the point he is making?

5. What is the point of paragraph 8? How does it set us up for paragraphs 9 and 10?

6. What is the function of paragraph 13? Is it too long? Explain.

7. In paragraph 22, Glazer says that immigrants will continue to assimilate, but one group, because of its historical treatment, "is not yet fully incorporated in this generally successful process of nation-building." How do we know what group he means?

8. How effective is Glazer's closing paragraph? Why does he make reference to Serbia, Croatia, and Quebec? What have they to do with his topic?

Evaluating the Author's Viewpoints

1. Glazer says that Spanish-speaking immigrants, while tending to support bilingual education, "are definitely junior partners in the fight for multiculturalism" (4) when compared with the demands of blacks. What does he mean? Do you agree?

2. The author defends multiculturalism, but is careful to define what he means by it. Do you agree with his "defense of multiculturalism"? Explain.

3. Glazer assures his readers that "whatever the strength of the multicultural thrust, I believe that American history in its main lineaments will have to be what it has been, and will not become completely alien to those of us educated in another time" (19). Do you agree? Why?

Pursuing Possible Essay Topics

Unless you already have an idea for an essay, wait until you have read all the selections on this issue and have studied the list of ideas at the end before deciding on your own topic related to multicultural education.

Preparing to Read

Before reading this selection, make certain you have read the introduction to Unit 10, pages 397–399.

Take a minute or two to look over the following reading selection. Note the title and author, read the opening *two* paragraphs, and check the length. Make certain you have time now to read it carefully and to do the exercises that follow it. Then, in the spaces provided, answer the following questions.

1. How do you define "ethnicity"? _____

_____

_____

2. What does ethnicity have to do with multiculturalism? _____

_____

_____

3. What do you think you will learn about multiculturalism from reading

   this selection? _____

   _____

   _____

4. Do you think you will agree or disagree with the author's viewpoints?

   Why? _____

   _____

   _____

Vocabulary

Good comprehension of what you are about to read depends upon your understanding of the words below. The number following each word refers to the paragraph where it is used.

ethnic (1) pertaining to racial, national, or tribal features

diversity (1) differences

salient (1) noticeable, crucial

unprecedented (4) new, not done before

promiscuous (5) diverse, jumbled, mixed up (as used here)

E pluribus unum (5) out of many, one

divisiveness (6) trouble, dissension

reconfigured (7) reshaped, made into something different

spurned (8) snubbed, ignored

inviolable (9) sacred, pure

Eurocentric curriculum (10) making European culture the center of course studies

redemption (10) the act of setting free or making up for a wrong

apocalyptic (11) predicting the end

ferment (11) simmering, seething, in a state of agitation

rent (13) torn apart, slashed

Now read the essay.

Multiculturalism Threatens the Ideal That Binds America

ARTHUR SCHLESINGER, JR.

1   The history of the world has been in great part the history of the mixing of peoples. Modern communication and transport accelerate mass migrations from one continent to another. Ethnic and racial diversity is more than ever a salient fact of the age.

2   But what happens when people of different origins, speaking different languages and professing different religions, inhabit the same locality and live under the same political sovereignty? Ethnic and racial conflict—far more than ideological conflict—is the explosive problem of our times.

3   On every side today ethnicity is breaking up nations. The Soviet Union, India, Yugoslavia, Ethiopia, are all in crisis. Ethnic tensions disturb and divide Sri Lanka, Burma, Indonesia, Iraq, Cyprus, Nigeria, Angola, Lebanon, Guyana, Trinidad—you name it. Even nations as stable and civilized as Britain and France, Belgium and Spain, face growing ethnic troubles. Is there any large multiethnic state that can be made to work?

4   The answer to that question has been, until recently, the United States. "No other nation," Margaret Thatcher has said, "has so successfully combined people of different races and nations within a single culture." How have Americans succeeded in pulling off this almost unprecedented trick?

5   We have always been a multiethnic country. Hector St. John de Crèvecoeur, who came from France in the 18th century, marveled at the astonishing diversity of the settlers—"a mixture of English, Scotch, Irish, French, Dutch, Germans and Swedes...this promiscuous breed." He propounded a famous question: "What then is the American, this new man?" And he gave a famous answer: "Here individuals of all nations are melted into a new race of men." *E pluribus unum.*

6   The U.S. escaped the divisiveness of a multiethnic society by a brilliant solution: the creation of a brand-new national identity. The point of America was not to preserve old cultures but to forge a new, *American* culture. "By an intermixture with our people," President George Washington told Vice President John Adams, immigrants will

"get assimilated to our customs, measures and laws: in a word, soon become one people." This was the ideal that a century later Israel Zangwill crystallized in the title of his popular 1908 play *The Melting Pot.* And no institution was more potent in molding Crèvecoeur's "promiscuous breed" into Washington's "one people" than the American public school.

7   The new American nationality was inescapably English in language, ideas and institutions. The pot did not melt everybody, not even all the white immigrants; deeply bred racism put black Americans, yellow Americans, red Americans and brown Americans well outside the pale. Still, the infusion of other stocks, even of nonwhite stocks, and the experience of the New World reconfigured the British legacy and made the U.S., as we all know, a very different country from Britain.

8   In the 20th century, new immigration laws altered the composition of the American people, and a cult of ethnicity erupted both among non-Anglo whites and among nonwhite minorities. This had many healthy consequences. The American culture at last began to give shamefully overdue recognition to the achievements of groups subordinated and spurned during the high noon of Anglo dominance, and it began to acknowledge the great swirling world beyond Europe. Americans acquired a more complex and invigorating sense of their world—and of themselves.

9   But, pressed too far, the cult of ethnicity has unhealthy consequences. It gives rise, for example, to the conception of the U.S. as a nation composed not of individuals making their own choices but of inviolable ethnic and racial groups. It rejects the historic American goals of assimilation and integration. And, in an excess of zeal, well-intentioned people seek to transform our system of education from a means of creating "one people" into a means of promoting, celebrating and perpetuating separate ethnic origins and identities. The balance is shifting from *unum* to *pluribus.*

10   That is the issue that lies behind the hullabaloo over "multiculturalism" and "political correctness," the attack on the "Eurocentric" curriculum and the rise of the notion that history and literature should be taught not as disciplines but as therapies whose function is to raise minority self-esteem. Group separatism crystallizes the differences, magnifies tensions, intensifies hostilities. Europe—the unique source of the liberating ideas of democracy, civil liberties and human rights—is portrayed as the root of all evil, and non-European cultures, their own many crimes deleted, are presented as the means of redemption.

11   I don't want to sound apocalyptic about these developments. Ed-

ucation is always in ferment, and a good thing too. The situation in our universities, I am confident, will soon right itself. But the impact of separatist pressures on our public schools is more troubling. If a Kleagle of the Ku Klux Klan wanted to use the schools to disable and handicap black Americans, he could hardly come up with anything more effective than the "Afrocentric" curriculum. And if separatist tendencies go unchecked, the result can only be the fragmentation, resegregation and tribalization of American life.

12   I remain optimistic. My impression is that the historic forces driving toward "one people" have not lost their power. The eruption of ethnicity is, I believe, a rather superficial enthusiasm stirred by romantic ideologues on the one hand and by unscrupulous con men on the other: self-appointed spokesmen whose claim to represent their minority groups is carelessly accepted by the media. Most American-born members of minority groups, white or nonwhite, see themselves primarily as Americans rather than primarily as members of one or another ethnic group. A notable indicator today is the rate of inter-marriage across ethnic lines, across religious lines, even (increasingly) across racial lines. "We Americans," said Theodore Roosevelt, "are children of the crucible."

13   The growing diversity of the American population makes the quest for unifying ideals and a common culture all the more urgent. In a world savagely rent by ethnic and racial antagonisms, the U.S. must continue as an example of how a highly differentiated society holds itself together.

Understanding the Content

Feel free to reread all or parts of the essay in order to answer the following questions.

1. Why does Schlesinger believe that multiculturalism threatens the ideal that binds America? What "ideal" does he mean?

2. What does the author mean when he says "the balance is shifting from *unum* to *pluribus*" (9)?

3. According to Schlesinger, how did the United States escape the trend toward multiculturalism in the past? Why is it different today?

4. What inference can you make about the author's views toward teaching a "Eurocentric" curriculum? Why?

5. Despite his concern over the trend toward ethnic separatism in society and in school curricula, Schlesinger says he remains "optimistic." Why? What does he think will happen?

Looking at Structure and Style

1. What is Schlesinger's thesis? Is it stated or implied? If stated, where?

2. What is the function of the first three paragraphs, especially paragraph 3? How do the last sentence of paragraph 3 and the first sentence of paragraph 4 work together? How important is the phrase "until recently"?

3. In paragraphs 4 and 5, the author quotes two foreigners. Why? What have they to do with the author's point?

4. What is the function of paragraphs 6 and 7? Is the information presented important in making Schlesinger's point? How?

5. How do paragraphs 8 and 9 work together? How important is the transitional word "But" that begins paragraph 9?

6. What negative adjectives are used in paragraph 12 that serve to "put down" those who press for multicultural fragmentation?

7. Is the closing paragraph effective? Why?

8. Did you find this selection easy or difficult to read? Explain why.

Evaluating the Author's Viewpoints

1. Schlesinger says, "Ethnic and racial conflict—far more than ideological conflict—is the explosive problem of our times" (2). Do you agree? Why?

2. Based on what you read, give Schlesinger's definition of "multiculturalism."

3. Reread paragraph 10. Schlesinger seems to support the teaching of a Eurocentric curriculum ("the unique source of the liberating ideas of democracy, civil liberties and human rights") and calls the teaching of multiculturalism "therapies whose function is to raise minority self-esteem." What is your opinion?

4. The author cautions in paragraph 11 that "if separatist tendencies go unchecked, the result can only be the fragmentation, resegregation and tribalization of American life." Do you think he is right? Explain.

5. According to the author, "The eruption of ethnicity is...a rather superficial enthusiasm stirred up by romantic ideologues on the one hand and by unscrupulous con men on the other..." (12). Does he support this statement? Do you agree with him? Explain.

Pursuing Possible Essay Topics

Unless you already have an idea for an essay, wait until you have read all the selections on this issue and have studied the list of ideas at the end before deciding on your own topic related to multicultural education.

📖 *Preparing to Read*

Before reading this selection, make certain you have read the introduction to Unit 10, pages 397–399.

Take a minute or two to look over the following reading selection. Note the title and author, read the opening paragraph, and check the length. Make certain you have time now to read it carefully and to do the exercises that follow it. Then, in the spaces provided, answer the following questions.

1. What do you think the title means? _____

_____

_____

2. What do you think you will learn from reading this selection? _____

_____

_____

3. Do you think you will agree or disagree with the author's viewpoints?

Why? _____

_____

Vocabulary

Good comprehension of what you are about to read depends upon your understanding of the words below. The number following each word refers to the paragraph where it is used.

Afrocentricity (1) placing African and African-American culture at the center of a school's curriculum

curriculum (1) all the courses of study offered by a school

infused (1) injected, put into, instilled

pejoratives (1) degrading or damaging statements

multicultural (1) made up of many cultures

anti-Semitic (2) against Jews

ethnocentrism (2) belief in the superiority of one's own ethnic group

resonates (4) rings, clangs, sounds out loudly

Now read the essay.

Putting Africa at the Center

MOLEFI KETE ASANTE

1   In its practical implications, Afrocentricity aims to locate African-American children in the center of the information being presented in classrooms across the nation. Most African-American children sit in classrooms, yet are outside the information being discussed. The white child sits in the middle of the information, whether it is literature, history, politics or art. The task of the Afrocentric curriculum is finding patterns in African-American history and culture that help the teacher place the child in the middle of the intellectual experience. This is not an idea to replace all things European, but to expand the dialogue to include African-American information. An Afrocentric curriculum covers kindergarten through 12th grade in every subject area. It can then be infused into an academic program cleansed of pejoratives like "Bushman" and "wild Indian" in order to have a truly multicultural curriculum.

2   Afrocentricity is neither racist nor anti-Semitic; it is about placing African people within our own historical framework. In none of the major works of Afrocentricity has there ever been a hint of racism, ethnocentrism or anti-anybody. Indeed, Afrocentricity believes that in order to have a stable society, we must always have a society that respects difference. One cannot argue that there is no difference—or that difference necessarily means hostility. One may be alien and yet not hostile. We only have to witness "E.T." to see the truth of that proposition.

3   **Imitative history:** Recent African-American history has shown that we have frequently been imitative of whites, following in the path of Europeans without understanding our own identities. Few African-American students or adults can tell you the names of any of the African ethnic groups that were brought to the Americas during the Great Enslavement; and yet prior to the Civil War there were no African-Americans, merely enslaved Africans. We know European ethnic names, but not these names, because we have seldom participated in our own historical traditions.

4   Afrocentricity resonates with the African-American community because it is fundamental to sanity. It is the fastest growing intellectual and practical idea in the community because of its validity when tested against other experiences. What could be any more correct for any people than to see with their own eyes?

Understanding the Content

Feel free to reread all or parts of the selection to answer the following questions.

1. How does Asante define an "Afrocentric curriculum"? What is it, and what is it *not*, in his view?

2. Why does Asante promote Afrocentricity? Why does he feel it is needed?

3. Does Asante want Afrocentricity to replace the present curriculum for all students or just black students? Explain.

4. Why, according to Asante, do few African-American students know the names of any of the African ethnic groups that were brought to the Americas during the Great Enslavement?

Looking at Structure and Style

1. What contrast does Asante draw in the first three sentences? How does this help make his case for Afrocentricity?

2. Find some statements in the essay that are made specifically to show that people should not be afraid that Afrocentrism is one-sided or racist.

3. Explain Asante's reference to "E.T." in paragraph 2. Why do you think he uses an "E.T." analogy to make his point?

4. What is the function of paragraph 3? How does it help support his view that an Afrocentric curriculum is needed?

5. The last sentence of the essay is really a question. Is it an effective way to conclude? Explain.

Evaluating the Author's Viewpoints

1. Do you think, as Asante does, that Afrocentricity should be included in the curriculum of all schools? Explain your views.

2. If Afrocentricity were placed in the kindergarten through twelfth grades, what would have to be taken out of the present curriculum? Does Asante address this issue?

3. Asante concludes, "What could be any more correct for any people than to see with their own eyes?" Does this mean that Asian-Americans should have an "Asiancentric" curriculum, Native Americans a "Native Americacentric" curriculum, Arab-American an "Arabcentric" curriculum, and so on?

4. Evaluate the pros and cons of Asante's argument for an Afrocentric curriculum.

Pursuing Possible Essay Topics

Unless you already have an idea for an essay, wait until you have read all the selections on this issue and have studied the list of ideas at the end before deciding on your own topic related to multicultural education.

Preparing to Read

Before reading this selection, make certain you have read the introduction to Unit 10, pages 397–399.

Take a minute or two to look over the following reading selection. Note the title and author, read the opening paragraph, and check the length. Make certain you have time now to read it carefully and to do the exercises that follow it. Then, in the spaces provided, answer the following questions.

1. What do you think the title means? _____

_____

_____

2. What do you think you will learn from reading this selection? _____

_____

_____

3. Do you think you will agree or disagree with the author's viewpoints?

Why? _____

_____

_____

Vocabulary

Good comprehension of what you are about to read depends upon your understanding of the words below. The number following each word refers to the paragraph where it is used.

   pharaohs (title) a term for kings of ancient Egypt, also used to mean tyrants

bemoans (1) regrets, groans about

polemicists (2) those skilled in argumentation or controversy

proliferation (2) a rapid increase or growth

ideological (2) having to do with ideas reflecting the needs of a certain class or culture

fundamentalism (2) a point of view characterized by a strict or rigid holding to basic principles

stigmatized (3) branded as disgraceful

shibboleths (3) common sayings or ideas

diaspora (3) those who left and have settled in other places

labile (5) open to change, adaptable

bogus (6) false

Now read the essay.

Beware of the New Pharaohs

HENRY LOUIS GATES, JR.

1   There's a scene in Woody Allen's "Bananas" in which the luckless hero, played by Allen, bemoans the fact that he dropped out of college. "What would you have been if you'd have finished school," a co-worker asks him. "I don't know," he sighs, "I was in the black-studies program. By now, I could have been black."

2   The truth is, too many people still regard African-American studies primarily as a way to rediscover a lost cultural identity—or invent one that never quite existed. And while we can understand these impulses, those in our field must remember that we are scholars first, not polemicists. For our field to survive, we need to encourage a true proliferation of rigorous methodologies, rather than to seek ideological conformity. African-American studies should be the home of free inquiry into the very complexity of being of African descent in the world, rather than a place where critical inquiry is drowned out by ethnic fundamentalism.

3   We need to explore the hyphen in African-American, on both sides of the Atlantic. We must chart the porous relations between an "American" culture that officially pretends that an Anglo-American *regional* culture is the true, universal culture, and the black cultures it so long stigmatized. We must also document both the continuities and discontinuities between African and African-American cultures, rather

than to reduce the astonishing diversity of African cultures to a few simple-minded shibboleths. But we should not lay claim to the idea of "blackness" as an ideology or religion. Surely all scholars of Africa and its diaspora are, by definition, "Afrocentric," if the term signals the recognition that Africa is centrally in the world, as much as the world is in Africa. But this is a source of the problem: all Afrocentrists, alas, do not look alike.

4   In short, African-American studies is not just for blacks; our subject is open to all—to study or to teach. The fundamental premise of the academy is that all things ultimately are knowable; all are therefore teachable. What would we say to a person who said that to teach Milton, you had to be Anglo-Saxon, Protestant, male . . . and blind! We do nothing to help our discipline by attempting to make of it a closed shop, where only blacks need apply. On the other hand, to say that ethnic identity is the product of history and culture is not to say that it is any less real. Nor is it to deny our own personal histories, to pretend that these are not differences that make a difference.

5   Nobody comes into the world as a "black" person or a "white" person: these identities are conferred on us by a complex history, by patterns of social acculturation that are both surprisingly labile and persistent. Social identities are never as rigid as we like to pretend: they're constantly being contested and negotiated.

6   For a scholar, "Afrocentrism" should mean more than wearing Kente cloth and celebrating Kwanzaa instead of Christmas. (Kwanzaa, by the way, was invented in Los Angeles, not Lagos.) Bogus theories of "sun" and "ice" people, and the invidious scapegoating of other ethnic groups, only resurrects the worst of 19th-century racist pseudoscience—which too many of the pharaohs of "Afrocentrism" have accepted without realizing.

7   We must not succumb to the temptation to resurrect our own version of the thought police, who would determine who, and what, is "black." "Mirror, mirror, on the wall, who's the blackest one of all?" is a question best left behind in the '60s.

Understanding the Content

Feel free to reread all or parts of the selection to answer the following questions.

1. What does Gates teach? How do you know?

2. What does Gates feel is needed for African-American studies to survive?

3. How does the author regard "blackness" as an ideology?

4. What is Gates's definition of "Afrocentric"?

5. Whom does Gates call "pharaohs of 'Afrocentrism' "? What does he mean by the term? Why does he call them that?

6. What is the thesis of the essay?

Looking at Structure and Style

1. Is the thesis stated or implied? If stated, where?

2. To begin his essay, Gates quotes a character in a Woody Allen movie. How does this tie in with his thesis? Is it an effective opening? Explain.

3. What does Gates mean in paragraph 3 when he says, "We need to explore the hyphen in African-American, on both sides of the Atlantic"?

4. Gates raises the question of who should teach Milton (a blind, seventeenth-century English poet) to make an analogy about who should teach African-American studies. Is this a valid analogy? What is his point?

5. How does Gates use a parenthetical comment in paragraph 6 to help support the point he is making? What is his point?

6. As in the previous essay by Asante, the essay conclusion centers on a question. How do the questions differ in use?

Evaluating the Author's Viewpoints

1. Gates says in paragraph 2 that "African-American studies should be the home of free inquiry into the very complexity of being of African descent in the world, rather than a place where critical inquiry is drowned out by ethnic fundamentalism." Rephrase his remark in your own words. Do you agree? Why?

2. The author believes that Afro-American studies is not just for blacks to study and teach. Why do you agree or disagree?

3. Why do you think Gates warns, "Beware of the New Pharaohs"? Why do you think he uses that term?

4. Gates contends that "nobody comes into the world as a 'black' person or a 'white' person" (5). Explain his statement. Is he right or wrong, do you think?

Pursuing Possible Essay Topics

Unless you already have an idea for an essay, wait until you have read all the selections on this issue and have studied the list of ideas at the end before deciding on your own topic related to multicultural education.

📖 *Preparing to Read*

Before reading this selection, make certain you have read the introduction to Unit 10, pages 397–399.

Take a minute or two to look over the following reading selection. Note the title and author, read the opening paragraph, and check the length. Make certain you have time now to read it carefully and to do the exercises that follow it. Then, in the spaces provided, answer the following questions.

1. What does the title tell you about the author's viewpoint on her subject?

_____

_____

2. What do you think you will learn about multiculturalism from reading

   this selection? _____

_____

_____

3. Do you think you will agree with the author's viewpoints? Why? _____

_____

_____

Vocabulary

Good comprehension of what you are about to read depends upon your understanding of the words below. The number following each word refers to the paragraph where it is used.

McCarthyism (1) the practice of using insufficient evidence to publicly accuse someone of disloyalty or subversion

fundamentalism (1) a reference to a religious movement characterized by a legalistic interpretation of the Bible

totalitarianism (1) a government in which one person has absolute rule over all spheres of human life

Jacobins (1) radical or extreme leftists

politically correct (1) a term used to describe being so sensitive to saying or doing something hurtful that nothing is said or done that could be mistaken as a negative comment (abbreviated **P.C.**)

backlash (2) a negative reaction to a prior action

monoculturalism (2) emphasis on one culture

poignant (3) impressive, snappy, touching the emotions

haughty (5) snobbish, arrogant

homophobic (5) expressing fear of homosexuals

signers (6) those able to use sign language to translate for the deaf

relentlessly (7) stubbornly, ceaselessly, continuously

parochial (9) limited, controlled

Now read the essay.

Teach Diversity— with a Smile

BARBARA EHRENREICH

1   Something had to replace the threat of communism, and at last a workable substitute is at hand. "Multiculturalism," as the new menace is known, has been denounced in the media recently as the new McCarthyism, the new fundamentalism, even the new totalitarianism—take your choice. According to its critics, who include a flock of tenured conservative scholars, multiculturalism aims to toss out what it sees as the Eurocentric bias in education and replace Plato with Ntozake Shange and traditional math with the Yoruba number system. And that's just the beginning. The Jacobins of the multiculturalist movement, who are described derisively as P.C., or politically correct, are said to have launched a campus reign of terror against those who slip and innocently say "freshman" instead of "freshperson," "Indian" instead of "Native American" or, may the Goddess forgive them, "disabled" instead of "differently abled."

2   So you can see what is at stake here: freedom of speech, freedom of thought, Western civilization and a great many professorial egos. But before we get carried away by the mounting backlash against multiculturalism, we ought to reflect for a moment on the system that the P.C. people aim to replace. I know all about it; in fact it's just about all I *do* know, since I—along with so many educated white people of my generation—was a victim of monoculturalism.

3   American history, as it was taught to us, began with Columbus' "discovery" of an apparently unnamed, unpeopled America, and

moved on to the Pilgrims serving pumpkin pie to a handful of grateful red-skinned folks. College expanded our horizons with courses called Humanities or sometimes Civ, which introduced us to a line of thought that started with Homer, worked its way through Rabelais and reached a poignant climax in the pensées of Matthew Arnold. Graduate students wrote dissertations on what long-dead men had thought of Chaucer's verse or Shakespeare's dramas; foreign languages meant French or German. If there had been high technology in ancient China, kingdoms in black Africa or women anywhere, at any time, doing anything worth noticing, we did not know it, nor did anyone think to tell us.

4   Our families and neighborhoods reinforced the dogma of monoculturalism. In our heads, most of us '50s teenagers carried around a social map that was about as useful as the chart that guided Columbus to the "Indies." There were "Negroes," "whites" and "Orientals," the latter meaning Chinese and "Japs." Of religions, only three were known—Protestant, Catholic and Jewish—and not much was known about the last two types. The only remaining human categories were husbands and wives, and that was all the diversity the monocultural world could handle. Gays, lesbians, Buddhists, Muslims, Malaysians, Mormons, etc., were simply off the map.

5   So I applaud—with one hand, anyway—the multiculturalist goal of preparing us all for a wider world. The other hand is tapping its fingers impatiently, because the critics are right about one thing: when advocates of multiculturalism adopt the haughty stance of political correctness, they quickly descend to silliness or worse. It's obnoxious, for example, to rely on university administrations to enforce P.C. standards of verbal inoffensiveness. Racist, sexist and homophobic thoughts cannot, alas, be abolished by fiat but only by the time-honored methods of persuasion, education and exposure to the other guy's—or, excuse me, woman's—point of view.

6   And it's silly to mistake verbal purification for genuine social reform. Even after all women are "Ms." and all people are "he or she," women will still earn only 65¢ for every dollar earned by men. Minorities by any other name, such as "people of color," will still bear a hugely disproportionate burden of poverty and discrimination. Disabilities are not just "different abilities" when there are not enough ramps for wheelchairs, signers for the deaf or special classes for the "specially" endowed. With all due respect for the new politesse, actions still speak louder than fashionable phrases.

7   But the worst thing about the P.C. people is that they are such poor advocates for the multicultural cause. No one was ever won over to a broader, more inclusive view of life by being bullied or relentlessly "corrected." Tell a 19-year-old white male that he can't say

"girl" when he means "teen-age woman," and he will most likely snicker. This may be the reason why, despite the conservative alarms, P.C.-ness remains a relatively tiny trend. Most campuses have more serious and ancient problems: faculties still top-heavy with white males of the monocultural persuasion; fraternities that harass minorities and women; date rape; alcohol abuse; and tuition that excludes all but the upper fringe of the middle class.

8   So both sides would be well advised to lighten up. The conservatives ought to realize that criticisms of the great books approach to learning do not amount to totalitarianism. And the advocates of multiculturalism need to regain the sense of humor that enabled their predecessors in the struggle to coin the term P.C. years ago—not in arrogance but in self-mockery.

9   Beyond that, both sides should realize that the beneficiaries of multiculturalism are not only the "oppressed peoples" on the standard P.C. list (minorities, gays, etc.). The "unenlightened"—the victims of monoculturalism—are oppressed too, or at least deprived. Our educations, whether at Yale or at State U, were narrow and parochial and left us ill-equipped to navigate a society that truly is multicultural and is becoming more so every day. The culture that we studied was, in fact, *one* culture and, from a world perspective, all too limited and ingrown. Diversity is challenging, but those of us who have seen the alternative know it is also richer, livelier and ultimately more fun.

Understanding the Content

1. What does Ehrenreich mean when she says that "something had to replace the threat of communism" (1) and that substitute is multiculturalism? Is she serious? Explain.

2. What is it about multicultural education that the author applauds with one hand? What about it does she disapprove with impatiently tapping fingers of the other hand?

3. What kind of education did she receive? Does she approve of it? Explain.

4. Based on what Ehrenreich says here, define what is meant by a "politically correct" person.

5. What can we infer about what is happening at some colleges and universities based on her statement, "It's obnoxious . . . to rely on university administrations to enforce P.C. standards of verbal offensiveness" (5)? How would she describe P.C. standards?

6. According to Ehrenreich, why are "P.C. people" such poor advocates for the multicultural cause?

7. Why does she feel both sides of the multicultural issue "would be well advised to lighten up"?

8. How do you think Ehrenreich defines "multicultural education"? According to her, what group of people will benefit most from teaching multiculturalism?

Looking at Structure and Style

1. How would you describe the author's tone and attitude toward her subject? Illustrate with some examples.

2. How well has the author prepared us for the first sentence of the second paragraph? Explain.

3. What is the function of paragraphs 3 and 4?

4. How does paragraph 5 serve to shift the author's point of view?

5. How well do paragraphs 6 and 7 support the author's shift in point of view? Explain.

6. Notice how frequently the author uses quotation marks around certain words and phrases (paragraphs 1, 4, 6, 7, 9). Why does she do this?

7. Did you find this essay easy or difficult to read? Explain.

Evaluating the Author's Viewpoints

1. In paragraph 2, Ehrenreich says that what is at stake when "politically correct" multiculturalism goes too far is "freedom of speech, freedom of thought, Western civilization and a great many political egos." As she defines "P.C.," do you think she is right? Is she exaggerating? Explain.

2. The author seems to demean her educational background. What did she receive academically that was good? What bad? Do you agree with her? Explain.

3. Read the last sentence in paragraph 5. Explain why you agree or disagree.

4. In paragraph 7, Ehrenreich explains why she is against what the P.C. people advocate. Is she right? Explain.

5. The author urges both sides to "lighten up." What does she mean? Are you more in favor of one side than the other? If so, which side? Explain your views.

6. What is your reaction to her concluding summary?

Pursuing Possible Essay Topics

1. Write an argumentative essay that supports or disagrees with the thesis of one of the essays on multicultural education. Begin your essay by summarizing the position of the essay you are writing about. Then discuss what you agree or disagree with, and why.

2. Write an essay that argues for multicultural changes in the K–12 educational system. What do you want to see omitted, added, or modified? Explain why these changes are needed and what good they would do.

3. Argue for or against an Afrocentric K–12 curriculum.

4. An administrator at the University of California at Santa Cruz has sought to ban such phrases as "a chink in his armor," "nip in the air," and "call a spade a spade" because they contain words that in other contexts might offend a Chinese, Japanese, or African-American person. Argue for or against such a ban.

5. Students who signed up for a course in Black Politics at San Francisco State College picketed it or dropped out, complaining that it was listed under Political Science rather than Black Studies. Argue for or against the students' position.

6. Read all or parts of one of the following works and write your reaction to it:
   a. Molefi Kete Asante, *Afrocentricity*
   b. Martin Bernal, *Black Athena*
   c. Allan Bloom, *The Closing of the American Mind*
   d. Henry Louis Gates, Jr., *Loose Cannons*
   e. E. D. Hirsch, Jr., *Cultural Literacy*

7. Brainstorm or freewrite on one or more of the following:
   a. multiculturalism   d. the Great Books
   b. political correctness   e. hyphenated Americans
   c. cultural similarities   f. *E Pluribus Unum*

8. Separate yourself from these ideas and find your own topic for an essay on multicultural education.

Student Essay

As you read the following student essay, look for answers to these questions:

1. Does the essay fit the assignment to write on some aspect of a controversial issue?

2. Is there a thesis? If so, is it well supported?

3. How well written is the essay? Does it hold your interest?

Stop Executing Juveniles

Trisha Toyoto

1   According to Tanya Coke in a recent editorial in the Mobil
Register, the legal system has executed three juvenile offenders
within the last ten years and placed 32 others to wait on death
row for their execution. We are the only western democracy to
apply the death penalty to young people. As hard as it may be to
believe, our laws, she says, are more harsh against juveniles
than countries that use capital punishment frequently, such as
South Africa and the Soviet Union.

2   In this country, only seven states disallow capital punishment for offenders under age 18 at the time of their crime. "The
other 30 states which allow the death penalty have either a
lower age limit or no limit at all," according to Coke. Our country
is virtually the only one in the world that executes children. In
fact, the Inter-American Commission on human rights ruled that
the United States "violated international standards in allowing
the execution of two teenagers" in 1986: James Roach in South
Carolina and Jay Pinkerton in Texas.

3   A poll taken in Georgia revealed that while 75 percent of
Georgians approve of capital punishment for murder, only 26
percent wanted the law to apply to juveniles. Most people in this
country, if polled, would probably feel the same way.

4   Why should juveniles be exempt from the death penalty? Our
entire legal system is set up with the understanding that juvenile
offenders are different from adult offenders. We have a separate
juvenile justice system. We are aware than juveniles are not capable of handling some situations and so have laws that limit
when they can drive, when they can drink alcohol, or when they
can enter into legal contracts. Juvenile offenders are sent to ju-

venile hall, not city or county jails when they break the law. Juvenile offenders are more prone to rehabilitation than hardened criminals and frequently leave their criminal careers behind. Why, then, do we put them to death if they commit crimes that call for the death penalty established for adults?

5   Some argue that the death penalty for juveniles is a deterrent. Victor Streib, an expert on juvenile execution and a lawyer who wants the U.S. Supreme Court to rule on this issue, says that "the deterrence theory is especially weak as applied to young people." He suggests that a better deterrent is the "prospect of a lengthy prison term—no telephone, no cars, no Saturday nights out—has more deterrent value for an adolescent than does a shadowy notion of death."

6   There are, according to Coke, some indications that states are changing. Indiana recently raised its minimum age for death sentencing from 10 to 16, and Maryland abolished capital punishment for those under 18. Still, this problem is one that concerns us all. We must stop letting our courts send children to the executioner.

Reaction

In the space below, write your reaction to the student essay. What would tell the student about her essay?

Commentary

Toyoto's essay does fit the assignment on writing about a controversial issue. Her slant is also a bit different in that she deals with one aspect of the death penalty, lawful juvenile executions. She has attempted to make the topic her own. She also takes a stance and makes her thesis clear. Those are things I like.

But there are some problems for me as a reader. First, her main source seems to be from "a recent editorial" in the *Mobil Register* by Tanya Coke. No date is given so I have no idea how recent this information is. Paragraph 2 is basically Coke speaking, not Trisha. That might pass, but paragraph 3 brings in statistics with no mention of their source. Are they again from Coke's editorial? The last sentence of that paragraph is also a rather sweeping statement. Does the poll taken in Georgia suggest the rest of the country would feel the same way?

I like paragraph 4. It attempts to answer a question readers would ask at this point. The author gives her viewpoints, not someone else's comments. I feel the writer at work here. But paragraph 5 brings in quotes from Victor Strieb. While we are told who he is, what is the source for these quotes? What else has Trisha read? Is this from the editorial mentioned earlier in the essay?

When I read the last sentence, "We must stop letting our courts send children to the executioner," I understand her viewpoint. It is a strong statement of position, but somehow it rings hollow. I'm left with the feeling that this essay was done because it was assigned, not because the author had any real passion for the topic. I'm not saying she doesn't, and I have no way of knowing. I'm simply saying that while the thesis and form of an essay are here, the way the essay is written contains more of the thinking and information of others than it does the writer's thinking and feeling.

Appendixes

APPENDIX A
Essay Format and Proofreading Guide

Essay Format

If your instructor does not tell you what form your final essay draft should take, follow these standard rules.

If you type or use a word processor

1. Use standard 8½″ × 11″ bond typing paper. Don't use erasable paper because it smears too easily. Make certain that your typewriter or computer printer ribbon makes a clear, dark imprint. Don't use script or unusual type, especially if you print out your paper on a dot matrix printer. Make certain all letters are distinguishable (for instance, some printers don't make clear p's or d's).

2. Double-space your paper to provide room for your instructor to make comments and corrections. This also leaves enough space for you to correct any typing, spelling, or punctuation errors you notice when proofreading your typed copy. (See proofreading correction symbols on page 464.) If your paper is very messy, retype it.

3. Leave at least 1″ margins all around your page.

4. Your name, your instructor's name, the course number, and the date should appear in the upper left- or right-hand corner on the first page. Double-space, then center your title, capitalizing the first letter of each word unless it is an article, conjunction, or preposition. Don't underline or place quotation marks around your title. (If other writers refer to your essay by title in their writing, then they should place quotation marks around your title to identify it as such.)

5. Indent the first line of each paragraph five spaces.

6. Leave two spaces after every period, question mark, or exclamation mark; use only one space after commas, semicolons, or colons.

7. Use quotation marks around short quotations that run less than five lines of your own manuscript. If the quote runs longer, then indent ten spaces from the left to set it off from your own writing;

no quotation marks are needed, but the quote should be followed by the source cited in parentheses (see Appendix B, "Quoting and Documenting Sources"). When the quote is completed, return to your regular margins.

8. Number all pages consecutively in the upper right-hand corner about ½" from the top. You may want to place your last name next to the page number. No page number is needed for the first page unless your instructor wants a title page. In that case, ask the instructor for more details on format. Title pages are generally used for lengthy research papers, which require outlines and footnote and bibliography pages.

9. Staple your pages together in order at the upper left-hand corner only. Don't use paper clips; they fall off or get caught in other students' essays when stacked in a pile. Don't bend the corners together with a little tear—it doesn't work.

10. Don't use binders or folders unless your instructor requests them.

11. Make a copy in case something happens to the original. If you use a word processor, be sure to save it on disk.

If your essay is handwritten

It's generally not a good idea to submit handwritten papers. If your instructor does permit it, you should follow the rules above for typed papers, with these differences:

1. Use white, wide-lined paper, no smaller than 8½" × 11".

2. If you write on paper from a spiral notebook, cut off the ragged edges before you submit it.

3. Write on every other line, using only one side of a page.

4. Use only black or dark blue ink.

5. If your handwriting is poor, print. If you can't write or print neatly, pay a typist. An instructor has many papers to grade and has little patience with papers that are difficult to read.

Following these essay format rules is fairly safe, but it is always a good idea to ask any instructors who require written essays what format they want you to use.

First Page of Manuscript Without a Title Page

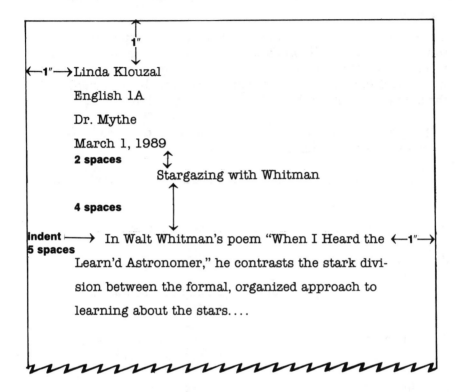

Numbering Subsequent Pages

Klouzal 2

To show these two distinct views, Whitman divides his eight-line poem into two parts. The first part consists of....

Proofreading Guide

Correction Symbols

Once you have finished typing your paper, be certain that you or someone else carefully proofreads it. Read it aloud or have it read aloud to you. If you notice many mistakes, you should type it over. If there are only a few errors, you can correct them by hand using the following symbols. Just be neat and use dark ink.

a. to insert an apostrophe or double quotation marks

  Is this the professor's book?

b. to insert a word, letter, or comma

  insert word, letter, or comma

c. to insert a period

  Insert a period

d. to delete

  delete

e. to indicate a new paragraph

  ... end of a sentence. The next sentence ...

f. to indicate no new paragraph

  ... end of a sentence.
  no ¶   The next sentence ...

g. to insert space

  insert space

h. to close up space

  close up space

i. to transpose (reverse) letters or words

  reverse

j. to indicate a capital letter

  september

k. to indicate a lower-case letter

  small letters

Proofreading for Mechanics

The following brief summary of some mechanical rules may be of help before you finalize your paper.

Underlining

In typing, underlining is reserved for the following:

a. to identify books, magazines, newspapers, films, or record albums

Herman Melville's <u>Moby Dick</u>

<u>TIME</u> magazine   (Notice that *magazine* is not underlined.)

<u>Los Angeles Times</u>   (Quotation marks are used around titles of chapters, articles, essays, or poems that appear in books, magazines, or newspapers.)

Woody Allen's <u>The Purple Rose of Cairo</u>

The Beatles' <u>Sergeant Pepper's Lonely Hearts Club Band</u>   (Quotation marks are used around titles of songs in an album.)

b. to identify foreign words not in everyday use

The Welsh call themselves <u>cymry</u>.

c. to call attention to a particular word

The word <u>run</u> has over twenty definitions.

The student used <u>affect</u> when she meant <u>effect</u>.

d. to denote sounds

With a <u>plunk</u>, the penny slowly dropped to the bottom of the well.

Numbers

In general, these rules apply to writing numbers and figures:

a. Spell out numbers that can be written in one or two words.

twenty

twenty-two   (hyphenated numbers are considered one word)

twenty-two thousand

b. Use numerals for numbers that require more than two words.

275   (two hundred seventy-five)

22,645   (twenty-two thousand, six hundred forty-five)

c. Numerals are almost always used for money: $35; occasionally they're written out: one dollar. There are times when the use of figures is more impressive looking. For instance, *one trillion* doesn't have the visual snap that seeing the figure *$1,000,000,000,000* has.

d. When starting a sentence, it's better to use words.

Forty-three people attended the lecture.

e. When referring to page numbers, prices, or scores, use figures.

From page 16 of <u>Newsweek</u>, he learned that the tickets were $15.

The Giants beat the Cardinals 10–4.

Capital Letters

Use capital letters:

a. to refer to persons, places, and brand names

Albert Einstein

Yellowstone National Park

Porsche

Harvard University

b. to refer to title or rank

Mayor Koch

Bishop Tutu

Prince Charles

c. to refer to names of religions and members of them

Buddhism, Unitarians, Jewish

d. to refer to titles of written works

Bloom's <u>The Lexington Reader</u>   (book)

Smith's "What Will Become of the Latchkey Kids?"   (essay)

Frost's "Stopping by Woods"   (poem)

Notice that the phrases "of the" and "by the" in the titles are not capitalized. Unless they begin the title, **articles** (a, an, the), **prepositions** (of, on, by, in, to, etc.), and **conjunctions** (and, or) are not capitalized.

e. for the names of the days and months

There are four Sundays in March this year.

Manuscript style manuals vary, but unless your instructor wants you to follow a particular style manual, these rules should be acceptable.

Quoting and Documenting Sources

Quoting Sources

Quotations from other sources are basically used for one of three reasons: (1) they contain authoritative information or ideas that support or help explain your thesis, (2) they contain ideas you want to argue against or prove wrong, or (3) they are so well-written that they make your point better than your own explanation could. However, before you use any quotations, ask yourself what purpose they serve. The use of too many quotations can be confusing and distracting to a reader. Quotations should not be used as a substitute for your own writing.

There are several ways of quoting your source material. One way is to quote an entire sentence, such as:

> In her article, "The State of American Values," Susanna McBee claims, "The recent U.S. News & World Report survey findings show that the questions of morality are troubling ordinary people."

Notice that the title and author of the quotation are provided before the quotation is given. Never use a quotation without providing a lead into it. Usually, verbs such as "says," "explains," "states," and "writes," are used to lead into a quotation. In this case, it is "claims." Notice, too, the placement of punctuation marks, especially the comma after "claims" and the closing quotation marks after the period.

Another way to quote sources is to incorporate part of a quotation into your own writing:

> In her article, "The State of American Values," Susanna McBee claims that a recent survey conducted by U.S. News & World Report shows that "the questions of morality are troubling ordinary people."

Quotation marks are only placed around the exact words of McBee. Since her words are used as part of the writer's sentence, the first word from McBee's quotation is not capitalized. Notice the way the

469

quotation marks are placed at the beginning and end of the quotation being used.

At times, you may want to make an indirect quotation. Indirect quotations do not require the use of quotation marks because you are paraphrasing, that is, rewriting the information using your own words. Notice how the McBee quotation is paraphrased here:

> In her article, "The State of American Values," Susanna McBee states that according to a recent survey conducted by U.S. News & World Report, the average person is bothered by what is and isn't moral.

When the exact wording of a quotation is not vital, it is better to paraphrase the quotation. However, be sure not to change the meaning of the quotation or to imply something not stated there. When paraphrasing, you must still provide the reader with the source of the information you paraphrase.

When quotations run more than five lines, don't use quotation marks. Instead, indent the quoted material ten spaces from your own margin and skip a line. This is called a **block quote** and it shows that the quotation is not part of your own writing:

> In her article, "The State of American Values," Susanna McBee concludes by stating:

>> Where individuals should be cautious, warn social scientists and theologians, is in forcing their standards upon others. In the words of the Rev. McKinley Young of Big Bethal AME Church of Atlanta: "When you find somebody waving all those flags and banners, watch closely. Morality, if you're not careful, carries a sense of self-righteousness. Whenever you pat yourself on the back, it creates all kinds of cramps."

Here, quotation marks are not needed for the McBee quotation. But because McBee's quoted statement contains a quotation by someone else, her quotation marks must be included in the block quote. This is a quotation within a quotation.

Try to avoid quotations within a quotation that is shorter than five lines. They are awkward to follow. But if you do need to, here is the way:

> McBee concludes by saying, "In the words of Rev.
>
> McKinley Young of Big Bethal AME Church of Atlanta:
>
> 'Morality ... carries a sense of self-righteousness. When-
>
> ever you pat yourself on the back, it creates all kinds
>
> of cramps.' "

Notice the position of the first set of quotation marks (")—just before the beginning of the McBee quotation. Then, when McBee begins quoting Young's words, a single quotation mark (') is used. Since the entire quotation ends with a quote within a quote, a single quotation mark must be used to show the end of Young's words, plus regular quotation marks must be used to show the end of McBee's words. You can see why it's best to avoid this structure if possible.

Look in the example above at the use of what looks like three periods (...) between the words "Morality and "carries." This is called an **ellipsis**. An ellipsis is used to indicate that part of the quotation is left out. When part of a quote is not important to your point, you may use an ellipsis to shorten the quoted material. Be sure, however, that you haven't changed the meaning of the original quotation. Furthermore, always make certain that the remaining quoted material reads like a complete thought or sentence, as in the example.

Documenting Sources

Most English instructors require that you document your sources by following the guidelines of the Modern Language Association. The following examples show how to document most of the sources you would probably use. However, it is not complete, so you may want to consult the *MLA Handbook for Writers of Research Papers* for further information.

When you use quotations in your paper, you are required to identify your sources. Documenting your sources lets your readers know that the information and ideas of others are not your own. It also lets readers know where more information on your subject can be found in case they choose to read your sources for themselves. You cite your sources in two places: in your paper after the quotation, and at the end of your paper under a heading entitled "Works Cited."

Citing Within the Paper

Here's how you would show where the examples above came from.

> In her article, "The State of American Values," Susanna
>
> McBee claims, "The recent U.S. News & World Report sur-
>
> vey findings show that the questions of morality are trou-
>
> bling ordinary people" (54).

The number in parentheses (54) refers to the page number in the McBee article where the quotation can be found. Since the author and article title are provided in the lead-in to the quote, only the page number is needed at the end. Readers can consult the "Works Cited" page at the end of your paper to learn where and when the article appeared. Notice that when the source ends with a quotation the parentheses and page number go *after* the quotation marks and *before* the period.

When paraphrasing a quotation, use the following citation form:

> In her article, "The State of American Values," Susanna
>
> McBee states that according to a recent survey conducted
>
> by U.S. News & World Report, the average person is both-
>
> ered by what is and isn't moral (54).

Here the parentheses and page number go after the last word and before the period.

If the quote is not identified by author, the author's name and page number should be included in the parentheses.

> A recent survey shows that the average person is bothered
>
> by what should be considered moral (McBee 54).

By including the author's name and page number, you let the reader know where to look on the "Works Cited" page for the complete documentation information.

The "Works Cited" Page

All the sources you used for writing your paper should be listed alphabetically by the author's last name on the "Works Cited" page.

If there is no author's name on the work, then alphabetize it using the first letter of the first word of the title, unless it begins with an article (*a, an, the*). Here are the proper forms for the more basic sources. Note especially the punctuation and spacing.

For books by one author:

Bloom, Alan. <u>The Closing of the American Mind</u>. New York: Simon, 1987.

As usual, two spaces are used after periods; single spacing is used elsewhere. A colon is used after the name of the city where the publisher is located, followed by the publisher's name. Book publishers' names can be shortened to conserve space. For instance, the full name of the publisher in the example above is Simon and Schuster. A comma is used before the date and a period after it.

If two or more books by the same author are listed, you do not need to provide the name again. Use three hyphens instead. For example:

---. <u>Shakespeare's Politics</u>. Chicago: U of Chicago P, 1972.

For books by two or three authors:

Jones, Judy, and William Wilson. <u>An Incomplete Education</u>. New York: Ballantine, 1987.

The same punctuation and spacing are used, but only the name of the first author listed on the book's title page is inverted. The authors' names are separated by a comma.

For books by more than three authors:

Gundersen, Joan R., et al. <u>America Changing Times</u>. 2nd ed. New York: Wiley, 1982.

The Latin phrase *et al.*, which means *and others*, is used in place of all but the name of the first author listed on the book's title page. Notice its placement and the use of punctuation before and after.

For books that are edited:

> Dupuis, Mary M., ed.   <u>Reading in the Content Areas</u>.   Newark:
>
> Int. Reading Assoc., 1984.

The citing is the same as for authored books except for the insertion of *ed.* to signify that it is edited rather than authored by the person named. If there is more than one editor, you follow the same form as for authors, inserting *eds.* after the last editor's name.

For magazine articles:

> McBee, Susanna.   "The State of American Values."   <u>U.S. News &</u>
>
> <u>World Report</u> 9 Dec. 1985: 54–58

When citing magazine articles, use abbreviations for the month. The order of the listing is (1) author, (2) article title, (2) magazine title, (3) date, and (4) page number(s) of the article. Note carefully how and where the punctuation is used.

For newspaper articles:

> Reeves, Richard.   "America Isn't Falling Apart."   <u>San Francisco</u>
>
> <u>Chronicle</u> 24 June 1987: C2.

The citing is basically the same as that for a magazine article. The difference here is that you include the letter of the newspaper section with the page number ("C2" in the sample).

For scholarly journal articles:

> Kellman, Stephen G.   "The Cinematic Novel: Tracking a Con-
>
> cept."   <u>Modern Fiction Studies</u> 33 (1987): 467–77.

The citing for a scholarly journal article begins the same as for a magazine article except that the journal volume number (33 in the example) and the date (only the year in parentheses) are cited differently. Volume numbers for journals can usually be found on the cover or on the table of contents page.

For an encyclopedia article:

"Television." <u>Encyclopedia Americana</u>. 1985 ed.

Since encyclopedias are written by many staff authors, no author can be cited. Begin with the title of the section you read, then the name of the encyclopedia, and the date of the edition you used. No page numbers are needed. Notice the position of the punctuation marks.

For an interview that you conducted yourself:

Stone, James. Personal interview. 9 Jan. 1988.

For a lecture:

Dunn, Harold. "Poverty of the Arts in an Affluent Society." Santa

Barbara City College. 3 May 1985.

If a lecture has no title, substitute the word *Lecture*.

For movies:

<u>Jules and Jim</u>. Dir. Francois Truffaut. With Jeanne Moreau,

Oscar Werner, and Henri Serre. Carrose Films, 1962.

The listing order is title, director, actors, distributor, and year the film was made.

For television shows:

<u>ABC Nightly News</u>. With Peter Jennings. KABC, Los Angeles.

2 May 1988.

Index

Instructor's Guide for

Viewpoints:

Readings Worth Thinking and Writing About

W. ROYCE ADAMS
Santa Barbara City College

SECOND EDITION

D. C. Heath and Company
Lexington, Massachusetts   Toronto

Address editorial correspondence to:

D. C. Heath
125 Spring Street
Lexington, MA 02173

Published simultaneously in Canada.

Printed in the United States of America.

International Standard Book Number: 0–669–27369–4

10 9 8 7 6 5 4 3 2 1

INTRODUCTION

This *Instructor's Guide* offers some suggestions for users of *Viewpoints: Readings Worth Thinking and Writing About*, Second Edition. Recommendations for assigning and helping students get the most from "Part I: Viewpoints on Reading and Writing Essays" appear here, along with commentaries on each of the reading selections in "Part II: Readings Worth Thinking and Writing About." These comments may help you decide which readings you wish to assign during the course and in which order.

The reading selections in *Viewpoints* have not been selected as "models" of excellent writing that students must then try to emulate. The selections are end-products and do not reflect the multitude of changes the authors may have gone through. Instead, the selections were chosen for the stimulation of thought they may stir in the student. Some readings are very well written, others are not. Your task is to show students why some authors do a better job than others. In that capacity, then, the readings can serve as "models." Thought, I believe, should come before concern for a rhetorical mode, and all the readings were selected because they provide students with various viewpoints on a topic they must ultimately think about before they express their own minds in writing.

Throughout this guide, you'll read frequent suggestions that call for small group or class discussions. While such an emphasis may seem strange in a book dealing with composition, my experience has shown that lively class discussions and a controlled exchange of viewpoints stimulate student thinking, thus effecting thoughtful student compositions by the end of the term.

I strongly recommend that you have students keep a reading journal in which they write their reactions to essays and their answers to the questions for the readings you assign. Encourage them to write down any questions or problems they have regarding selections so they can bring them to class for clarification. Let them know that capturing their initial thoughts as they read as well as after is important and could ultimately lead to a topic for an essay of their own. You may also want them to use their journals for keeping a record of the vocabulary words taken from the readings that they need to learn.

As you read through this *Guide*, you may notice some redundant comments. It seems unavoidable. Remarks made for one reading selection or unit may also apply to another, and since instructors will no doubt skip around in the text or omit certain readings from their course syllabus, repetition of some suggestions has to occur.

All the approaches presented here have worked for me, but they are never meant as the way you should use the book. My hope is that *Viewpoints* is designed so that all users find it compatible with their own teaching styles.

RATIONALE FOR PART I

Many years of teaching freshman composition have led me to believe that most students lack the necessary analytical skills required to read and react to assigned readings as we would like. In addition, many students have little or no understanding of the writing process or what good writing entails. Since one of the goals of *Viewpoints* is to teach the interrelationship of reading and writing skills, Part I is divided into two units for this purpose. Unit 1 teaches students how to read essays; Unit 2 teaches how to write them. Every effort has been made to show how these two basic skills complement one another.

For some students, Unit 1 serves as an introduction and for others a review of such fundamentals as the essay structure, the difference between a topic and a thesis, paragraph patterns or modes used for developing topic sentences, and transitional devices required of certain patterns. The same fundamentals presented when teaching composition are presented here as tools for better reading comprehension. In addition, Unit 1 shows students how to separate main ideas from supporting details, how to distinguish fact from opinion, and how to draw inferences. These reading skills are, of course, the same skills a writer must consider when composing. Finally, ways to retain comprehension through notetaking, textbook marking, and journal keeping are explained and encouraged. In effect, Unit 1 is a mini-course on how to read analytically with frequent references to the writing connection.

Unit 2 builds on the content of Unit 1 by showing how the methods and qualities of a good essay reader can be applied to essay writing. The unit provides the student with what are generally accepted as the three basic writing stages: prewriting, writing, and rewriting. Again, this unit serves as an introduction or a review of the writing process, continually reminding students that writing is a recursive process.

My experience has been that many freshman students need a sense of direction, an example to follow in order to get started on safe ground. Unit 2 does this by taking students through the entire writing process, showing them how someone might begin an essay and work through several revisions before arriving at a final draft. In so doing, students are taken step by step through prewriting techniques (such as using questions or reactions from their reading journals, brainstorming, clustering, and freewriting), to writing techniques (such as discovering a working thesis, developing and organizing support, and writing a first draft), to revising techniques, including editing and proofreading. The text points out, as you will no doubt wish to do,

1

that there are as many ways to approach writing as there are writers, and that students must discover what works best for them.

Part I, then, provides a background and a useful resource for students that establishes a sense of direction and an understanding of what is expected of them when they are assigned the readings in Part II and the writing of full-length compositions.

Using Unit 1: Viewpoints On Reading Essays

Unit 1 supplies students with the analytical reading skills necessary for reading the essays in *Viewpoints* as well as other sources by teaching them what an essay is, how it is structured, how to read with greater comprehension, and how to retain and use an essay's content. For this reason, I recommend that Unit 1 be assigned the first week of class.

The Writing Exercises   Interspersed with the discussion of reading to understand topic, thesis, supporting evidence, paragraph patterns, and order of support are opportunities for students to interact by responding to questions that test their understanding. Because these questions are followed by explanatory answers, it is possible to assign all or parts of Unit 1 for out-of-class reading. However, in order to monitor students' comprehension of this information, three brief one-paragraph writing exercises have been provided at appropriate intervals. Rather than assigning the entire unit at once, you may prefer to use the writing exercises as a breaking point for three separate assignments. This would depend on the ability of the class and how thoroughly you want to cover this unit.

These three writing exercises can be used in several ways. On the one hand, you can use them as a diagnostic tool, a means to discover the strengths and weaknesses of the class so that you have some idea what skill areas need more coverage than others. On the other hand, you may prefer that students return all three for grading, as an assurance before moving on that the material has been understood. The results of the paragraph writings may reveal a need to go over all or parts of the unit in class, or they may reflect that the class is ready for Unit 2. Another approach is to use the exercises as "pop" quizzes, surprising the students to see if they did read and understand the assignment. Or, as the students work through the unit, have them write the three exercises in their reading journals. You then can read them during a later journal check.

The Reading Journal   You'll notice that I encourage students to keep a reading journal. The unit emphasizes why and how to write summaries of assigned readings, the need for recording any personal reflections after reading, and the maintenance of a vocabulary list for study. Reading–journal-keeping may not be an approach you wish your students to take; if so, mention it as something they may want to do on their own if they feel it will help them. However, it *will* help them, and I strongly recommend that students be required to maintain a reading journal, at least in part. If journal-keeping is done correctly, students become more actively involved in the reading process. You can modify the journal assignments by selecting certain readings for which you want entries, rather than requiring entries for all assigned readings. The reading journal can also be used for other items for which you wish a student response, such as writing answers to any of the questions that follow the reading selections, freewriting, or in-class writing practices. (For ideas, see *The Journal Book*, edited by Toby Fulwiler, Boynton/Cook, 1987.)

Marking Notes in the Text   Another reason for assigning Unit 1 first is that it illustrates for students how to separate main ideas from supporting details, how to separate facts from opinions, and how to draw inferences. Students are also shown how to read with pen in hand, to make thoughtful notations, and to have a dialogue with the author as they read. This information lays the groundwork for careful reading of all the assigned selections in Unit 2.

Even though students are provided with practice in marking up Pete Hamill's essay, "The Wet Drug" (page 34), it might be efficacious during the first or second week to select one or two essays from any unit in Part II for additional practice of the skills taught in Unit 1. Since the units do not have to be read in any order, you could, for example, assign Kathleen Neville's "A Primary Lesson on Sexual Harassment" (page 319) and Jean Shepard's "The Endless Streetcar Ride Into the Night . . ." (page 169). They are distinctly different in structure, tone, and language. Neville's piece has a clear thesis and a standard organizational pattern, using definition, examples, description, and cause-effect passages that can be easily pointed out in class. Shepard's first-person narrative reflects a different tone and attitude, uses many short, one-sentence paragraphs and dialogue, and on the surface may seem to reflect no thesis.

Pointing out these differences, discussing thesis and its location or implication, main ideas and supporting details, implied statements, facts versus opinion, and so on, would aid students when called upon to read on their own. Such an approach would reveal some of the range and diversity of authors and point up the need for analytical reading comprehension.

Initially, students need to be shown how to read and mark assigned reading selections. Frequently I've found it's helpful and fun to read certain passages from the readings aloud, providing the necessary tone and attitude students must learn to provide for themselves when reading silently. We can't assume that students know how to read the way we want them to read; thus, we must show them. Only then can we begin to use the readings as a means for exposing them to humanistic ideas and the range of viewpoints that exist on many topics.

Some students are reluctant to mark up their textbooks. But I show them how one of my books looks after I've read and reacted to an author. I try to convince them, as Mortimer Adler does so well in his classic "How to Mark a Book," that the benefits of marking up a book far outweigh any price they may receive during the campus bookstore buy-back period. I share with them the Herman Ebbinghaus "curve of forgetting" that appears in most freshman psychology textbooks, which reveals how quickly we forget what we learn if we don't reinforce our memory (over 40 percent within twenty minutes, over 55 percent in one hour, and around 70 percent after nine hours).

If you have students keep a reading journal, you may want them to share their entries either in small groups or with the entire class. Students will see that not everyone responds to a selection the same way, nor comprehends the same meaning. This serves to make clear that some reading selections require more than one reading, and that through exchange of thoughtful discussions, most everyone can eventually come to an agreement on what an author's thesis is, without necessarily agreeing with the viewpoint.

I contend that the time spent dealing with the reading skills taught in Unit 1 will result in better student compositions. My recommendation is that you don't assign any full-length essays until after you have covered both Units 1 and 2.

Using Unit 2: Viewpoints on Writing Essays

Don't assign Unit 2 until at least a week has been spent on Unit 1 and after the class has undertaken a close examination of two or three selected essays in Part II. Rather than leaving students on their own, it seems best to make certain they have some guided practice applying the skills taught in Unit 1. At least the same amount of time should be given to Unit 2, depending upon the level of your students. Obviously, some classes may require more time, some less.

There are four writing exercises, similar to those in Unit 1, appearing periodically after specific information on composition has been presented. The exercises call for a written application or a summary of the material read. You may want to use these exercises as a way to divide the unit into four separate assignments, each one followed by the completion of the writing exercise. As in Unit 1, these exercises can be graded, used as quizzes, or assigned as journal entries. I favor collecting them so that student comprehension can be monitored, using them as a gauge for the amount of time needed to be spent on the unit. These exercises also serve as an indicator of which students are keeping up with the assignments.

The Prewriting Activities   While many prewriting heuristics exist, three rather universally accepted ones are presented for students in *Viewpoints*: reacting to questions and statements from the readings recorded in their journals, brainstorming (listing and clustering), and freewriting. (If you are unfamiliar with freewriting and clustering as prewriting activities, Peter Elbow's *Writing with Power*, Oxford Press, 1978, and Gabriele Lusser Rico's *Writing the Natural Way*, J. P. Tarcher, 1983, are highly recommended.) Once presented with various prewriting methods, students seem to favor one of these three approaches.

It's been my experience that students need practice in prewriting beyond what they get in the text. Take the time to do some prewriting board work in class. For instance, I ask students to give me a topic, any topic, which I then write on the board. Next, I ask them to provide some possible working theses based on the topic. This activity helps clarify the difference between a topic and a thesis, plus reveals for them the wide range of directions one can take on any given subject. Then I ask students to provide some ideas or supporting evidence that can be used to support one of the thesis statements we formulate together. Sometimes we brainstorm, sometimes we cluster. When thoughts are exhausted or time infringes, we look over our list or clusters, erasing those points that fail to relate to the thesis. I can never anticipate what the results will be, any more than the students can. Together we discover what will work and what won't. The students thus take part in the prewriting stage and learn what is expected of them when given their first full-length essay writing assignment.

Follow this type of board work with the next phase, organizing those ideas left on the board that relate to the thesis. Students learn that there is a variety of ways to organize supporting evidence for an essay and that it may take several drafts to figure out which approach reads best. After such a class activity, I call their attention to pages 47–52 to show the parallel between what we've done on the board and the example in the text itself.

Whatever way it is done, the teaching of prewriting activities is an invaluable lesson. Practices in one or more of these prewriting exercises before assigning full-length essays benefit both the student and you when the full-length composition is finally assigned.

The Nutshell Statement   You may not want to require students to complete a nutshell statement as described on pages 60–62 in the text. However, I find it helpful to them and to me when I require that one be attached to every essay, at least during the early stage of the course. When I have individual conferences with students, I use the nutshell statements to point out where their strengths and weaknesses are in relation to their purpose (thesis), support (organization and logic), and audience (tone and style). Once students are writing well enough, I no longer require the nutshell statement unless they find it helpful.

If you do want to use nutshells, you will probably find that students need some help in preparing ones that are not vague or hurriedly written. Sometimes I distribute handouts with examples of nutshell statements from previous students' work. I usually share in class both good and bad student examples without identifying the authors.

I frequently ask students to write a nutshell statement for one of the reading selections in the text as a writing assignment. Sharing their written nutshells in class leads to interesting discussions of the assigned reading, often revealing biases and discrepancies in their comprehension of the reading selection. It is also revealing to have students exchange their own essays, requesting that classmates write nutshell statements for comparison with the student author's, showing the students how others perceive their work and making them aware that the instructor is not the only audience for whom they are writing.

Paragraph Patterns   The information on rhetorical modes on pages 63–68 should be compared with that on pages 9–20 in Unit 1. It serves as a reinforcement of the reading-writing connection.

I find it rather artificial to ask students to write using a particular rhetorical mode. It seems to place the pattern before thought and content. After students write a rough draft, I then ask them to see if some pattern appeared naturally. When they revise, I remind them they may need to express their thoughts using a different pattern. Still, there may be a place for requesting students to use a particular paragraph pattern as a drill or an exercise in understanding that pattern.

You may want to select examples of various modes reflected in paragraphs from essays in Part II as models to share in class. See the Rhetorical Table of Contents for a classification of essays according to the various rhetorical paragraph modes found within the readings.

Viewpoints approaches the use of paragraph patterns as a way to develop information based on the way a topic sentence is written. The text itself says all that need be said here.

The Student Model Essay   It's worth class time to look carefully at the various drafts of the model student essay on pages 69–85 as a way to discuss recursive writing. Point out the various changes from draft to draft, stressing the importance of revision. Although the text visually illustrates these changes, it is recommended that you make certain through class discussion that students see and understand the changes and additions that were made. Many students will not actually notice some of the changes unless they are pointed out.

The student model essay offers an opportunity to emphasize the need for revision, but it also provides you with a tool for discussing how you would respond to and grade the essay, and provides students with a better understanding of your own particular demands and expectations.

In addition to the model student essay in this unit, there is one at the end of every unit in Part II. Some are well written, some flawed. I think students can learn from the mistakes that appear on the essays as well as from the positive aspects. All are followed by commentaries explaining my reaction to them. These views are based on my perspective; certainly you should provide your own commentary as well, especially if you disagree with me.

The Revision and Editing Checklists   You will probably want to discuss in class the checklists provided to help clarify any terminology or points students don't understand. The checklists are of little value if the students can't interpret what they are meant to check.

Brief versions of the expanded revision and editing checklists are provided at the end of Unit 2 for the convenience of the student. You can request that the students apply these checklists to each of their essays before they submit their work to you.

RATIONALE FOR PART II

The eight units that comprise Part II fulfill several of this book's objectives. The readings provide a variety of viewpoints, thematically arranged, on contemporary issues with four types of follow-up questions that stimulate or suggest to students ideas for their own essays; they contain a wide range of examples of professional and student writing; and they directly or indirectly offer possibilities for simple research projects. The units can be read in any order, and, if you wish, you can skip around through the units ignoring the themes altogether. Having more essays in the book than you will have time to cover during the course allows you to choose only the selections you want to assign or use in class.

Each unit contains a broad theme with which all students will have some familiarity. When assigning essays from any unit, spend some class time and attention on the photos, quotes, and short prefatory comments that open each unit. They introduce the unit's theme and help focus student attention on the unit readings. For instance, Unit 4, which deals with human behavior, begins with a husband's letter to Ann Landers describing his wife's strange habits. Discussing it and Landers's answer is fun and focuses the students' attention on the unit's theme. Unit 4's prefatory comments also explain how social scientists, sociologists, psychologists, and economists define human behavior. You can remind students that their textbooks from these classes might contain a wealth of stimulation for an essay or possible research paper. Students will begin to see that ideas for essays don't have to come from among those suggested in the book, that there is a connection between the English course they are taking and the "real world."

Many students often have difficulty concentrating on assigned readings unless the subject truly interests them. As a way to prepare students for a reading assignment, prereading questions require a brief survey of the selection and a prediction about the content. The questions are based on two well-known reading techniques, the DRTA (Directed Reading-Thinking Activity) and the first steps of the SQ3R (Survey, Question, Read, Recite, Review). Requiring students to answer these prereading questions forces them to concentrate on what they are about to read. Just as a camera must be focused before taking a picture, the reader must focus on what is about to be read. Remind students that the prereading questions are part of each reading assignment. In fact, you may want to go over the prereading questions with the students at the time you assign the reading selection, a sort of preview of coming attractions.

A list of key vocabulary words provided before the selection itself permits students to preview the definitions and note the essay paragraphs where the words appear. Some instructors like to discuss these words with the students at the time the reading assignment is given. Others prefer to deal with vocabulary after students have read the piece. Still others leave the learning of vocabulary up to the individual student. I like to go over the words with the students when I assign the essay, answering any questions they may have and assuring correct pronunciation. It seems to make the reading of the essay easier for them.

The four sets of questions that follow each reading selection reinforce the skills presented in Part I. The first set, **Understanding the Content**, deals with basic comprehension elements: recognizing thesis, main ideas, supporting evidence, fact and opinion, and so on. They are questions for which answers can usually be agreed upon.

The next set, **Looking at Structure and Style**, focuses on the author's organization, paragraph patterns, language usage, transitional techniques, and the like: in effect, most of the composition fundamentals taught in Unit 2. The third set of questions, **Evaluating the Author's Viewpoints**, calls for personal reactions, critical thinking, and evaluation of what was read. **Pursuing Possible Essay Topics**, the last set, offers a variety of ideas or starting points for student essays or research projects dealing with the unit's theme.

The first three sets of questions can be used in several ways. Some can be selected for reading journal entries, some for class discussion, others for "pop" quizzes. Some instructors like to break the class into small groups, making each group responsible for providing answers to specific questions, or to assign individuals specific questions to answer orally in class. More ways to use the questions are mentioned later in this guide when individual essays are discussed.

For those instructors introducing their students to the research project, the fourth set of questions frequently contains suggestions that require more reading. Some of the items offer specific book titles or library sources for students to pursue. You may want to divide your class into groups, assigning each group one of the questions to brainstorm or discuss, then have the students share their ideas with the entire class.

Part II provides more than enough reading selections for a one-term course. The abundance and diversity of style and difficulty are intentional, allowing you to choose the readings most appropriate for the level of your class and the length of your course. I have found that students can, if interested in the subject, often read above their expected level. Don't let a seemingly difficult selection deter you from assigning it. If they are to develop their skills, students need the challenge of more difficult reading. The intent is to provide instructors with interesting material useful in teaching students how to read and write at a higher level than they could handle when they entered the class. Good instruction requires students to be challenged, not just fed easy material because they are "underprepared." How else will they ever get prepared?

Using Unit 3: Viewpoints on Learning

While it is not necessary to begin with this unit after finishing Part I, to do so can be useful because most students at this point in the course are experiencing a new kind of learning—adaptation to college life. If you are assigning essay topics on themes, learning is an appropriate starting place. Discussing in class the Doonesbury cartoon, the quotation, and prefatory materials will focus students on the broad theme of learning and will prepare them for any of the essays you assign.

When assigning a reading selection, periodically remind students of the reading skills taught in Unit 1. Go over the prereading questions and vocabulary words with the students. You may want to look at some of the words in context as part of a prereading activity. Although it may not be practical to do this with every reading assignment, it helps to do this with the more difficult reading selections.

Following are some comments and suggestions for using the essays in this unit.

"Salvation" by Langston Hughes

A classic of sorts, appearing in many other reading anthologies, it's a touching narrative of a type of initiation rite into adulthood that most of us go through. A simple story on the surface, other deeper implications and analogies can be made from the story. Discussing content questions 5 and 6 is especially important in teaching this selection.

The narrative is well done; consequently, assigning or discussing all the questions dealing with "Looking at Structure and Style" may be called for. None of the other readings in this unit deals quite as effectively with description (note paragraphs 3 and 4 especially) and dialogue (paragraphs 8–10) in the way Hughes does here. Most students can remember an epiphany of their own they can write about if you want to assign a narrative essay.

If you want to teach the different ways narrative is used, assign the Hughes piece with Sharon Whitley's essay on Anne Frank's diary.

"Students' Love Affair with Anne Frank" by Sharon Whitley

Unlike Hughes in "Salvation," whose narrative implies and suggests through a story, Whitley uses narrative up to paragraph 11, then switches in the last paragraphs to statements of others to back up her argumentative thesis that *The Diary of Anne Frank* is a useful teaching tool and must not be banned from the classroom. The Hughes essay and this one serve to show the differences in the way "I" can be used.

You may want to read a passage or two from Anne Frank's diary, particularly passages that some might find objectionable, although I don't know what they would be. You may also want to discuss journals or diaries and their possible importance to the future, perhaps not at a global level, but certainly at a personal or family history level.

Because this essay deals with censorship as well as learning, it makes for a healthy class discussion of the subject of censorship. Is censorship ever warranted? If so, when and by whom? What do we mean by censorship? Who should be the censors? If students are stimulated to write about censorship rather than learning, why not let them? Suggest that students may want to read the book, looking for reasons some people want it suppressed.

Your college librarian will no doubt have information on books that frequently come under censorship attacks. Share some of the titles with students.

"To Err Is Wrong" by Roger von Oech

If you can't assign all of the essays in this unit, this is *not* one to skip. The subject of failure and success is on the minds of most students—indeed, most all of us. The idea that failure can bring success is important, especially to student writers who struggle with the fear of failure or live with their past failure. I recommend at least reading paragraph 26 aloud and discussing the four tips in class.

In paragraph 8, von Oech quotes the baseball player Yaz, "If you want hits, be prepared for misses," and equates this comment to the way the game of life goes. Remind students that that's also the way writing an essay goes—lots of false starts, lots of errors, lots of revisions before that successful final draft. Emphasize that errors can be stepping stones to success.

Because of the variety of paragraph patterns used—cause/effect, comparison/contrast, examples, use of anecdote—the selection can be used to discuss and reinforce rhetorical modes. The questions under "Looking at Structure and Style" provide for such an approach. As an aside, you might want to point out the difference in handling a lengthy quotation (the block quote in paragraph 17) and in citing shorter quotations (those in paragraphs 11 and 19).

Students who respond favorably to this selection may want to read *A Whack On the Side of the Head* (Warner Books, 1983), the book from which this essay was taken.

"In Praise of the F Word" by Mary Sherry

Sherry says, "Passing students who have not mastered the work cheats them and the employers who expect graduates to have basic skills," a statement that usually provokes discussion. Many of my students have this complaint. "Why was I passed on? Why wasn't I made to learn? I'm in this class because I wasn't taught the skills I needed." I'm certain you have your own favorite retorts to their anger and excuses for not learning, which leads to some lively class discussions.

This essay raises the issues of the grading system, attitudes toward learning, teacher competency, parental responsibility, and the levels of literacy, all good topics for possible essays. Ask students to get into groups and discuss their various learning experiences. Have them argue for or against grades or one of the issues mentioned above. You could use this piece as a way to discuss an argumentative essay: What is Sherry's thesis? Is it supported with sound arguments? What are they? What's wrong with her argument? Would she feel this way if her son hadn't been threatened with an F? and so on.

Take time to discuss all the questions under "Looking at Structure and Style."

"School vs. Education" by Russell Baker

To help students recognize Baker's sarcastic and cynical tone, read this one orally in class. Because of its brevity, there is time to discuss most of the questions that follow it. Particularly important under the content questions are items 3, 5, and 6, dealing with thesis and tone. All the questions under "Looking at Structure and Style" seem important if the selection is used at an early stage in the course.

One way to facilitate coverage of all the questions is to divide the class into small groups, assigning each one certain questions you wish to emphasize. Then have each group report its findings to the entire class. Ask some students to research more about Russell Baker, then report back to class with some other examples of his work.

You may wish to assign a student composition at this point by asking students to use the list of possible essay topics as thought provokers. I prefer to wait until we have discussed all the essays in a given unit so that students can choose from all of the "Pursuing Possible Essay Topics" lists. These lists of suggestions can also be used for in-class writing exercises or journal writings. If you want a more controlled essay-writing assignment, pick the item yourself. Personally, I find this approach too stifling for the student; worse, it usually results in student writing that reflects what they think I want to hear.

"Bilingualism's Goal" by Barbara Mujica

Although placed in the unit on education, this essay also touches on cultural heritage and family. You may want to refer to it again when you deal with those units (Units 5 and 7).

Many students have experienced bilingual education and can contribute some firsthand accounts in a class discussion. But beyond the topic itself are other aspects of education this essay can open up: Just what is the role of the schools? What should the schools teach and what should they not? Who should teach sex education? Should prayer be allowed in the schools? Who is responsible for a student's failure? Mujica's essay makes a nice bridge into these and other areas.

"The Practicality of the Liberal Arts Major"
by Debra Sikes and Barbara Murray

Even though the authors intended this essay for college teachers, students will find this essay interesting because it reflects what research has discovered about the practicality of the liberal arts degree. Paragraph 5 discusses where and what the research project was about. Paragraph 7 shows the skills, in order of importance, that a college student should acquire for future jobs. Paragraph 8 provides the authors' recommendations to students based on their findings.

It can be a useful essay for getting students to rethink their college goals. You might want to call their attention to the key points in paragraphs 7 and 8. Ask them if they are presently taking or planning to take the courses that will benefit them the most. Do they believe it is possible to be "overeducated"? Such questions get students to see that the reading selection can and does relate to them personally.

Good follow-up writing drills and/or essay topics are numbers 2, 4, 5, and 6, as they direct the students to consider their reasons for attending college, their learning skills, and the benefits derived from a college education.

Calling attention to the stylistic differences between this and the Baker essay may prove valuable. Structure, as well as tone and attitude, are quite different.

STUDENT ESSAY: **"The Vast Emptiness at the Core of Today's Liberal Arts Education"** by Max A. Boot

Be certain that you assign the student essay, requiring students to write their reactions where it is called for. A class session could easily be spent looking carefully at the four prereading questions, having students share their written responses, and sharing your own comments as well as reacting to the text commentary. Grading varies from instructor to instructor. My criteria may not be yours. But in order for students to understand yours, discuss the grade you would give the student essay. If you disagree with my commentary, explain why to your students. I wouldn't mind hearing from you, either.

Boot's essay is certainly not an example of the type of writing I usually get at the beginning of a course, but the content follows up the Sikes and Murray selection on liberal arts education. I remind students that some of the qualities found here are those for which students should strive. Don't shy away from this essay because it may appear too difficult. Go over it carefully with students; don't let Boot's complaint become theirs later in their academic careers.

Freshman students may not understand Boot's complaint here, so you may have to help explain what Boot thinks he has missed (paragraph 3). While Boot is mainly attacking UC Berkeley, what he says is a commonly heard complaint from students at major universities. (You may want to read some passages from Page Smith's *Killing the Spirit: Higher Education in America*, Viking, 1990, as a back-up to Boot's complaint.) Go over paragraphs 6 and 7 carefully. You will need to help them with paragraphs 9 with his discussion of "deconstructionists" and "revisionists."

This also may be an appropriate place to discuss the form you wish students to follow when preparing full-length essays, for submission. You may want something different from the model explained on pages 461–467.

Using Unit 4: Viewpoints on Human Behavior

The theme of human behavior appears after the one on learning simply because it, too, is broad and familiar enough for all students to relate to without much strain. Should you use the topic for a full-length essay assignment, the unit's introductory comments help reflect the wide explanations for human behavior frequently given in textbooks. You might remind students that if they are taking psychology, sociology, or anthropology, they are studying human behavior and may find ideas and sources for essay topics from their other textbooks and lectures as well as from this book.

The two pictures at the beginning of the unit, along with the Shakespeare quote, generate some humorous responses. The letter to Ann Landers at the beginning of the unit commentary and her response at the end can be used to begin thinking about human behavior. You may want to clip a few "advice" columns and bring them to class to stimulate discussion of the theme.

"The Seven Dwarfs and I" by Cara M. Egan

While Egan calls our attention to the way we react to dwarfs, she indirectly makes us think about our reactions to any people who are different from what we think of as the "norm." Her article stimulates discussions of our reactions to the disabled, the disfigured, the homeless, foreigners, and others we look upon as "different."

Her essay begins and ends with references to Walt Disney World and the Seven Dwarf dolls. Structurally, I find her essay analogous to a hearty sandwich. She uses the opening and closing paragraphs like two pieces of bread, between which she provides tasty food for thought. Using familiar subjects such as the Seven Dwarfs, the Munchkins from *The Wizard of Oz*, and the dwarfs in the movie *Willow*, she provides another perspective on real dwarfs.

Point out her use of definitions in paragraphs 2 and 6. Ask how these paragraphs differ from her narrative.

"Sexual Bigotry" by Roger Rosenblatt

Although Rosenblatt's essay does touch on sexual harassment and sexual bigotry at the work place, he deals with the issue at a broader level, so it appears here under the theme of human behavior. It is certainly an essay to which you can refer when you teach the unit on work.

You can use this selection to touch on several issues: men's fears that women may take over their jobs, jealousy, the difference between sexual harassment and sexual bigotry, and bigotry against races and foreigners.

Use the questions under "Looking at Structure and Style" to illustrate some writing techniques Rosenblatt uses.

"Superstitious Minds" by Letty Cottin Pogrebin

An easy essay to read and understand, Pogrebin's piece makes a nice model for students who wish to write a first-person narrative about a family member or themselves. Most of us think we're rational but, if probed far enough, will admit to some type of superstition. Ask students what some of their superstitious quirks are, where they came from, what support they provide.

This is a good essay for discussion of tone, question 7 under "Structure and Style." Call attention to the way Pogrebin uses words to give us feelings for her mother. Ultimately, ask if this essay is really about superstition or the author's mother.

The essay can also be used to stimulate some library research on topics such as black magic, voodoo, the occult, astrology, ESP, reincarnation (Shirley McLaine's "other lives"), and those beings from outer space the *National Enquirer* always reminds us are out there.

"Night Walker" by Brent Staples

Staples's opening paragraph is very well done—so well done, in fact, that after reading only the first sentence, one of the early reviewers of the *Viewpoints* manuscript said that she would not read or teach this essay. Staples, of course, deliberately leads us to think he is some sinister person, probably a rapist or murderer. But as we read on, we learn as he did, "his unwieldy inheritance, the ability to alter public space" by just being a black man among fearful whites.

Have students deal especially with questions 2–6 under "Looking at Structure and Style." Some readers may find it overly descriptive, a good discussion point. All the questions under "Evaluating the Author's Viewpoints" create some lively discussions, especially item 3.

You might, if you have time, get students to do some non-library research. Have them keep track for a week or two of the number of street violence episodes being reported on national and local television news, in daily papers, and in national news magazines. Is such news frequent? Can it create more fear than it deserves? Does it seem biased in presentation, as Staples suggests?

You might want to point out the connection of this essay with "The Seven Dwarfs and I" in regard to the way we perceive people and where we get our perceptions.

"Slow Descent into Hell" by Jon D. Hull

Excerpted from a longer essay in *TIME* magazine (February 2, 1987), this portion illustrates good use of descriptive techniques as well as a way to discuss the growing homeless situation. You or your students may want to research the article and share more of it in class.

For those of you teaching rhetorical modes, Hull provides a fine example of descriptive writing. You may want students to look through it for examples of passages that utilize our five senses.

At the time of this printing, the problems of the homeless were receiving much publicity, thus providing some possible sources for outside reading assignments. Not much regarding the homeless has changed since 1987, has it?

"Fun. Oh, Boy. Fun. You Could Die from It." by Suzanne Britt

Despite the essay's brevity and ease of reading, some students may not really grasp Britt's point because of her tone. (They wonder what the grouch is complaining about. People *should* have fun, right?) It helps to combat such reactions by pointing out paragraphs 4, 5, and

13 to help clarify her thesis. Have them think back for other examples of "fun" that bombard us daily by elaborating more specifically on paragraph 10.

Get a discussion going on what fun is. Do television beer ads portray fun? Is watching a football game fun? Can we deliberately set out to have fun? Do children have more fun than adults?

Ask students how Britt defines fun in paragraph 14. This is a good springboard for dealing with essays that define if you're interested in teaching modes.

"The Endless Streetcar Ride into the Night..." by Jean Shepherd

Students have fun with this one, even though there are some vocabulary difficulties. Use it to discuss tone, attitude, narration, description, and story entertainment. The subject is one that most all of us have experienced or might someday.

If there is time, try to read aloud those passages in the essay that require the proper intonations and pacing. Show them how words can create tone, how sentences have rhythm. Doing so helps students see what they need to bring to such a reading selection if they are to fully appreciate it.

Most of the students will probably find that the suggestions for "Pursuing Possible Essay Topics" are more than enough to tap ideas for an essay on human behavior.

STUDENT ESSAY: "Man and Woman: A Soap Opera with Real Soap" by Cindy Evans

As mentioned before, it is important to have students carefully read the student essay and for you to provide class time for them to share their written reactions called for in the text. The student model essays reflect what other students have done with the topic, revealing their strengths and their weaknesses.

The commentary following Evans's essay points out three strengths: she makes the topic her own, she uses the comparison/contrast pattern appropriately, and she pays attention to word choice. You may want to discuss how Evans does this by going over the essay with your class. One reviewer thinks this essay is too descriptive. Whatever you think, use it to teach what you want and don't want to see in your students' essays.

Compare/contrast this essay with the student essay in Unit 3. Ask students which one they think is better written and why.

Using Unit 5: Viewpoints on Cultural Heritage

If the make-up of your class is culturally diverse, consider using this unit early in the course. As the unit's introduction states, a great immigrational surge to this country, both legal and illegal, has occurred since the 1970s. The United States is now the fifth largest Spanish-speaking country in the world. Soon major cities, such as Los Angeles and Miami, will have more Spanish speakers than English ones. Over twelve million Asians will have immigrated here by the year 2000. The great change in the cultural make-up of our country that is in process makes for a current theme of interest to many students. Set the groundwork for this unit by referring to the unit's prefatory comments. Ask students their reactions to the Statue of Liberty and immigrant pictures and the caption.

The diversity of cultural heritage is reflected in this unit's reading selections: one recounts the history of the German and Dutch influx of immigrants here in the mid-1800s; another offers some Native Americans' reaction to the celebration of Columbus Day; another shares a reader's discovery of African-American literature; another gives the views of a Chinese man who lived in the United States for two years; one focuses on "black English"; another narrates the experience of an Armenian growing up in two cultures; and still another presents the problems some Indochinese immigrants are having adjusting to America. The student essay, written by a Vietnamese, describes the hardships of his family's flight to this country.

Cultural heritage makes a rich topic for outside reading. You might want to call for some non-library research, suggesting that students interview family members for more information about their own culture, or interview students on campus from a culture different from their own.

The controversy over multicultural education is treated in Unit 10. You may want to follow up with those readings after covering this unit.

"Settling in the Cities" by Albert Robbins

Since this work is based on research, it can be used for historical background, for making comparisons with the reactions of todays' immigrants to this country with earlier ones, and for introducing students to the way quoted information is presented.

This selection is different from most of the others in that the author stays in the background. Most of the information is drawn from the writings of others. Show students how information from other sources can be drawn together to make the point made in the last paragraph. Point out how long quotations are handled in block quotes (paragraphs 2, 3 5, and 6); how ellipses and brackets are used (paragraph 3); and how sources are cited in footnotes. If you teach the MLA style, show the differences between the method used here and what MLA requires.

Item 2 under "Pursuing Possible Essay Topics" provides some sources for a possible library research project. Of course, items 3 and 4 could also be a different type of research project, using people instead of printed material.

The quotations used from various sources contain some interesting comparisons with life then and life now. Many students may find these historical accounts revealing and may discover in them challenging ideas for essays.

"Don't Celebrate 1492—Mourn It" by Hans Koning

Although the quincentennial celebration of 1492 mentioned in the opening paragraph is over, the essay remains contemporary because it deals with the whole idea of our yearly celebration of Columbus Day. Paragraphs 4, 5, and 6 present Koning's opposing reasons, some graphically described, as to why some people should think twice about Columbus as a "hero."

To back up the comment in paragraph 7, there were over six new books printed in 1991 alone dealing with Columbus. Some continued to exalt Columbus a hero, others faulted him. You may want to balance this essay's viewpoint by explaining what life was like in 1492, especially in Spain, and what was considered moral and immoral in those times. Does that excuse Columbus for his "sins"?

Considering it's such a short essay, it can generate quite a heated discussion and can lead to some historical inquiries for those interested. Many students may feel Koning is making too much of a small thing. Unless students are aware of the abuse American Indians have taken, his comments in the last paragraph regarding economic deprivation, powerlessness, discrimination, and gross injustice will not mean much. However, he seems to base much of his argument on the belief that his audience is aware of certain historical facts.

For those students who become interested in historical injustice or in the culture or literature of the American Indian, a list of a few resources is provided in "Pursuing Possible Essay Topics."

"African-American Literature: Much to Be Proud Of"
by Terry McMillan

McMillan edited *Breaking Ice: An Anthology of Contemporary American Black Fiction*, Viking, 1990. This selection is from her introduction.

Structurally, it can be used to show chronological narration and effective use of examples. The content can be used to discuss self-discovery and success as well as to introduce the names and works of many American writers. If there is time, encourage students to explore some of the authors mentioned by requiring some library drills in the use of the card catalog, computer retrieval, biographical index, and so forth.

The set of follow-up questions you emphasize will depend on what aspect of the selection you wish to underscore.

"After Two Years in the Melting Pot" by Liu Zongren

I cheated some here. This "essay" is taken from two portions of the author's book *Two Years in the Melting Pot* (China Books, 1988). I find it interesting because it provides students with a look at America by an outsider, a man from China who spent two years here away from his family and then gladly went home. Zongren's book contains many more passages such as this one if you care to read some to your class or recommend it to them.

There are some excellent comparison and contrast examples in this selection dealing with cultural values. If you have any non-native speakers in your class, this essay can help them open up with examples of their own. Ask students who have traveled to other countries what customs they found strange or familiar.

"What's Wrong with Black English" by Rachel L. Jones

Some students may have to be shown why this essay is presented in a cultural heritage section, thinking it belongs better in a section on language. They have a point, but black English (or to be more "politically correct," African-American English) is a living example of one aspect of cultural heritage for a large number of people. The subject prompts some great discussions, especially if you have some vocal African-Americans in class. Ask: Is there such a thing as "black English"? Is it incorrect to speak black English? Is speaking black English similar to speaking "Spanish English"? Should black English be preserved? Why is there such a phenomenon as black English?

A counterargument to Jones can be found in James Baldwin's "If Black English Isn't Language, Then Tell Me What Is?" which appears in many other anthologies. It's worthwhile to read portions of Baldwin's viewpoints to compare with Jones's.

"A Story of Conflicts" by Yeghia Aslanian

Aslanian's essay raises many worthwhile issues: humiliation caused by cultural differences, language barriers, the need to know more than one language in today's world, and the value of studying another language.

Question 4 under "Evaluating the Author's Viewpoints" should get some interesting responses. Then explore some of the "Pursuing Possible Essay Topics" in class.

"Trouble for America's 'Model' Minority" by David Whitman

Based on interviews with Indochinese, much of this selection contains quotations, with long passages in italics. It might be necessary to distinguish for students how a magazine handles these long quotations compared with the way students are expected to in their own writing and with the way Robbins does in the first essay in this unit. If students are conducting personal interviews as a form of research, they can be shown how Whitman paraphrases as well as quotes directly.

More important, however, might be the discussion of the plight of these people, both past and present, and the courage involved in beginning a new life in a country so foreign to them in language and culture. Many students of mine seem woefully ignorant of the effects the Vietnam War has had and is having on the United States today. An excellent book from which you might read passages, or at least recommend to students, is *Haing Ngor: A Cambodian Odyssey*, by Haing Ngor. The author was the subject of the movie, *The Killing Fields*. You might wish to show parts of that movie, now on videotape, in your class.

STUDENT ESSAY: **"Coming to America"** by Hieu Huynh

When we have foreign students in our classes, we should take every opportunity to make use of their experiences as a way of broadening both our students' and our own awareness of other cultures. I have found that most Asians are a bit shy about talking in class or discussing anything about themselves, but once made to feel comfortable, they open up and add much to a class.

The student essay in this unit may not stand as an example of college-level writing, but it reflects much worth discussing: the struggle to escape persecution, the struggle to get to this country, the struggle to survive in a new country, and the struggle to learn a new language. Most of our students have never experienced what this young man has had to deal with. The essay speaks for itself.

Using Unit 6: Viewpoints on Some Social Concerns

This unit is intended as an extension of Unit 5, although it doesn't have to be taught that way. It moves from cultural heritage into social concerns that stem from differing cultural values. In addition to discussing the two brief newspaper reports in the introduction to the unit, you might want to read the following passage from David Bender's *American Values: Opposing Viewpoints:*

> It is important to consider every variety of opinion in an attempt to determine the truth. Opinions from the mainstream of society should be examined. Also important are opinions that are considered radical, reactionary, minority or stigmatized by some uncomplimentary label. An important lesson of history is the fact that many unpopular and even despised opinions eventually gained a widespread acceptance. The opinions of Socrates, those attributed to Jesus, and Galileo are good examples of this. To have a good grasp on your own viewpoint, you must understand the arguments of those with whom you disagree.

Because this unit contains differing opinions on social issues, students should be asked to set aside their own biases when they read the essays and discuss the topics brought up in this unit. Essays included range from opinions on racial and ethnic prejudices to the AIDS epidemic.

Go over the definitions of values, norms, and roles provided in the unit's prefatory comments before assigning any essays in this unit.

"Debating Moral Questions" by Vincent Ryan Ruggiero

Generally it doesn't matter what essay you teach first in any given unit, but in this case it seems most appropriate to start with Ruggiero's. Once students have been exposed to the question of morals through this essay, they tend to let the concept filter into the other essays presented.

In this selection from his book *The Art of Thinking* (Harper & Row, 1988), Ruggiero raises the question: Is it legitimate for us to pass judgment on the morals of another culture? Quite provocative, the subject of moral issues can be extended into such topics as the morality of abortion, capital punishment (see Unit 10), apartheid, selling arms to warring countries, business ethics, morality in politics, and on and on. For instance, you might ask your class whether or not America has a right to tell other countries what form of government they should have. Another way to phrase the question is to ask whether or not we have a moral obligation to bring democracy to underdeveloped countries. Lively class or small group discussions on morality often lead to some thoughtful student essays.

Ruggiero cites four sources in his essay. You might want students to research these in the library.

"A Long Way to Go," by Rosa Parks

Here is an excellent piece raising the issue of civil disobedience. Thoreau's viewpoints and his famous night in jail can be used for historical perspective.

Rosa Parks was arrested in Montgomery, Alabama, on the evening of December 1, 1955, for refusing to give up her bus seat to a white man. The seamstress's act of defiance touched off a boycott of the city's buses, led by Martin Luther King, Jr. Some say that Parks's refusal to give up her bus seat was the beginning of the civil rights movement. Now 76, she lives in Detroit, working as an assistant to a Michigan congressman.

Her essay provides a rather succinct three-generation history of blacks in the South, especially eye-opening for those students unaware of the reasons behind the 1960s civil rights movement. The essay can lead to many thought-provoking areas: racial prejudice, black history, the Statue of Liberty, the NAACP, Martin Luther King, Jr., and apartheid to name a few.

"Eggs, Twinkies and Ethnic Stereotypes" by Jeanne Park

This essay, written when Park was a junior at Stuyvesant High School, serves as a nice little piece for teaching both the narrative essay form and for dealing with stereotypes at three levels: her own superiority complex, the teacher's belief that all Asians are smart in math, and racial bigotry. Dealing with all the questions under "Looking at Structure and Style" and "Evaluating the Author's Viewpoints" is worth your time.

Some of these issues are very sensitive ones, depending on your class make-up. But why bother teaching composition if the bottom line isn't to get students to deal thoughtfully and intelligently with the very issues Park explores?

The next essay by Kang can be used successfully with Park's since they deal with the social problems caused by cultural differences. You may want to hold off on the "Pursuing Possible Essay Topics" until after you have discussed both essays.

"A Battle of Cultures" by K. Connie Kang

Along with the growing number of Asian immigrants coming to the United States come the problems of social misunderstandings and adjustments. Kang's essay focuses on our need for what she calls "cultural insight" (paragraph 6). She provides a good example of cultural differences that can cause misunderstanding in paragraphs 7–11. Paragraphs 12–15 help explain why it may appear to some Americans that newly arrived Asians starting businesses here are rich. She touches on philosophical differences between Asians and Americans in paragraph 16. Without "blaming" anyone for cultural misunderstandings, she provides a balanced account of the need for everyone to "celebrate our similarities as well as our differences."

If you use both this essay and the previous one by Parks, you might want to explore both sets of questions under "Pursuing Possible Essay Topics."

"Severing the Human Connection" by H. Bruce Miller

Miller's essay raises the issue of honesty and integrity. "Is it that the people are simply incorrigibly dishonest," he asks, "that the glue of integrity and mutual respect that holds society together is finally dissolving?" A good question for us to consider.

I find it interesting to mention to my classes that in my youth we never locked our house or our cars. It was safe for a youngster to ride the city bus alone or walk the streets at night. Storekeepers trusted us to pay the next time if we happened to be short on a purchase. Then I ask why life has changed, and in what direction we seem to be going. I get some interesting answers.

This selection works well for a discussion of tone, attitude, and style. Point out that the author was prompted to write by his reaction to an ordinary event. Students often overlook such personal incidents and perspectives as possibilities for interesting compositions.

"America Discovers AIDS Is Real" by Richard Rodriguez

Some of your younger students may not remember the shock that America, and much of the rest of the world, felt the day Magic Johnson announced he was retiring from basketball because he was infected with the HIV virus. Suddenly AIDS was no longer just a problem for gays and "junkies." You may have to fill students in on how the media were mesmerized by the story.

The Rodriguez piece, one of many that appeared that week, took a unique slant. While most people hailed Johnson as a hero of sorts, Rodriguez wants to tell us "about some other heroes I know" (paragraph 7). His vivid descriptions of the fear and suffering of AIDS victims is graphic and touching at the same time. "Why," he asks, "do we need a celebrity to tell us of such a thing?" Paragraphs 14–15 should be probed deeply beyond just the AIDS issue.

STUDENT ESSAY: **"Can Magic Breach the Wall of Denial?"** by Tatiana Litvin

Not one of my students, Litvin was attending the University of Southern California when she wrote this piece, which appeared in the *Los Angeles Times*. Because it is another reaction to Magic Johnson's announcement that he was infected with the HIV virus, and because it deals with the nonchalant reaction by some students to the growing AIDS epidemic, it seems appropriate to include it here. See the textbook itself for my commentary. Again, your reaction might be quite different and you should share it with your students.

Using Unit 7: Viewpoints on Family Relationships

As with the other reading selections, this unit's theme is broad and significantly familiar to most students. It contains an assortment of writing styles and viewpoints on family relationships. The introductory comments to the unit discuss six major qualities shared by healthy families universally. One way to get students interested in the unit's theme would be to discuss these in class, or have students react to them in a writing exercise as a warm-up before assigning the readings.

"Pre-Wedding Syndrome" by Jane Whitney

Most students will enjoy the humor in this piece. The narrative takes us through the trauma of what Whitney calls "P.W.S." It has stimulated students to write their own accounts of rituals they have gone through that only seem humorous in hindsight.

Whitney uses a lot of details and examples to describe her encounter with P.W.S. Point out to students how cleverly she takes the usual details of planning a wedding—selecting the food, the table-ware, the music, the guest list, clothing, budget—and makes us laugh through her agony.

The connection with the theme of family relationships becomes pretty obvious in paragraphs 11–14.

"The Importance of Family" by Sam Keen

Keen's essay is, of course, more serious and more sophisticated in presentation than Whitney's. Some students may "feel" that Keen's essay is too difficult to follow after reading about Whitney's "P.W.S.," but it isn't if you walk them through it. Besides, students need to read challenging material if they are to expand their reading abilities.

You may need to discuss briefly why Keen mentions Plato, Marx, and Mao as anti-family in his first paragraph since one of his points is that "So long as men's and women's prime loyalty is to family and kin, they cannot be controlled by the state or any other institution" (paragraph 1). Good readers will be able to infer what those thinkers proposed from Keen's comments about "ideal republics."

Paragraph 2 establishes the importance of the family unit. Paragraph 3 then cautions us that we may be voluntarily "eroding the freedoms and surrendering the loyalties no tyrant could take from us" because of our "devotion to the competitive goals of the corporation over loyalty to family."

In paragraph 4, Keen gives an extended definition of "economics," which has changed because "factory, store, office, bank" have "usurped the loyalties" that belong to the home. In paragraph 5, Keen begins to show what is needed to keep the family at the core of our lives. Paragraph 6 and 7 acknowledge counterarguments but point out their invalidity. His last two paragraphs tell us what he thinks men need to do to keep the family unit from disintegrating. You may want to have students read Barbara Brandt's essay, "Less Is More: A Call for Shorter Work Hours," in Unit 8 along with this one. Her reason for calling for fewer work hours is so that people can spend more time with their families, reinforcing Keen's point that we sometimes make work more important than our family.

Taken from Keen's book, *Fire in the Belly*, the essay's audience is mainly men.

"Escaping the Daily Grind for Life as a House Father" by Rick Greenberg

Despite the fact that more and more men seem to be staying home while the women work, many of my male students rebel against the concept. Thus, Greenberg's essay often creates a stir among male students. For some male students the traditional roles, defended by traditional clichés, still abound: a woman's place is in the home; the man "brings home the bacon"; something is wrong when a woman has to support a man; and so on. Consequently, the essay sometimes leads into discussion of changing values as well as changing roles in family relationships.

Greenberg's use of the first-person provides a narrative model. You can also use the essay to teach more mundane skills: punctuation within quotations (paragraphs 1, 3, 17, 21), punctuation of dialogue (paragraphs 4, 7, 18, 27, 30), the use and effectiveness of one-sentence paragraphs (paragraphs 13 and 19), and transitions (paragraphs 4, 7, 18, 27, 30).

"One Son, Three Fathers" by Steven O'Brien

Many students can relate to O'Brien's essay. While it reflects a warm relationship between stepson and stepfather, the selection deals with some of the emotional traumas and effects of divorce on both child and adult. O'Brien doesn't solve any issues or take any stands here, but rather leaves us with a revelation of his own life-style and its effect on his stepson. It's interesting that O'Brien never uses the word *stepson* or *stepfather*.

It's suggested that you deal with all of the questions listed under "Looking at Structure and Style," as well as those under "Evaluating the Author's Viewpoints."

"The Way" by Forrest Carter

After enjoying Forrest Carter's *The Education of Little Tree*, labeled a true story about a Cherokee boyhood in the 1930s, and after selecting this passage for use in *Viewpoints*, some evidence surfaced that has called into question the authenticity of the story and the true character of the author. Nonetheless, I decided to use the passage because it stands as a lovely and tender account of a young boy's relationship with his grandparents.

The book, which has become a cult classic of sorts, has been praised for its "humor, tragedy, tenderness and most of all, love," for the "memorable reading experience" it affords, and for its "love and respect for the Indian way of life." Evidence now suggests that Carter was not an Indian at all, but instead a racial bigot who wrote speeches for Alabama Governor George Wallace and at one time was affiliated with the KKK.

Should this take away from "The Way"? A good question to discuss in class.

"Mother Love" by Nancy Friday

Some instructors may want to skip Friday's essay, feeling that it is too difficult for the level of their students. I disagree; students need to be challenged, to be faced with the type of reading they must do in their other classes. Some misreading of certain statements may occur, with students concluding that Friday hates her mother, or blames her mother for failing her in some way. But a closer look at some of her statements, especially the last paragraph, is in order. It seems to me it is not her mother, but the illusion of some type of perfect love between mother and daughter, that Friday comes to realize has kept her from clearly seeing her true relationship with her mother.

The "Understanding the Content" questions, if looked at carefully, can put students on safe ground. Her definition of "mother love" focuses more on what it is *not* than what it is. Her comparisons of a woman's traditional roles—her grandmother's, her mother's, her own—are used to help her define "mother love." And her implications call for drawing inferences. It is, then, a good reading teaching tool.

STUDENT ESSAY: "In Defense of Motherhood" by Rosa Avolio

The commentary following Avolio's essay explains what I find is a common problem in many student essays—a lack of development and a tendency to drift away from a clearly stated thesis. As an exercise, you can ask students to outline the essay. The difficulty they'll face will give them with an understanding of the need for organizational control.

Don't, however, overlook the plus side to Avolio's paper, which admittedly is more on the mechanical area.

Using Unit 8: Viewpoints on Work

These reading selections deal with process ("How to Take a Job Interview"), definition/illustration and example ("A Primary Lesson in Sexual Harassment"), argumentation ("Less Is More: A Call for Shorter Working Hours"), classification ("What You Do Is What You Are"), comparison/contrast ("Workers"), and narration ("My Mother Never Worked"), thus supplying a variety for those who like to teach rhetorical modes. Of course, paragraph examples of other patterns appear within these selections.

Since many students have worked, are presently working, or are in college preparing for some type of employment, familiarity and interest in the work theme are built in. However, if you've been teaching long, you know that many students don't know what type of career for which to prepare, or they have grandiose expectations for future professions they probably will never achieve. This unit offers students an opportunity to reflect on their work goals.

"How to Take a Job Interview" by Kirby W. Stanat

The "How to . . ." of the title leads one to believe that the author will provide a step-by-step procedure for taking a job interview, but it isn't quite that straightforward. Stanat uses first-person narration, establishing himself in a position to watch and relate how a job recruiter conducts interviews on a college campus. He then presents his "how to . . ." or rather "how *not* to . . ." by describing the recruiter's reactions to "Sidney Student" and then "you," the reader, before and during the interview process. In so doing, Stanat makes his point that most recruiters have made up their minds about an interviewee before the actual interview begins. The essay takes a rather interesting twist on the use of process analysis.

Whether you assign it as an essay or a writing practice of some sort, item 2 under "Pursuing Possible Essay Topics" is a valuable one for students to think about.

"A Primary Lesson in Sexual Harassment" by Kathleen Neville

Neville opens with a definition of two types of sexual harassment at the work place and then proceeds to give numerous examples of different types of harassment that occur. A straightforward essay, easy to follow, it contains some clever "plays on words" you will want to point out.

As this edition of *Viewpoints* was forming, the repercussions over the sexual harassment charges by Anita Hill against then Supreme Court Justice nominee Clarence Thomas were still in the news. It should be interesting to see whether or not sexual harassment awareness is still on the rise or has diminished by the time you discuss this selection.

"Less Is More: A Call for Shorter Work Hours" by Barbara Brandt

Brandt's argument is that more free time is the best way to nurture our families and rebuild our communities. This essay makes an interesting parallel to Sam Keen's essay, "The Importance of Family," in Unit 7. Brandt, as does Keen, feels that as mothers and fathers spend more time on the job, "we are beginning to recognize the deleterious effects—especially on our young people—of the breakdown of social ties and community in American life" (15). It is interesting to show students how two writers argue the same point but from different directions.

Brandt brings in many examples. You will probably want to look closely at the structure of this essay as well as its content.

"What You Do Is What You Are" by Nickie McWhirter

After reading this essay, students can be asked to do a little introspection. Why do they want to get into a particular profession or job? Money? Status? Power? What do their answers say about their values?

Paragraphs 3 and 7 make good springboards for a discussion of stereotyping people based on our sense of values and class system.

The selection can also be useful if you wish to deal with argumentation and classification. Because it is short, you can go over the entire essay, pointing out rhetorical and stylistic devices McWhirter uses.

"Workers" by Richard Rodriguez

Rodriguez basically compares and contrasts the *gringo* construction worker with those he calls *los pobres*, the Mexican itinerant workers. But this first-person narrative also uses classification (paragraphs 9 and 16) and description (paragraphs 5, 10, 12–16) well, and indirectly defines and contrasts "real work" as known by his father with the type of work he does for the summer. Thus, the essay is a blend of rhetorical modes. However, labeling these passages as such seems to diminish their content, so I prefer first to point out and deal with the content, then look at the modes later.

Rodriguez has written many essays arguing against affirmative action and bilingual education. In his book, *Hunger of Memory: The Education of Richard Rodriguez*, he recounts how he was offered several university positions after graduating from Stanford, but "he could not withstand the irony of being counted a 'minority' when in fact the irreversibly successful effort of his life had been to become a fully assimilated member of the majority." It may be of interest to students to learn that Rodriguez eventually was rejected by his Mexican-American immigrant parents, who, unable to speak English, thought they had failed in their efforts to educate him because of his stance on these issues.

"My Mother Never Worked" by Bonnie Smith-Yackel

The structure of this essay is worth pointing out to students. It opens and closes with a conversation between the author and someone in the Social Security Office. The opening conversation establishes the mother's death through the author's request for a death-benefit check. While she is on hold, the author reminisces in a kind of flashback on her mother's long and arduous life. When the Social Security clerk gets back on the line to explain that there will be no death-benefit check because the mother "never worked," we feel the irony of the situation.

All the questions under "Looking at Structure and Style" are useful for discussion of the essay's structure.

STUDENT ESSAY: **"Oh, I'm Just a Housewife"** by Roy Wilson

For the reasons mentioned in the commentary, the Roy Wilson essay is a fruitful one for class discussion. While not powerful or erudite, it does contain the elements of essay writing taught in composition classes and is rather typical of the freshman student fare I get. But as stated before, make your own commentary of the essay to help students better understand the qualities you want to see in their writing.

Using Unit 9: Viewpoint on the Media

Many students are unaware of the media's influence on our thinking and values, so you may want to give some emphasis to the theme. Several informative books mentioned in the unit's preface are useful references for you or for student research projects. In addition, many of the items under the section "Pursuing Possible Essay Topics" contain leads to sources on various aspects of the media. Given the extraordinary power of the television medium, the essays in this unit lean more in that direction.

Because most students have grown up with television as a natural part of their environment, they seldom evaluate what they have grown accustomed to seeing. As an eye-opener of sorts for students, I play back in class a videotaped broadcast of the national evening news from the night before. I then have the students count the number of commercials, keep track of the actual amount of time devoted to news, note what news is emphasized, and evaluate the style of the commentators. This sometimes requires running portions of the tape more than once. For some students, this is the first time they have watched the news; for others, it gives them new viewing eyes.

I also play back some commercials, discussing the audience for whom they are intended, the honesty and values being displayed, the need for the product, and the quality of the presentation. Try turning off the monitor and have students listen to the news without the video portion. Is there much difference? Such activities create some interest in the media theme.

You can also ask students to bring in a particular edition of a newspaper. Go through the paper with them, looking at the attention given to hard news as opposed to the space devoted to such features as advice columns, movie reviews, garden ideas, recipes, advertisements, and other non-news. Take this opportunity to point out the editorial section, letters to the editor, syndicated columnists, and essay contributions. For some students, it's a revelation to discover that essays appear in places outside of textbooks.

You might wish to compare the depth of news coverage presented in the newspaper with that on the news videotape, especially if they both deal with the same day's news. As a way to tease students, ask them why sports coverage gets a section of its own. Why isn't sports coverage included in the business section, since professional sports is really big business? What does such an emphasis on sports say about our values?

Ask students to compare some news magazines, such as *TIME* and *Newsweek*. Or, bring in some copies of *Harper's*, *Atlantic Monthly*, *Utne Reader*, or *The New Republic*, for example, to expose students to magazines they may not find at the checkout counters. This may also be an appropriate time to look at the sources for the essays in *Viewpoints* by reading the acknowledgments.

"Murder on the Dial: Does Television Set the Killers Loose?" by Neal R. Peirce

You can use this essay to show how writers use something they read as the basis for an essay. In this case, Brandon Centerwall's research—which purports to show that 10 to 15 years after television is introduced to a country, its murder rate skyrockets—becomes the basis for an essay on television's influence. Point out that Peirce covers himself in paragraph 6, admitting the research may not be conclusive, but proceeds to build his argument on the basis that it is as he slides into paragraph 7.

Discuss paragraph length. Could any paragraphs be combined? This piece appeared in a newspaper, thus the short paragraphs.

Other issues are raised here that can be discussed or written about, among them media censorship, responsibility in broadcasting, and education on how to watch television without being seduced by it.

"Do You Still Want Your MTV?" by John Leland with Marc Peyser

An article in the *Los Angeles Times* in November 1991 discussing the changes taking place in magazine journalism, especially *TIME, Newsweek,* and *U.S. News & World Report,* stated that most of the reporting in *Newsweek* had a "Gee-whiz,-mom,-look-I'm-writing" quality about it. This piece appeared in *Newsweek* about that time. You might want to ask students if that applies to this selection. Is it reporting, commenting, criticizing, being clever?

Before assigning this selection, videotape a sixteen-minute segment (see paragraph 6) of an MTV program and play it for the class. Discuss student reaction to it. Then ask them to read the article and react to the questions under "Evaluating the Author's Viewpoints." Still another approach is to have students read both this and the next essay, by Caryl Rivers, before getting into class discussions or giving an essay writing assignment.

You could also use the "Murder on the Dial . . ." essay as a model and have students react to "Do You Still Want Your MTV?"

"The Issue Isn't Sex, It's Violence" by Caryl Rivers

Rivers's essay touches on the negative effects of some rock lyrics. With the advent of MTV, rock videos now bring the lyrics to life. Her argument that some rock lyrics incite listeners to violence is not new. But unlike those who call for censorship, Rivers provides her own solution to what she sees as a problem (see paragraph 15 especially). In this piece, written for the *Boston Globe,* Rivers uses several paragraphs to define the problem and present her view, always anticipating those who may disagree with her by presenting and refuting counterarguments.

Some students who disagree with Rivers fail to really examine her arguments because their own bias prevents them from accepting what she presents. Naturally, they don't have to agree with her, but a careful look at her arguments, how she orders and presents them, is worth some class time as an exercise in understanding the argumentative essay. Students may want to know her credentials. Rivers is a professor of journalism at Boston University, a novelist, and frequent essay contributor to newspapers and magazines.

"TV or Not TV" by Dave Barry

Barry's humorous essay disguises (well, sometimes) some of the craziness he sees in the television business. He frequently makes fun of himself, but not without making fun of television journalists and production. I like to read this essay aloud, since some of my students seem not able to inject the humor where it belongs and I find myself laughing alone.

Barry has several books of essays. You may want to share others he has written with your class.

"Did the Media Buy a Military Spin on the Gulf War?" by Terry Pristin

Actually, this is not an essay; it's a jumbled piece of reporting. Still, I think the information in it is important to consider. Pristin reports on a conference entitled "Macho and Media Coverage of the Gulf War" sponsored by USC's School of Journalism and the Institute for the Study of Women and Men. He reports the accusations made against the government regarding its media coverage of the Gulf War and defensive rebuttals by government officials. In addition, he raises the issue of whether or not news coverage about women in Desert Storm was slanted.

Properly used, this selection can lead students into thinking about government censorship, the role of the media in reporting the news, the responsibility of journalists, slanted news coverage, government propaganda, and the power of television images and news coverage. Assign it with Cohen's essay, discussed below.

"Bohemian Grove: Off-Limits to News Coverage" by Jeff Cohen

Cohen's essay works well in conjunction with the previous essay by Terry Pristin on military news spin. Pristin's piece is a report; Cohen's is an essay making a charge against the powers that be and their control of the media. Cohen is the executive director of Fairness & Accuracy in Reporting, the New York based media-watch group that publishes the journal *Extra!* In the June 1987 issue of that publication, Ben Bagdikian pointed out that just 26 corporations control half or more of all media, including book publishers, TV, radio, newspaper, and movie production companies. That figure is down from 50 corporations in 1982. You or some of your students might want to read and report on Bagdikian's *The Media Monopoly*, published by Beacon Press. The inferences being made in Cohen's essay are worth discussion in class.

"TV + Telephone = Electronic Democracy" by Duane Elgin

Whereas most of the other selections approach the media with a rather negative bent, this one proposes some positive uses for television. It recognizes the power of television and prescribes a method whereby television could be used to the benefit of democracy.

Use this one to lead students into a discussion of apathy at the polls, the growing negativity and lack of interest in politics, the responsibilities of the people in a democratic society. Ask them if Elgin's idea would work in their community, whether they would telephone in and take part in such a project. Ask students if they feel they are a part of a democratic institution, if they are doing their part in making democracy work.

STUDENT ESSAY: **"TV News: Journalism or Propaganda?"** by Jim Stone

A full commentary appears in the text. Again, you will no doubt want to add your comments.

Using Unit 10: Viewpoints on Two Controversial Issues

As the preface to Unit 10 states, two controversial issues are to be presented: capital punishment and multicultural education. You may wish to deal more thoroughly with one of the issues rather the other. Regardless of whether you assign one or both sets of essays, make certain that you go over the preface to Unit 10, discussing the seven questions students are directed to answer as they read.

Both issues make excellent topics for research projects. The issues are contemporary ones, and students will have no trouble finding source materials for whatever position they desire to defend or investigate.

ISSUE I: VIEWPOINTS ON THE DEATH PENALTY

Two good sources on the issue of capital punishment you may want to share with your students are *The Death Penalty: Opposing Viewpoints*, 2nd ed., edited by Carol Wekesser (Greenhaven Press, 1991), and *A Punishment in Search of a Crime*, by Jan Gray and Moira Stanley (Avon, 1989).

"Death to the Killers" by Mike Royko

Royko lets it be known from the first that he has written columns in favor of the death penalty for murderers. Then, stating that he doesn't like to make fun of people who oppose his views (paragraph 3), he spends most of his essay doing just that. He follows a pattern of quoting someone's question or argument, then attacks or ridicules it with sometimes flippant answers, making his opponents sound naive or stupid.

Royko does use a good argumentative technique. He takes his opposition's arguments, then shows or attempts to show why those arguments aren't valid. However, some of Royko's answers need to be examined for their bias and reasoning. Ask students how much of Royko's argument is based on logic and how much on emotion. Such a question can elicit lively class discussions and compositions.

You may want to assign Koch's essay, "Death and Justice," along with Royko's. Koch uses the same argumentative technique that Royko does, but with less emotion and bias. They both argue for capital punishment. Or, you may want to have students read pro and con arguments back to back, the way they are presented in the text.

"Death Penalty's False Promise" by Anna Quindlen

Quindlen opposes the death penalty, but confesses that if a loved one of hers were murdered, although she would feel that urge for revenge, she believes at her rational level that such an emotional response is wrong. Quindlen makes several references to Ted Bundy, the handsome young man who was finally caught and convicted for the murder of several young women in many states. She even says that had she been in the wrong place at the right time, she could have been one of Bundy's victims. She admits that had her daughter been one of his victims, she would "with the greatest of pleasure" kill him herself. She gets rather graphic in paragraph 9 when she describes the gruesome killing of six-year-old Adam Walsh. Despite the horrors committed by some people, Quindlen opposes the death penalty to punish them. You will no doubt want to point out to students that this is a good writing technique: it lets her readers know she shares the same emotions as those who favor capital punishment, but she feels it is "stooping to the level of the killers" (paragraph 10).

If you want to present two arguments opposing the death penalty together, assign King's essay, "The Death Penalty Is a Step Back." Students can compare the argumentative techniques used by both authors.

At the time of this printing the father of Adam Walsh, the murdered boy mentioned in the essay, hosts a popular television program that recreates real, unsolved crimes and has helped lead to the arrest of many suspects.

"Death and Justice" by Edward I. Koch

As noted under the comments for Royko's essay, Koch takes six arguments usually presented in opposition of capital punishment and examines them through counterarguments. At many points, he seems to be using "facts" to prove his points. Have students look carefully at Koch's arguments and ask them if they satisfactorily dismiss the arguments against.

Koch raises the question of responsibility that comes with law enforcement (paragraphs 13–16). Students who tend to be disinterested in the issue of capital punishment as something too far removed from their own lives can be drawn into the conversation with more interest when discussion turns to their own responsibility in law enforcement.

"The Death Penalty Is a Step Back" by Coretta Scott King

King looks at capital punishment as both immoral and unconstitutional, but the basis of her argument is built around three "practical reasons" presented in paragraphs 6–9. In paragraphs 10 and 11, she anticipates and states counterarguments and, like Royko, she answers back but more gently. She also makes it clear in paragraph 4 that she has suffered loss of loved ones at the hands of murderers. In effect this seems to imply that even though she has cause for favoring the death penalty, she looks at the subject objectively, not emotionally. Have students compare King's technique and arguments with Quindlen's.

It helps students if you list both pro and con arguments from the essays on the board. Then have them create a list of arguments of their own. As a class or in small groups, have students examine the arguments for and against, take sides, and debate the issue.

"A Hanging" by George Orwell

Unlike the other essays in Part I, Orwell's contains little direct commentary, yet he manages through his descriptions to express his feelings toward capital punishment. Because most of us would rather not think about the subject, we tend not to think about it, to let others deal with it. Orwell's essay provides a great contrast. You may want to assign this essay before the others as an attention-getter for the subject.

Have students discuss each witness's reaction to the hanging. Point out the difference in the way each views the hanging: the stoic prisoner; Francis, the head jailer; the fawning "hangman"; the stern, impatient Superintendent; the Eurasian boy; Orwell himself; even the dog. Raise the issue of carrying out your duty, even though it may be a task you morally oppose. You may want to venture into discussion of whether or not one country has the right to impose its morals and laws on another country, which is what is taking place in this essay.

Above all, don't avoid looking closely at the description used.

ISSUE II: VIEWPOINTS ON MULTICULTURAL EDUCATION

Make certain students have read the preface to Unit 10 before assigning these readings. Students may find that the essays in this section are more difficult to read than those in other units. You may have to spend more class time going over them, but students need to be exposed to more challenging reading levels than they presently can handle if they are to develop their reading versatility.

In addition to the books mentioned in some of the commentaries below, you or your students might want to read "Upside Down in the Groves of Academe" in *TIME*, April 1, 1991, and the lead story in *Newsweek*, September 23, 1991, "Was Cleopatra Black?"

"In Defense of Multiculturalism" by Nathan Glazer

Glazer offers a definition of what multiculturalism is and is not in paragraph 2, but goes on to say that he does not believe that multiculturalism "in its present form" is being driven by the new immigration but rather by black educators. After a rather balanced, I think, coverage of what is occurring in education and the reasons for it, he ultimately decides that perhaps those black educators have a good reason for pursuing more balanced cultural diversity in education.

This is a rather long and, for some, a difficult essay compared to most in the text, so I suggest going over the "Understanding the Content" questions first and then moving into the "Looking at Structure and Style." If you do this, the essay doesn't seem as formidable.

The essay provokes a great deal of discussion regarding all African-American schools and all male African-American schools that exist in some areas. Is this segregation in reverse? Are such schools necessary?

"Multiculturalism Threatens the Ideal That Binds America" by Arthur Schlesinger, Jr.

As his title indicates, Schlesinger is opposed to multicultural education. He argues that the whole point of America was "not to preserve old cultures but to forge a new *American* culture" (paragraph 6). After giving a mini-history of America's multiethnic beginnings, his dissension begins in paragraph 9. He plays with the phrase *E pluribus unum*, stating the "the balance is shifting from *unum* to *pluribus*," terms you may have to explain. In paragraph 10, he defends the Eurocentric curriculum that many multiculturalists abhor. His argument seems to be that democracy, civil liberties, and human rights are Eurocentric concepts and the ideals that bind America.

Discuss paragraphs 10 and 11 in class, especially if your class contains students of many ethnic backgrounds.

"Putting Africa at the Center" by Molefi Kete Asante

A short selection, this one nevertheless is difficult for some students to read on their own. Still, it contains some provocative thoughts that stimulate student thinking. I read this one aloud in class and students interrupt when they agree or disagree with some of Asante's remarks. The question of what exactly is "Afrocentricity" always comes up. What is its place in the educational curriculum? Should only African-Americans be taught Afrocentricity? Will such a curriculum create more or less racial prejudice? These are some of the questions students usually raise and they make for lively discussions.

This essay should be read along with Gates's "Beware of the New Pharaohs."

Asante is chair of the Department of African-American Studies at Temple University and author of *Afrocentricity*. You may want to read some selected passages from his book.

"Beware of the New Pharaohs" by Henry Louis Gates, Jr.

Assign this with Asante's essay. Ask if Asante could be considered "a new pharaoh." Gates argues less for Afrocentricity, it seems, and more for "rigorous methodologies." Paragraph 4 argues that African-American studies are not just for blacks and argues against those who want to turn such studies into "ethnic fundamentalism." You will need to explain some of these terms and concepts to your students, but the results are worth it.

The "Looking at Structure and Style" questions will help students get a better grasp of this essay.

Gates is chair of Afro-American Studies at Harvard University and author of *Loose Cannons*. An interview with Gates entitled "A 'Race Man' Argues for a Broader Curriculum" appeared in *TIME*, April 22, 1991. Assign a student to compare what Gates says in this essay with his comments in that interview. Also see the references to sources at the beginning of Part II in this unit.

"Teach Diversity—with a Smile" by Barbara Ehrenreich

Ehrenreich's essay strikes a balance between both extremes on the multicultural education issue. It appears last in the unit and should be assigned last. She uses a term being thrown about at the time of this printing that may need some clarification: "political correctness." A definition of P.C. can be drawn from the comments she makes, particularly in paragraphs 1, 2, 5, 6, and 7.

She also makes reference to "the great books approach," another term you may need to clarify, although after discussions on the other essays, I'd be surprised if the term hadn't already come up.

After studying these essays, you might ask your class to create a college curriculum that would "prepare us for a wider world."

STUDENT ESSAY: "Stop Executing Juveniles" by Trisha Toyoto

As usual, my comments appear in the text following the essay.